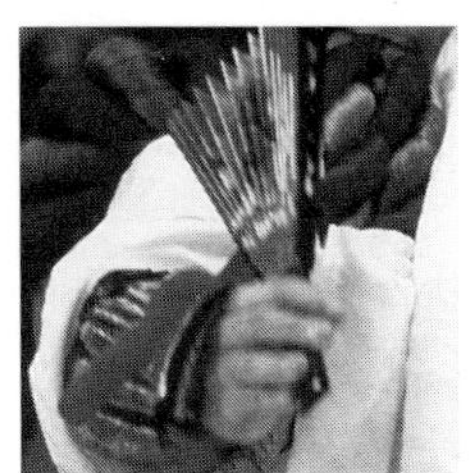  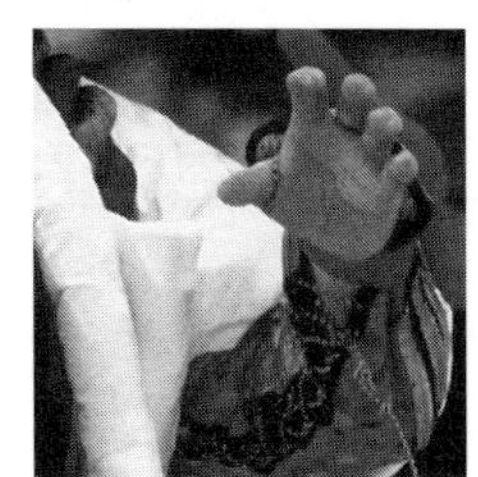

Drama and Theatre Studies at AS/A level

Jonothan Neelands and Warwick Dobson

Hodder & Stoughton

A MEMBER OF THE HODDER HEADLINE GROUP

The editors and publishers would like to thank the following for permission to reproduce copyright material:

Copyright text:
pp27-29 The Prologue from *Antigone*, from 'The Thebans' translated by Timberlake Wertenbaker, Faber and Faber Ltd; pp56-58 *The Crucible*, Arthur Miller, Methuen; pp75-76, 80, 82-87 *Mother Courage and her Children*, Bertolt Brecht, Methuen; pp110 *Yerma* from Lorca – three plays translated by Gwynne Edwards and Peter Luke, Methuen; pp129-130, 133-137, 208 *A Doll's House*, Henrik Ibsen, Methuen; pp149-151 *Hedda Gabler*, Henrik Ibsen, Methuen.

Copyright photographs:
p8 © Camera Press, London (8475-1); p9 © Donald Cooper/Photostage; p11 Poster for *Playboy of the Western World* as produced by Pure Design (Hull) for Leicester Haymarket Theatre; p11 reproduced by kind permission of *Chicago The Musical*, Aldelphi Theatre, London; p15 © Donald Cooper/Photostage; p17 Sarah Ainslie/Photostage; p19 © John Haynes; p20 © Donald Cooper/Photostage; p21 © Bridgeman Art Library; p24 © Donald Cooper/Photostage; p25 © Life File; p34 © Donald Cooper/Photostage; p40 © Catherine Ashmore; p45 © Hutchinson Library; p47 © The Illustrated London News Picture Library; p48 © Donald Cooper/Photostage; p56 © Donald Cooper/Photostage; p71 © Donald Cooper/Photostage; p78 © Hainer Hill (Bertolt Brecht Archiv, Berlin); p88 © Corbis; p91 © Corbis; p93 © Bristol University Theatre Collection; p96 © Archiv der Akademie der Kunste, Berlin; p97 © Corbis; p106 by kind permission of the University of Northumbria; p166 © Ruth Berlau (Bertolt Brecht Archiv, Berlin); p169 © Donald Cooper/Photostage; p170 © Donald Cooper/Photostage; p172 © Welfare State International/Chris Hill; p175 © Corbis; p192 © Donald Cooper/Photostage; p210 © Donald Cooper/Photostage; p211 © Ronald Grant Archive; p222 © The National Gallery, London; p222 © Frick Collection; p223 © Catherine Ashmore.

Every effort has been made to trace copyright holders of material reproduced in this book. Any rights not acknowledged here will be acknowledged in subsequent printings if notice is given to the publisher.

Orders: please contact Bookpoint Ltd, 78 Milton Park, Abingdon, Oxon OX14 4TD. Telephone: (44) 01235 827720, Fax: (44) 01235 400454. Lines are open from 9.00 – 6.00, Monday to Saturday, with a 24 hour message answering service. Email address: orders@bookpoint.co.uk

British Library Cataloguing in Publication Data
A catalogue record for this title is available from The British Library

ISBN 0 340 75860 0

First published 2000
Impression number 10 9 8 7 6 5 4 3
Year 2005 2004 2003 2002 2001 2000

Cover photo © CORBIS, London/Michael S. Yamashita
Typeset by Fakenham Photosetting Limited, Fakenham, Norfolk NR21 8NN
Printed in Great Britain for Hodder & Stoughton Educational, a division of Hodder Headline Plc, 338 Euston Road, London NW1 3BH by Redwood Books Ltd, Trowbridge, Wiltshire.

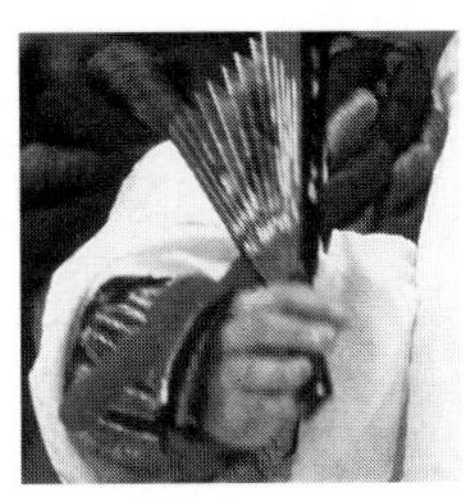

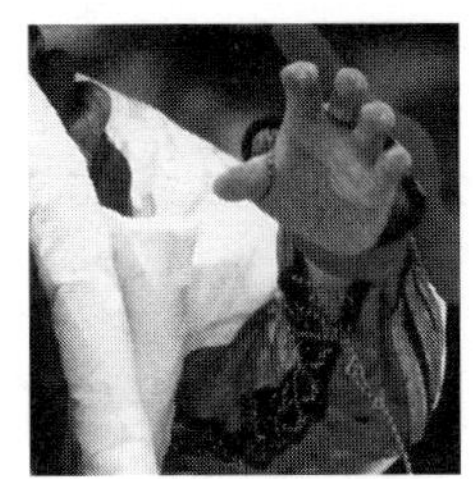

Drama and Theatre Studies
at AS/A level

We shall make lively use of all means, old and new, tried and untried, deriving from art and deriving from other sources, in order to put living reality in the hands of living people in such a way that it can be mastered.

(Bertolt Brecht 1938)

Acknowledgements

We are grateful to our colleagues and students at the University of Warwick and the University of Northumbria for their patience, guidance and critical vigilance during this project.

Particular thanks go to Tony Goode who has, once again, been our not so silent partner.

This book has gone through a long process of re-editing based on ideas, criticisms and suggestions from our readers group who have generously given their time and extensive experience of teaching A level to this project.

We would also like to thank Judith Ackroyd of University College, Northampton; Alice Bayliss of Josiah Mason Sixth-Form College, Birmingham; and Duncan Fewins of Colmer's Farm School, Birmingham. Particular thanks go to Duncan who not only gave us detailed feedback but also gave us practical suggestions and resources, which in many cases were better than our own!

Our special thanks go to Professor Harvey Miller, University of Victoria, BC, Canada, who gave us expert advice and encouragement for the chapters on directing and textual analysis.

Our special thanks also go to our research assistant Anna Brown, who compiled the glossary, for her diligent rooting out of definitions, facts and dates.

Theatre Directions is a companion reader for this textbook. It contains short extracts from the writings of theatre practitioners and theorists which will support your study of Drama and Theatre at A/S and A level. The table on p. 3 indicates where there are connections between this text and *Theatre Directions*.

CONTENTS

Introduction

Welcome to your A/S and A level studies in Drama and Theatre. This book has been specially written for you. It offers a course of study which covers all the aims and objectives for the current specifications in Drama and Theatre Studies. The book is a mix of practical and theoretical material which taken together will give you a thorough understanding of how drama and theatre work; it will also prepare you for success in your exams both practical and written.

The book is organised into six sections and ten chapters, which together cover the skills and knowledge you will need to be successful in your studies and practical work.

Overview

Section One, 'The Foundations of Drama and Theatre' serves as an introduction to your subject. In Chapter 1, The Infinite Variety of Theatre, we begin with everyday and technical definitions of drama and theatre. We go on to look at the variety of theatre which is on offer today and then introduce you to the technical terms that you will need to use in your studies. In Chapter 2, The Origins of Drama and Theatre, we look at the roots of the modern art-form both in fifth century Athenian culture and also in other forms and traditions of performance. These two chapters provide the foundations for the rest of the book and for your course.

Section Two, 'Acting Workshops and Scene Work' gives you practical experience as an actor in two contrasting styles of acting and performance. In Chapter 3, Playing the Given Circumstances, we introduce you to the ideas and rehearsal methods developed by Konstantin Stanislavski and Lee Strasberg. These ideas are applied practically to a short scene from Arthur Miller's *The Crucible*. In Chapter 4, Finding the *Verfrumdungseffekt*, we offer a contrasting workshop based on the ideas and rehearsal methods of Bertolt Brecht and apply these to scenes from his play *Mother Courage and Her Children*.

Section Three, 'The Work of the Director' introduces you to directing and the twentieth century history of great directors. In Chapter 5, The Emergence of the Director, we tell the story of how directors first emerged as the new artist of the theatre in the nineteenth century and introduce you to the ideas of many of the twentieth century's most famous and important directors. In Chapter 6, From Page to Stage, we look at the director's work and the processes that lead from page to stage. This chapter includes a case study of a production of *Yerma* written by a director.

Section Four, 'Textual Analysis' offers you strategies for reading plays for performance and a model for analysing play texts. In Chapter 7, Reading for Performance, we identify the strategies that are used to read plays as potential texts for performance rather than as literature; there is a wide range of practical tasks to help you. In Chapter 8, A Director's Model for Textual Analaysis, we provide you with a step-by-step process for analysing play texts from a director's point of view. Finally you will find the first of our three questionnaires – The Textual Analysis Questionnaire – which provides you with a detailed checklist of questions to help in your own analysis of a text. Like the other questionnaires it also draws your attention to the assessment criteria that will be applied to your textual analysis work.

Section Five, 'Devising and Analysing Performances' equips you with clear and thorough processes for devising theatre and for the critical analysis of performances you have seen. In Chapter 9, Devising Theatre, we offer you a ten-stage framework that covers everything in the devising process from first ideas through to the evaluation of the performance. The Devising Process Questionnaire is there to help you check what you need to do at each stage and how to match the assessment criteria. In Chapter 10, Reading the Signs of Performance, we introduce you to semiotics and performance theory as a means of helping you to make your analysis and evaluation of performances that you see more thorough and effective. This chapter will also help you to check that your own performances are even more effective! The Performance Analysis Questionnaire will help you organise your responses and note-taking.

Section Six, 'Resources' provides you with additional resources to assist in your studies and practical work. Appendix 1, the Glossary, gives you explanations and definitions for important practitioners, genres, periods, styles and other specialist terms used in the book. The important words in ***bold italic*** have an entry in the Glossary and also in the Index at the end of the book. Appendix 2, Theatre timeline, gives you a brief history of European and non-European theatre from 600BC to 1910. This will be a useful reference which will help you see when new ideas were first introduced, what styles of theatre are associated with particular historical periods, and how the history of European theatre compares with the great non-European traditions such as Noh, Kabuki and Kathakali. Finally, there is a Webliography to help you in your further research and interest in theatre and drama.

How To Read and Use This Book

All names and technical words associated with drama and theatre are in *italics*. Most of these words have an entry in the Glossary/Index at the end of the book so you can look for more information if you need it. The sidebars in the margins of most chapters describe the content in the neighbouring paragraphs. Bold has been used to pick out the important points being made which you should take particular note of.

There are three ways in which we hope that you will find this book useful. In class you will want to use the book for the wealth of practical tasks, exercises and extracts from plays. You may also take the book home and read the theoretical and historical material in preparation for your next class, or to help you in writing assignments, or in your private study of texts. Finally, we believe that this book is an excellent foundation and resource for your future studies, or lifelong interest in theatre. Keep it as a trusted friend that you can refer back to long after your AS and A levels are finished with!

Your teacher will guide your reading of the book. It is not written so that the sections have to be read in order, although we have assumed that you will begin your studies with the first three chapters. Your teacher will know the details of your particular specifications and therefore how best to guide and sequence your reading and practical work. We hope that there will be something new for your teacher in this book as well and that you will enjoy using it together.

We suggest that certain chapters are more suited to AS level and others to A level. Again this will depend on which specifications you are following. On the following page we indicate the level of difficulty of the chapters, but even the most difficult sections can be understood with guidance, discussion and practical experimentation. We have also included a reference to the relevant extracts from the companion reader *Theatre Directions*. In order to help you we have signposted the text with sidebars which give you a quick reference to the content of that section.

Key Skills

In every chapter you will find that the practical work encourages you to develop and use your communication and group skills. Tasks involving group discussion,

Chapter	Level	Relevant extracts from *Theatre Directions*
1	AS	1, 2
2	AS	3–17
3	AS	18–25
4	A	25–32
5	AS	35–46
6	A	35–46
7	AS	–
8	AS, A	42, 43, 44
9	AS, A	47–52
10	A	11, 12, 13, 38, 44

presentations, recording and using information in a variety of ways and problem solving are clearly marked in the text. We have also included tasks that will develop your information technology (IT) skills; particularly your use of the World Wide Web (WWW).

Authors Health Warning!

We have tried in this book to provide you with models and frameworks that you can use in your study and practice of drama and theatre. Often these frameworks suggest categories and labels that you can use to describe the differences between play texts and performances – to distinguish between the genres of Comedy and Tragedy for instance. Sometimes we break complex processes like devising and textual analysis into easy-to-follow stages. But be warned. The Western theatre tradition observes few rules and those that are made will be broken. Artists have resisted labels and categories and frequently blur the boundaries between style and genres. The models and frameworks we suggest are there to help you organise and make sense of your studies, but nothing is cast in stone!

Drama and Theatre Studies is a young subject in schools and universities and it hasn't yet got an established vocabulary of terms to describe its history and practices. You may find quite different words used to describe the same ideas. There are for instance considerable differences in the glossaries provided by the exam boards. We have made every effort to check out our definitions and vocabulary with expert academics and authoritative theatre dictionaries and technical manuals. You may, however, have to use slightly different terms from those we use in order to satisfy the requirements of the specifications you are following.

Have Fun!

Finally, we wish you every success! Work hard but also enjoy your practical work and studies. We believe that theatre is the most human of all art-forms – in studying, making and appreciating theatre we discover more about ourselves, who we are and who we are becoming. Theatre and drama are living art-forms and you will find pleasure and intellectual challenges ahead and also provide the same for your audiences. In these pages we have shared both our knowledge and also our love and enthusiasm for theatre and drama. We hope that you too will come to love and understand the subject you are about to do and study together.

Below is a list of the photographs used in this book to provide a quick reference:

SECTION 1

The Foundations of Drama and Theatre

1

The Infinite Variety of Theatre

According to the Dictionary

We will begin by thinking about what it is that you will be studying as you read and use this book. 'Theatre' and 'drama' – what do we mean when we use these two terms? What do they cover?

When you hear the word 'theatre' what picture comes to mind?

Do you see theatre as a building?

Do you see a 'play' being performed by actors for an audience?

What about 'drama'? Is it the same thing – does it bring the same pictures to your mind?

How are the terms 'drama' and 'theatre' used both in everyday speech and within the world of 'theatre' itself? On the left, you will find some definitions from the *Oxford Dictionary*. The definitions are followed by the tasks below which will help you to begin to define and identify what you will be doing and discovering in the next months.

Some definitions

A Theatre (from the Greek *theatron* = to behold):
1 a) a building or outdoor area for dramatic performances, b) a cinema
2 a) the writing and production of plays, b) effective material for the stage (*makes good theatre*)
3 a room or hall for lectures etc.
4 an operating theatre
5 a scene or field of action (*the theatre of war*)
6 a natural land formation in a gradually rising part-circle like ancient Greek and Roman theatres

B Theatrical:
1 of or for the theatre; of acting or actors
2 (of a manner, speech, gesture, or person) calculated for effect; showy, artificial, affected

C Drama (from the Greek *drao* = to do):
1 a play for acting on stage or for broadcasting
2 the art of writing and presenting plays
3 an exciting or emotional event, set of circumstances etc.
4 a dramatic quality (*the drama of the situation*)

D Dramatic:
1 of drama or the study of drama
2 (of an event, circumstance etc.) sudden and exciting or unexpected
3 vividly striking
4 theatrical, overdone, absurd

Task 1: Working with the definitions

Working from your own experiences of drama and theatre, both in school and out of it, make a list of those definitions which you would say are *accurate* and *relevant* to the study of theatre and drama.

Make an alternative list of definitions, which you think are not appropriate to your course of study. For instance, is the definition of theatre as a 'scene or field of action *(the theatre of war)*' relevant? Why is the word 'theatre' used to describe such different places as a building that houses performances, a battlefield and the operating theatre in a hospital – is it just a coincidence or is there some connection?

Some of these everyday definitions offer a view of drama and theatre as something 'showy', 'overdone' and 'affected'. Why do you think that the terms 'drama' and 'theatre' have become associated with exaggerated and emotional forms of behaviour? Is this a true reflection?

Organise yourselves into three groups with each group taking responsibility for one of the following three tasks based on three of the given definitions:

1 What is effective material for the stage? (A2(b)) What makes 'good theatre'? Brainstorm the kinds of themes or stories which you think make *good* theatre. Choose one and make three different *still-images* to share with the group, which illustrate different takes on the possible 'drama' of

the theme or idea you have selected. If you choose 'love', for instance, the images might include:

- separation and loss;
- a single image that contains different kinds of love;
- a character torn between the love for two people;
- a more abstract picture that captures the opposites of joy and pain in love.

Share the images with the group and talk through the other suggestions that you had.

2 What kind of events or sets of circumstances (situations) make for exciting and emotional drama? (**C3**). Brainstorm the kinds of situations and events which make for **exciting** and **emotional** drama. These situations might include: having to make a tough choice; being persecuted; mistaken identities; an act of betrayal or conflict. Events might include births, deaths, weddings; historical events; a moment of truth or point of no return; the revealing of a secret or a sudden disaster that will change lives.

Create three very short scenes to illustrate some of your ideas. The scene should do no more than introduce the actors with three or four lines of dialogue to establish what kind of situation, or event, is being represented. For example:

(*Man sits at a table with his head in his hands. Woman enters, looks at him, and begins to clear up the table in front of him*:)

Woman: When will we see you again, then?

Man: I'm not sure, in a few days. (*Pause*) Perhaps.

Woman: Can't I help?

Man: Look, I just need some time on my own.

Woman: On your own?

(*Pause*)

Man: I don't know who to trust any more.

Share the scenes and the other ideas you had with the group. You might want to see what ideas people have about how to develop one of your scenes into a *plot* or storyline. What might have already happened; what might happen next?

3 How do we turn an ordinary event such as a meeting between two friends into a situation that has a **dramatic quality** for an audience or for a drama workshop? (**C4**). Brainstorm the ways in which an ordinary, everyday event can be made 'dramatic'. What do we **add**, or **take away**, in order to get a dramatic effect? Your ideas might include tension and conflict; mystery and suspense; a sense of impending doom or surprise; interesting characters; or unusual settings.

Take the meeting between friends and make three short scenes in which you will add different kinds of dramatic quality to the seemingly ordinary meeting. For example:

First Friend: I said I would be here to meet you.

Second Friend: What do you want?

First Friend: C'mon, we can still be friends can't we?

Second Friend: After all this time? (*Pause*) Did you really think we could just carry on as before?

First Friend: If I'd known (*tries to touch his friend, then stops)* I would never have asked you in the first place!

Share the three versions with the group and ask them to identify what you have added to each to make a different kind of dramatic quality.

Technical Definitions

Now we will look more closely at how the terms 'drama' and 'theatre' are used both by those working in theatre and drama and also by those who study it and write about it. These are the specialist definitions that you will need to understand and use in your studies.

Historically, 'drama' has often been used to refer to dramatic literature and 'theatre' to refer to the performance of dramatic literature. This distinction tells us something about the particular history of Western theatre, which has developed as a 'literary' art as well as a performance art.

Since the time of the great tragedians in fifth-century Athens, the playwright has tended to dominate the development of the Western tradition of theatre. It is only in recent times that 'theatre' – the 'performance' and the 'performers' – has become a field of serious study. Even now we tend to tell the story of theatre in terms of the succession of playwrights who have shaped the development of the art-form. Many students in school today still study 'drama' as part of their study of English literature rather than doing 'drama' – looking at how to produce and understand performances.

The 'play' (as a written text) remains, whereas the performance (the live experience) only exists in the moment of performance. The 'play' as literature can be read and reread as well as performed, so it provides a more permanent record for future generations. The plays of ***Shakespeare*** have been in print since 1623 and generations of scholars have pored over his words and discussed his importance as a 'dramatist'.

The dominance of the playwright in the history of theatre is also a result of the historical relationship between the different producers of drama and theatre. The first Greek playwrights were referred to as 'teachers' rather than as 'writers'. Their job was to 'teach' the chorus and actors how to perform by providing a narrative, speeches and directions for the actors to follow. This was the beginning of a tradition in which the playwright was established as the true 'author' of both the play and the performance; actors merely served the playwright and were of little importance. Indeed, actors were often seen as having the same social status as tinkers and beggars.

As we shall see in Chapter 7 it was only in the nineteenth century that 'directors' began to be identified as playing a part in the 'authorship' of a performance, and in modern times the director, rather than the playwright, is often seen as being the most important 'author' or ***auteur*** of the performance itself.

Konstantin Stanislavski

Task 2: Who is involved?

As we have seen, the playwright has traditionally been given the highest status in Western theatre. But what about the other people involved in the creation of a performance? Theatre is unique in the sense that it is the collective achievement of a group of people who perform different kinds of roles in the production process. Once the play is written, who else gets involved? Make a list of the kinds of work or contribution that the following roles make to the creation of a theatre performance:

Role	Contribution
Director	
Actor	
Designer	
Stage manager	
Choreographer	
Lighting/sound technician	
Audience	

Which of these roles do you and the rest of your group have some experience of?

Are some roles more 'vital' than others? Do you need a designer for instance?

Which is your favourite/least favourite role? Do you prefer directing to acting, for instance?

The Play Text and the Performance Text

The importance of the director has increasingly led to the idea that there are two kinds of text in performance: the play text and the performance text. The **play text** refers to the original play, or other written score, produced by a writer or by a devising group. The **performance text** refers to what is done with the play text by the performers in performance. Sometimes the performance text will try to faithfully represent the playwright's ideas and intentions, and sometimes a performance text will tell us more about the director's, designer's and actors' views, intentions and ideas than those of the playwright. This modern tradition of directing has been closely influenced by the rise of the status of the director in film: we speak of who directs and stars in a film rather than who wrote the screenplay. In the modern theatre the performance text may not be based on a play text at all – it may be a devised performance or an adaptation of non-dramatic literature.

Cate Blanchett as Susan Traherne in *Plenty* (***Hare***). Albery Theatre April 1999.

An interest in actors and what actors bring to the performance text is also a modern idea that belongs to the same historical period as the rise of the director. Remember that acting was once considered to be a very lowly and dubious occupation. The first actors in fifth-century Athens were called *hypocrites*, meaning 'answerer' or 'interpreter', from which we get the word 'hypocrite', meaning someone false or duplicitous. In the early days of the travelling theatre companies in America, actors were buried at the crossroads with a stake in their hearts. ***Moliere*** was the first French actor to be buried in consecrated ground in 1673, and the first actor to be knighted was *Sir Henry* ***Irving*** in 1895. It is only since the beginning of the twentieth century that the actor has been seen as a professional artist with a similar social status to writers, painters and others. The model for ***Stanislavski***'s system of actor training was based on the performances of a serf-actor (a feudal slave) called *Mikhail* ***Shchepkin***.

In our own time, partly because of film, we are more conscious of the actor as the creator of the performance. We go to the theatre and watch films because of who the actors are as much as because of who has written or directed the piece. We also expect more of our actors in the modern age. They are not just the mouthpieces for the playwright's words or puppets to be controlled by the director.

Actors are often referred to as 'performers' in recognition of the wide range of skills that they need in the modern theatre: singing, dancing, acrobatics and musicianship. Actor training, acting styles and increasingly *physical* forms of performance have become increasingly central to our understanding and appreciation of theatre.

It is important to remember that we have, so far, been talking of the Western tradition of theatre. **There are other great performance traditions in other cultures which have not developed as 'literary' arts**. They are not based on the written score of a playwright but on genres and styles of performance. The performer, and performer training, are at the heart of these traditions and the first analyses and training manuals for performers were produced in India and Japan: the *Natyastra* in India in the first century BC and the writings on ***Noh*** performance written by *Zeami* in fifteenth century Japan. The performer-centred traditions of India (***Kuttiyattam*** and ***Kathakali***; of Bali (*Gumbuh* and *Topeng*); and of Japan (*Noh* and ***Kabuki***) are all living traditions of theatre that place the performer rather than the playwright at the heart of theatre. In the European tradtion of ***Commedia dell'Arte***, the actors improvise their performances based on *stock characters* and situations and their own *lazzi*, or stage tricks of great physical dexterity.

It is no longer customary to accept that drama refers to dramatic literature and theatre to performance. We know now that we cannot understand a play text without thinking about how it will be performed and that the performance of a play cannot be separated from a consideration of the structure and conventions of the play text. The emergence of new and distinctive forms of drama since the invention of film and TV has also led to new meanings for the term drama. **It has become more usual to use the term drama as a generic, or umbrella, term to cover all that is associated with the making, performing and responding to performance, whether it is live or recorded on film or TV**.

Drama is the big heading which includes a wide variety of subheadings, which in turn include not just dramatic literature, but drama on TV and film, dramatic events in the news and in our lives, live theatre and all that is associated with the training, preparation and working practices of those involved in the making and performing of enacted fictions. This broad definition of drama will include the dramas that you will be used to from your first years at secondary school and the kinds of exploratory drama work that you will have experienced at GSCE level and which you will continue to enjoy in your AS and A level study of the subject.

Theatre on the other hand is now often seen as one of the subheadings of drama. It is used to refer to the live performance of a drama, which is shared with an audience. In this usage, the term theatre is used to make a distinction between recorded performances on film and TV and the immediate experience of live performance. It may also refer to anything to do with the preparation for a live theatre experience or performance; this would include rehearsals rather than workshops; research into character and period, etc.

What's On?

Even if we limit the usage of 'theatre' to the live performance of drama we must still recognise that there are many different forms of theatre available to us. Take a look at the 'what's on' section of a national newspaper such as the *Guardian* or of a regional newspaper that covers a large urban area – what is advertised? Musicals, revivals, comedies, thrillers, pantomimes? The variety of theatre that you will find is often classified, or categorised, in order to make distinctions between the different forms it takes. This classification is often made clear in the publicity for a show, so that the publicists can target the audience they think will most enjoy the performance.

What follows is a description of two different shows from an issue of the *Guardian* and a simple chart to help you to distinguish between these two shows or any other that you might find.

Who is producing the entertainment for whom?		**Distinction can be made between:**
Chicago	**Playboy**	**1** amateur/professional; **2** local/national/touring companies; **3** adult/family/youth/childrens' theatre. **4** These distinctions might be further reinforced by different venues: **5** National Theatre (RNT, RSC); repertory/ West End; **6** civic/arts centre/community/environmental (outdoor, museums, streets, etc.)
• Professional/ international company; • Big well-known stage stars; • Major London West End theatre	• Professional/local company; • Features well-known TV actor; • Regional repertory theatre	
What genre, or type, is it?		**Distinction can be made between:**
American Broadway musical.	Revival of classic Irish tragi-comedy.	Musical, pantomime, mime, tragedy, comedy, adaptation, revival, classic, physical theatre.
How 'arty' is it?		**Distinction can be made between:**
'*Razzle dazzle the West End*' suggests that it will be commercial as does the West End venue. American musicals tend to be entertaining.	When it was first written and performed the play was experimental/avant-garde. But this revival seems to have commercial appeal: '*A riotous Irish comedy . . . Irish nights at the Haymarket*' and the sponsorship by a brewery all suggest 'commercial' and the comic exploitation of Irish cultural stereotypes.	*Experimental/**avant-garde***, which seeks the **cutting edge** or outer limits of what can be done in theatre; it will go against popular and accepted tastes in theatre. *Mainstream*, which is produced by critically acclaimed 'serious' actors, directors and companies and is often based on the performance ideas introduced by earlier *avant-garde* movements: the *Royal Shakespeare Company* and the ***Royal National Theatre*** for instance. These companies depend on government subsidies. *Commercial*, which often stresses its 'light' entertainment and enjoyment value; it seeks to be accessible and pleasurable to a broad audience. It also seeks to be profitable.
What period, or style, does it represent?		**Distinction can be made between:**
A modern musical which evokes the golden period of the American musicals and the gangster years in Chicago in the 1930s and 1940s. The style is likely to include big dance routines and set piece songs.	The play was an attack on the moral constraints of Irish society. In 1902 when it was first performed there was a riot. ***Synge*** was associated with the development of modern Irish drama. The style will be ***realist***, possibly sentimentalising Ireland and playing up the comic aspects of this classic ***tragi-comedy***.	The periods of theatre associated with the playwright or the artistic and historical influences on the first performance (e.g. ***Naturalism***, ***Symbolism***, Expressionism, Epic, Theatre of the Absurd). The historical period associated with the work (e.g. Classical, Medieval, Renaissance, Restoration, Modernist, Post-Modernist.

These distinctions help us to identify the expectations that we might have of the two different performances.

If you have already decided to go to a performance, but haven't yet decided what to see, you may find yourself going through the 'what's on' section looking for a play that is:

- from a particular historical **period** – Elizabethan or contemporary for instance.
- representative of a particular **genre** – comedy, farce or musical, for instance. When we choose a genre such as comedy we expect the performance to share certain characteristics with other examples of comedies. Genres change over time (new characteristics are added, and old ones discarded) so we also combine **period and genre** when we speak of *Greek tragedy* as opposed to *Elizabethan and Jacobean tragedy*.
- Performed or written in a particular **style** – a distinctive style of play writing associated with a particular playwright or a group of playwrights from the same period, or a performance style such as *physical theatre*. But 'style' may also be used more loosely to refer to the most obvious characteristic of a play or performance which might be original or might be borrowed – a performance of *Grease* which calls for a 'fifties' style, for instance.

In this process of identifying similarities and differences between plays and performances, period refers to a historical epoch; genre refers to the general category of theatrical form and style to the particular work or particular performance. Plays of a particular *period* may be in different *genres* (***Shakespeare*** wrote comedies, tragedies and histories) and have quite distinctive *styles* (*Shakespeare's* tragedies were written in the same period as Christopher ***Marlowe's*** but they have a very different style to them).

Period, genre and style can be used to distinguish works in other art-forms too. A song like Oasis' 'Morning Glory' has it's own distinctive style but it is also retrospective of the music of the 1960s in terms of *period*, a 'ballad' in terms of *genre* and associated with the *style* of the *Beatles* ballads. Dance music is a style which is sometimes divided into periods like 'seventies disco' and is also divided into genres like 'house', 'garage', and 'trance'.

Task 3: What's on?

Use the entertainment section of a national or regional newspaper to identify five current productions. Make a grid to analyse these productions with the following headings:

Production	Venue	Period	Audience appeal	Genre/style	Other features
Title: Author: Company:					
Title: Author: Company:					
Title: Author: Company:					
Title: Author: Company:					
Title: Author: Company:					

As an extension activity you could also look up any reviews of these productions to see if they give further clues as to the nature of the performances. The review might be in the same edition of the newspaper. Most national daily and weekend newspapers have a website that will give you access to the reviews section.

Conventions are the Key!

At the heart of these categories of period, genre and style is the idea of conventions, the tricks, devices, techniques and formal elements used to communicate the performance's intentions to an audience. **Conventions in drama and theatre refer to the 'means' used to make particular kinds of 'meanings' for an audience.**

The conventions of the performance are a kind of agreement between the performers and the audience about the possibilities of dramatic representation. It is because of convention that we accept a ***soliloquy***; in reality we tend not to speak our innermost secrets out loud to a large crowd – but in the theatre we accept the convention because it is a device for communicating the character's inner speech. We want to know what the character thinks so we accept the convention of the *soliloquy*.

There is a 'convention' or agreement that the plays of ***Shakespeare*** can be set in other times and places. We know that the plays were written for an Elizabethan audience but we accept modern-day dress as a commentary on Shakespeare's ideas, which a director thinks is relevant to understanding the play.

You may be familiar with the idea of 'conventions' from your GCSE drama work: *tableau, thought-tracking, soundscape* and *role-on-the-wall* are common examples of the 'conventions' used in classroom drama. They are the 'means' used to represent the meanings that are explored and communicated in the drama.

Task 4: Thinking about conventions

Here are four popular conventions that you will be used to from your experiences of drama in school. In order to make the convention work, what do the actors need to do and what do the audience need to understand? Follow the example that is given and fill in the columns for the three other conventions. (If a convention is unfamiliar, choose another that you do know.)

Convention	Actors	Audience
Role-play	Actors must improvise the words and behaviour of the roles according to the given circumstances of the situation. They cannot drop in and out of role in order to plan or discuss what's happening.	This is an unrehearsed attempt to respond to the given situation and roles. The actors are not playing fully developed characters and it is what is said and done that is important not the quality of the acting. The audience understands that the actors are 'in role' rather than speaking as themselves.
Teacher-in-role		
Still-images		
Thought-tracking		

The 'Means' and 'Meanings' of Theatrical Communication

The 'conventions' of a drama may be just that – conventional, familiar and well-known means of communicating, such as the ***soliloquy*** – or they may be quite new and radical inventions by the artist who is trying to find new means of communicating.

Stephen Dillane in *Hamlet*. Gielgud Theatre 1994.

Many of the playwrights and practitioners that you will meet in your study of theatre are remembered because they introduced *new* conventions into drama and theatre. It is always important to remember that in their time these artists were radical and revolutionary in their practice – they changed the way that people saw and understood themselves by developing new 'means' for representing the human condition on stage.

In your studies of drama and theatre you will often be asked to recognise the 'conventions' used by a playwright or in a performance and to suggest which period, genre or style they are associated with. At its most simple you are being asked to identify the 'means' that are used to make 'meanings' for an audience. The 'means' of masks produce different kinds of meanings from the 'means' of song, dance or narration.

Conventions may refer to the 'means' of:

- Characterisation and speech
- Staging
- Design
- Actor-audience interactions
- Structuring the play text or dramatic narrative
- Acting style.

When we group two or more pieces of work together and say that they are representative of a period, genre or style we are saying that these works share **the same, or similar, conventions**.

So, we can talk about the typical conventions of a **period** such as the *Jacobean* theatre by looking to see what new conventions were invented during this historical period and used by a number of artists of the time. However, the story of the theatre is not to be found in the conventional or mainstream theatre of a period but in the *struggle* between periods. At those times in history, some artists began to break with the conventions of their time and to invent new ones, thus laying the ground for the next period of theatre in which their new conventions will become the 'conventional' theatre of the next generation.

In the early nineteenth century, for instance, a number of playwrights reacted against the conventions of ***romanticism*** by abandoning verse, introducing ordinary rather than aristocratic heroic characters, and using realistic settings. By the end of the century this realist revolution would become the next conventional theatre and a new group of ***symbolist*** artists would abandon the conventions of realism and introduce more abstract and theatrical conventions. At the time of their first introduction, the conventions of realism, which we are now so used to, were considered shocking, strange and radical by audiences.

When considering the conventions of a period, then, we need to look at the 'conventional' theatre of the time and also at what was happening in the ***avant-garde*** theatre. The *avant-garde* is the term used to describe the experimental, progressive and alternative theatre of a period, which seeks to break new ground and to turn against the 'conventional' – the safe, the commercial.

We can talk about the conventions of a particular **genre** of theatre such as *tragedy* by looking at the conventions of play structure, characterisation and plot that are associated with that genre. When we speak of a genre like *tragedy* we may also focus on how the genre has changed and developed over time because artists have introduced new conventions into the genre.

We can see, for instance, that there are differences between the conventions of the classical Greek tragedy and those used by ***Shakespeare***. Shakespeare introduced comic characters and scenes into his tragedies and ignored the classical unities of time, place and action (see page 23). Although they come from different periods and use some different conventions we can say that *Antigone* and *Hamlet* both belong to the genre of tragedy because they share a common set of conventions that have become associated with that genre. Both plays have an aristocratic main character, both have unhappy endings that result from some decision or choice taken by the main character, and the mood of both is predominantly despondent and sad.

The relationship of convention to **style** is not quite as straightforward. When style refers to a practitioner, as in ***Brechtian***, we mean that a performance uses conventions first associated with *Brecht*'s work. The performance may include storytelling and song, for instance, or the structure of the play may be *episodic*. *Brecht* developed the genre of *epic theatre* which has a particular set of conventions, but another practitioner may use *some* but not *all* of the conventions of *epic* in order to give a performance a *Brechtian* style. The conventions of a style can be combined with the conventions of a genre. Hence, *Macbeth* can and has been played in a number of different styles including those of gangster and samurai warrior films.

Style may also refer to design references to a particular historical period as in the *Grease* example we gave earlier. A play may be given a 1960s style or a 'Victorian' style.

Style may also refer to the conventions associated with a particular performance tradition; *Joan* **Littlewood** and *Theatre Workshop* used the conventions of the Victorian music-hall to give a style to her treatment of World War I in *Oh! What a Lovely War*. One aspect of *Peter* ***Brook***'s characteristic and eclectic style is his use of conventions from Indian, Japanese and Chinese performance traditions.

The *Mahabarata*, directed by *Brook*.

When we talk of the characteristic style of a practitioner or company we recognise that they will use certain kinds of convention regardless of the period or genre of performance that the company or practitioner is working with. *Brecht* applied the conventions of *epic* to his productions of musicals and *Shakespeare*'s plays.

Companies like the Royal Shakespeare Company tend to have a 'house' style, which is recognisable in quite different performances. Companies like the masked group *Trestle*, the physical theatre group ***Teatre de Complicite*** and the storytelling theatre of ***Shared Experience*** and *Method and Madness* have a house style; whatever the period or genre, we expect these companies to give a certain characteristic style to their work.

Task 5: Make your own definitions

Before moving on you need to make sure that you are clear about the terms convention, period, genre and style.

- **Write your own definitions based on the notes we have given you and use them to guide you in the future. If you are unsure of your definitions check them out with the group.**
- **Apply your definitions to a genre or style of music that you like – can you find examples of period, style and genre in your collection?**

Causing a Riot!

In your own practical work you will make decisions about the conventions, or 'means' that will best express and communicate your intentions to an audience. You may well want to try and develop new 'conventions', either because you want your work to be original and different or because you are dissatisfied with the 'conventional' means of communicating in theatre. If this is the case you are part of a long line of artists who have sought to change the theatre of their time by introducing new conventions. But, be warned – a new convention has to be accepted by the audience! If it's too far beyond what they are capable of accepting there will be trouble. Here are some examples of artists and performances that introduced conventions that the audience was not ready for!

In 1907, *The Playboy of the Western World* caused real riots when it was first shown at the ***Abbey Theatre*** in Dublin, because it was taken as an attack on the hypocrisy of Irish morality. Now, performed in Leicester, it has become a much safer '*riotous irish comedy*'!

In 1912 Igor Stravinsky used a new and radical twelve-tone scale in the music for *The Rite of Spring*. There was a riot on the first night, which prevented the piece being finished.

In 1922 the dancer Isadora ***Duncan*** finished a performance in New York by baring her breast and waving a red scarf; this also resulted in a riot!

In 1935, Antonin ***Artaud*** staged his version of *The Cenci* with animal movements, noises and graphic scenes of violence; once again there was a riot!

In 1965 Bob Dylan performed a concert of folk songs at the Albert Hall in London. The first half was a conventional set played solo and acoustically. After the interval Dylan returned in a black suit and dark glasses, carrying an electric guitar and fronting a five-piece band. Some of the audience, who had enthusiastically applauded the first half, began to shout 'Judas' at Dylan as he began his electric set.

Susan Fleetword and Stephen Rea in *Playboy of the Western World*, Royal National Theatre 1975.

The Cooking Pot that is Theatre

Most modern performances will consist of a mix of styles – a cocktail of conventions associated with different periods, genres and practitioners. However radical or inventive a new work might be it will still contain traces of earlier experiments and directions in theatre. Imagine the theatre of today to be like an old cooking pot, which is deeply crusted with all the meals that have been cooked in it over the years. When a new meal is cooked it will be flavoured by the residues and juices left by previous meals. The same is true of a play or performance – it will reflect modern trends but will be made out of conventions that have a long history. We have already noted that ***Shakespeare*** wrote radically new forms of *tragedy* but despite the 'moderness' of his plays there are still echoes of the ways in which tragedies were conventionally written in earlier times.

There are few rules in theatre and such rules as do exist become the target for radical artists! **The boundaries between genres, styles and periods are always slippery and changing**. As we have seen, in any period of theatre there will be a variety of different styles and genres at work – some will be dominant and mainstream while others will be experimental and ***avant-garde***. Playwrights do not like to be restricted by the rules of genre either. *Shakespeare* introduced some conventions from comedy into his tragedies and ***Chekhov*** developed ***tragi-comedy*** as new cross-breed of the genres of tragedy and comedy. Terms like 'genre' and 'period' are useful guides but they are never rigid and fixed definitions. You will always find examples of artists 'breaking the rules' in order to offer fresh and original dramas of the human condition.

Most of this book is concerned with developments in theatre in the twentieth century. But these developments were influenced by the theatre of earlier centuries**. In Appendix 2 we offer a brief history of pre-twentieth century periods, genres and styles**. The timeline gives you an overview of major developments in Western theatre between AD600 and 1910. You can follow the story or use the timeline to see when a new period begins and when new conventions first emerged. We have also included an account of the origins of the great non-European performance traditions, many of which have had profound influence on twentieth century Western practitioners. As you begin to study particular plays and practitioners, take the time to use the timeline to find out more about the other artists and developments of that period and the periods before and after.

Kathakali – King Lear, Shakespeare's Globe Theatre, July 1999.

2 The Origins of Drama and Theatre

How often have you seen this symbol of theatre? Perhaps you have a version yourself. Maybe someone who knew you were interested in theatre and drama bought you jewellery or a T-shirt with the symbol on. Throughout the Western world the masks of comedy and tragedy are used to refer to theatre and the performing arts. The common recognition of these signs tells us something about the story of theatre and the origins of the performances that we see now in our own time.

Comedy and tragedy first developed in ancient Athens

The masks suggest that these origins are to be found in the golden age of Athenian drama during the fifth and fourth centuries BC. It was during these times that the two classical dramatic genres of tragedy and comedy were first developed. It is sometimes said that the origins of theatre itself are to be found in the sacred rituals of ancient Athens, which later developed into the earliest forms of comedy and tragedy. This belief that *all* forms of theatre stem from sacred rites and festivals is very strong in the English theatre in particular. In fact there is little concrete archaeological evidence to suggest that drama and theatre originated in these sacred events. Nor can the early dramas of Athens be seen as the only origins of our theatre which in recent times has become more inclusive of other great cultural performance traditions and often includes elements of more recent European performance traditions – carnival, ***Commedia dell'Arte***, music-hall and musicals for instance. However, it is still worth looking at the Athenian drama because it helps us to understand some general points about theatre and performance which are relevant to a wide range of cultural traditions, including the forms of theatre that we find in our own time.

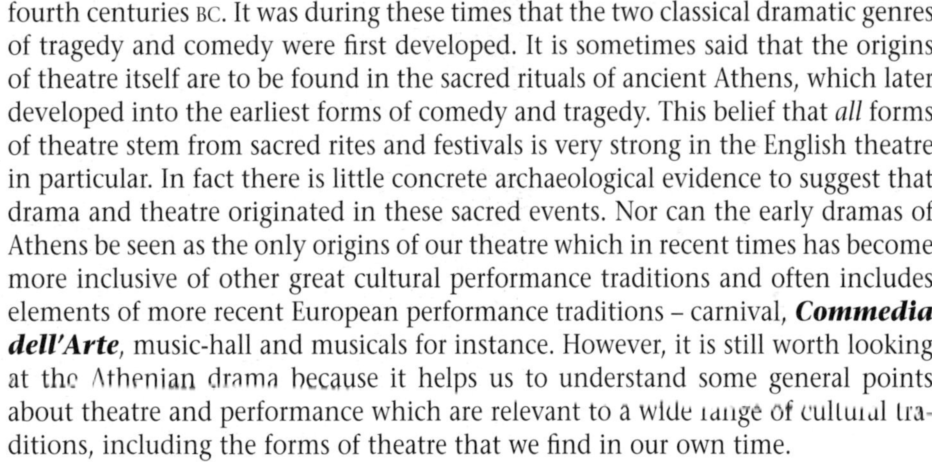

Aristotle's Theory of Tragedy

Aristotle described how comedies and tragedies should be written

Much of what we know about the origins of comedy and tragedy have been influenced by the theories of ***Aristotle*** who was a fourth century Athenian philosopher. *Aristotle* wrote on a wide range of aesthetic issues and only a small part of his work was concerned with the analysis of drama and theatre. *Aristotle* described how comedies and tragedies should be written. He did this partly by looking closely at the structure of the great plays of ***Aeschylus*** and *Sophocles* and partly by making his own rules. *Aristotle*'s account of comedy has never been fully recovered but his writings on tragedy have been very influential in the development of Western theatre and drama since they were rediscovered in the fifteenth century.

Aristotle defined tragedy as:

> **a representation of an action that is worth serious attention, complete in itself, and of some amplitude; in language enriched by a variety of artistic devices appropriate to the several parts of the play; presented in the form of action, not narration; by means of pity and fear bringing about the purgation of such emotions**

Aristotle's theories are still relevant today

In this short definition, Aristotle establishes certain features of tragedy, which we can still recognise in some genres and styles of today's theatre.

Many plays are based on the serious exploration of **a significant action** taken by the central character, which brings about their downfall or changes them and those around them in some profound way. Theatre, while it may often tell a story, is the **art of actions** – things happen rather than being merely described as they might be in a novel. In *Aristotle*'s analysis, actions in tragedy were not by chance or accident; they were made inevitable or necessary because of the characters and situations in the drama. Many plays still work on this idea of showing that characters behave as they do because of the social and psychological circumstances that they face.

Aristotle said that the central action should be of '*some amplitude*'. We now speak of certain kinds of action as being *dramatic* and by that we often mean **'larger than life'**. Often plays and other forms of drama depend on some big event to grab our interest and stir up the lives of the characters involved. In *Macbeth* a king is murdered. In disaster movies, some terrible natural calamity changes the course of people's lives. Sometimes we are struck by the magnitude of human choices which lead to death and destruction; sometimes by the tragedy of cataclysmic natural disasters and their effects.

Theatre seeks to move us, to make us feel strong emotions in response to the actions of the characters. For *Aristotle*, the purpose in arousing these strong emotions in the audience was to relieve or purge the same emotions in them – to allow the audience to experience strong emotions without having to suffer them as we do in everyday life. *Aristotle* called this process *catharsis*. This is a term we still use today and the dictionary defines it as '*an emotional release in drama or art*'. We still enjoy cathartic drama – think of a film like *Titanic* and how much you enjoyed crying at the climax! As we will see in Chapter 4, in the twentieth century ***Brecht*** would argue against *catharsis* and suggest that the purpose of theatre was to arouse the audience's thinking so that they would consider what action to take to change the world, rather than be purged and released from their feelings and emotions.

Greek tragedies were based on explorations of conflict between characters, groups of people or ideas. This idea that theatre is based on the struggle between opposing sides, represented by individual characters or groups, or on a tension created by conflict of some kind, is still a common principle in Western theatre.

The idea of a theatre based on some kind of conflict is included in the terms ***protagonist*** and ***antagonist***. The *protagonist* is the Greek term still used today to identify the main character, or 'hero', in the play who initiates the main action and around whom the rest of the characters and plots revolve. The *antagonist* is the character who opposes the *protagonist*'s objective or the main action of the play.

Many theatre words are Greek in origin

Many of the words that we use to speak about drama and theatre today, came into our language because they were made popular through *Aristotle*'s writings: for example, theatre, drama, tragedy, comedy, poet, critic, scene, rhythm and catharsis.

Epic storytelling evovles into tragedy

The tragedies of *Aristotle*'s time had their origins in the choral singing and storytelling of the great Greek myths. These performances became drama when ***Thespis*** turned the leader of the chorus into a character from the mythic story being told by the chorus for the first time. We still use the word *thespian* to describe an actor. **The actor wore a mask to show that he was now a character in the narrative rather than a storyteller.** At first, then, the dialogue between the main character and the chorus created the drama; the chorus would comment on, question or challenge the actions taken by the character, or *protagonist*. Later, *Aeschylus* invented a second actor, the *antagonist*, so that the conflict, or opposition of ideas, between two characters could be dramatically represented. *Sophocles* added a third actor (the *tritagonist*) and reduced the role of the chorus. This further developed the dramatic potential of tragedy.

Some of *Aristotle*'s principles, while they survived into the eighteen and nineteenth centuries, are no longer in use. He suggested that a tragedy should be in five acts and of sufficient length to properly represent the 'journey' or events which '*allows the hero by a series of probable or necessary stages to pass from misfortune to happiness or from happiness to misfortune*'.

The unities

Aristole also suggested that there should be: **unity of time** – the events of the play should take place within a 24-hour cycle; **unity of place** – the events should all be set in the same place; and **unity of action** – there should be a single plot which should have a clear beginning, middle and end.

Few modern plays still observe these unities, but both eighteenth century ***neo-classicism*** and the *Irish theatre* of the early twentieth century revived their use. Unity of action means that there should only be one main plot or storyline in the play; even if there are sub-plots they should still be part of the main story. In the twentieth century, ***Stanislavski*** would adapt this idea in talking about a play's '*through-line of action*'.

Within *Aristotle*'s idea of unity of action there is a second point which is important. The main character is always completely exhausted by the mental, physical and emotional demands of the action or plot. This means that the character's life is finished within the time period of the play. This idea that a character's life, or career, ends when the play does is still common in modern drama. For instance, in reality Macbeth's life would last longer than the three hours of the play. But the unity of action means that his stage life is completed within the span of the play. When there is a sense of the lives and destinies of characters concluding with the ending of the play we call it a **closed structure**.

In some modern plays, like *Waiting For Godot* or *Marat/Sade*, there is an alternative sense of the characters carrying on 'living' beyond the end of the play – we are watching an *episode* rather than a completed story. Most *soap operas* work on this principle – we imagine the lives of the characters to continue even if we are not watching. This is called an **open structure**.

The 'unites' of action, time and place together with the emphasis on the life of a single heroic character distinguishes the Athenian genre of tragedy from the *epic* genre of narrative. In *epic*, the story may involve a whole people's history or many different characters, span across decades of time and be set in a number of places – *Homer*'s *Illiad* and *Odyssey* are examples of *epic* and both ***Shakespeare*** and *Brecht*, among others, incorporated or substituted elements of the *epic* into their 'tragedies'.

Comedies were often crude and considered inferior to tragedies

The fragments of Aristotle's writings on comedy which have survived reveal that he **considered comedies to be inferior to tragedies** because they were bawdy and frivolous, based on chance, fantasy and comic errors. While tragedy sought to reveal the truth of human existence, comedy served to make fun of and escape from the realities of life. The Greek word *komos* literally meant a drunken revel! Tragedy served a serious purpose whereas comedy was for pure entertainment. This distinction between 'serious' and 'light' forms of theatre and drama and the idea that one is more elevated and sacred than the other still persists very strongly in our discussion of today's theatre and drama. Some people look down on comedies and other pieces of entertainment while others

Lysistrata by ***Aristophanes***, Old Vic Theatre, London 1993.

prefer to be entertained rather than being asked to take everything very seriously.

Aristophanes was a famous writer of comedies like *Lysistrata* in which the women refuse to have sex with their husbands unless they give up fighting!

The *satyr play* is the third genre of theatre with its origins in fifth century Athens. A *satyr play* was performed after a tragedy. The *satyr plays* were more informal, often crude with phallic imagery. The plays satirised, or were *parodies* of, myths, legends, historical heroes and even the tragedies that would have been performed before them. *Satyr plays* combined songs, dances and sketches and laid the basis for the later development of both modern *farce* and *burlesque*.

Recent studies of Athenian comedy and *satyr plays* reveal some remarkable connections with the modern theatre. The buffoonery and clowning of the comedy can be seen in the development of ***Commedia dell'Arte*** and more recently in the work of Dario ***Fo*** and ***Teatre de Complicite***. The gross emotions, phallic references and the distorted and ugly facemasks of the *satyr play* would reappear in the work of a playwright like Alfred ***Jarry***, and traces of both the *satyr plays* and the Athenian comedy are also to be found in the ideas of Antonin ***Artaud***.

The use of savage satires and parodies reoccurs throughout the history of theatre drama and mirrors the popular entertainment forms of *carnival* and the old English custom of *charivari* in which masked gangs would parade the streets mocking adulterers, profiteers, fraudsters and others in the community. The same spirit is to be found in the work of companies such as ***Welfare State International***. The actors in comedy would also come out of character, during the *parabasis*, or interval, to comment on topical events or to make a joke or aside directly to the audience just as *Brecht*'s actors would do in the twentieth century. The comedies also ignored, as much modern drama does, the unities of time, space and action.

The Athenian Influence on 'Serious' Theatre Today

Influences and comparisons in today's theatre

It was suggested at the beginning of this section that it is often assumed that our modern theatre originated in the dramas of fifth century BC Athens. Perhaps this is because there were important features of theatre of this period which closely resemble some aspects of the modern theatre. In addition to the features of tragedy, comedy and the ***satyr play*** that we have already considered there are some other general comparisons that can be made.

The plays were the work of playwrights and the Western tradition of theatre is, as we noticed in the first chapter of this book, based on a **literary tradition**. In other words it is remembered, principally, in terms of a long succession of playwrights and their literary works – the plays they wrote.

The literary tradition

The **emphasis on language** in Athenian drama led to the emergence of actors whose main purpose was to 'speak' or 'deliver' their 'lines' – the words given to them by the playwright. The audience came to listen to the words rather than to watch a play. They listened attentively and quietly. Actors were judged by their ability to speak their lines appropriately rather than by their ability to physically 'characterise' their parts. Even in ***Shakespeare***'s time people would talk of going to 'hear' a play rather than to 'see' a play, as we would. Many performances now are still based on the actors' skills in 'delivering' their lines to an audience that listens attentively and quietly.

The Athenian dramas began the tradition of **representing universal themes and ideas about human experience** through presenting the story of particular characters and their journeys. This idea that theatre should focus on a small group of characters and their particular story as a means of commenting on or explaining the world at large still underpins much modern drama.

The first theatre buildings

The Athenian dramas took place in theatres just as many of our plays do. The creation of **theatre buildings** was the result of the development of the city as a

Epidaurus Theatre, Greece.

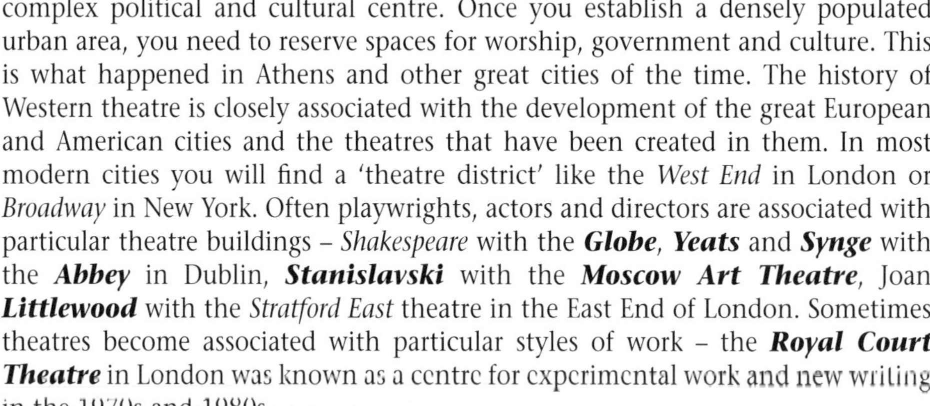

complex political and cultural centre. Once you establish a densely populated urban area, you need to reserve spaces for worship, government and culture. This is what happened in Athens and other great cities of the time. The history of Western theatre is closely associated with the development of the great European and American cities and the theatres that have been created in them. In most modern cities you will find a 'theatre district' like the *West End* in London or *Broadway* in New York. Often playwrights, actors and directors are associated with particular theatre buildings – *Shakespeare* with the ***Globe***, ***Yeats*** and ***Synge*** with the ***Abbey*** in Dublin, ***Stanislavski*** with the ***Moscow Art Theatre***, Joan ***Littlewood*** with the *Stratford East* theatre in the East End of London. Sometimes theatres become associated with particular styles of work – the ***Royal Court Theatre*** in London was known as a centre for experimental work and new writing in the 1970s and 1980s.

Athens became a progressive democratic state

During the fifth century BC, Athens became a progressive democratic state in which citizens of a certain rank and class were allowed to vote for a group of representatives who would then govern the city. Here lie the origins of our modern democracy. During this period, going to the theatre was seen as an important part of public life. Citizens were expected to go to the theatre just as they were expected to contribute to the public good of the city. The Theatre of Dionysus at Athens in its final form could house an audience of 20,000. The theatre was seen as offering citizens a mirror of the concerns and issues that faced them.

Although, like our own middle-class theatre, the Greek theatre depended on a wealthy audience of slave owners, the great Athenian leader *Pericles* established the *theoric fund* to subsidise the cost of a seat for the poor – the first government-subsidised theatre!

Theatre contributes to debates about society

The idea that theatre should contribute to debates about society and the directions in which it is going is very strong in the history of Western theatre. At different times, playwrights from *Shakespeare* through to ***Ibsen***, ***Strindberg*** and ***Brecht*** have sought to explain or challenge the times in which they lived. In order to do this, playwrights and others have often needed to introduce **new conventions** in order to reflect the changes that are occurring in society.

Western Theatre evolves and changes

This tradition of a progressive art form that seeks new methods and new conventions for representing our private and social lives has its origins in Athenian drama. However, in many of the world's great performance traditions, particularly those of Asia and Africa, the emphasis is on tradition and continuity – the idea is to preserve and recreate performances rather than to invent new conventions and ideas about performance. But as we have seen, in Athens during the fifth century BC there was a rapid development of drama and theatre because playwrights were encouraged to invent and develop new ways for the audience to see themselves and the swiftly changing circumstances of their lives.

Antigone: An Example of Greek Tragedy

The plot of *Antigone*

Antigone (442–441BC) was the first of a *trilogy* of plays that *Sophocles* wrote to tell the tragic story of the royal house of Thebes. At the heart of this story is the tragedy of Oedipus. Oedipus was brought up by foster-parents and set out on a journey to find his natural parents. Through a tragic series of unwitting mistakes, Oedipus kills a stranger in an angry quarrel only to discover, much later, that the stranger was in fact his father King Laius of Thebes. He also marries the widow

Jocasta who bears him two sons and two daughters, only to discover that Jocasta is his natural mother. As a result of this shame Jocasta kills herself and Oedipus blinds himself and goes into exile; eventually he 'dies' in mysterious circumstances.

Oedipus passes over control of Thebes to Jocasta's brother Creon, but his sons, Polynices and Eteocles, will not accept this decision and both make rival challenges to Creon's power. Eventually, Polynices joins forces with the city of Argos, the enemies of Thebes, and invades. Despite his differences with Creon, Eteocles bravely defends Thebes against his brother's attack and both end up killing each other.

In order to deter any further treason and to bring order back to Thebes, Creon decrees that Eteocles should be buried with full honours while his brother's body must be left to rot outside the city gates. Anyone who tries to bury Polynices shall be stoned to death. The Greeks believed it to be vital for a body to be properly buried and taken to the 'underworld' below. It was the responsibility of the family to ensure that there was a proper burial ritual. The story of *Antigone* begins with the *Prologue* in which Oedipus' two daughters, Antigone and Ismene, discuss Creon's decree.

(*Thebes*)

Antigone: My own sister, dear sister, Ismene.
Tell me this: are there any evils coming from Oedipus that Zeus does not fulfil through us – the two still living?
Pain, ruin, shame
All of these
I see in your evils and mine

And now what is this proclamation the general has made to all of Thebes?
Have you heard anything? Are you aware that evils appropriate for our enemies are to be endured by our loved ones?

Ismene: I have no word, Antigone, concerning our loved ones. Nothing sweet, nothing bitter, has come my way since we two were bereft of our two brothers – one day's double blow of a double death. And with the departure of the armies from Argos last night, I do not know whether to feel more fortunate or more distressed.

Antigone: I know –
and I've brought you outside the gates of the house so you alone can hear.

Ismene: What is it? You're troubled – brooding over some story.

Antigone: We have two brothers. Hasn't Kreon honoured one with a tomb and shamed the other?
Eteocles, they say, has been buried, with due observance of justice and custom, under the ground, to be honoured amongst the dead.
As for Polyneikes, they say it is forbidden by decree to bury him, or mourn him, but he is to be left unwept, unburied, a sweet morsel for the birds as they look down – their treasure store of tasty meat.

That is the good Kreon's proclamation to you and to me – yes, to me – and he is coming here to make this clear to those who may still not know.
And this is no small matter.
Whoever does these things anyway will be stoned in front of the people of the city. That's how it is for you as well and you will soon show whether you are well born or the bad shoot of good stock.

Ismene: If these things are so, my poor sister, what can I do? Not do?

Antigone: Think if you will share in the work, the act.

Ismene: Share in what? What do you mean?

Antigone: Will you help this hand to lift the dead?

Ismene: You are thinking of burying him – and this has been forbidden?

Antigone: He is my own brother, and yours too, even if you do not wish it. I will not be known as the one who betrayed him.

Ismene: Such purpose – and Kreon has forbidden it.

Antigone: Not for him to keep me from my own.

Ismene: *Oimoi.*
Think,
sister
how our father died –
hated, in shame
shunned
uncovering himself his own guilt and striking his two eyes with his own hands. And then the mother, wife, double name, mangling her life in that tangle of ropes.
And finally, our two brothers, in one day each miserably slaying the other, trapped in a shared fate wreaked by their own hands.
We are the two left behind. Alone. We too will die most miserably if we violate the decree and defy the power of the tyrant.
We must remember we are born women and are not meant to do battle against men.
And then that we are ruled by those who are the stronger and we must obey this and things even more painful.
And so I beg forgiveness of those below, I am compelled: I have to obey those in power.
There is no sense in the excessive gesture.

Antigone: I won't urge you any more – no, even if you changed and wanted to do it – you would no longer be welcome.
Think as you will.
I will bury him.

And I will die well doing this.
I will lie with him I love, my friend, my kin – guilty, yes, but of a holy crime.
I believe I owe more of my time to pleasing the dead below than those here: there, I shall live for ever.
Think as you will, but you will be guilty of dishonouring the gods.

Ismene: I am not doing them a dishonour.
I cannot act against the will of the city.

Antigone: Such is your excuse.
I will go and raise a tomb for my beloved brother.

Ismene: Hard suffering, I fear for you.
Antigone: Don't fear for me; straighten out your own destiny.
(Continues)

Antigone Workshop

1. Work with a partner and read through the extract together at least twice.
2. Decide with your partner what each character's *objective* might be in this scene: What does Antigone want to happen, or make happen, next? What does Ismene want to happen next?
3. Read through the extract again, but now think about the characters' objectives and how this will affect the way in which the lines are spoken and responded to by the characters. Try to make your reading of the play lifelike, in the sense that if you think that Antigone is trying to persuade Ismene or that she gets angry with her this should be reflected in the way that you speak your lines.
4. Now join together with another pair and share your ideas about the way to play the lines. Let one pair read through the extract, expressing the objectives in your voice, while the other pair improvise the physical actions of the two characters. How do they move around the stage? When are they close? When might they move away from each other? What about facial and other gestures? Work together until you feel that the actions and the words match together, then share your work with other groups.

Remember that ***Aristotle*** based many of his ideas about tragedy on the plays of *Sophocles*. Go back to *Aristotle*'s definition of tragedy on page 21. What do you think is the action, in this extract, that is worth serious attention. Where is the language enriched by a variety of artistic devices (imagery, metaphor)? Is the plot presented in action rather than narration? What emotions do the characters express? And what emotions do you think an audience might experience during this scene?

Aristotle broke down the structure of tragedy into six parts, and again we still use some of these terms in our discussion of today's theatre. We have described the six elements and their contemporary usage on the next page and asked you some questions about how the six elements relate to this extract.

Element	Questions
1. Plot (*mythos* from which we get the word 'myth'): this was 'the soul of tragedy' for ***Aristotle*** and referred to the incidents and sequence of events in the play which would include crises, conflicts, reversals of fortune, climaxes, tensions and suspense, exposition and denouement. *Aristotle* also suggested that the plot should have a beginning, middle and end.	This Prologue offers the 'exposition' of the play's plot. This is the essential information about characters' past lives and relationships and a foreshadowing of events to come. What events are re-told? What events are foreshadowed? What conflicts and tensions are there? What crises and climax do you think there will be later in the play?
2. Character (*ethos* from which we get 'ethics'): there were four aspects of character: • a character should be 'good' which often meant being of noble birth; • being 'good' also meant that characters should have a moral purpose for their actions; • characters should be 'typical' of the people they represent rather than odd or different; • they should be 'real' not fantastical or magical and they should be 'consistent' – they should behave 'in character', as we would say – their actions should be probable, credible and plausible.	Both Antigone and Ismene are aristocrats. Many plays until the nineteenth century were about princes, kings and queens and other aristocratic heroes. What are Ismene and Antigone's moral purposes in this scene? What does each consider to be the right/wrong thing to do? In what ways are Ismene and Antigone 'typical'? What kind of person does each represent? The idea of 'consistency' of character would become one of the principles of ***Stanislavski***'s system of acting. In modern times character is more usually discussed in terms of the psychology and morality of a character and the social relations between characters. What clues are there that the characters will behave consistently for the rest of the play?
3. Thought (*dianoia*): we would now use the term 'theme', which describes the ideas of the play, or issues raised, and how the drama-world of the play relates to or illuminates the actual world in which we live. Discussion of a play's 'thought' is often concerned with an exploration of the spiritual, political or social content of a play. This translation is by the contemporary playwright Timberlake ***Wertenbaker***. Many different generations have found connections between the story of Antigone and their own times. During the 1940s both Jean ***Anouilh*** and ***Brecht*** adapted the play as a commentary on the decline into fascism.	What are the issues and themes that are raised in this extract? Why might these themes and issues have been of interest to a woman writing plays today and a Marxist playwright in fascist Germany? Do any of these issues have relevance for you, living today?
4. Diction (*lexis* from which we get 'lexicon' meaning a dictionary or vocabulary): this describes the literary aspects of the drama – how it is written, the language and poetry, the imagery and metaphors of speech.	Look closely at Ismene's speech beginning: *Oimoi . . . .* Why has Wertenbaker laid the lines out in this way? What is intended by the line breaks? How can the intentions of the written format be played in performance? What is the effect?
5. Music (*melos* from which we get 'melody'): *Aristotle* didn't dwell on *melos* but a consideration of the 'acoustic' elements of a performance – what we hear in terms of music and other sounds – has become increasingly important in modern theatre.	Is there a 'melody' in the language? As you read through were you conscious of the rhythm, or sound, of the words? What music or other sound effects might you add to this scene in a modern production?

Element	Questions
6. Spectacle (*opsis* from which we get 'optics' and 'optical'): again, *opsis* was not an important category for *Aristotle* but the visual elements of a play are now seen as being essential to the 'theatre' of a performance and both music and spectacle are of great importance in genres such as pantomime, opera, musicals and physical theatre.	The Greeks used very little in terms of scenery and other visual clues of the play's setting. The main scenery was provided by the *skene* (from which we get the word 'scene'), which was a wooden building at the back of the *orchestra* or stage. The *skene* looked like a real house and was the territory of the female characters as it was in Athenian culture. Which of Antigone's lines refers to the *skene* as a house? What other elements of setting or props might you introduce into a modern production that would be in keeping with the play's setting and themes?

The functions of the chorus

The first chorus, which speaks of the same events, follows this Prologue but from the perspective of the citizens of Thebes who support Creon's actions. **In *Sophocles'* tragedies the chorus serves a number of functions:**

- they place the events of the story in a more universal theme;
- they raise anxieties, on behalf of the audience, about what is happening;
- they act as a silent and public witness to private acts (such as this conversation between sisters);
- they speak for the citizens of Athens (the audience).

For the final exercise you are going to use a modern idea that the chorus might work visually rather than vocally – they might show through images rather than comment in words.

1. Prepare a series of still-images based on the content of the two sister's dialogue – events and ideas – that the chorus might present during this extract. You will need the whole group to work together in the following way. Two pairs will provide the words and actions for the scene. The rest are the chorus who form their images at appropriate moments in the scene. Practise the timing so the images either foreshadow the events the two sisters talk about or comment, as outsiders, on the events they have already expressed their opinion about. The actors may need to freeze to allow the images to be made, and the chorus may also repeat lines as a *caption* or heading for their image.
2. Run the sequence together when you think you have an effective sequence in which the work of the chorus is satisfying some of the functions described above.

Task 1: From Athens to today's theatre

- **What are the main similarities and differences between the fifth century Athenian theatre culture and our own? What has changed and what has remained the same?**
- **How does the history of the Athenian theatre help us to understand and talk about today's theatre?**

There is an excellent website to visit which gives you information, animations and text about this period of Greek stagecraft: http://didaskalia.berkeley.edu./stagecraft/greek.html

Different Performances

In Chapter 1, The Infinite Variety of Theatre, we talked about the ways in which different kinds of plays and performances can be organised into periods, styles and genres. We can add to these by introducing three new categories for broadly distinguishing between different performances and styles. These categories are also to be found in the theatre of fifth century Athens.

Once again we need to remind you that while it is useful to be able to talk about the differences in performance, categories and labels are always slippery and changeable! Performances are never either one category or another. But they are often more or less one category or another.

The categories are:

Realist and non-realist styles and genres	Making a distinction between 'lifelike' and abstract or 'stylised' performance styles
The social function of the performance	The intended purpose or effect of the performance on the audience
Presentational and representational theatre	The difference between recreating another 'world' in 'another time' on stage and communicating directly to the audience 'here and now'

Realist and Non-realist Styles in Theatre

Mimesis* is the origin of *realism

The various genres of ***realism*** in theatre, film and TV are based on the Aristotelian concept of ***mimesis***, which is often taken to mean **a lifelike representation** of how people behave and respond to experience. *Mimesis* is the origin of *realism*, which is still the most commonly used style of theatre and is certainly the dominant style of TV and film drama.

In a *mimetic*, or *realist* style of drama we only see and hear what we would actually see and hear in life – people look as they would do, they often, though not always, use the same language that we hear in our everyday lives and they are realistically presented in their natural surroundings. The ambition of *realism* is to remove all traces of theatricality so that the drama and performance can be experienced as 'real life' rather than as a representation or construction of real life.

The opposite of the *realist* tradition in theatre can be most simply described as ***non-realist***. *Non-realist* theatre, like some styles of painting, doesn't try to represent the world as we actually see and hear it. Instead, it tries to represent the invisible and imagined world of thoughts, ideas, dreams and fears through mask, dance, mime, symbolic gestures and costumes, props and set design.

Most of the great non-European performance traditions such as ***Kathakali***, ***Noh*** and ***Kabuki*** are non-realist in style. Look at the *Kabuki* actor on the cover of this book. This is not a 'lifelike' representation of character in the *realist* tradition. The costume, mask and colours represent instead the spirit, the demons, the fantasy and power evoked by the character, but rather you can actually see when looking at a character, but rather what you can imagine when you think, or dream, about the character.

The ambition of the *non-realist* style is well summed up by ***Stanislavski*** who described the problems of presenting ***Maeterlinck***'s *The Blue Bird* to his actors in this way:

> **There are three main difficulties to overcome. First of all, we must express on the stage the *inexpressible* ... Second, the sensibilities of the audience are not ready to receive and comprehend**

abstract thoughts and feelings. Third we have to _personify_ sleep, a dream, a presentiment, a fairy tale. This is lace work, woven of fine threads like a cobweb, while the scenic means of modern stage technique (realism) are coarse and clumsy.

Non-realism is not always as obviously symbolic and abstract as this quote suggests. **_Non-realism_ also refers to any performance style which stresses the _theatricality_ of the performance.** In other words, rather than seeking to persuade the audience that the events on stage are real-life, the performance emphasises that it is theatre, not life. This means that the performance will stress movement, props and costumes, lighting and design and stlylised performance traditions like masks, puppets and ***Commedia dell'Arte*** that are obviously stylised and theatrical – only experienced and seen in the theatre rather than borrowed and copied ***mimetically*** from life.

Practitioners associated with this style of *non-realism* would include ***Craig***, ***Meyerhold***, ***Brecht***, ***Grotowski***, ***Brook*** and most of the great twentieth century practitioners who sought to rebel against the *realism* of *Stanislavski*'s system. For this reason the work of these practitioners is sometimes referred to as ***post-realist***. The great Russian director Vsevlod *Meyerhold*, describes this form of *non-realism* in these words in 1912:

The public comes to the theatre to see the art of man, but what art is there in walking about the stage as oneself? The public expects invention, playacting and skill. But what it gets is either life or a slavish imitation of life. Surely the art of man on stage consists in shedding all traces of environment, carefully choosing a mask, donning a decorative costume, and showing off one's brilliant tricks to the public – now as a dancer, now as the intrigant at some masquerade, now as the fool of old Italian comedy, now as a juggler.

Although in this book we will use the terms *realist* and *non-realist*, you will find that there are different terms used to describe this basic difference between 'lifelike' and 'non-lifelike' or stylised theatrical forms of theatre. Sometimes the difference is expressed as 'naturalistic' and 'non-naturalistic'; or 'stylised' and 'symbolic' are used to describe non-realist theatre. **These terms are interchangeable; there is no general agreement about which terms to use.** But it is important to remember that *realism*, ***naturalism*** and ***symbolism*** also refer to specific genres and styles of late nineteenth century theatre practice.

One difficulty is that when the term *'naturalism'* is used it can mean either a general 'lifelike' style of theatre or a specific genre of theatre associated with the writers Maxim ***Gorki***, Leo ***Tolstoi***, Gerhart ***Hauptmann*** and others. In some cases you will find these genres spelt with a capital letter (Realism) to indicate the historical genre rather than a general style (realism).

Task 2: Differences between realism and non-realism

Look at the two illustrations overleaf. One is from a performance that is generally considered to be in the _realist_ style, the other is _non-realist_. What are the key differences in the pictures? What do you imagine would be the different effect, or _impact_, of each production?

Realism is not real; naturalism is not natural

It is important to remember that *realism* is a style of theatre. It presents the **illusion** of reality. It is no more **real** than the most abstract and stylised forms of *non-realist* theatre; *realism* will always be artificial and 'unreal' precisely because it is a **representation**, or construction, of reality on the stage rather than life as it is actually experienced and lived on the street. We are often reminded of how 'artificial' and 'unnatural' realism is when we see a play or drama that is based on our own

The Weir, Royal Court/Duke of York's, February 1998.

Nancy Crane and Stephen Dillane in *Angels in America*, Royal National Theatre 1993.

experiences. Teachers, police officers and doctors probably don't think that *Grange Hill, The Bill* and *Casualty* are lifelike at all! And you may not find the representation of school in film and TV to be true to your own experience. As we have seen, drama is often based on 'larger than life' characters and events – everyday experience becomes dramatised for our entertainment. But we are also made conscious that however realistic the style, drama is always an **interpretation** of life *not* life itself. Theatre is always made; it is never 'natural'.

Different generations view realism differently

Throughout history, theatre artists have struggled to show their audiences the world as it really is – to find the most truthful way of showing the audience who they are and who they are becoming as a society. Every generation has imagined that its theatre is more real or realistic than that of previous generations. What the Greeks took to be realism, or *mimesis*, would now seem quite unrealistic to us – masks, chorus, verse, etc. Many of the classic plays that you will study may seem strange and quite unreal as pictures of the human condition. But always remember that in their time these plays would have seemed to be highly realistic pictures of life to their audiences. In the same way those old black and white movies shown on Sunday afternoons may seem absurd and unreal to you, but they were realistic for the cinema audiences of 40 and 50 years ago.

Task 3: What counts as 'realism' today?

- **Which current TV or film drama would you say is the most *realistic*? How is the sense of *realism* created – character, plot, settings, language, camera angles?**
- **Choose a genre such as police dramas and compare the *realism* of today's examples of the genre with those you can remember from childhood. How have ideas of *realism* changed?**

***Realism* in nineteenth century theatre**

Different generations have different ideas about what is real in their lives and what is realism in theatre. In the late nineteenth century, for instance, many people believed that science alone could resolve all the unanswered questions and mysteries of life. The turn against religion and mysticism led to a way of thinking called *positivism*. The basis of *positivism* is that all true knowledge is scientific. Everything can be measured and classified according to scientific principles. *Empiricism* is the term used to describe the *postivist* method of inquiry.

In *empiricism* the truth can only be established if it can be proved by actual experience – in other words, the truth only exists in the material world of rational thinking and the evidence of our senses: touch, taste, sight, and hearing. *Realism* in nineteenth century theatre, then, was based on the idea that the instantly recognisable characters, settings, language and situations on stage were 'truthful' because they were scientifically accurate descriptions of human experience and behaviour. But if we look more closely at *realism* as a style we can see through this illusion.

Most plays in the *realist* style are based on the following elements.

A strong **plot** or story in a lifelike setting	**But,** we know that life is more complex than a story. Stories neatly organise experience into a beginning, middle and end. But our everyday experience is often more muddled and uncertain than this! We don't live in a story, even if stories are the main means we have of explaining our

	experiences to each other. A poet would argue that a poem could be just as 'truthful' a means of representing human experience as a story. The idea that characters can be explained in terms of their physical setting – the environment in which they live – is also a superficial idea of personality and behaviour.
Unified and consistent **characterisation** based on the idea of the 'well rounded individual' (this is the basis of ***Stanislavski***'s acting methods)	**But**, the basis of the 'realist' character is the idea that characters should behave with a degree of consistency (in the same way) whatever the situation or setting. The purpose of rehearsal is to 'iron out' any rough edges, or inconsistencies, in the character to create the illusion of a predictable, well rounded and unified personality. In reality of course, we know that people are not like that – they often behave 'out of character', and you know that there are many quite different 'sides' to your own personality. We also know that people change – they are never complete in the way that the *realist* character is presented.
A cultural and class specific **perspective**	The 'reality' of the world that is presented in ***realist*** theatre is always based on how the world appears to a particular culture and class. There are exceptions, but more often than not, *realist* plays and performances seek to make a white, European, middle-class view of the world look like the only 'natural' and 'truthful' perspective. This is also the basis of ***naturalism*** as a genre. In *naturalist* plays the effects of environment and poor health on the morality and fortunes of the lower classes are scientifically analysed and presented for the benefit of the middle-class audience. This reflects their view of the lower classes.

Realist and _non-realist_ styles are often mixed

Although the origins of modern *realism* are to be found in the theatre of the ancient Greeks it is important to remember that the Greeks mixed elements of *realism* and *non-realism* in their performances, and this tradition has continued through history. ***Shakespeare*** wrote *realist* plays that mixed prose (*realism* in speech) with poetry (*non-realism* in speech). ***Chekhov*** included ideas associated with ***symbolism*** in his *realist* plays. *Brecht* is often considered to be a *non-realist* practitioner but he called his theatre *scientific realism* even though he often used *non-realist* settings and costumes.

In contemporary theatre we often find a mix of *realist* and *non-realist* ideas. The characters and speech may be realist but not the setting, or costumes or stage design. **It is often more appropriate to talk of a continuum between *realism* and *non-realism* when discussing the style of a performance**; to say that the performance was more *realist* than *non-realist*, for instance. It is also important to think about the logic behind the choice to make some elements *realist* and others *non-realist*. *Shakespeare* reserved verse for his aristocratic characters and for creating particular effects of atmosphere. *Brecht* used some *non-realist* costumes and scenery to emphasise the political messages in his plays.

Task 4: Is *Macbeth* a realist or non-realist play?

1. **Remind yourself of the plot of the play; remember all the supernatural happenings: the witches, Hecate, the ghosts.**
2. **Make a line to represent the *realist/non-realist* continuum. Let each member of the group stand on the line according to where they think the play is on this continuum. Discuss your positions.**

Getting Results and Fooling Around – The Social Function of Theatre

Theatre serves different social functions

We have seen that theatre played an important role in the lives of the Athenians. It had different social functions. Sometimes, as in the tragedies, the social function was to both educate and create serious debate among the citizens. In *Antigone* for instance, the conflict between the interests of the city government and the interests of family life which is represented in the conflict between the characters of Creon and Antigone was intended to both instruct and create debate among the audience of Athenian citizens. The comedies and ***satyr plays*** had a different function in entertaining and amusing the Athenians, providing pure pleasure rather than instruction.

Theatre and drama have continued since Athenian times to serve a variety of social functions, from providing a forum for debate and for promoting changes in cultural attitudes or unjust laws to the pleasurable experiences of whodunits, farces and slapstick clowning. The social function of ***Ibsen***'s plays *A Doll's House* and *Hedda Gabler* was to try and change society's attitudes towards women as domestic slaves who were 'owned' like property by their husbands. The social function of his play *Ghosts* was to raise the taboo subject of venereal disease. ***Brecht***'s plays had a strong political social function in seeking to promote a Marxist analysis of society. His purpose was not to simply show the world as it was but to *change* it into a better world for workers and other oppressed groups. Early in his career he wrote a series of plays called *Lehrstucke* or 'learning plays'. The *Lehrstucke* offered very clear and unambiguous lessons to the audience and are an example of *didactic* theatre. The social function of *didactic* theatre is clearly educational, often political, rather than for amusement or entertainment.

Later in his career, *Brecht* would argue that for a play to be educational and instructive it should also be entertaining. Indeed, most plays and performances which have a social function to educate or promote social reform also have the secondary function of providing entertainment. **But you can still distinguish, just as the Athenians did, between plays and performances that emphasise a political or educational function and plays and performances which offer pleasure and fun** to the audience without asking them to do much thinking about the world and its problems.

We use the term 'social function' but you may also find terms like 'playwright's intention' or 'overall purpose' used in some texts. Again there is no general agreement about which term to use to describe the different functions of performances.

Task 5: Thinking about social function

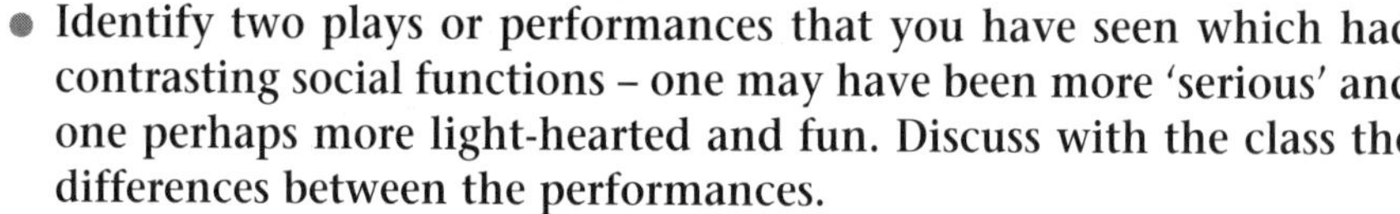

- Identify two plays or performances that you have seen which had contrasting social functions – one may have been more 'serious' and one perhaps more light-hearted and fun. Discuss with the class the differences between the performances.

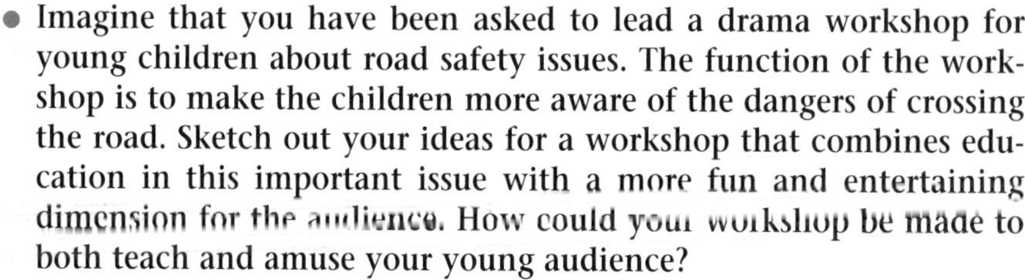

- Imagine that you have been asked to lead a drama workshop for young children about road safety issues. The function of the workshop is to make the children more aware of the dangers of crossing the road. Sketch out your ideas for a workshop that combines education in this important issue with a more fun and entertaining dimension for the audience. How could your workshop be made to both teach and amuse your young audience?

Presentational Theatre and Representational Theatre

This distinction refers to the relationship between the performance, the performers and the audience. A broad distinction can be made between performances that include, or make direct use of, the audience and what is happening to them, and performances which ignore the audience and offer an alternative 'stage reality', a different reality from that of the audience.

Performances that directly address the audience and their actual reality are termed ***presentational***; they focus, and often comment on, the present, **here-and-now experience** of the audience. The effect of a presentational performance will be that the events on stage are happening 'here' among us, as we watch.

Performances that create a fictional 'world' that is entirely divorced from the audience and their reality are termed ***representational***; they *re*-present a different experience which is happening **somewhere else** in a parallel, or virtual reality that is not the same as the actual place and time of the performance itself.

Realism **and** ***naturalism*** **require representational performances**

The plays and performances of the genres of ***realism*** and ***naturalism*** in the second half of the nineteenth century are purely *representational*; the 'fourth wall' of the proscenium arch separated the fictional world represented on the stage from the darkened and silent world of the audience in the auditorium. **In representational theatre there is no direct contact between the actors and the audience**. The actors are in a different world and in a different time from the audience, so there can be no contact between them. A *representational* style of theatre often depends on the use of acting styles based on the ***psycho-realism*** of ***Stanislavski***'s system. Indeed, as we shall see later in this book, *Stanislavski* developed his system precisely in order for his actors to play in the *representational* mode – completely 'being' in character and completely unaware of the audience. (See Chapter 3 for a more detailed explanation of this acting style.)

Epic and other popular forms require presentational performances

The plays and performances of *Brecht* on the other hand sought to directly include the audience by presenting events and characters directly to them. The actors would comment on their characters to the audience and address the audience directly through songs and stories. Presentational theatre is often associated with popular forms of entertainment like *burlesque, music-hall, musicals* and *stand-up comedy*; those forms of entertainment which seek to give the audience an experience rather than to represent another place and time. A presentational style of theatre often depends on the use of acting styles associated with *Brecht*. He developed a style of *scientific realism* in acting which mixed 'being' in character with 'showing' or presenting characters to the audience, so that his actors could both represent another world to the audience while at the same time including the audience directly in the representation. (See Chapter 4 for a more detailed explanation of this acting style.)

Again, many contemporary and historical performances mix elements of presentation and representation, just as the Greek theatre did. In *Antigone* the scene between the two sisters is *representational* in the sense that the sisters do not acknowledge the audience – they pretend 'as if' the meeting is really happening and that there is no one else watching. But the first chorus that follows on immediately from this scene does directly address its speech to the audience, as an audience of fellow citizens; it is therefore *presentational*. The chorus in Greek tragedy often switches from being *representational* – part of the reality of the play – to being *presentational* – directly addressing and including the audience.

In Greek comedies, the plays are broken into two by the *parabasis* in which the actors and chorus step out of role to directly address the audience about political and social issues, just as they would in *Brecht*'s dramas.

Shakespeare also mixed the *representational* and *presentational*. In *A Midsummer Night's Dream*, for instance, he mixes the representation of the world of Athens and the woods inhabited by the fairies with presentational sequences like the mechanical scenes which are addressed to the audience to make them laugh. The play closes with Puck's famous *presentational* address to the audience:

If we shadows have offended
Think, but this, and all is mended,
That you have but slumbered here
While these visions did appear . . .
So, good night unto you all.
Give me your hands, if we be friends
And Robin shall restore amends.

The Alternative Origins of Today's Theatre

In order to make and understand theatre in our time it's important to know something of the origins and structures of the Athenian forms of tragedy and comedy. But to claim that the modern theatre originates entirely in the fifth century theatre of Athens is to ignore the many other cultural traditions of performance which have influenced theatre's development in modern times. In general terms there are five other major influences which we can still recognise today even though their origins lie in the deep past of Western history (many of these influences would be more recognised in modern cultures which have maintained traditional forms of performance).

The five influences that need to be considered alongside comedy and tragedy are:

- Stories and storytelling
- Ritual
- Shamanism
- Dance
- Martial arts contests of skill and strength

Storytelling

Both stories and storytelling – the ways in which stories can be told – have had a profound influence on the development of theatre. Most of the world's great performance traditions are based on the stories and/or the storytelling styles of earlier times. We have seen that Athenian drama developed from the stories told by the great, blind, *Homer* who sang his epic tales to the accompaniment of a *lyre*. The *Sanscrit* performance tradition in India was, and still is, based on episodes from the epic tales of the *Mahabharata* and the *Ramayana*. Similarly, the traditions of Chinese theatre and *Noh* performances are based on the playing of traditional stories. ***Shakespeare*** is an example of a playwright who based many of his plays on traditional stories and classical histories borrowed from *Ovid*, *Plutarch* and others.

Many plays and dramas use a *narrative form*

Many plays and dramas use a *narrative form* in which there is a clear sense of a beginning, middle and end. Narrative is the most common way for us to share and understand experience. You tell your friends what has happened to you in the form of a narrative. You listen to their stories and understand something of their experiences as a result. Story, then, is the most commonly used and generally understood way of representing experiences.

There are common characteristics in both drama and story, but also some important differences.

The similarities are:

- Events are put into a *context* of time and place. Things happen at certain times in a particular place. We talk about a play's **setting**.
- We are introduced to the characters of the people involved – we find out what the people involved in the story are like from how they behave and respond to the events in the story. We talk about **characterisation**.
- There is often an appeal to our emotions; the story is told to arouse pity, fear, laughter and anger in us. We talk about the playwright or performance's **intention**. In the *Sanscrit* tradition, intention is referred to as *rasa* meaning the 'flavour'. The same story can be given different intentions or 'flavours' according to the audience.
- The storyteller has a voice in the story that is used to give us a particular

The Lion King, Lyceum Theatre, London 1999.

perspective on the people and events involved. The story will be told in the interests of the person telling it! The storyteller will tell the story in such a way that it persuades us that the storyteller's own view is the right one. **A play will be stamped with the playwright's own values, attitudes and experiences of the world.** When you devise a performance as a group, it will inevitably reveal something about you and the group to an audience.

- **Stories are often told to illustrate *themes* or ideas**, or told as particular examples of a more general *theme*. Through the particular story we are led to think about and reflect on the bigger *theme*. So, *Romeo and Juliet* is a particular story about the theme of young love and family disputes. We may tell stories from our own experience in order to illustrate a theme such as 'life is unkind', or 'boys always get their own way', or 'the pains of growing up'.

The differences are:

- **In drama and theatre, stories are usually, but not always, told in the *present*** – as if the events were happening here and now for the first time. In most other forms of story, including films and TV, the events are in the *past* – the story is a record of what has already happened. When a play begins it is often like being suddenly thrust into things and lives that are happening *now* on stage. We watch and listen carefully to what *is* going on and who is involved, and after a while we begin to find out what has happened before the play began and what might happen next. In the *Antigone* workshop we noticed that the play begins with two sisters meeting to discuss events. This meeting happens 'here and now' on stage as if it was actually occurring, but during this meeting the two sisters provide the audience with information about what has already happened and also begin to foreshadow what will happen later in the play.
- When you tell a story to your friends you rely almost entirely on words. You may use some gestures and even speak like the characters in your story, but essentially it is through words that your story will be understood. **Theatre, on the other hand, uses more than words to tell its stories.** Actors physically become the people in the stories and will adapt their voices and bodies and gestures to suit the *character* of the person they are playing. They may use all sorts of costumes and props to help them. The *space* is used to tell the story; there maybe a *set* that helps us to imagine the story's setting or the space may be used to visually create the atmosphere or *mood* of the story. A play also uses *timing* to assist in the storytelling – we talk of a comedian's timing, but in a play we also talk of *rhythm* which refers to the changing *tempo* of the play; the alternation between slower and faster moments in the play. Lighting, sounds and significant objects are also used to tell the story in theatre – again, lights and sound may be used to add to the realism of the setting and/or to amplify the mood of the performance.

In theatre, then, the 'story' is presented using the *dramatic elements* of:

- Time
- Space
- Physicality
- Lights
- Sounds
- Objects

Because theatre is a live performance, the way in which these elements are used will produce an *impact* or *effect* for the audience. Different performances of the same play will have a different *effect* or *impact* according to the different ways in which the elements have been used. When you are producing drama as actors, directors or designers you need to think about the impact that you want to have on your audience and how to achieve it through your use of the *dramatic elements*. When you experience drama as an audience you need to try and think about the effect that the performance has had on you and how this effect was created through the use of the *dramatic elements*.

Task 6: Creating a performance based on a story

The exercises that follow will help you to practise some of the ideas about story that have been introduced. We begin with some simple *story-theatre* exercises based on the folk-tale of *Little Red Riding Hood*, and then move on to a short performance project based on the same folk-tale.

1. In a group, organise your memory of the story under three headings: *People*, *Places*, and *Events*. Spend a short time discussing what is in your lists – what kind of people are involved; how do you imagine them? What are the woods like, for instance?

2. Write down the eight most important events in the story in the correct sequence (beginning, middle and end) on a large sheet of paper.

3. Now, elect one member of the group to be the storyteller. The storyteller is going to begin to tell the tale *but* in the present tense. In other words, instead of 'Little Red Riding Hood lived with her mother . . . her mother asked her to take that basket' the storyteller will say: 'Little Red Riding Hood lives with her mother . . . her mother asks her to take a basket . . . she leaves the house and she walks into the woods'.

4. As the storyteller tells the tale, the rest of the group must act out the story as a group as it is told! No time to discuss or cast, just get on with it! Everything the storyteller speaks of must be played – flowers, baskets, smoking chimneys, everything! If you wish, you can act out scenes from the story as you go, so that when the storyteller says 'Little Red Riding Hood turns around and sees a wolf – she asks the wolf . . .' this scene could be improvised before the storyteller moves on to the next event.

5. Now, prepare a set of ***monologues*** for different characters in the story. The idea is to think about the story from the different perspectives of the characters and then to create a monologue based on each character's version of events. Each member of your group could take responsibility for one of the following:

   - Little Red Riding Hood's mother explains to her friends – some of the other mothers – what happened.
   - Little Red Riding Hood explains to her school friends what happened.
   - The woodcutter boasts of his bravery to the guests in the local inn.
   - The wolf's wife explains what happened to her children, the wolf cubs.

6. Perform the monologues to each other. When you're done you might want to *hot-seat* each character by asking them questions

about their version of what happened, which must be answered in character. Finally, discuss how the story has changed for you following these exercises.

7. In the next phase of this project you are going to work with a series of short extracts from two stories written by Angela ***Carter***. The stories are *The Company of Wolves* and *The Werewolf* from *The Bloody Chamber*, which are both based on *Little Red Riding Hood.* There are four extracts, so you could share them out among the class, or try them all if you are in a small group.

   - You may use all the words in the extract or only a few – but the *sense* of your extract must be fully communicated to the audience. There are two further objectives for the work. You must *vocalise* and *physicalise* your extract(s) as effectively as you can. This will mean working out how best to use the voices in the group to speak words, to repeat or echo them and also to provide any other sounds which you think appropriate. Then think about how the people in your group can be used to make shapes, gestures and movements that will provide the 'visual' dimension of your work.
   - Before you begin, consider your extract alongside the headings that we used earlier:

     - Events
     - Context
     - Characters
     - Emotions/mood
     - Author's perspective
     - Theme

   - Then discuss the *impact* you want to have on your audience and how you will use the dramatic elements to achieve it.
   - Finally, rehearse and perform, paying close attention to the audience's feedback – were they *affected* in the way that you hoped? If not, what would you now change to strengthen your performance?

From The Bloody Chamber *by Angela Carter*

1. It is a northern country; they have cold weather, they have cold hearts. Cold, tempest; wild beasts in the forest. It is a hard life. Their houses are built of logs, dark and smoky within. There will be a crude icon of the virgin behind a guttering candle, the leg of a pig hung up to cure, a string of drying mushrooms. A bed, a stool, a table. Harsh, brief, poor lives.
2. Children do not stay young for long in this savage country. There are no toys for them to play with so they work hard and grow wise but this one, so pretty and the youngest of her family, a little latecomer, had been indulged by her mother and grandmother who'd knitted her the red shawl that, today, has the ominous if brilliant look of blood on snow.
3. The good child does as her mother bids – five miles' trudge through the forest; do not leave the path because of the bears, the wild boar, the starving wolves. Here take your father's hunting knife; you know how to use it.
4. The child had a scabby coat of sheepskin to keep out the cold, she knew the forest too well to fear it but she must always be on her guard. When she heard that freezing howl of a wolf, she dropped her gifts, seized her knife and turned on the beast.

Although stories in theatre are usually told as if they were happening rather than as reported events in the past, there are playwrights and practitioners who have been interested in using storytelling as part of the play. In this way they can combine events in the past (which are told to us by a *narrator* who may or may not be a character in the play) with events in the present (dramatised scenes from the story that occur in the present). **Bertolt *Brecht* is famous for using narrators, songs and other devices so that his plays are a combination of events from the past with events played in the present.** Contemporary practitioners who take an interest in using storytelling as part of their theatre include Mike ***Alfreds*** and Nancy ***Meckler*** who both have worked for ***Shared Experience***; Brian ***Friel*** and other playwrights associated with the ***Abbey Theatre*** in Dublin; Simon McBurney and the work of ***Teatre De Complicite*** and *Theatre Alibi*.

Ritual

Since the beginnings of time, rituals have been used as communal events that celebrate or confirm the shared beliefs, customs and taboos of a community. Rituals usually require that all who are present must participate in, or believe in, the ritual. Taking part in a ritual is like saying 'this is what we believe in, this is the group that I belong to and by taking part I am showing the world that I agree to live by this group's rules and beliefs'. The rituals of a society may include examples such as: the Catholic Mass, funerals, calls to prayer, circumcision and bar mitzvah, Diwali, Eid and Ramadan rites, weddings, coronations, investitures, school prize-giving ceremonies, protest marches, chanting at football matches, trick or treat and other Halloween rituals.

The purpose of rituals may be to transform or change something or someone

Rituals may be no more than the customs and courtesies of everyday life – the way that we greet each other or show politeness to each other. But the purpose of rituals may also be to transform or change something or someone, forever. Through various symbolic acts, through the participation and belief of those who are present, it is imagined that some lasting change can be made. In the Catholic Mass, for instance, the bread and wine become transformed into the body and blood of Christ. In the wedding ceremony, a spinster or bachelor becomes a bride or groom – a wife or a husband. In many societies there are rituals, or rites of passage, which transform boys and girls into men and women, The ritual is a way of showing that from now on this person has joined the world of adults and left childhood behind.

Rituals share common features with theatre. They are both social rather than private events, they both use symbols and symbolic gestures, and they both comment on and explain the culture they belong to. In the twentieth century, many theatre practitioners have been drawn to the idea of ritual and ritual performances because of their transformational power and the sense of community associated with ritual. **Imagine how attractive the idea is that through your play or performance you could change or transform people forever!** Theatre artists have also been interested in harnessing the spirituality and sense of shared experience in rituals that celebrate or mark the changing seasons or rhythms in the natural world – rituals to mark winter, harvest, births and deaths. ***Meyerhold***, ***Grotowski***, ***Antonin***, ***Barba***, ***Brook*** and ***Wilson*** are among well-known twentieth century practitioners who have included ritual ideas and forms in their work. There is also a long tradition of playwrights who have focused on the negative effect of our everyday rituals, which they have sought to reveal as oppressive, reactionary, or false. Such authors would include ***Ibsen***, ***Chekhov***, ***Synge***, ***Beckett***, ***Pinter*** and others.

A ritualistic performance will seek to appeal to the audience's sense of the spiritual and may use the elements of fire, water, earth and air in highly symbolic ways. The audience in ritual theatre will be treated more as a congregation or as a community than as a paying audience of individuals.

Shamanism

The shaman transforms into a spirit – the spirit takes on the physical form of the shaman

The shaman is a special kind of priest who officiates in healing rituals. Sometimes the shaman is referred to as a 'witch-doctor', 'sorcerer' or 'medicine man'. The shaman enters into a trance by taking hallucinogenic drugs or by fasting and meditating. It is believed that powerful spirits take hold of the shaman while he/she is in the trance – in other words the shaman transforms into a spirit – the spirit takes on the physical form of the shaman. There are two important connections with theatre here. First, the shaman brings the invisible world of sprits and demons into the actual world, which is also the ambition of some forms of ***non-realist*** and ***symbolic*** theatre. Second, the shaman, from the audience's point of view, transforms into another character for the duration of the trance. This idea of the shaman transforming into another being is very like the ***Stanislavskian*** and ***Grotowskian*** styles of representational acting which seek to convince the audience that the actor has *become* the character.

In many Western cultures people are suspicious of the idea of spirits, demons or ghosts – anything that can't be seen or heard or touched or proved to exist, but that hasn't stopped theatre practitioners from trying to physically and visually represent both the visible world and the invisible worlds of dreams, nightmares and fantasies. Artists who have sought to combine these worlds in their work would include ***Ibsen*** in *Peer Gynt*, ***Strindberg***, Antonin ***Artaud***, and Eugenio ***Barba***.

A Witch Doctor from Cameroon.

The transformation of the shaman into another spirit-being is closely related to those forms of acting in which the actor is skilful enough to create the illusion that she or he has literally become or turned into the character he or she is portraying. Practitioners associated with the 'shaman' model of acting would include Eugenio *Barba*, Jerzy *Grotowski* and Peter ***Brook***.

Dance

From the earliest of times people in many cultures have been both entertained by dance and also have used it for ritual and communal activity. When you go 'clubbing' with your friends on a Saturday night you are participating in an ancient tradition! The fifth century Greeks combined dance and drama in the performances of the tragedies, comedies and ***satyr plays***, and in other cultures the imitation of animals, the introduction of masks and the miming of human behaviours in dances blurred distinctions between what we would now call dance, drama and storytelling.

The idea that dance and drama are two different art-forms is particular to Western culture. In many non-European performance traditions there is a mix of drama, dance, songs and music, which together make a single performance style.

The performers of the *Commedia dell'Arte* were highly skilled dancers

The idea that dance and drama are different art-forms is also relatively modern. The earliest ideas about dance as an art-form in its own right emerged in Italy in the fifteenth century, and in 1661 the rules and principles of *ballet*, which are still in use today, were developed by the Academie Royale De Danse in Paris. In the *Renaissance* period of theatre, no distinction was made between actors and dancers and indeed performers were expected to be skilled actors, dancers and acrobats. The performers of the ***Commedia dell'Arte*** were highly skilled dancers and much of the pleasure of a performance came from the acrobatic dance routines. ***Moliere*** is best known now as an actor and playwright but in his own time he was also famous as a mime artist and dancer. We do not know as much about the training of actors in the past as we do about the playwrights, but it can be assumed that professional performers have always been trained in dance as well as in acting.

In the chapter on directing (see Chapter 5), we shall see that many of the great directors of the twentieth century have been drawn again to dance and mime as key elements in theatrical performance. The focus on developing the actor's use of *movement* to convey meaning is based on the tradition of *Commedia dell'Arte* actor training.

The influence of dance in twentieth century theatre

Dancers and mime artists have had a considerable influence on the development of ***non-realist*** theatre styles. At the turn of the twentieth century there was an extraordinary dancer called Isadora ***Duncan*** whose free use of movement and the body shocked audiences. She rejected the formalism of the *ballet* and sought to create the dancer of the future who would 'dance the freedom of women'. She was also responsible for introducing her lover Gordon ***Craig*** to ***Stanislavski***.

Craig saw dance and movement as being the essential language of the stage and proposed removing ***realist*** actors entirely and replacing them with *uber-marionettes* or dancing puppets. As a result of these theories and *Craig*'s contact with the ***Moscow Art Theatre*** (MAT), Vsevlod ***Meyerhold*** developed his *non-realist* acting style of *bio-mechanics*, based on the principle that movement rather than words conveyed the 'reality' of behaviour. *Meyerhold*'s actors trained in *Commedia dell'Arte* techniques, acrobatics, fencing and throwing the discus in order to develop a highly balletic acting style.

Isadora ***Duncan*** and her School of Greek Dancing, 1908.

The work of other great dancers like Mary ***Wegman*** and Pina ***Bausch*** is often referred to as *dance theatre* because their work blurs and crosses the boundaries between the two art-forms. Between 1914 and 1942, *Wegman* performed her own solo dances but she also choreographed for the stage. She said:

> **I feel that the dance is a language which is inherent, but slumbering in every one of us. It is possible for every human to experience the dance as an expression in his own body and in his own way.**

Contemporary dance performances by Pina *Bausch* and the Wuppertal Dance Theatre often attract a theatre audience and are reviewed as theatre. *Bausch* represents 'characters' and 'settings' in her work through attention to the detail of gestures and body movements. She seeks to discover 'not how people move but what moves them'. Her sets are often highly *realist* or covered in natural materials like earth, flowers and water.

In recent times, *non-realist* directors (***Artaud***, ***Grotowski*** and ***Brook*** for example), have continued the tradition of highlighting the physical movement and gestures of the actor as the core of performance. The Italian director Dario ***Fo*** has reclaimed the skills and techniques of the *Commedia dell'Arte* in his energetic and stylised physical performances of *Mistero Buffo*. Many modern *physical theatre* practitioners like ***Teatre de Complicite*** and ***DV8*** combine elements of the *Commedia dell'Arte* style with ideas from the great twentieth century mime teachers Etienne ***Decroux*** and Jacques ***Lecoq***.

Martial Arts/Contests of Skill and Strength

In many cultures, exhibitions and contests of martial arts and other physical skills are a popular form of entertainment and are closely related to theatre and drama. We have already noted that Athenian drama developed the idea of a conflict or tension between characters, groups or ideas, and that most plays have some sort of contest at their core. The Athenians had a lively sporting culture as well as an interest in the theatre – our modern Olympic games have their origin in this same period of history.

The Street of Crocodiles, Téâtre de Complicité, Royal National Theatre 1992.

In some forms of Chinese, West African and Latin American theatre, the skills, grace and dexterity of a martial art are included as part of the performance style. In the modern Western tradition of theatre actors are often now expected to have the same physical capabilities as athletes. The increasing influence of *physical theatre* and the tendency towards blurring drama and dance in theatre has led to a much more acrobatic style of acting that requires a strong physique and great stamina. Some contemporary Western performers will use exercises taken from *t'ai chi, kung fu, aikido* and other systems of physical training based on the martial arts.

In earlier times, audiences would enjoy both theatre and the spectacles and excitement of physical contests and displays of skill. The ***Globe*** and ***Rose*** theatres of ***Shakespeare***'s time, for example, staged wrestling matches and bear-baiting contests alongside plays. In the unlicensed theatres of the eighteenth century, extracts from plays would be performed as part of a mixed evening of entertainment that would also include jugglers and acrobats and tests of strength. This tradition was kept alive in the nineteenth and early twentieth century by *music-hall* and ***vaudeville*** performances.

Task 7: The Keeper of the Keys exercise

In this exercise you are going to use the old children's game of 'Keeper of the Keys' to explore the similarities and differences between games, contests and theatre.

1. **To play the original game, set a chair in the middle of a large circle of spectators. A volunteer is placed on the chair and blindfolded. A large set of keys, or other object that will jangle, is placed under the 'keeper's' chair. The 'keeper' is given a stick or rolled sheet of paper to help 'protect' the keys. Ask for silence and then ask for a second volunteer who will try and creep forward and 'steal' the keys without being hit by the 'keeper'!**

2. Try playing the game a few times, then pause for reflection. What is the difference between a game such as this in which there are only two 'players' and an audience as opposed to games in which everyone participates? What holds our interest as the audience? What emotions do we experience as we watch?

   The game has a clear link to sporting events, which also involve two or more players in a contest which has an unknown result – part of our interest in watching is to see who will win. In this game, as in many other forms of entertainment, there are two sides competing against each other and there is a clear sense of what will be lost and gained from victory.

3. Now play the game again but this time the two players should try and 'show' the audience that there is some sort of contest going on in which both players have a 'stake' – they both need to win. How does the contest change now that it is being 'acted'? In other words, now that the players are trying to show what it would be like to be the 'hunter' and the 'keeper'. Are we still interested as an audience? Is there anything added to what we experience as we watch?
4. Now play the game for the third time but this time without the blindfold! You could either work in pairs to choreograph your movements and consider how to make the 'game' interesting for the audience, or improvise in front of the group. You should still leave the outcome of the game to be worked out between the players as the 'game' develops. What is the interest for the audience now? What are we watching? Is this now a drama?

The model for much theatre and drama, which is based on the idea of conflict, can be found in games and contests, but drama does more than present us with a simple trial of skill and strength. **In drama, we are conscious that we are watching a 'representation' of a contest – a story about a contest rather than the contest itself.** We are interested in the characters, their motives, backgrounds, strengths and weaknesses. Sometimes the 'contest' at the heart of the drama might make us laugh at the vanity or foolishness of the competing characters; sometimes we are moved to tears or anger by the tragedy or futility of the contest. The simple game model of drama is sometimes a useful way of checking that your own devised performances or scenes will be interesting to follow. Try using these questions about your own work:

- **Who are the players?**
- **What is the nature of the contest between them?**
- **What is at stake for the players – what will be won and lost?**
- **What will interest the audience in this contest (why should they be 'bothered' by what goes on)?**
- **How will the contest be played out (the scenes or events of the drama)?**

Section 2

Acting Workshops and Scene Work

3 Playing the Given Circumstances

Outline

In this chapter we are going to look at, and practise, ***realist*** styles of acting. *Realism* is still the most popular acting style in film and TV and we will begin, in Part 1, by considering the core concept of **given circumstances** and how the actor identifies and plays them.

We will focus on the ideas of two of the greatest practitioners of the *realist* style of acting: Constantin ***Stanislavski*** and Lee ***Strasberg***. Both developed specific approaches to realist acting which focused on building a complex psychological understanding of character – *Stanislavski*'s *system* and *Strasberg*'s *method*. The work of both these directors and theatre teachers is complex and we will only be introducing ourselves to the basic techniques associated with their work. We will return to the ideas of *Stanislavski* in particular in our more advanced work on directing in Chapter 6 and on textual analysis in Chapter 8.

Part 2 is a workshop in *realist* acting based on a scene from Arthur ***Miller***'s *The Crucible* in which we will explore how to play a scene in the *realist* style and practically explore some of the ideas presented in Part 1.

Part 1 *What are the Given Circumstances?*

The 'given circumstances' is the term that ***Stanislavski*** gave to the essential information about characters' past lives and relationships, the circumstances and incidents which are revealed by the playwright, particularly near the beginning of the play in the ***exposition*** but also as the play develops. **In most *realist* styles of drama it is understood that the characters behave in ways that are 'true' to their given circumstances.** In other words, what characters do and say and how they react to others is a consequence of their past lives and relationships. The 'given circumstances' determine how a character will react to each new event in the plot of the play. When you look at a scene from a *realist* play, the problem is to know how the words and directions given by the playwright should be 'played' rather than merely read through. The 'given circumstances' tell you how the lines and other directions should be delivered.

Stanislavski tried to present characters who behaved 'consistently'. **He tried to make his characters credible for an audience by ensuring that every action and reaction was part of a consistent pattern of behaviour** – the character would respond to new events in ways which were consistent with how they responded to similar events in the past. This method of working required his actors to undertake deep research into the psychology of character – searching the text for clues, thinking about the character's past, imagining the character in a variety of different situations. The effect of this style of direction is to produce characters that are predictable, unified and constant.

The American director Lee ***Strasberg*** developed his *method* from *Stanislavski's* work, but with a difference. *Strasberg* believed that characters often experienced a conflict between their own inner feelings and sense of truth and the behaviour that is socially or culturally expected of them. In *Strasberg's* style of direction, characters may sometimes behave unpredictably, or have sudden outbursts of strong emotions which may seem 'out of character' but which help an audience to understand the inner turmoil (or 'inner circumstances' as *Stanislavski* called it) of a character's life. In both forms of *realist* acting, close attention to the 'given circumstances' is essential in the preparation and rehearsal of character. The actor is expected to play the 'given circumstances' for the audience – in other words, the actor must find ways to physically express as much of the information in the 'given circumstances' as possible.

Identifying the Given Circumstances

The simplest way of identifying the 'given circumstances' of a scene is to record:

- Who is present?
- When is it happening?
- Where is it happening?
- What is happening?
- What has happened/what might happen next?

Making notes in response to these questions will help you to identify the basics of the 'given circumstances' of a scene. This simple list also tells us something about the depth and complexity of the work that actors and directors need to do in order to create a performance that is really consistent with the 'given circumstances' of the play.

Who is present?	How a character behaves in a scene will depend on who else is present. The status, age, dramatic importance and previous shared experiences of the characters will all influence how each actor plays their character in the scene. In thinking about how to play the scene you must consider how to play with the other actors so that the relationships between characters are made clear for an audience. Sometimes, the actors must also think about other characters in the play who are not present but whose influence will be strongly felt by those involved in the scene.
When is it happening?	The 'when' of a scene is also complex. What **period** of time is the scene/play set? People behaved and thought differently in different historical periods. The actors may need to research the customs and manners of a particular period in order to play the character in the context of their, rather than our, time. 'When' also refers to the place of the scene in the play. In playing the scene the actors must remind the audience of what has already happened and also lay the ground for what will come later on in the play. A play 'unfolds' and actors must take care to let their characters develop as it does. How an actor plays a particular scene will therefore depend on the place of the scene in the overall structure of the play or the stage in the character's development. 'When' will also refer to the **actual time** of the scene – a morning scene may have a different feel to an evening scene. The scene may be leisurely and relaxed or it may have a sense of urgency and pace.

Where is it happening?	**The place that the scene is set in will also have an important influence on how the actors play it.** Is it a public place, requiring formal behaviour, or is it an intimate and private place that will allow actors to reveal their true feelings and thoughts? The physical characteristics of the scene must also be considered – is it outdoors/indoors, is it cold/warm, and is it threatening/ claustrophobic? Does this place have a particular significance for a character or characters? Have they been there before? Are they likely to have memories that might influence them now?
What is happening?	At a simple level, what is happening refers to the most obvious level of 'doing' in the scene. A family dinner, for instance, or a meeting. But in most ***realist*** plays we also expect there to be a *sub-text* which refers to what is happening underneath the surface. The family dinner might also be a power struggle between two characters. The meeting might be an opportunity to reveal a character's true motives. **The actors have to play both the surface and the sub-text.** This often means working out what each character's motives are – why do they do what they do. This in turn may lead to thinking about what a character's objective is for the scene – what is this character trying to make happen in the scene?
What has happened/what might happen next?	A scene is always written as if it is happening 'here and now' rather than as a record of some past event. The actors need to create the illusion that the scene is actually taking place now. But in most forms of realism, the 'here and now' is different from the 'here and now' of everyday life. **The scene will also reveal what has happened and suggest for the audience what will happen later on in the play.** When a play begins, the audience seems to be suddenly involved in what is happening to the characters on stage, but the playwright will need to give information that will help the audience understand the 'given circumstances' – the history and other significant factors which will help the audience understand what they are seeing and create an interest in what might happen next. In other words, what will be the consequences of what we are seeing now? **The problem for the actors is how to play the scene as an immediate 'here and now' experience while also expressing what has happened prior to the play's beginning and hinting at what is to come.**

Making a list of the given circumstances is only the beginning for the actor and director. In order to play the given circumstances, both use all the available elements of drama to physically create the scene for the audience. Timing, use of space, objects, sounds and lighting can all be used to help in this creation. For the actor, the body will be the principle means of conveying the given circumstances for the audience. The actor will 'physically' experience the circumstances – physically respond to the place, for example. This often means doing a lot of 'sensory' work in rehearsal. The actor who plays *King Lear* on the verge of madness alone with the fool on the storm-swept moors might need to try (and physically through the senses) answer the following questions:

- What does the moor look like? What and how far can you see?
- What would the cold and wet feel like?
- What does it smell of?
- What can you hear?
- Is there a wind blowing, is it raining, how does the rain feel when it touches you?

- Does a madman experience the moor in the same way as a sane man?
- If you fall to the ground, how would it feel – soft/hard, wet, brambly?
- How easy/difficult is it to walk across the moor – would you stumble or need to jump over holes and dips?

The director and designers may assist in the creation of the illusion of a storm-swept moor by using design, objects and sound and lighting effects, but in the end **it is the actor who must convince us that he is experiencing the physical reality of the scene.** For each of the 'What' questions above, the actor needs to experiment and play with the sensory details – it is not an intellectual exercise in making lists of relevant information, it is about discovering how a character experiences the touch, sound, sight and smells of a scene. What ***Stanislavski*** wanted was for his actors to physically and mentally *live through* the characters and the situations in a play; to behave '*as if*' they had become the characters and were actually living their lives.

Exercises

Both ***Stanislavski*** and ***Strasberg*** created exercises to help actors develop their physical and sensory experience of the 'given circumstances' of their character. Actors in rehearsal still commonly use some of, or variations on, these exercises.

	Stanislavski's system
Magic if	This is based on the human ability to imagine what it would be like to be in a different situation, to walk in someone else's shoes – if *I* were King Lear on the moor what would *I* do, what would it be like, how would *I* feel? In the **system** the actor builds a character on his or her own self – she or he finds themselves in the character and finds the character in themselves!
Emotion memory	The actor and director identify the **dominant emotion** that the character will experience in the scene. The actor then tries to remember a time in their own life when they felt that emotion – of great sadness, of loss, of uncontrollable rage, of joy. The actor then tries to recall the experience in as much detail as they possibly can; they keep on concentrating until they can re-experience the emotion as if it was happening now.
Units and objectives	Each actor plots the major experiences and turning points in the character's development across the whole play. These are the milestones that establish the character's **through-line of action** – the path this character will travel, changing and evolving as the play develops. Discussion then leads to each actor defining **the super-objective** for his or her character – what is at stake for this character (the motivation) and what the character is trying to make happen in the play. Once the super-objective is established the actor then looks at each scene of the play, or smaller **units** within a scene of the play and decides on the character's objective for that scene or unit. The objective for each scene or unit must be named. For example, I want to convince X or I want Y to trust me. Finally, the actor compares the objectives for each scene with the super-objective and through-line of action in order to make sure that the super-objective will be realised through the objectives for each scene. In other words, if the objectives for each scene are taken together, do they add up to the super-objective?

Circle and/or object of attention	These exercises are designed to help actors to overcome their self-consciousness of the audience and to prevent them from self-consciously playing the characters. They are intended to produce performances that are 'natural'; the actors lose themselves behind the mask of the character. In the first exercise, the actors work in a blacked-out studio – a small space is lit around the actors who focus on every detail of the space. As the actors improvise or play the scene their attention remains entirely focused on the lit space rather than on the darkness and audience beyond. Gradually, the space is increased and the actors take in more and more detail until they become 'unconscious' of what lies in the darkness beyond. In the object exercise, the actor focuses entirely on a significant object or prop while improvising or playing the scene. The actor gives total concentration to how the character would touch and feel the object, how they would gaze at it and what thoughts and feelings the object might arouse for the character.
Communion	The above exercises are intended to help actors create what *Stanislavski* called 'communion', which describes the total attention that the actor must give to something or someone other than the audience. For *Stanislavski*, there were five types of communion that actors might focus on to help their concentration: 1 With oneself as in a soliloquy between the character's heart and mind. 2 With another 'soul', meaning another actor. 3 With a real object. 4 With an imaginary object (the dagger in *Macbeth* for instance). 5 With a crowd or chorus.
Method of physical actions (MPA)	The *system* often resulted in actors spending a great deal of time working on the text at an intellectual level – making notes and identifying objectives and the given circumstances from their reading of the text prior to rehearsals. At the end of his career *Stanislavski* invented the MPA to encourage the actors to begin with physical work on the character. The actor would be asked to perform a simple stage direction like entering a room. As the actor tries to execute this action they are forced to consider the given circumstances – why am I entering the room? How would I enter the room? What's my objective for doing so? As the actor continues to work on the action they begin to work out the physical and psychological life of the character. The MPA led to the breaking down of each scene into three or four key actions, each of which was given a name or motive – for example, I open the door to attract X's attention.
	Strasberg's method
Sense memory	*Strasberg*'s exercise is similar to 'emotion memory' but with a greater emphasis on the actors' abilities to forcibly express strong and painful emotions. The actors recall an experience that was a powerfully strong emotional event for them. They build up all their sensory memories of the event – how it felt, how it smelt and looked. They talk about the experience of how they felt physically and any other sensory information they can recall, until they are able to trigger the emotion in themselves. The idea was to keep working on a range of powerful memories in this way so that the actor could have a set of emotions that they could trigger when needed – pain, loss, tears, laughter, etc.
Singing the words	*Strasberg* believed that the text and the words were often blocks to the actor's characterisation, so he developed a series of exercises

	to help. These included playing the scene but using 'gibberish' language so that the actors would focus on the details of action and the expression of emotion. Actors might also be asked to speak their lines, or recite a poem or monologue while performing a number of completely different activities suggested by the class – having a shower or shopping in the supermarket, for example.
The scene	*Strasberg* placed great emphasis on improvisation as a means of helping actors to discover and play the inner depth of their characters. 'The scene' is a semi-prepared improvisation involving one or more of the characters in a usually very ordinary or domestic scene. The idea was for the actors to be given time on stage in front of an audience to 'become' the character – to explore how the character would sit and how they would respond to the detail of the stage and the other characters. This exercise helps actors to 'naturally' become the character on stage.

Part 2 The Crucible *Workshop*

Tom Wilkinson and Zoe Wanamaker as John and Elizabeth Proctor, *The Crucible*, National Theatre 1990.

Identifying the Given Circumstances

The Crucible, by the American playwright Arthur ***Miller***, is set in the village of Salem in the State of Massachusetts, USA, in 1692. The plot of the play is based on the historical facts of a witch-hunt of the time that resulted in many innocent people being hung for witchcraft. At first the accusers were a group of adolescent girls, but many people became accusers in order to settle old scores or to try and gain more land and property. The play was written in 1953 when many Americans felt that the House Un-American Activities Committee under Senator Joseph McCarthy was imprisoning and ruining innocent people on trumped-up charges of being communists. The scene that follows is taken from the opening of the second of the play's four acts. It involves John and Elizabeth Proctor – a husband and wife who farm near to the village of Salem.

> ***(The common-room of Proctor's house, eight days later)***
> ***At the right is a door opening on the fields outside. A fireplace is at the left, and behind it a stairway leading upstairs. It is the low, dark, and rather long living room of the time. As the curtain rises, the room is empty. From above, ELIZABETH is heard softly singing to the children. Presently the door opens and JOHN PROCTOR enters, carrying his gun. He glances about the room as he comes towards the fireplace, then halts for an instant as he hears her singing. He continues on to the fireplace, leans the gun against the wall as he swings a pot out of the fire and smells it. Then he lifts out the ladle and tastes. He is not quite pleased. He reaches to a cupboard, takes a pinch of salt, and drops it into the pot. As he is tasting again, her footsteps are heard on the stair. He swings the pot into the fireplace and goes to a basin and washes his hands and face. ELIZABETH enters.***

There is a tradition in ***realist*** playwriting of using detailed stage directions to provide the details of setting and action for actors to follow. Like ***Chekov***, ***Ibsen***, ***Shaw*** and others, *Miller* prefaces the scene with these directions. They are meaningful signs of the 'given circumstances' of the scene that follows. Begin by working practically, using the MPA technique with these directions.

Task 1: Working the stage directions

Begin with a copy of the directions and mark any words, actions or descriptive details that you think will prove to be significant to the scene that follows. Does the description of the room as being 'low' and 'dark' matter? Is it important that we hear Elizabeth singing off-stage? Once you have marked your directions discuss your ideas with your friends and discuss how the marked sections might become significant in the scene that follows. Now, prepare a list of questions about the directions that might include: Why is Proctor 'not quite pleased'? Why does he add salt to the pot? Why does he wash his hands afterwards? Keep this list for future reference.

You will need to work in a group of three for this task. Two of you will act the characters of Elizabeth and John while the third reads the stage directions. You can alternate these roles as you go through the task.

1. Arrange the space with objects and furniture to represent the room, the staircase and the room above where Elizabeth is singing to her children. The actors go through the actions exactly as the reader of the directions describes them. Try this a couple of times until you are familiar with the sequence.
2. Now go back to your annotated copies of the directions and the list

of questions and consider them again. How can the actors draw attention to the highlighted words? Are the questions any clearer now? Begin the sequence again but this time the actors must try to draw attention to the significant details. You might also try playing the sequence until one of the characters reaches a question at which point he or she stops and asks: 'Why am I doing this?'. Anyone present can make suggestions to the actor before they carry on: 'Because you don't like her cooking'; 'Because you haven't heard your wife singing before'; etc.

3. Play the sequence again but this time the reader will add directions on pace and timing: QUICKLY enters; SLOWLY walks to the fireplace; swings a pot out of the fire and PAUSES; HURRIES to the basin; Elizabeth enters VERY SLOWLY.

   Discuss and make notes on the dramatic potential of this sequence – why should it hold an audience's interest? What potential tensions or 'sub-texts' are there?

This is the dialogue that follows.

1 *Elizabeth*: What keeps you so late? It's almost dark.

2 *Proctor*: I were planting far out to the forest edge.

3 *Elizabeth*: Oh, you're done then.

4 *Proctor*: Aye, the farm is seeded. The boys asleep?

5 *Elizabeth*: They will be soon. (*and she goes to the fireplace, proceeds to ladle up stew in a dish*).

6 *Proctor*: Pray now for a fair summer.

7 *Elizabeth*: Aye.

8 *Proctor*: Are you well today?

9 *Elizabeth*: I am. (*she brings the plate to the table, and indicating the food*) it is a rabbit.

10 *Proctor*: (*going to the table*) Oh, is it! In Jonathan's trap?

11 *Elizabeth*: No, she walked into the house this afternoon; I found her sittin' in the corner like she come to visit.

12 *Proctor*: Oh, that's a good sign walkin' in.

13 *Elizabeth*: Pray God. It hurt my heart to strip her, poor rabbit. (*She sits and watches him taste it)*

14 *Proctor*: It's well seasoned.

15 *Elizabeth*: (*blushing with pleasure)* I took great care. She's tender?

16 *Proctor*: Aye. (*He eats, she watches him)* I think we'll see green fields soon. It's warm as blood beneath the clods.

17 *Elizabeth*: That's well.

18 (*Proctor eats then looks up)*

19 *Proctor*: If the crop is good I'll buy George Jacob's heifer. How would that please you?

20 *Elizabeth*: Aye, it would.

21 *Proctor*: *(with a grin)* I mean to please you, Elizabeth.

22 *Elizabeth*: *(it is hard to say)* I know it, John.

23 *(He gets up, goes to her, kisses her. She receives it. With a certain disappointment, he returns to the table)*

24 *Proctor*: *(as gently as he can)* Cider?

25 *Elizabeth*: *(with a sense of reprimanding herself for having forgot)* Aye! *(She gets up and goes and pours a glass for him. He now arches his back)*

26 *Proctor*: This farm's a continent when you go foot by foot droppin' seeds in it.

27 *Elizabeth*: *(coming with the cider)* It must be.

28 *Proctor*: *(drinks a long draught, then, putting the glass down)* You ought to bring some flowers in the house.

29 *Elizabeth*: Oh, I forgot! I will tomorrow.

30 *Proctor*: It's winter in here yet. On Sunday let you come with me, and we'll walk the farm together; I never see such a load of flowers on the earth. *(With good feeling he goes and looks up at the sky through the open doorway)*. Lilacs have a purple smell. Lilac is the smell of nightfall, I think. Massachusetts is a beauty in the spring!

31 *Elizabeth*: Aye it is.
(There is a pause. She is watching him from the table as he stands there absorbing the night. It is as though she would speak but cannot. Instead, now, she takes up the basin. Her back is turned to him. He turns to her and watches her. A sense of their separation rises)

Task 2: Identifying the given circumstances

Read through the scene, take time to discuss with the others how the scene clarifies or changes the ideas and questions that came from the previous task. Now begin to fill out the given circumstances of the scene based on the information you have. Wherever possible you should provide line references to support your views. Leave yourself room to add to the given circumstances later in the workshop.

Who is present?	There are only two characters present but what can you tell about the characters from this scene? Are there any clues about their relationship? Look at the words spoken and the directions to help you.
When is it happening?	Are there any clues about the historical period of the scene – in the language perhaps, or in the status relationship between man and wife? Is it important that the scene is set in the evening? How does the time of day affect the pace of the scene – does it seem rushed or leisurely to you?
Where is it happening?	Again the setting is obvious, but what is the relationship between the setting and the feel of the scene? Could the same scene have occurred in a public or outside setting?

	Does the language and mood of the scene fit the setting? Does the description of the room contribute to the mood of the scene?
What is happening?	On the surface the scene is of a man returning from the fields and being given his supper by his wife, but what else is going on in this scene? What is the '*sub-text*'? Make a note of any lines that you think provide a clue to what is going on beneath the surface (e.g. 23, 21 and 22). Try to build a theory or idea about what is happening beneath the surface of the meal.
What has happened/ What might happen next?	Does the playwright provide any clues in this scene as to what has happened previously or what might be going to happen later in the play? Again, pick out the lines that you think provide the clues and try and imagine what has happened/will happen.

Look through your notes and compare with others where there are points of difference. Look together at the text. Words, actions and directions in ***realist*** drama are often ambiguous – i.e. they can be understood in more than one way. Now read on! Below, the given circumstances of the scene have been fleshed out by adding details from the rest of the play. Read through this new information and think about how it changes the given circumstances that the two actors would need to respond to in order to play the scene.

John Proctor is a key character in the play. When we first meet him, *Miller* describes him thus:

> **Proctor was a farmer in his middle thirties . . . powerful of body, even-tempered and not easily led . . . there is evidence to suggest that he had a sharp and biting way with hypocrites . . . a man in his prime . . . with a quiet confidence and an unexpressed, hidden force.**

In the first act of the play it seems as though the rest of Salem has gone mad – everyone seems willing to believe the girls and their wild accusations of witchcraft, except John Proctor. He suspects that the girls are lying to cover up their own mischief. They had been discovered dancing naked in the woods by **Thomas Putnam**, the father of one of the girls. Such an activity, in a Puritan society, would have led to a severe whipping for the girls. So, they invent the charges of witchcraft. Proctor is a well-respected leader in the community. He has the power to stop the witch-hunt, and people will listen to him. But he does nothing. Why?

Miller also says of Proctor:

> **the steady manner he displays does not spring from an untroubled soul. He is a sinner, a sinner not only against the moral fashion of the time, but against his own vision of decent conduct.**

What troubles his soul? He has had a sexual relationship with **Abigail Williams**, who is the leader of the girls; she is described by Miller as:

> **Abigail Williams, seventeen, enters – a strikingly beautiful girl, an orphan, with an endless capacity for dissembling.**

Abigail worked for the Proctors as a maid until Elizabeth suspected that her husband was having an affair with her. She then threw Abigail out onto the streets. Proctor has tried to end his relationship with Abigail. He says to her:

> **I will cut off my hand before I'll ever reach for you again.**

But Abigail still has strong feelings for Proctor and believes he still 'loves' her (and maybe he does!). Her reason for dancing in the woods was to cast a charm on Elizabeth to kill her and get her out of the way.

So, the problem for Proctor is that in order to reveal the truth he must publicly declare himself to be a lecher – a middle-aged man who seduced a 17-year-old girl employed as his servant – and so destroy his reputation in the community. It is possible to read the play and feel some sympathy for Proctor's dilemma while blaming Abigail for leading him on. Abigail is responsible for the accusations of witchcraft and she will go on to accuse both Elizabeth and John with tragic results. But, it should be remembered that Abigail is young and vulnerable. She is an orphan with no father of her own and seeing her own parents die traumatised her:

I saw Indians smash my dear parents' heads on the pillow next to mine.

Elizabeth Proctor is not introduced in detail. We have to pick up on the clues in the text. It appears that John had his affair while his wife was ill from childbirth. In other words he wasn't enjoying a sexual relationship with her at the time. But is this a good enough excuse for the affair? There are frequent references to Elizabeth being cold towards John. For example:

She is a cold, snivelling woman (Abigail to Proctor);

Oh. Elizabeth, your justice would freeze beer (John to Elizabeth).

Even Elizabeth herself seems to excuse John because of her own temperament:

It needs a cold wife to prompt lechery.

And in the scene we are studying, John seems to refer to Elizabeth's coldness again when he says:

It's winter in here yet (line 30).

In Act 1 there is a sexually charged and very intimate, private scene between John and Abigail in which she reveals that the charges of witchcraft are a cover-up. The next time we see Proctor is in the scene that we are studying. So he carries any feelings Abigail may have aroused from the first scene into this one. His wife may also strongly suspect that he is still seeing Abigail. She certainly hasn't forgotten what he has done. In this sense there are really *three* characters present. Abigail haunts the scene.

Remember how the scene begins. John enters and *secretly* adds salt to the pot and keeps this secret from Elizabeth. This is a very important action, because it exactly describes the present relationship between John and Elizabeth. He is keeping secrets from her and he has added to the pot/plot without her knowledge.

As the scene begins, Elizabeth knows the dilemma that John is in, and when he enters she expects him to tell her the news from Salem but he does not, nor does she ask. Why?

Task 3: Working with the new information

Discuss with the class your reactions to this new information, what are your feelings towards the three characters and their dilemma? Now, read through the scene again and make notes on how the scene changes because of what we now know.

1. **Work on a *still-image* that will show the rest of the class what you think the relationships are now between Abigail, John and Elizabeth. How can you mould the actors to show their dilemmas, passions, fears and insecurities?**
2. **Go back to your list of given circumstances and add this new information. Finally, highlight the given circumstances that you think are essential to the scene – how much of the information given should the actors' concentrate on expressing in the scene?**

So far, we have made an intellectual analysis of the scene. Now we must think about the emotional levels that will need to be played. It's one thing to understand the scene, quite another to be able to play it as if it was actually occurring to flesh and blood characters.

Playing the Given Circumstances

We now understand a great deal about the scene, but the biggest problem is still to come – how must the scene be played so that the performance itself will express our understanding of the play to an audience. In theatre there is only what we see and hear on the stage – all that you might want to say about the scene (the characters, the ideas you have) must now be translated into a living performance for an audience. The tasks in this section will work best if you can work in a group of three; two of you will be cast as John and Elizabeth and the third will work as the director. **The two actors now need to learn the lines! And the director needs to review all the material so far produced.**

Task 4: Dominant emotions

1. **You will have begun to feel for John and Elizabeth and their given circumstances. Perhaps you pity Elizabeth as a woman betrayed by her husband, or feel pity for John, because his passions have destroyed his relationship with the wife he loves. But what of the characters themselves? What emotions do they experience during this scene? How would you react to your wife/husband if you were in this situation? Use the grid below to brainstorm the possible feelings experienced by each character during the scene.**

	John feels	Elizabeth feels
Before		
During		
After		

2. **Are there any key moments in the scene where you think a definite change of emotion takes place for either character? Mark these lines.**

3. Without raising any painful memories for yourself, can you think of a time when you also experienced any of these emotions? Guilt, perhaps, or fear of losing someone? Think about that time; try and recall your sense memories – what was said, the sights, smells, tactile sensations and the taste it left in your mouth. How close can you get to the emotions of John and Elizabeth in this scene?
4. Finally, decide on the **dominant emotion** for each character in this scene. In other words, John may feel frustrated, sorry, frightened and ashamed but the strongest emotion might be guilt. Now work with three others – two of you will read the scene carefully and slowly while the other two silently play John and Elizabeth. Both pairs, the readers and the actors, should try to express the dominant emotions as the scene progresses. Discuss your experience.

Task 5: Reflections on the scene

1. Look again at the closing stage directions:

   (*There is a pause. She is watching him from the table as he stands there absorbing the night. It is as though she would speak but cannot. Instead, now, she takes up the basin. Her back is turned to him. He turns to her and watches her. A sense of their separation rises*)

2. Arrange two actors to represent John and Elizabeth at the end of the scene, and use the rest of the class to make two *still-images*: the first will appear behind John as Elizabeth watches him in the doorway, the second will appear behind Elizabeth when John turns and watches her at the basin. The directions include the words: 'she would speak but cannot'. In your work, Elizabeth might now speak her thoughts as she watches John and her image. Then let John speak as he watches her. You could end by repeating the image you made earlier of Abigail, John and Elizabeth. Present your work as a dramatic sequence in which we see the actors watching each other in turn and the images of what each sees forming on stage.

Task 6: Structure of Language

We are going to pause and go back to look at how the text is written. In the previous section we began to generate our own ideas, as performers, about the characters and the situation they are in and to make connections with our own experience. The performance of a play such as *The Crucible* will be a meeting between the ideas and intentions of the performers and those of the playwright. We have already noticed that it is common in ***realist*** plays for the playwright to give very detailed directions to the players and director. ***Miller*** has *written* the play to be performed and the given circumstances provided through the words and directions are the principal means by which *Miller* tells actors how to perform his written play text. **As a writer, *Miller* uses all the conventions of writing to help guide the actors.**

1. Look again at the scene and notice how punctuation is used. What is *Miller* telling the actors to do with his use of commas in lines 21 and 22? Why are they there? What effect do they have? Look at

when *Miller* uses exclamation marks – why? With what effect? It is not enough to learn the lines in this scene, you must learn the punctuation as well!

Miller's punctuation and the length of each character's line also help us to understand the **pace** and timing of the scene. Read the scene again. But this time pay very careful attention to the punctuation and line length: if there is a full stop, exaggerate the pause; if there are no marks exaggerate the pace. Can you sense a rhythm of fast, slow exchanges or moments? Make notes about the pacing of the scene to remind you of where the rhythm is.

Task 7: Scene objectives

In order to play the scene effectively it is important to work out what the objectives for each character might be. You will remember that there are two levels of objective in the ***Stanislavskian** system* of acting: the super-objective and scene/unit objectives. Below are suggestions for the super-objectives of John and Elizabeth. Now suggest what the **objective** will be for each character in this scene. The objective is always expressed as an action; something the character wants to try and make happen.

If the super-objective is . . .	**John**: I want to use my good reputation to stop the madness in this village and I want to forget my mistake and make my wife love me again. **Elizabeth:** I want my marriage back but I must make him face up to what he has done instead of trying to bury his head in the sand.
Then the scene objective is . . .	**John:** **Elizabeth:**

Task 8: Strategies, obstacles and tactics

Having decided on the objective for each character in the scene, you now need to decide how the character will try and achieve their objective. This means identifying a *strategy*. **The strategy is the means of achieving the objective.** If your objective for Elizabeth is to make John feel relaxed enough to open up to her, by what strategy will she do this? By trying to please him perhaps, or trying to make him laugh and forget his troubles, or getting him to show some affection? If you decide on a different objective – to make him feel guilt for his betrayal, for example – you will obviously suggest different strategies.

In order for a strategy to work, we often need to adopt different *tactics*. Imagine a game of football: the objective for each team is to win, but they may adopt different strategies for doing so – playing defensively or attacking, for instance. But as the game develops, each team might need to use a range of tactics to achieve their objective. If a player is injured or sent off, if the opposing team's strategy is more successful, a team might need to adopt a new tactic. **In drama, there are two principle tactics that are used by characters: threats and lures** (sticks and carrots). Look at the scene again. Can you identify the tactics? Isn't John using a lure in lines 14 and 21? And threat, or reprimand, in lines 28 and 30?

One reason for a character to change tactics is because another character creates an *obstacle* that must be overcome in order for the character to achieve their objective. Earlier in the play, one imagines that John was trying to achieve his super-objective by avoiding any contact with Abigail and staying at home with Elizabeth, hoping that time would heal the wounds. But the witch-hunt becomes an obstacle and he has to change his tactics. In this scene, line 23 seems to suggest that Elizabeth's lack of enthusiasm for John's kiss is an obstacle to his tactic of showing her physical affection. In the same way John, drawing attention to the lack of flowers and cider, seems to be an obstacle to be overcome for Elizabeth.

Let us now review the whole scene in terms of objectives, strategies, tactics and obstacles.

	John	Elizabeth
Objective		
Strategy		
Obstacle	1 2 3	1 2 3
Tactic	1 2 3	1 2 3

Try rehearsing the scene a few times and experimenting with the information you have collected. With the help of the director, try and work out how best to express the objectives and strategies and when tactics change. You should aim for a dynamic piece that feels as if it is driving forward – a keen sense of both characters developing their own strategy as they respond to each other.

Task 9: From scene to scene

If you have copies of *The Crucible* go back to the scene between John Proctor and Abigail towards the end of Act 1. Use the strategies that we have introduced to work on the scene. Run the two scenes together. Then answer these questions:

1. How will the actor playing Proctor in the second scene be affected by the experience of the first scene. How will the first scene effect how the second scene is played?
2. Let Elizabeth sit in on the first scene, witnessing how her husband behaves. Let Abigail sit in on the second scene, witnessing her 'lover' with his wife. *Hot-seat* both characters immediately after each scene.
3. Now play the second scene again. How has the acting of the scene changed as a result of these further rehearsals?

Finally, if you want to find out more about *The Crucible* and the work of Arthur ***Miller*** try visiting: http://www.levity.com/corduroy/millera.htm

4 Finding the *Verfrumdungseffekt*

Outline

Having looked at ***realist*** styles of acting and ***representational*** theatre in the previous workshop, we now turn our attention to the ***non-realist*** acting style and ***presentational*** theatre which ***Brecht*** developed as part of his theory of *epic theatre*. Like ***Stanislavski*** and ***Strasberg***, *Brecht* was both a practitioner (he wrote and directed plays) and a theatre teacher. We know of *Brecht*'s ideas about theatre from his theoretical writings. We also know about the detail of his own productions because he kept a *modelbook* for all of his major plays. The *modelbook* is the play text with illustrations and explanatory notes, made during *Brecht*'s own rehearsals. These notes and photographs interpreted the play's characters, settings and actions for the actors and designers and were intended to be used by others who wished to perform his plays. They are, if you like, an interesting example of the kind of working diary you will be expected to keep of your own practical work!

In **Part 1**, we will consider the two fundamentals of *Brechtian* theory: the *epic* and the *verfrumdungseffekt*. It is important to remember that, although *Brecht* had tremendous respect for *Stanislavski*'s work, his theories were developed largely in reaction against *Stanislavski*'s 'theatre of empathy'. We will see how *Brecht*'s political convictions led him in a very different direction. **Part 2** is a workshop designed to help us understand the complex workings of the *verfrumdungseffekt* in practice.

Mother Courage and Her Children

In our work we will be exploring a scene from ***Brecht***'s famous play *Mother Courage and her Children*, which was completed in 1939. It is set in Europe during the Thirty Years' War (1618–1648) and tells the story of a woman who makes her living by trailing around the battlefields with her canteen wagon, buying and selling whatever goods she can lay her hands on. At the beginning of the play she is accompanied by her two sons, Eilif and Swiss Cheese, and her dumb daughter, Kattrin. The play tells the story of how Mother Courage eventually loses all of her three children to the war. As the Sergeant prophetically says to her at the end of the first scene:

> **Like the war to nourish you?**
> **Have to feed it something too.**

Brecht was a committed Marxist and he intended his theatre to be ***dialectical***, because *dialectics* lies at the heart of Karl Marx's philosophical thinking and revolutionary politics. Broadly speaking, *dialectics* refers to the clash of **opposites**, and the **contradictions** which are bound to arise when opposites come into conflict.

Mother Courage herself embodies a clash of opposing ideals – a *dialectic*: she is a walking contradiction. She needs the war in order for her business enterprise to thrive, but, at the same time, she fears it for the threat it presents to the safety of her children. **She is caught in the contradiction between being a merchant and being a mother.** So, essentially, the play is about the contradictory claims of business and motherhood; and about the inevitable loss that the mother suffers as she tries to negotiate these contradictory demands.

Task 1: The mother-merchant

In the *modelbook* for *Mother Courage, Brecht* describes Mother Courage's situation thus:

> She longs for the war but at the same time fears it. She wants to join in but as a peaceable businesswoman, not in a warlike way. She wants to maintain her family during the war and by means of it. She wants to serve the army and also to keep out of its clutches.

In each of these sentences *Brecht* expresses the contradictions in Mother Courage's character. The basic contradiction of course is between her role as a mother and her ambition as a merchant. *Brecht* uses the exceptional circumstances of war as a means of forcing the contradictions in her character to the surface; to dramatically confront and reveal the contradictions through the brutal events of war.

Make *still-images*, based on each of the sentences, which explore and represent clearly the contradictions in Mother Courage's character. An image that shows the two faces of mother and merchant for instance.

Discuss what kind of scenes or situations might force the contradictions to the surface. What might happen as she tries to serve the army which will also put her in their 'clutches'? What might happen as she tries to make money for her family from the war which would also threaten her family? *Remember* that she loses all of her children to the war, one by one, as the story develops.

Part 1 *The Fundamentals of Epic Theatre*

Circumstances are Changeable, not Given

We have seen how ***Stanislavski***'s concept of the 'given circumstances' is one of the cornerstones of ***realist*** acting; but this was precisely the point at which ***Brecht*** believed that it was necessary to part company with *Stanislavski*'s methods. For *Stanislavski*, it is the given circumstances that ensure consistency of characterisation, and determine how a character will behave; for *Brecht*, circumstances which are 'given' are, ultimately, inescapable. To state the case even more forcefully: the 'given' circumstances imprison the character in fairly fixed patterns of behaviour, and suggest that the world is beyond her or his control.

Stanislavski's brand of *realism* is a theatre of empathy which produces a number of effects on the spectators:

- it seeks to draw them into the stage illusion and not to question the picture of life on the stage;
- it encourages them to share and empathise with the experiences of the characters;
- it provokes a degree of emotional involvement and emotional release (catharsis);
- it implicates and entangles them in the stage action – it presents the stage world as being 'natural' and unchangeable.

According to *Brecht*, this kind of theatre produces a passive, accepting, uncritical attitude in the audience. They are drawn into a world which seems natural, inevitable and unalterable. Their tolerance of this world prevents them from seeing the circumstances they encounter there as being subject to question and criticism. The last thing *Brecht* wanted was a tolerant, suggestible, empathic spectator; he needed an active, enquiring, thinking audience.

It was *Brecht*'s studies in Marxism, and his revolutionary politics, that led him to imagine a new kind of spectator. Traditionally, the theatre audience (under *Stanislavski*'s spell), was content to accept the world depicted on the stage as a true picture of the world as it really is; something which simply has to be accepted as 'natural'. *Brecht* wanted a theatre that would show that, in any set of circumstances, a number of different options exist for the characters; and the job of the spectator was to judge the validity of the characters' selected course of action. ***Stanislavski*'s theatre tended to create submission in the spectator; *Brecht* wanted to create dissent.** In political terms, submission produces acquiescence, deference and conformity to the *status quo*; dissent produces defiance, protest and a desire for change.

The two elements in *Stanislavski*'s theatre that elicit submission in the spectator are: **identification** and **cause and effect.** Because the spectator is encouraged to identify with the plight of the characters, he or she begins to see them as victims of circumstance; helpless individuals, with no real power to shape their own destinies. This sense of helplessness is reinforced by the logic of 'the through-line of actions' in an endless chain of cause and effect, whereby action A will inevitably cause action B, and the effect of action B will be to cause action C.

For *Brecht*, it was these two elements in *Stanislavski*'s system that produced its politically 'conservative' nature. Consequently, he had to develop techniques that would counteract these politically reactionary tendencies which he had identified in *Stanislavski*'s work. **The overriding principle in *Brecht's* theatre is a commitment to fundamental social change;** and, consequently, he set out to develop a theatre which presents the world and human nature as knowable and alterable. As we shall see, it is the device of the *verfrumdungseffekt*, and the *epic* form that provide him with the tools for achieving this end.

Brecht wore his politics on his sleeve. He directly addressed his audience and challenged them to look at what happens in the world of human affairs not as being 'natural', like the weather or the changing of the seasons, but as being man-made, socially unjust and therefore changeable. Many of his ideas both about politics and a new 'anti realist' theatre are contained within this prologue to his *Lehrstucke*, or 'learning play', *The Exception and the Rule*. Notice the ***presentational*** style of performance. The players directly address the audience; they present themselves and their story, rather than beginning by creating the illusion of another place and time.

We are about to tell you
The story of a journey. An exploiter
And two of the exploited are the travellers.
Examine carefully the behaviour of these people:
Find it surprising though not unusual
Inexplicable though normal
Incomprehensible though it is the rule.
Consider even the most insignificant, seemingly simple
Action with distrust. Ask yourselves whether it is necessary
Especially if it is usual.

We ask you expressly to discover
That what happens all the time is not natural
For to say that something is natural
In such times of bloody confusion
Of ordained disorder, of systematic arbitrariness
Of inhuman humanity is to
Regard it as unchangeable.

Task 2: Playing with contradictions

- What clues are there in the prologue that there will be differences between ***Brecht***'s style of theatre and the ***realist*** style we have explored in the previous workshop?
- What can you tell about *Brecht's* politics, or world view, from this prologue?
- Who might the 'exploiter' and the 'exploited' be in this story – a master and slaves; a ruthless guide and innocent travellers? What events do you expect to happen during the journey? How will *Brecht* use these characters and what happens to them as a means of teaching his political view? Remember that *Brecht* used ***dialectics*** – contradictions and opposites – to show how the powerful try to make their exploitation of the powerless look 'natural' and 'unchangeable'.

1. The prologue is spoken by the players; the actors in the story that follows. Work in two groups. The first group will try to find the most effective way of speaking the lines. How will you allocate the words to different voices so that the intentions of the words are clearly emphasised for the audience? Meanwhile, the second group will work on a series of images to illustrate the words. These images will show the 'exploiter' and the 'exploited' and some of the events or changes in their relationship as the journey unfolds.
2. When both groups are ready, find the most effective way of combining both groups' work into a dramatic sequence.

The *Verfrumdungseffekt* and the *Epic*

For ***Brecht***, the *verfrumdungseffekt* is the antidote to identification and empathy; it is designed to cultivate in the audience a more clinical, detached and objective form of socially critical spectatorship. When reading about *Brecht* and his work, you will often find this term translated as 'alienation effect', which is inaccurate; we prefer the more literal translation, **'strange-making effect'** (either of the words 'estrangement' or 'defamiliarisation' would be more in keeping with the spirit of the German term).

Brecht did not invent this concept himself. It was first used by the *romantic* poet, William *Wordsworth*, as long ago as 1802. And, in the early years of the twentieth century, Victor Shklovsky, the Russian formalist, wrote about defamiliarisation in ***realist*** novels. **The *verfrumdungseffekt* forces the spectator to look at ordinary, familiar, everyday things in a striking, peculiar or unexpected way;** its aim is to encourage the audience to step back from its habitual, obvious ways of seeing, in order that they might see the world afresh.

The second concept essential in helping the audience to view the play in a thinking, rather than a feeling, way is *Brecht*'s idea of the *epic*. The *epic* form was first identified by ***Aristotle*** in his *Poetics*. In an epic narrative, the separate story elements are broken up in such a way that the different events are recounted outside of the traditional time sequences that we find in other poetic forms; in other words, **'epic time' is not linear, sequential, chronological time.**

This form suggested itself to *Brecht* because of the way in which it disrupts the chain of cause and effect which is indispensable in ***Stanislavski***'s theatre of empathy. *Brecht* believed that the 'through-line of action' fostered in the spectator the illusion that the play's final outcome was always inevitable; that things could never have turned out otherwise. *Brecht*'s solution to this problem was to dislocate the 'through-line of action' by ensuring that each scene in the play was self-contained and free-standing. This technique places demands on the spectator that he or she should make his or her own connections between different episodes. **An 'episode' is a scene, complete in itself, which is set in a single location and deals with one particular event.** In the gaps between such episodic scenes, *Brecht* wanted the spectators to exercise their judgement and arrive at their own conclusions about the events they had just witnessed.

The *verfrumdungseffekt* and the use of the *epic* then, work together to counteract the essential *Stanislavskian* features of identification and causality. The important question for us to consider in this workshop is: how, in practice, are they able to do this?

In order to give a full answer to this question, it is necessary to consider three crucial aspects of *Brechtian* theatre:

- its **style of presentation**;
- the **structural devices** which *Brecht* used in his playwriting;
- the **function of the actor**.

Style of Presentation

Everything about a ***Brechtian*** production is designed to remind the audience that it is sitting in a theatre, watching a series of fictional events unfold in the form of a play. In stark contrast to the theatre of empathy, it is **anti-illusionistic**, it is ***presentational***.

For *Brecht*'s own production of *Mother Courage*, the first thing the audience noticed was the bare, grey stage, backed by a pale cyclorama. On the floor was a large circular revolve (or turntable) representing Courage's world. Each scene took place inside the circle, and the travelling was represented by a wagon moving around the revolving circumference. The wagon was made to look as authentic as possible, being constructed of materials that were consistent with the seventeenth century setting. The goods that hung from the wagon changed from scene to scene, reflecting Courage's changing fortunes. The costumes were realistic without being historically authentic; *Brecht* expressly ruled out any 'folksy' tendency or excessive concern with historical accuracy. **Scenery and props were mostly authentic, but the most important thing was that they should be *usable*.** They were also minimal: a stool for a scene in which someone was required to sit down; a roof for Kattrin to climb on in the scene where she warns the villagers of Halle of the imminent attack.

***Brecht* used bright, white light for every scene**, irrespective of whether it was a spring afternoon in Sweden or the dead of night in Saxony; and the lanterns, hanging from a metal grid, were plainly visible. Also visible to the audience was a four-

Judi Dench as Mother Courage, Royal Shakespeare Company, Barbican 1984.

piece orchestra in one of the side boxes, although some of Paul Dessau's music was played on a backstage record-player. All of this was intended as a constant reminder to the spectators that they were attending a theatrical presentation.

The famous *Brechtian* half-curtain ran the whole length of the stage on a wire. The curtain was drawn whenever there was a scene change. As the stage hands set up the next scene, a sign dropped in from above. Crude letters scrawled on a frame, made up of what looked like metallic branches, indicated the location: 'SAXONY'; and other summary details were projected onto the half-curtain:

> January 1936. The emperor's troops are threatening the Protestant town of Halle. The stone begins to speak. Mother Courage loses her daughter and trudges on alone. The war is a long way from being over.

The important thing to note here is that the scene summary tells the audience exactly what is about to happen. *Brecht* did not want the spectators wondering '**what** happens next?'. There should be no surprises in the action which was about to unfold; knowing that Courage loses Kattrin in the forthcoming scene allows the audience to focus on **how** things happened.

By using signs and projected captions, *Brecht* is effectively **labelling** the events about to be portrayed. He draws attention to them and implies that they call for an explanation. *Brecht* likened these disruptions to a **footnote** in a piece of text; something that breaks the reader's stream of thought and forces her or him to pause for further consideration.

Structural Devices

As with the overall presentational style, many of the structural devices that ***Brecht*** used in his writing were also calculated to ensure that **the audience remained critically alert during the performance.**

The epic structure	As we have already noted, the use of the *epic* form itself is essentially a structural device for disrupting the flow of action. In **Brecht**'s own words: **the individual episodes have to be knotted together in such a way that the knots are easily noticed. The episodes must not succeed each other indistinguishably but must give us a chance to interpose our judgement.** This kind of strategic interruption in the flow of the narrative subverts the sequence of cause and effect and, more importantly, it also helps unmask the nature and the momentum of the **social forces** that are at work on the **individual** characters.
Types **that are socially real, not** ***characters*** **that are psychologically real**	Whereas ***Stanislavski***'s theatre of empathy focuses on the individual and her or his psychological make-up, *Brecht*'s attention is firmly directed towards the **historical** and **social** pressures that make the individuals what they are. Whereas *Stanislavski* was concerned to develop highly individual characters who were unique in their psychology and other characteristics, *Brecht* presented universal **types** of character. Mother Courage represents all poor working-class mothers struggling to make ends meet in times of war – she is not a particular woman with a name, but a mother who shares the same characterisitcs as other mothers of her social class and historical circumstances. Whereas in *Stanislavski*'s theatre we are fascinated by **who** the character *is*, in *Brecht*'s theatre we are shown **what** a character *does*, and through their actions we come to understand history and the class system at work.
Narrators, music and singers	Aspects of the *verfrumdungseffekt* can also assist in this process of disruption. We have already mentioned *Brecht*'s use of music in *Mother Courage*. He is highly specific about how actors should perform the songs in his plays. He recommends that the actor should not 'drop into' song (in the manner of the Hollywood musical); rather, he or she should clearly mark it off from the surrounding lines of dialogue. In *Mother Courage*, **the songs serve a variety of purposes:** both Yvette's 'Song of Fraternisation' and Courage's 'Song of the Great Capitulation' tell us about each character's past, but they also provide a biting comment on the harshness of seventeenth century life. The 'Song of the Girl and the Soldier' acts as a warning, whereas the 'Song of Solomon' neatly summarises one of the play's major themes – that the rewards of virtue are meagre in corrupt times; there's no use trying to be an angel when you live in hell! *Brecht* did not use a storyteller or narrator in *Mother Courage*, although it was a device which he sometimes employed – for example, in *The Caucasian Chalk Circle*. In *Brechtian* theatre, song and storyteller function in much the same way. As with the songs, the storyteller addresses the audience directly. In so doing, she or he can comment on the action, alert us to any important details we should be paying particular attention to, and offer us a different viewpoint from those that the characters hold. Alternatively, he or she can pose questions for us to consider.

The Function of the Actor

However, by far the most important means of achieving the *verfrumdungseffekt* is to be found in the work of the actor. In the rest of this workshop we will explore and understand the techniques that ***Brecht*** used in order to develop the style of acting best fitted for his *epic* theatre.

As we have already emphasised, because *Brecht* does not want the audience to empathise with the characters, in performance the actor must avoid any measure of identification between the actor and her or his character. This is a contrast with ***Stanislavski*** who sought to create in his actors a very strong and personal identification with the character; finding the 'I' in the character.

***Brecht*, on the other hand, insisted that a definite distance has to be created between the actor and the role.** This means that the actor, instead of identifying with the role to create the fully rounded character, should demonstrate the role instead. In *Brecht*'s theatre, representation gives way to presentation.

This separation between actor and role is most vividly illustrated in the way the actor Charles ***Laughton*** played the part of Galileo in *Brecht*'s play, *Life of Galileo*. Laughton, the actor, is present on stage smoking a cigar; each time he is required to take on the role of Galileo, he sets the cigar down in order to show us some aspect of Galileo's behaviour. By means of this simple device the smoking of the cigar comes to be associated with the actor, and the absence of the cigar tells us we are watching the character, Galileo.

Demonstrating the role is only one aspect of the *Brechtian* actor's job; the other is finding a way to let the audience see exactly what attitude the actor has to the role he or she is playing. In order to provide his actors with a model of how this should be done, *Brecht* used the example of a street scene in which an eyewitness explains to passers-by how an accident occurred.

In 'The Street Scene', the eyewitness *demonstrates* the sequence of events surrounding the accident, and *shows* how the driver and the victim behaved. The eyewitness does not get carried away in describing the detail of the incident; she or he does not 'become' any of the people involved; and he or she does not attempt to create the illusion in the passers-by that they are watching the real accident. Instead, she or he relates the detail of the incident in a detached manner; impersonates, or even caricatures, the people involved; and probably offers an opinion as to the rights and wrongs of the accident, and who was to blame.

Task 3: Telling and showing a story

1. **Think of an incident that actually happened to you in the last few weeks: it could be something amusing that happened at school; some argument that took place at home; or something unusual that happened to you and your friends on a night out.**
2. **Take a few minutes to remember the detail of what happened and then give as full an account of the incident as you can to your partner, using gestures, voices and actions to fully illustrate what happened. Make sure they know who was involved, what the sequence of events was, and what you thought about the incident.**
3. **As your partner describes their incident, watch carefully how they tell the story, paying particular attention to how the people involved are presented. What did you notice?**

4. **Now join together with another pair and take it in turns to show and tell the story that your partners told with all the mannerisms and gestures they used in the original retelling. *But* also exaggerate your partner's gestures and way of telling the story so that you are now showing your partner showing the story! As an actor, these exaggerations show us that you are commenting on the 'character' (your partner) who tells the story as well as showing the story itself.**

In summary then, *Brecht* wanted his actors to:

- use their natural abilities as storytellers and mimics;
- appear, in performance, as themselves, impersonating the characters as they speak the playwright's lines;
- stand outside of the character;
- adopt a definite, objective, critical attitude towards the role they are playing;
- invite the audience to make their own critical judgements, which may or may not be consistent with the actor's own attitude and evaluation.

Rehearsal Techniques

In his work with actors, ***Brecht*** *did* make use of some of ***Stanislavski****'s* techniques. In the early stages of rehearsal, *Brecht* knew it was important for his actors to go through a stage of identification with the character before they could go beyond it. Once the actor had gone through the stage of identification, they were ready to try to see the character from the outside, from the point of view of society, and to generate a critical attitude towards that character.

In order to help his actors achieve this *verfrumdungseffekt* (simultaneously being and not being the character), *Brecht* developed a number of rehearsal techniques. These techniques created for the actors the sense of detachment from the characters that is essential to the *verfrumdungseffekt* in *Brechtian* acting.

Whereas *Stanislavski*'s starting point was the given circumstances, Brecht's was the social relevance of the events depicted in the drama. Actors were encouraged to analyse their lines by asking four questions:

1. Who is the sentence of use to?
2. Who does it *claim* to be of use to?
3. What does it call for?
4. What practical action corresponds to it?

These questions are designed to help the actors understand the relationship of the fictional world of the play to the real world in which they live.

Task 4: Comparison with Stanislavski's given circumstances

1. **How are these questions *different* from the questions used to identify the given circumstances in *Stanislavskian* theatre? Go back to these questions on page 51 and compare the kinds of information that the two sets of questions throw up.**
2. **In the light of your work on *The Crucible* scene, apply *Brecht*'s questions to the following lines from the scene we studied and discuss how this new information might change the way that the lines would be played in a *Brechtian* style:**

1 ***Elizabeth*: What keeps you so late? It's almost dark.**

22 *Elizabeth*: (*it is hard to say)* I know it, John.

For example:

8 *Proctor*: Are you well today?
The sentence is of use to Proctor who is trying to make things right with Elizabeth. The sentence claims to be of use to Elizabeth – it shows that Proctor cares. The sentence calls for Elizabeth to reciprocate with a kindness towards Proctor. Proctor tries to please Elizabeth with a kiss which 'she receives'.

Like *Stanislavski, Brecht* also divided his scenes up into units. But whereas for the *Stanislavskian* actor the units are primarily designed to help determine the character's motivation and objective in the scene, for *Brecht*, each unit sketches in the basic actions and the relationships between all the characters.

We will be using the following extract from *Mother Courage* to describe four exercises that *Brecht* used to help his actors find the appropriate acting style. It is a 'unit' taken from Scene 5, in which The Chaplain wants to help a peasant family who have lost their farm in the war. Although Kattrin is keen to help rescue the injured family, Mother Courage is reluctant to let them use linen shirts as bandages.

A peasant:	(*brought in by the chaplain*): My arm's gone.
The Chaplain:	Where's that linen?
Mother Courage:	I can't give nowt. What with expenses, taxes, loan interest and bribes. (*Making guttural noises, Kattrin raises a plank and threatens her mother with it.*) You gone plain crazy? Put that plank away or I'll paste you one, you cow. I'm giving nowt, don't want to, got to think of meself. (*The Chaplain lifts her off the steps and sets her on the ground, then starts pulling out shirts and tearing them into strips.*) My officers' shirts! Half a florin apiece! I'm ruined! (*From the house comes the cry of a child in pain.*)
The peasant:	The baby's in there still! (*Kattrin dashes in.*)

Rehearsal Exercise 1: Speaking the Stage Directions

In a group of four, read through the above extract enough times for it to become familiar (remember that, although Kattrin is unable to speak, her actions form a vital part of the scene). Play the sequence through three or four times to get a sense of the dynamic of the incident. Now read the following version of the same extract:

A peasant:	The peasant entered with the Chaplain, and seeing the two women, told them that his arm was hurt.
The Chaplain:	The chaplain made an urgent enquiry about linen.
Mother Courage:	Mother Courage dismissed his enquiry, saying that her expenses made it impossible for her to give linen away.
Kattrin:	As Kattrin made rasping noises in her throat, she picked up a plank of wood and held it over her mother in a threatening manner.
Mother Courage:	Mother Courage enquired whether her daughter had taken leave of her senses. She told Kattrin to put the plank of wood down, adding a few threats of her own. She repeated that she could not afford to give her linen away.
The Chaplain:	The Chaplain lifted Mother Courage from the steps of

	the wagon and placed her firmly on the ground. He then pulled four linen shirts from the wagon and began to tear them into strips.
Mother Courage:	Mother Courage protested and lamented the loss of two florins, saying that the Chaplain's actions had ruined her.
The peasant:	The peasant heard the sound of a child's cry from inside the house. He remembered that the baby was still inside.
Kattrin:	Kattrin rushed into the house in search of the baby.

Try to play this version of the scene. You will notice that the characters now speak the stage directions aloud and that the content of the speeches have been included in these directions.

When you play the scene you still play to the other characters, so use a change of voice for words or phrases that are directly addressed to other characters. For instance, the first line might be: 'The peasant entered with the Chaplain, and seeing the two women, told them that *(different voice)* HIS ARM WAS HURT'.

Rehearse the sequence until you have a version that you are happy with. With the other members of your group, discuss the effect of playing the scene in this way, and compare it with your original version. What was the impact of speaking the stage directions aloud on the physical action of the extract?

Rehearsal Excercise 2: Paraphrasing the Text

This time, play ***Brecht***'s original scene but **paraphrase** the text. Try paraphrasing it in a number of different ways: you could turn *Brecht*'s everyday language into ***Shakespearean*** verse (e.g. 'Methinks I have no sensation in my arm'); try the scene using different dialects (e.g. Cockney, Birmingham, Geordie), or accents (e.g. American, Australian); strip the dialogue down to its absolute essentials (e.g. **reduce each sentence to a single word**).

When you have experimented with the sequence, find a way to play the extract that really brings out the **differences in social background** between the characters.

Exercise 3: Making the Present Historical

Return to ***Brecht***'s original text, but try to put the lines into the **past tense** (e.g. *A peasant*: My arm *was* gone; *The Chaplain*: Where *was* that linen? etc.). Because Kattrin doesn't speak any lines, make sure that she speaks her own stage directions at the appropriate time (the other three should only speak the dialogue). Don't worry if this sounds strange (you're playing with a 'strange-making effect', remember). In this version, the characters are looking back on events that happened in the past. Discuss how playing the scene in the past tense changes it. What is the effect of playing it in this way?

Exercise 4: Working in the Third Person

Play the sequence one last time. Retain the **past tense**, but also put each speech into the **third person** (e.g *A Peasant*: *His* arm was gone etc.). Once again, discuss how this effects the scene.

Task 5: Reflecting on the rehearsal techniques

- **What is the effect of these excercises for you as an actor? In what ways have they helped you to both identify and not identify with the characters?**

- **Remember your experiences in rehearsing the scene from *The Crucible*. How are these two approaches to acting different?**
- **From an actor's point of view, what is the difference between rehearsing in a *realist* style in which you are 'being' the character and rehearsing in a *Brechtian* style in which you are 'showing' the character?**

These four exercises were designed to help actors *avoid* identification with their roles, encouraging them instead to *stand outside* of them, producing the critical objectivity that is so vital to *Brechtian* theatre. Having already done the *playing the given circumstances* workshop you should already be developing a sense of the different demands that *Brecht* placed on his actors. We will shortly have the opportunity to push our explorations a little further, but first we need to consider one final, crucial distinction between *realist* forms of acting and *Brechtian* acting.

Contradiction, Changeability and the *Gestus*

We have seen how **consistency** in characterisation is a vital part of ***Stanislavski***'s approach. For ***Brecht***, the opposite is true: he wanted the audience to see the many different, often **contradictory**, sides of a character.

If you were to chart Mother Courage's different moods throughout *Brecht*'s play, you would find her, by turns: confident; thoughtful; flirtatious; doubting and sceptical; amused; preoccupied; conceited and full of herself; egotistical; shy; devastated and desolate. Her changes of mood happen quite suddenly (a factor that calls for great versatility in the actor, of course).

At the end of Scene 1, having seen her eldest son recruited against her wishes, she is dismayed, but at the beginning of the second scene we see the shrewd businesswoman bargaining (and flirting) with the Cook. Each scene shows a different side of Courage, and we are forcibly struck by her changeable moods. Being a Marxist, **change**, of course, is a key word for *Brecht*: Mother Courage changes; her wagon changes from scene to scene; circumstances can change; and, above all, **the world can change**.

So, the changeable and contradictory natures of *Brecht*'s characters is a vital ingredient in *epic theatre*. **But, we see contradiction not only in the changing sides and moods of the characters, but also in the smallest physical gestures.** Hans Curjel watched *Brecht* at work on his 1948 production of *Antigone*. He was struck by *Brecht*'s attention to the smallest physical detail:

> **The directorial method was based on investigation and varied experimentation that could extend to the smallest gestures – eyes, fingers . . . Brecht worked like a sculptor on and with the actor.**

Contradiction then, is also to be found in the actors' gestures, and, in order to formalise this concept, *Brecht* invented the word ***gestus***. It is based on the German word for gesture (*'geste'*), but is somewhat confusingly defined, even by *Brecht* himself. We can, we think, narrow *gestus* down to two essential components. The first is that it must contain a **contradiction**.

In *Brecht*'s 1950 production of *Der Hofmeister* (*The Private Tutor*), the character Lauffer, in an attempt to secure work, tries to ingratiate himself with the Mayor. He respectfully approaches the Mayor, who is in conversation with someone else, and bows in a most exaggerated fashion. The Mayor sees Lauffer, but chooses to ignore him; so Lauffer repeats the same exaggerated bow three more times. On the final bow, exasperated with the Mayor's indifference, he mutters under his breath, 'Go to the devil, louts!'. The contradiction lies in between the respectful bow and the impertinent insult: the physical gesture says one thing, which is contradicted by the words which are spoken.

The second component of *gestus* is that the physical action also stands for a **social relationship**. Lauffer's exaggerated bow to the Mayor emphasises the difference in social status between the two characters.

Brecht's 1949 production of *Mother Courage* contains probably the most famous and celebrated *gestus* in the whole history of *Brechtian* theatre. Courage was played by Helene ***Weigel*** (*Brecht*'s wife). In Scene 3, when Courage hears the volley of shots that signals the execution of her son, Swiss Cheese, *Weigel*'s response was **the Silent Scream**.

Weigel's Courage is seated on a stool with her hands in her lap. She grabs the coarse material of her skirt and leans forward with a straight back. At the same time, she thrusts her head back and opens her mouth as if to scream. But no sound comes out.

A member of the audience later described the scream in these words:

> **A harsh and terrifying, indescribable sound issued from her mouth. But in fact, there was no sound. Nothing. It was the sound of absolute silence. A silence which screamed and screamed throughout the theatre, making the audience bow their heads as if they had been hit by a blast of wind.**

The **contradiction** is contained in the idea of a scream that is silent; and the physical action indicates that Courage's **social position**, as a helpless mother unable to save her son, means that she is powerless to prevent the soldiers from carrying out the execution. She silently refuses to recognise her son, but she cannot refuse to recognise *and* express her horror at what happens – so the scream is silent.

It is also interesting to note that *Weigel* played with the positioning of the silent

Helene Weigel's Silent Scream in *Mother Courage and her Children*, Berlin, 1951.

scream in the scene. There are accounts of performances in which she used the scream at the end of the scene when her son's body is brought on stage by the soldiers and she silently shakes her head, twice refusing to acknowledge the dead boy as her own. As the soldiers take off the body, *Weigel* turns away and does the silent scream.

This shows us that as a *Brechtian* actor, *Weigel* could both identify with the character by expressing the pain and horror felt by Mother Courage and also be detached enough from the character to use such a powerful *gestus* as a staging device which could be 'turned on' at different places in the scene's development.

Task 6: *Gestus* in *The Crucible*

The idea of *gestus* was used by other playwrights, even in the *realist* tradition. Remember in the scene from *The Crucible* when Proctor secretly adds salt to the cooking pot?

- **What does this action tell us about the social relations between Proctor and Elizabeth and how does it comment on what Proctor has been up to prior to this action?**
- **In what sense is this action contradictory? In other words, does it go against the grain of Proctor's other actions and words in this scene?**

Having grasped the fundamentals of *Brecht's epic theatre*, and the major implications for the *Brechtian* actor, we move on explore how the *verfrumdungseffekt* can be made to work in practice.

Part 2 *The* Mother Courage *Workshop*

The best-known scene in *Mother Courage and her Children* is Scene 11, sometimes called the 'drumming scene', in which Kattrin saves the townspeople of Halle but loses her own life in the process. Before proceeding to the workshop, you might like to familiarise yourself with the whole scene. We gave you the location and caption for the scene on page 71. The dialogue is spread out over the next few pages.

To complete the workshop, you will need to form groups of at least eight, corresponding to the eight characters in the scene (Kattrin, The Peasant, The Peasant's Wife, The Young Peasant, The Ensign, First Soldier, Second Soldier, Third Soldier).

You will also need to construct a makeshift set to work on, and find some essential props. You will definitely need the following: stage right, the roof of the peasants' house, sturdy enough to bear Kattrin's weight; a ladder to reach the roof, which Kattrin can then pull up; a drum and two beaters; a chopping block, in front of the roof, and something to chop with; pikes for the soldiers; a piece of wood; a musket. *Brecht* would, of course, insist on props that have been 'lovingly made', but serviceable rehearsal props will suffice for our purposes.

Task 7: Marking off the fixed points

The cart is standing, much the worse for wear, alongside a peasant's house with a huge thatched roof, backing on a wall of rock. It is night.

An ensign and three soldiers in heavy armour step out of the wood.

The Ensign:	I want no noise now. Anyone shouts, shove your pike into him.
First Soldier:	Have to knock them up, though, if we're to find a guide.
The Ensign:	Knocking sounds natural. Could be a cow bumping the stable wall. (*The Soldiers knock on the door of the house. The peasant's wife opens it. They stop her mouth. Two soldiers go in.*)
Man's voice:	(*within*) What is it? (*The soldiers bring out the peasant and his son.*)
The Ensign:	(*pointing at the cart, where Kattrin's head has appeared*) There's another one. (*A soldier drags her out.*) Anyone else live here beside you lot?
The peasants:	This is our son. And she's dumb. Her mother's gone into town to buy stuff. For their business, 'cause so many people's getting out and selling things cheap. They're just passing through. Canteen folk.
The Ensign:	I'm warning you, keep quiet, or if there's the least noise you get a pike across your nut. Now I want someone to come with us and show us the path to the town. (*Points to the young peasant.*) Here, you.
The Young Peasant:	I don't know no path.
Second Soldier:	(*grinning*) He don't know no path.
Young Peasant:	I ain't helping Catholics.
The Ensign:	(*to the second soldier*) Stick your pike in his ribs.
The Young Peasant:	(*forced to his knees, with the pike threatening him*) I won't do it, not to save my life.
First Soldier:	I know what'll change his mind. (*Goes towards the stable.*) Two cows and an ox. Listen, you: if you're not reasonable I'll chop up your cattle.
The Young Peasant:	No, not that!
The Peasant's Wife:	(*weeps*) Please spare our cattle, captain, it'd be starving us to death.
The Ensign:	They're dead if he goes on being obstinate.
First Soldier:	I'm taking the ox first.
The Young Peasant:	(*to his father*) Have I got to? (*The wife nods.*) Right.
The Peasant's Wife:	And thank you kindly, captain, for sparing us, for ever and ever, Amen. (*The peasant stops his wife from further expressions of gratitude.*)
First Soldier:	I knew the ox was what they minded about most, was I right? (*Guided by the young peasant, the ensign and his men continue on their way.*)

In this short extract, under orders from The Ensign, the three Soldiers round-up The Peasant, his Wife, their Son and Kattrin, who has been sleeping in the wagon.

1. Play the scene through, from the beginning up until the stage direction *A soldier drags her out*. At this point freeze the action. Pay particular attention to the physical and spatial relationships between the military characters and their captives. Spend a few moments sculpting this image, so that the attitudes of the captives are reflected in their physical positions and relationships to the soldiers. At this point, we know that the son is in a defiant mood, but what of The Peasant and his Wife? What do you think Kattrin's attitude is at this moment?
2. When you are happy with your 'sculpture', use it as the starting point for the next short extract, which runs from The Ensign's line, 'Anyone else live here beside you lot?' to the First Soldier's, 'I'm taking the ox first'. Once again, freeze the action on this line. How defiant is the son now? What is the attitude of the father and mother? Has Kattrin's attitude changed? Once again, sculpt the image so that these new attitudes are made clear in the physicality of the captives.

Immediately afterwards, the mother indicates to the son that he should follow The Ensign's order to show the soldiers the way to the town. When the son agrees, The Peasant's Wife says: 'And thank you kindly, captain, for sparing us, for ever and ever, Amen'. She is immediately stopped from any further expressions of gratitude by her husband, and almost immediately the soldiers leave.

3. Remember our comments on ***Brecht***'s concept of ***gestus***. It is a *physical action* that stands for a *social relation*, which also contains a *contradiction*. Together, help the actor playing The Peasant's Wife to find an appropriate *gestus* to accompany her line (the action needs to stand in contradiction to the expression of thanks). When you are satisfied with The Peasant's Wife's *gestus*, try to find an appropriate physical action for The Peasant, The Young Peasant and Kattrin to perform as the woman delivers her line.

For this short extract, you now have three **fixed points:** the initial attitude of the captives; the attitude when the son is in the greatest danger; and the mother's expression of gratitude.

4. Rehearse the extract, and try to find a way of marking off these fixed points from the surrounding dialogue (perhaps by using a momentary freeze, or some kind of sound cue). Discuss what the effect of marking off these fixed points is. *Brecht* used the analogy of a **knot** to indicate points at which the flow of action is disrupted. How does this 'marking off' help distinguish the 'knots' between the different parts of the episode?

Task 8: Using Brecht's idea for a scene

Following the departure of the son with the soldiers, the peasants are left wondering what is about to happen. This is the quietest passage in the whole scene, and one which directors tend to gloss over. ***Brecht***, of course, did not make this mistake; and we are going to use one of the techniques that *Brecht* himself used when rehearsing his own 1949 production of the play.

The Peasant: What are they up to, I'd like to know. Nowt good.
The Peasant's Wife: Perhaps they're just scouting. What you doing?
The Peasant (*putting a ladder against the roof and climbing up it*) Seeing if they're on their own. (*From the top.*) Something moving in the wood. Can see some thing down by the quarry. And there are men in armour in the clearing. And a gun. That's at least a regiment. God's mercy on the town and everyone in it!
The Peasant's Wife: Any lights in the town?
The Peasant: No. They'll all be asleep. (*Climbs down.*) If those people get in they'll butcher the lot.
The Peasant's Wife: Sentries're bound to spot them first.
The Peasant: Sentry in the tower up on the hill must have been killed, or he'd have blown his bugle.
The Peasant's Wife: If only there were more of us.
The Peasant: Just you and me and that cripple.
The Peasant's Wife: Nowt we can do, you'd say ...
The Peasant: Nowt.
The Peasant's Wife: Can't possibly run down there in the blackness.
The Peasant: Whole hillside's crawling with 'em. We could give a signal.
The Peasant's Wife: What, and have them butcher us too?
The Peasant: You're right, nowt we can do.
The Peasant's Wife (*to Kattrin*) Pray, poor creature, pray!

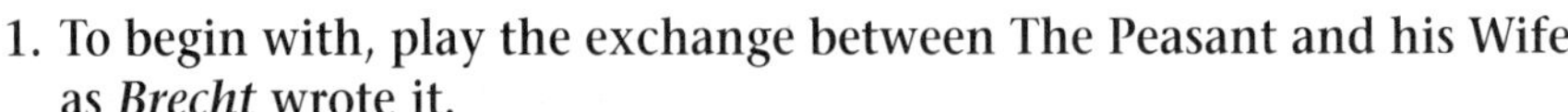

1. To begin with, play the exchange between The Peasant and his Wife as *Brecht* wrote it.
2. Replay the scene, but this time the actor playing The Peasant should add the words, '... said the man' following each of his speeches; and, similarly, the actor playing The Peasant's Wife should add the words '... said the woman'. Try this out a few times.

- What is the effect of adding these words each time a character speaks?

1. *Brecht*'s reason for doing this, he said, was to make the actors emphasise the peasants' failings, to show how they reassure each other that there really is nothing that they can do. Play the scene once more, with *Brecht*'s intention firmly in mind.

As the peasants wonder what is happening, the stage directions give us no sense of what Kattrin is doing. Go back to the third fixed point in Task 7, where the captives' different physical actions accompany The Peasant's Wife's expression of gratitude. This time, just work with the peasant, his wife and Kattrin.

2. Begin the scene with the words, 'What are they up to…'. Play the scene with the peasants using 'said the man/woman', but this time leave a pause in between the spoken lines. In this pause, the actor playing Kattrin is going to use **action narration**. She simply speaks aloud any action that Kattrin performs, even if there is apparently *no* action. It might go something like this:

The Peasant:	What are they up to, I'd like to know. Nowt good, said the man.
Kattrin:	Kattrin remains motionless.
The Peasant's Wife:	Perhaps they're just scouting. What you doing, asked the woman.
Kattrin:	She looks at the wife, and then at the peasant.
The Peasant:	(*putting a ladder against the roof*) etc.

Note that it is only *actions* that are narrated. **In this technique, you should always avoid telling us what the character is thinking or feeling. We are only interested in the action.** By using 'action narration' you can build up a sense of what Kattrin is doing as The Peasant and his Wife discuss the situation.

- What does the action narration exercise tell you about Kattrin's response to the events at the peasants' farmhouse?

Task 9: The drumming scene

We will be looking at the drumming sequence in two parts: the first is a very short section, just after Kattrin begins, where the only other characters present are The Peasant and his Wife. The longer, second part is when the soldiers return.

In the first part, the Peasant's Wife has been praying. During the course of her prayer, she mentions her brother-in-law and his four children. We have already seen, in the extract from Scene 5 that we worked on earlier, that Kattrin is prepared to endanger herself in order to rescue a baby; so, once she realises that children are at risk in the town, she steals away to the wagon, takes a drum and climbs onto the roof of the house to warn the townspeople.

The Peasant's Wife:	Forget not the children, what are in danger, the littlest ones especially, the old folk what can't move, and every living creature.
The Peasant:	And forgive us our trespasses as we forgive them that trespass against us. Amen. (*Sitting on the roof, Kattrin begins to beat the drum which she has pulled out from under her apron.*)
The Peasant's Wife:	Jesus Christ, what's she doing?
The Peasant:	She's out of her mind.
The Peasant's Wife:	Quick, get her down. (*The peasant hurries to the ladder, but Kattrin pulls it up onto the roof.*)
The Peasant's Wife:	She'll do us in.
The Peasant:	Stop drumming at once, you cripple!
The Peasant's Wife:	Bringing the Catholics down on us!
The Peasant:	(*looking for stones to throw*) I'll stone you.

The Peasant's Wife: Where's your feelings? Where's your heart? We're done for if they come down on us. Slit our throats, they will. (*Kattrin stares into the distance towards the town and carries on drumming.*)

The Peasant's Wife: (*to her husband*) I told you we shouldn't have allowed those vagabonds on to farm. What do they care if our cows are taken?

1. Kattrin should begin drumming immediately after the word, 'Amen' is spoken. Allocate the parts to three members of your group. Play the first, short sequence with the drumming continuing throughout the dialogue between The Peasant and his Wife. Find out, from the other five members of your group, how the scene works when you play it this way. What are the problems that need to be addressed?

In rehearsal, ***Brecht*** knew that this whole sequence demanded clarity and precision; and it is important to avoid creating a scene that is just plain messy, noisy and chaotic. **Careful orchestration is required to get the clarity that *Brecht* wanted.** Clearly, the drumming cannot continue throughout the dialogue, because a stage direction tells us that Kattrin pauses to pull the ladder up onto the roof to prevent the peasant from climbing up to stop her; but, other than this, there are no further indications as to how the drumming is to be orchestrated.

2. Use the **action narration** technique again, so that you can work out the detail of the action sequence that takes place as The Peasant and his Wife try to work out how they can stop Kattrin. In this version, Kattrin should *describe* what she is doing. At the same time she should make the *action* of drumming, but *not* actually strike the drum-skin. Try this as a starting point:

The Peasant's Wife: She gets up from her knees, looks at Kattrin, looks at her husband, and says, 'Jesus Christ, what's she doing?'.

Kattrin: She looks at the peasant woman and keeps on drumming.

The Peasant: He looks at the roof, and says, 'She's out of her mind'.

Kattrin: She looks at the peasant and continues drumming, etc.

Make sure that you create enough space for Kattrin to narrate her actions after every spoken line. We know she has to stop drumming to pull up the ladder, but does she stop at any other point in this sequence?

3. As you begin to develop a more detailed sense of what the three characters are *actually doing* throughout this sequence, you can work your way back to playing the scene as *Brecht* wrote it. When you have arrived at a version in which the drumming and the spoken dialogue are effectively orchestrated, ask the members of your group who have been watching to describe their feelings towards Kattrin as she tries to warn the people of Halle. The key question for them to address is: **as a spectator to these events, are you able to maintain the kind of critical detachment and distance that *Brecht* wanted from his audience?**

Task 10: Sympathy or detachment?

The Ensign: (*runs in with his soldiers and the young peasant*) I'll cut you to ribbons, all of you!

The Peasant's Wife: Please, sir it's not our fault, we couldn't help it. It was her sneaked up there. A foreigner.

The Ensign: Where's the ladder?

The Peasant: There.

The Ensign: (*calls up*) I order you, throw that drum down. (*Kattrin goes on drumming.*)

The Ensign: You're all in this together. It'll be the end of you.

The Peasant: They been cutting pine trees in that wood. How about if we got one of the trunks and poked her off . . .

First soldier: (*to The Ensign*) Permission to make a suggestion, sir! (*He whispers something into The Ensign's ear.*) Listen, we got a suggestion could help you. Get down off there and come into town with us right away. Show us which your mother is and we'll see she ain't harmed.
(*Kattrin goes on drumming.*)

The Ensign: (*pushes him roughly aside*) She doesn't trust you; with a mug like yours it's not surprising. (*Calls up.*) Suppose I gave you my word? I can give my word of honour as an officer.
(*Kattrin drums harder.*)

The Ensign: Is nothing sacred to her?

The Young Peasant: There's more than her mother involved, sir.

First Soldier: This can't go on much longer. They're bound to hear in the town.

The Ensign: We'll have somehow to make a noise that's louder than her drumming. What can we make a noise with?

First Soldier: Thought we weren't s'posed to make no noise.

The Ensign: A harmless one, you fool. A peaceful one.

The Peasant: I could chop wood with my axe.

The Ensign: Good: you chop. (*The peasant fetches his axe and attacks a tree-trunk.*) Chop harder! Harder! You're chopping for your life. (*Kattrin has been listening, drumming less loudly the while. She now looks widely round, and goes on drumming.*)

The Ensign: Not loud enough. (*To the first soldier*): You chop too.

The Peasant: Only got the one axe. (*Stops chopping.*)

The Ensign: We'll have to set the farm on fire. Smoke her out, that's it.

The Peasant: It wouldn't help, captain. If the townspeople see a fire here they'll know what's up.
(*Kattrin has again been listening as she drums. At this point she laughs.*)

The Ensign: Look at her laughing at us. I'm not having that.

I'll shoot her down, and damn the consequences. Fetch the harquebus.
(*Three soldiers hurry off. Kattrin goes on drumming.*)

The Peasant's Wife: I got it, captain. That's their cart. If we smash it up she'll stop. Cart's all they got.

The Ensign: (*to The Young Peasant*) Smash it up. (*Calls up.*) We're going to smash up your cart if you don't stop drumming. (*The Young Peasant gives the cart a few feeble blows.*)

The Peasant's Wife: Stop it, you animal!
(*Desperately looking towards the cart, Kattrin emits pitiful noises. But she goes on drumming.*)

The Ensign: Where are those clodhoppers with the harquebus?

First Soldier: Can't have heard nowt in town yet, else we'd be hearing their guns.

The Ensign: (*calls up*) They can't hear you at all. And now we're going to shoot you down. For the last time: throw down that drum!

The Young Peasant (*suddenly flings away his plank*) Go on druming! Or they'll all be killed! Go on, go on . . .
(*The soldier knocks him down and beats him with his pike. Kattrin starts to to cry, but she goes on drumming.*)

The Peasant's Wife: Don't strike his back! For God's sake, you're beating him to death!
(*The soldiers hurry in with the arquebus.*)

Second Soldier: Colonel's frothing at the mouth, sir. We're all for court-martial.

The Ensign: Set it up! Set it up! (*Calls up while the gun is being erected.*) For the very last time: stop drumming! (*Kattrin, in tears, drums as loud as she can.*) Fire! (*The soldiers fire. Kattrin gives a few more drumbeats and then slowly crumples.*)

1. Use the methods we employed in the previous task to help you orchestrate the climax to the drumming scene. You will find that this section is much more complicated, simply because now you have *eight* characters to worry about, instead of three.

2. When you have worked out the mechanics of this section, try to find a way of performing the scene which helps the audience maintain the critical distance and detachment that we talked about in our reflections on Task 9.

- Do you think it is possible to minimise the emotional impact of the scene, and prevent the audience from empathising with Kattrin? If so, how?

Task 11: Contradictory emotions

Look at the last two lines of the spoken dialogue.

The Ensign:	That's the end of that. (*But Kattrin's drumbeats are taken up by the town's cannon. In the distance can be heard a confused noise of tocsins and gunfire.*)
The First Soldier:	She's made it.

After the drumming stops, The Ensign enjoys a moment of triumph, but his pleasure is short-lived as we hear the town's cannons firing in the distance. When we talked about the importance of contradiction in ***Brecht***'s plays, we noted the many different sides of Mother Courage's character, and how her mood changed quite markedly from scene to scene. Here, The Ensign's mood changes from triumph to dismay in the blink of an eye.

- Play the second section of the drumming scene once more. But continue the scene right to the end. As Kattrin crumples following the musket shot, show each character's immediate reaction to The Ensign's line, 'That's the end of that'. Hold the reactions, frozen, for a few seconds. At the sound of a single drumbeat (representing the town's cannon) each character should show, in a *five-second slow motion* sequence, how the reaction to The Ensign's words changes as the cannon-fire registers. Make sure that the reaction is expressed *physically* (you may even want to *exaggerate* the physical reaction to heighten the effect). The end of the slow motion sequence should be marked by The Soldier's line, 'She's made it'.

- What do you notice about the changes that are registered in this five-second period? How would you describe the change in each of the characters' reactions? Whose reaction changes the most? Whose is the least perceptible? What do these changes indicate about the various characters?

SECTION 3

The Work of the Director

The Emergence of the Director

Playwright as Director

We have already noted how the director only came to prominence in the last quarter of the nineteenth century. We have also seen how, in the classical theatre of fifth century Athens, the entire production of the play was under the supervision of the playwright, who was commonly referred to as a 'teacher'. ***Aeschylus***, in particular, was noted for his brilliance in instructing the performers in their intricate dance movements, in their speaking of his poetry and in the orchestration of what, today, we might call the ***mise en scene***.

The emergence of the director

For centuries to come, the playwright continued to assume major responsibility for the mounting of his plays. Hamlet's advice to the travelling troupe of players who arrive to perform at the castle of Elsinore is often taken to be evidence of ***Shakespeare***'s own directorial approach; and we know that, in the great French theatre of the seventeenth century, ***Moliere*** was especially noted for the precision of his instructions to actors. But the playwright who, perhaps, came closest to the modern idea of the director was ***Goethe***, supervisor of the productions

Johann Wolfgang von ***Goethe***.

at the ***Weimar Court Theatre***. *Goethe*'s rehearsals were meticulously planned and rigorously organised; so much so that he, reputedly, used a baton at rehearsals and conducted his actors in much the same way as the conductor of an orchestra controls the musicians.

When we use the term 'rehearsal' in relation to the above theatre practices, we are using it very loosely. **The kind of carefully planned, meticulously detailed rehearsal process that we are used to in today's theatre is a relatively recent phenomenon**. Historically, the preparation period for mounting a play was usually very short, and, therefore, there was little time for exploration, experimentation and discussion. It was literally a case of entering, speaking the lines and making an exit. With the coming of the actor-manager, rehearsal practices slowly began to change.

Actor as Director

In the late eighteenth century, the balance of power began to change in the English theatre. Up until that point, the playwright had always been the central figure in the production process. But, with the emergence of a number of dazzlingly talented performers, the 'star' actor (who was often also the manager of the theatre) began to replace the playwright in importance. David ***Garrick***, who took over the Theatre Royal in ***Drury Lane***, was the first great actor-manager. He devoted rather more time to rehearsals than was customary, and paid much greater attention to the casting of minor roles. Following in *Garrick*'s footsteps came John Philip ***Kemble*** and Charles Macready – both of whom insisted on rehearsals being a testing ground for dramatic ideas, rather than just a mechanical run-through of lines. Charles ***Kean*** became known as the 'Prince of Managers' not only because his productions were thoroughly researched to achieve historical accuracy in settings and costume, but also because of his beautifully orchestrated stage pictures.

The Modern Director

The *Meininger*: the first disciplined ensemble

Although the early years of the nineteenth century saw massive changes in the whole process of theatrical production, it was not until 1874 that the modern idea of the director really began to take shape. It was on 1 May of 1874 that George II, Duke of Saxe-***Meiningen***, brought his then unknown company to perform in Berlin. What was striking about the work of the company was the **complete integration of every aspect of the production into a coherent, unified and harmonious performance**. The disciplined acting, painstakingly choreographed crowd scenes, a continuous and fluid flow of action, historically accurate sets and costumes, and meticulous attention to detail all contributed to the triumphant success of the company's first appearance in Berlin.

Here, for the first time in European theatre history, the audience was able to witness a true ensemble, with every actor submitting to the iron discipline of the company, tirelessly striving to serve the needs of the play and working flat-out for each other. The artistic vision for each new production came from the Duke himself, assisted, no doubt, by his actress wife, Ellen Franz; but Ludwig ***Chronegk***, employed as stage manager, was the disciplinarian who drilled the actors to achieve the highest possible standards of performance.

Following the success of the *Meinigen* company's work, the new director came to be seen as the key figure in the process of production. The roles of both playwright and actor began to be seen in a new perspective. In the hands of some directors, the playwright's words became a pretext for daring, new interpretations, although others were intent on creating faithful reproductions of the writer's intentions. The demands of performance became much more strenuous as different directorial approaches required greater discipline, dedication and versatility in actors.

The work of the *Meiningen* company inspired the great directors Andre ***Antoine*** (in France), Otto ***Brahm*** (in Germany) and Konstantin ***Stanislavski*** (in Russia).

Behind the Fourth Wall: The Great Realist Directors

***Antoine*: The first *realist* director**

Antoine founded the *Theatre Libre* in Paris in 1887. The disciplined approach of the *Meiningen* company became one of the hallmarks of *Antoine*'s theatre, but he had a broader vision. His aim was to create an experimental, scientific, theatre 'laboratory' in which the ideas of the ***naturalist*** writer, Émile ***Zola***, could be put into practice. In keeping with *Zola*'s theories, ***Antoine* set out to create the realistic environments that shaped the life and actions of the characters.** This meant reproducing the exact physical details of everyday life (he even transported the furniture from his own home to the theatre in order to create the setting for *Zola*'s play, *Jacques Damour*). Having created his environment in minute detail, *Antoine* would then decide which of the four walls he would remove, in order to provide the audience with the best view of the dramatic events that would unfold there.

In Germany, Otto ***Brahm*** followed in *Antoine*'s footsteps, founding his *Freie Buehne*. ***Brahm* understood the importance of creating detailed and realistic stage settings** but left this aspect of the work to his two assistants, preferring, instead, to concentrate his own attentions on the development of new plays, and on detailed rehearsals with actors.

Antoine's preoccupation with the creation of the visual setting was an important feature of ***Stanislavski***'s early work. **He would begin his preparations by producing extremely detailed production notes, which were then transposed to the stage during the process of rehearsal.** *Stanislavski* originally modelled himself on ***Chronegk***, who he had seen at work during the *Meiningen* company's visit to Moscow in 1890. But *Stanislavski* soon became dissatisfied with this autocratic style of directing, with its emphasis on reproducing the details of *external* reality. Consequently, he turned his attentions to developing a style of acting whose aim was to produce a sense of inner (or *psychological*) reality.

***Stanislavski* and psychological realism**

The realist dramas of Anton *Chekhov*, which had become a cornerstone of the work of the ***Moscow Art Theatre*** (founded by *Stanislavski* and ***Nemirovich-Danchenko*** in 1898), **demanded more true-to-life character portrayals.** *Stanislavski*, therefore, set himself the task of researching and codifying the principles of the acting style which has come to be known as ***psycho-realism***. *Stanislavski* thus came to share *Brahm*'s concern with the richness of the rehearsal process, and his research led him to develop valuable rehearsal techniques (some of which are used in the acting workshop on playing the given circumstances see page 51).

Antoine, Brahm and *Stanislavski* may be seen, therefore, as the foremost ***realist*** directors at the turn of the nineteenth century; the artists who attempted to put the theatrical flesh on the bones of *Zola*'s *naturalistic* theories. But another important theatrical movement was also under way during these years. Based on the work of Richard ***Wagner*** (the nineteenth century composer of operas), directors like Edward Gordon ***Craig***, Jacques ***Copeau*** and Vsevolod ***Meyerhold*** were pushing theatrical boundaries in other directions.

The Quest For the 'Idea of a Theatre': Early Non-realist Directors

Wagner had attacked the decaying theatre of his own time, saying that it was no longer capable of expressing humanity's noblest aspirations and deepest spirituality. The ancient Greeks provided *Wagner* with his template. He set out to develop the idea of a **total theatre**, rooted in the old Northern European mythologies, which would bring together into a coherent work all of the elements of theatre: action, poetry, music, movement, design and visual spectacle. ***Wagner* gave the name, *Gesamtkunstwerk* (or total art work) to what he believed would be 'the art of the future'.**

***Craig's* theatre of visions**

In 1905, Edward Gordon ***Craig*** (son of the great actress, Ellen ***Terry***) published *The Art of the Theatre*. Craig's book was a manifesto for the new 'art of the future'. In it, he argued that the demands of the new theatre required a new kind of '**theatre artist**' (or director) – a visionary, who would be capable of bringing together the diverse elements identified by *Wagner* into one harmonious whole. In

Richard ***Wagner***.

keeping with ***Wagner***'s theories, ***Craig*** **wanted to create 'a theatre of visions'** rather than 'a theatre of sermons'; an art-form that would say less, yet show more. *Craig*'s own approach to directing was very much a hit-and-miss affair. He admitted that, in preparing his productions, he worked in an illogical manner, preferring to work by intuition rather than by analysis. Consequently, as a director, it would probably be true to say that *Craig* himself achieved little. Yet, as a serious thinker about the possibilities and potentialities of theatre, *Craig* remains a major figure in twentieth century European theatre history.

***Copeau* sees the director as a specialist in interpretation**

In many ways, it was Jacques ***Copeau*** who embodied most fully in his practice the qualities *Craig* envisaged in his 'theatre artist'. *Copeau* created the ***Vieux Colombier*** in 1913, in order to bring together an ensemble of young, dedicated performers whose one ambition was to serve the art of the theatre. In his own directorial work, ***Copeau*** **sought to clarify the nature of the relationship between playwright and director – who, he argued, were involved in two distinct stages of the same intellectual operation**. He acknowledged that the great playwrights of the past (***Aeschylus, Shakespeare, Moliere***) had been able to successfully combine both functions. But he claimed that modern playwrights needed the expertise of the director as a specialist in interpretation. Unlike many of his contemporaries, *Copeau* was especially concerned to produce interpretations which kept faith with the playwright's original text. He was also concerned with developing a more intimate performer-audience relationship. And, in order to do this, he designed a small platform stage with a permanent architectural background, appropriate for the staging of any play.

Copeau and Vsevolod ***Meyerhold*** were both engaged in a search for what Copeau called 'the idea of a theatre': the unchanging, essential heart of theatre, capable of capturing the universal life of the human spirit.

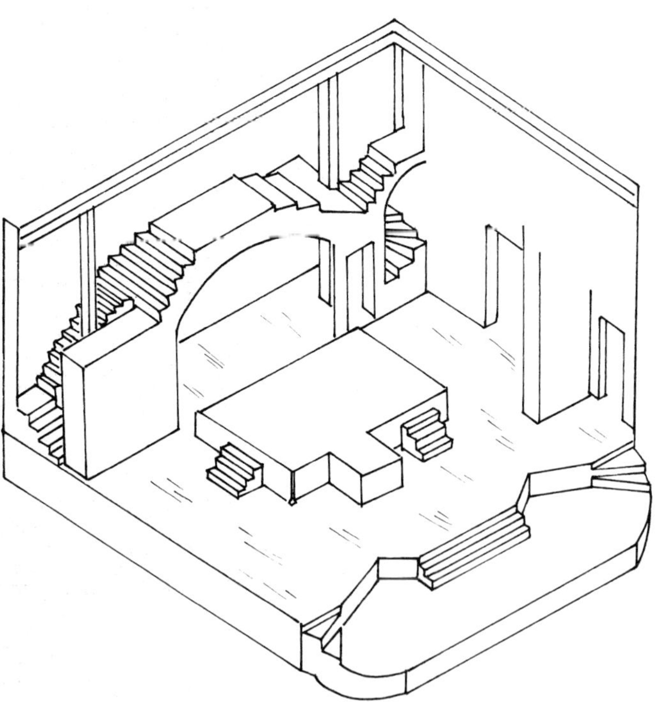

Copeau's stage at the ***Vieux Colombier***.

Meyerhold and Constructivism; the mechanical stage

Meyerhold, one of the original members of the ***Moscow Art Theatre***, had worked extensively with ***Stanislavski***, who saw *Meyerhold* as his natural heir and successor. Having performed in the early *Moscow Art Theatre* productions, *Meyerhold* became dissatisfied with the limitations of ***realist*** theatre and branched out. He worked with both Vera ***Komissarzhevskaya***'s company in St Petersburg and as director of the new Studio Theatre of *Moscow Art Theatre*. *Meyerhold*, in his search for a new theatre, conducted a number of daring theatrical experiments, many of which were considered to be failures. He mounted a ***symbolist*** production of ***Ibsen***'s realist play, *Hedda Gabler* and championed the theatrical work of the *symbolist* poet, Alexander ***Blok***. He researched earlier popular forms of theatre, including 'the grotesque' and ***Commedia dell'Arte***; and eventually arrived at a new concept which he called *constructivism*.

In keeping with the scientific and technological spirit of the times, *Meyerhold* wanted to develop 'a machine' upon which actors could perform. He designed and developed a flexible construction consisting of platforms, walkways, ramps and steps which could, theoretically, be used for the staging of any play. And, in order that his performers could exploit the full potential of this 'machine', he devised a system of movement exercises which he called *biomechanics*. Each day's rehearsal began with the *biomechanical* exercises, which were designed to foster flexibility and versatility, giving the actor perfect control over his bodily movements.

As a director, *Meyerhold* did not favour the meticulous preplanning of ***Antoine*** or the early *Stanislavski*. He preferred to arrive at rehearsals with a sense of what he wanted to explore, and was quite prepared to rework the scene the following

Meyerhold's 'Machine for acting'.

day incorporating ideas that had arisen during his experiments. He viewed each rehearsal as a preliminary sketch, reworking scenes over and over again until he arrived at a version that would find its way into the final product. *Meyerhold*'s approach led to startling new productions of plays, which featured prominently in the repertoires of many European theatres and were already well-known to theatre-going audiences. One Russian commentator suggested that his production of *The Government Inspector* owed very little to the original text written by Nikolai ***Gogol***, and should be re-christened *Meyerhold's Mental Associations Apropos The Government Inspector*.

***Meyerhold*'s experiments lead to the firing squad**

Meyerhold*'s revolt against the restrictions of *realism* led him to strike out in a multitude of new and daring theatrical directions.** His boldness eventually brought him into dispute with Soviet officialdom and, despite his own vigorous defence of his work, he was imprisoned and finally executed by the KGB during one of Stalin's purges in 1942. As a result of his artistic rehabilitation in 1956, scholars have been able to painstakingly reconstruct *Meyerhold*'s whole theatrical career, and it is now quite clear that many of the new and innovative developments in late twentieth century performance practice (including ***Brecht's *epic* theatre, Peter ***Brook***'s *A Midsummer Night's Dream* and the whole contemporary physical theatre movement) owe a considerable debt to *Meyerhold*'s adventurous and audacious experiments.

Measures of Control: Reinhardt and Vakhtangov

***Reinhardt* develops a highly detailed and technical theatre**

Max ***Reinhardt*** was renowned for the dazzling diversity of his many productions. Unlike ***Copeau*** and ***Meyerhold***, who, in their individual quests for an 'essential idea of theatre', eventually designed all-purpose, permanent 'platform stage environments' on which to mount their productions, *Reinhardt* was of the view that such a quest was futile. The richness of the world's drama could never be reduced to a single essence; each different theatrical form demanded its own unique approach, and the job of the director consisted in realising the specific atmosphere and ambiance of the play. Each new directorial challenge provided him with the opportunity to create a new world, with its own light and shadow, its own beauty and ugliness, its own heaven and hell.

***Reinhardt*'s overall approach was characterised by a determination to fully exploit all of the resources that theatre has to offer.** His brilliant theatrical effects were produced as a result of carefully mobilising and orchestrating all of the elements at his disposal: the text of the play; the dramatic action; the performers' skills; mass movement; music; light; costume; stage setting; and environment (for his production of *The Miracle*, he turned the theatre into a Gothic cathedral). Such effects could never have been achieved without the thorough preparation that was *Reinhardt*'s trademark. He arrived at the first rehearsal with his blueprint, and proceeded to mould every aspect of the production according to the master plan he had drawn up in his study. According to one of his actors, in the early stages of rehearsal *Reinhardt* treated actors as though they were puppets, controlling their every movement and intonation until their performances began to conform to the interpretation he had conceived in his mind's eye. Unlike *Copeau*, whose respect for the playwright's text was legendary, *Reinhardt* saw the play as a pretext for his own bold interpretations.

Vakhtangov's collective style of direction

Reinhardt's controlling directorial style stands in marked contrast to the approach of Eugene ***Vakhtangov***, another of ***Stanislavski***'s protégés from the ***Moscow Art Theatre***. Although both sought to achieve a highly vigorous theatricality in their productions, the means by which they pursued their aims were quite different. *Vakhtangov*, working in the immediate aftermath of the October Revolution in Russia, built **a theatre collective whose working style was intended to be in keeping with the new socialist ideals.** *Vakhtangov* saw himself as an efficient, theatre craftsman rather than an autocratic, controlling director. He reputedly never lectured his performers, preferring instead to participate fully and actively in the creative work of rehearsals.

Unfortunately, *Vakhtangov* never lived to see his own ideals realised. But, following his death in 1922, his successor, Boris ***Zakhava*** translated these ideals into a working practice. The decision about which plays were to be produced was left in the hands of the collective; each play was then assigned to one of the company's directors.

The director was first required to submit, for formal approval, his production plans. At a meeting of the collective, and (if possible) the playwright, the plans were considered (and perhaps revised and modified in the light of discussion) before the director was permitted to go into production. But, even at this point, the director did not assume complete control. The first rehearsals consisted of a series of detailed discussions with the actors on how the different roles were to be interpreted. Ideas submitted by other company members were incorporated into the director's production plans and rehearsals proceeded in consultation with the whole company.

Task 1: Discuss the different directorial approaches of Reinhardt and Vakhtangov

Drawing on your own experiences of being directed, consider the advantages and disadvantages of the two directing styles and record them on a chart similar to that shown below.

REINHARDT'S APPROACH		VAKHTANGOV'S APPROACH	
Advantages	Disadvantages	Advantages	Disadvantages

Political Directors

The Workers Theatre of *Piscator*

During the 1920s, Erwin *Piscator* joined *Reinhardt* in the front rank of German theatre directors. His early work consisted of small-scale touring productions of *agit-prop* (short for 'agitational-propaganda') plays, which were intended to instruct the workers in the key political issues of the day. He also toured 'Living Newspapers', which were, quite simply, enacted news stories for workers who were unable to read the real, printed newspapers. These touring pro-

Piscator's Living Newspaper Performances, 1927.

ductions would be performed at factory gates, workers' canteens and meeting halls, and, literally, on street corners.

In 1924, *Piscator* took over as director of the *Volksbuehne* in Berlin. Here, *Piscator* developed larger-scale documentaries dealing with pressing, current social and political issues. ***Piscator*'s use of new stage devices and technology was one of the most striking features of his new, documentary style.** The stage action was enhanced and supplemented by the use of charts, maps, placards, large-scale written slogans, conveyor belts, slides, film and newsreel inserts. Dismissed from his post at the *Volksbuehne* in 1927, *Piscator* moved to his own theatre where he adapted the Czech novel, *The Good Soldier Schweik*, which tells the woeful, wartime adventures of an ordinary soldier. This production, using filmed cartoons of drawings by the famous artist George Grosz, gave *Piscator* his greatest popular success.

One of *Piscator*'s collaborators on the adaptation of the novel was the playwright-poet-director, Bertolt ***Brecht***, shortly to become a major figure in twentieth century theatre history.

***Brecht* took ideas from his early work with *Piscator* and transformed them**

Brecht* took ideas from his early work with *Piscator* and transformed them into a fully developed set of theories.** Some theatre theorists were unable to put their ideas into practice (Edward Gordon ***Craig as we have seen; and Antonin ***Artaud***, the writer who conceived the idea of the 'Theatre of Cruelty'), but *Brecht* was a practical man of the theatre and his theoretical ideas were tried and tested in the rehearsal room, and in the legendary productions of his own plays. *Brecht* would often say 'The proof is in the pudding!'

As we know from the acting workshop on finding the *verfrumdungseffekt*, *Brecht*'s politics led him to react sharply against ***Stanislavski***'s approach. As far as *Brecht* was concerned, the *feeling* connection, essential in *Stanislavski*'s theatre of empathy, impaired the spectator's ability to view the play in a detached, objec-

Bertolt ***Brecht***.

tive, *thinking* manner. Empathy is the enemy of thought because it produces an inability in the spectator to make considered judgements about those circumstances and conditions that have contributed to the problems and dilemmas that the characters face. It also encourages the spectator to accept that these circumstances are beyond the control of the characters in the play, something that simply had to be put up with.

We have seen that *Brecht*'s studies in Marxism led him to think differently. The point of *Brecht*'s theatre was *not* to offer his spectators a view of the world which seemed given (as in the 'given circumstances') and unchangeable, but rather to present them with the possibility that circumstances *could* be changed by the actions of the characters. *Brecht* adopted the words of Karl Marx as his guiding principle in his work: **'it is not just a matter of interpreting the world, the point is to change it'.** *Brecht*'s purpose in making theatre, then, was openly political. His revolutionary outlook demanded that the spectators should open their eyes, see the extent of the inequity and injustice in the world and understand that there was an urgent need to change it.

Brecht* develops the *epic* and the *Verfrumdungseffekt

***Brecht*'s theatre, therefore, was designed to cultivate in the audience a more clinical, detached and objective form of spectatorship,** and we have already outlined the two concepts that are vitally important in achieving this end. The first is the concept of the *verfrumdungseffekt*, which forces the spectator to look at ordinary, familiar, everyday things in a new light. The second is the *epic* which dislocates the 'through-line of action' by ensuring that each scene in the play is self-contained.

In accounts of modern European theatre, the theories of *Stanislavski* and *Brecht* are almost always presented as being ***antagonistic*** to each other. But this is only partly true. The political distance between the two men meant that each was working towards different political (and, ultimately, theatrical) ends. But *Brecht* wrote a series of *Notes on Stanislavski*, and in these notes made it clear that ***Stanislavski's* ideas about empathy were vital to his own theories.**

Stanislavski*'s influence on *Brecht

Brecht was in no doubt that, in his own theatre, the illusions fostered by the realist theatre of *Stanislavski* had to be broken; but he also understood that an illusion had first to be created before it could be broken. He therefore devised a three-stage rehearsal programme (significantly entitled *'Building a Character* – also the title of the second of *Stanislavski*'s books on acting) for his actors. In the first stage of the process, the actor must become intimately acquainted with the character that is to be played. The second stage is that of empathy (in *Stanislavski*'s terms, becoming one with the character). The final stage is where the actor, now being thoroughly familiar with the role, is able to *stand outside* of it and offer the audience a more detached, critical insight into the character being played.

The Late Twentieth Century Directors

***Grotowski*'s theatre set out to probe the question: 'how should one live?**

Jerzy *Grotowski*'s theatre set out to probe the question: 'how should one live?'. His productions were designed to offer the audience some insight into this problem. In order to do this, he expected his actors to confront this same question through the process of rehearsal, and in performance. His aim required a thorough investigation into the nature and process of acting. His early work was undertaken in his 'Theatre of the Thirteen Rows' which was established in 1959 in a small Polish town.

Grotowski believed that authenticity, in life as in the theatre, was essential. **To live and perform authentically meant peeling away what he called the 'life mask' – that set of social roles that we assume in our everyday encounters with others.** This process of stripping away allows the performer to come face to face with that inner core of being that is the **true self.** Rehearsals are designed in such a way that each actor undertakes a creative exploration of the self.

But *Grotowski* recognised that it is impossible to view the self directly. He understood that in order to become thoroughly acquainted with the self, an *other* was required. This is because, in everyday life, we measure ourselves alongside other people. For example, we understand our own weaknesses by recognising the strengths in others, and vice versa. In *Grotowski*'s early work, the character in the play provided this 'other': as the actor struggles to find a connection between her or his own qualities and characteristics and those of the character, the performer inevitably learns something about him- or herself.

***Grotowski* believed that the world's great plays open doors for the actors to achieve greater self-knowledge**

We have already seen how in ***Brecht*'s** rehearsal programme, the ***Stanislavskian*** stage of empathy was vital. Similarly, the first stage of *Grotowski*'s rehearsal process requires the actor to become one with the character. However, as with *Brecht*, *Grotowski* soon parts company with *Stanislavski*. Whereas the *Stanislavskian* actor uses parts of the self to bring the character (or 'other') into being, the *Grotowskian* actor uses the 'other' (or character) to bring about a greater understanding of self. *Grotowski* believed that the world's great plays open doors for the actor (and the spectator) to achieve greater self-knowledge.

At the end of the 1960s, *Grotowski*'s thinking began to change. 'The Theatre of the Thirteen Rows' became an 'Institute of Research into Acting Method – Laboratory Theatre'. The shift in *Grotowski*'s thinking can perhaps be best summarised as follows: **'I am myself when I do not think about myself'**. Since *Grotowski* believed that 'thinking' did not help in the search for self, he sought the means of self-discovery in 'action'. For the actor, this means immersing her- or himself in action and in 'existence'. Therefore, *Grotowski* removes the character and **places the actor in the situation of the character**. In other words, the actors play their characters by playing themselves. At this point, *Grotowski* declares that acting has been abandoned.

Gradually *Grotowski's* company became preoccupied with self-exploration and less concerned with public performance

The repercussions of this renunciation of acting were tremendous. We should remember that *Grotowski's* aim, throughout, was to help both actor and spectator in their search for their authentic selves. The demands that *Grotowski* placed on his actors in the *Laboratory Theatre* were enormous, but the technical virtuosity and powerful intensity of the performers was often met by incomprehension in the audience. One critic wrote that he learned nothing about human suffering from watching the actors suffer. During this period, *Grotowski* set his actors increasingly difficult physical challenges until they eventually become impossible. For example, actors were asked to punch holes in the wall using only their voices! But, here again, the physical skill and technical wizardry had the effect of alienating the audience, forcing them to confront their own limitations in the face of extraordinary expertise.

Grotowski realised that the mesmerising physical abilities of his actors did not permit the act of self-revelation that was his ultimate goal; all that was revealed in performance was the actors' skills. *Grotowski's* solution to this problem was to veer towards the opposite extreme, and in so doing he developed the concept of the **via negativa** ('the negative way'). *Grotowski* continued to set his actors difficult challenges, but his aim changed: instead of asking themselves 'How do I do this?', the performers were required to discover what obstacles prevented them from meeting the challenge. In other words, they had to know what *not* to do. Gradually *Grotowski's* company became more and more preoccupied with self-exploration through intensive workshop sessions, and less and less concerned with public performance.

But it soon became obvious that the company's introversion and isolation could not last for long. In his early writings, *Grotowski* had emphasised that theatre was defined by the nature of the encounter which took place between actor and spectator, adding that everything else was supplementary. Several of *Grotowski's* productions attempted to draw the spectators into the dramatic action: *The Ancestors* for example; and *Kordian*, in which the audience were threatened with a cane if they did not join in the singing! Later, **the spectators were given roles**, but in keeping with their passive status as audience members. In *Dr Faustus*, the spectators were asked to act as the central character's 'witnesses'.

***Grotowski* abandons performance for rituals**

Frustrated at his inability to find a satisfying and productive kind of encounter between actor and spectator, *Grotowski* abandoned the idea of theatre altogether and embraced, in its place, the notion of meeting. From this point, his encounters with the public took the form of communal events in which the 'guests' were invited to participate in creative activities (improvisations, movement exercises and music-making) alongside the performers. In this creative contact **the social masks were intended to fall away as guests and performers embarked together on individual and shared journeys of self-discovery**. Theatre historians have tried to explain *Grotowski's* change of direction as an attempt to rediscover, through these events, forms of authentic human contact which have been lost in the course of civilization's development.

Peter *Brook*: gathering the fragements of theatre

We have seen how a number of the early ***non-realist*** directors were in search of an essential 'idea of a theatre' (***Craig***, ***Copeau***, ***Meyerhold***). Towards the end of the twentieth century, Peter ***Brook*** took up this challenge. In his book, *The Shifting Point*, Brook observes that 'nowhere in the world is there a complete theatre but only fragments of a theatre'. One could argue that *Brook*'s long career has been dedicated to bringing these fragments together into one complete whole: from his ground-breaking production of *Romeo and Juliet* in 1947, through the 1960s' attempts to bring ***Artaud***'s 'Theatre of Cruelty' to life, the flamboyant *Meyerhold*-inspired production of *A Midsummer Night's Dream*, the journey through Africa with *Conference of the Birds*, to the magnificent achievement of *Le Mahabharata*.

***Brook* develops his minimalist and poetic style of theatre**

In terms of the rich diversity of his theatre work, *Brook* can perhaps best be compared to Max **Reinhardt**. But *Brook*'s contribution to twentieth century theatre goes far beyond *Reinhardt*'s. **Having thoroughly absorbed the influences of *Stanislavski* and *Brecht* into his early work, Brook went on to find close affinities with *Grotowski*'s approach.** For *Brook*, acting was never a process of 'building'. Rather, it was a question of removing the blocks and obstacles that stand in the way of creating the role. Once these obstacles are removed, the character is able to 'penetrate' the actor. The production process itself required the removal of everything that was inessential. *Brook* records that in his preparations for the 1962 production of *King Lear* he systematically eliminated scenery, costume and music, and, finally, colour. Nineteen years later, in his production of *Carmen*, his watchword was still simplicity.

***Brook* develops an interest in intercultural performances**

In 1968, *Brook* was invited to Paris to run a workshop with actors from a variety of different countries and cultural backgrounds. Two years later, he moved to Paris where he set up the *Centre Internationale de Recherche Theatrales* ('International Centre for Theatre Research'), and soon afterwards the *Centre Internationale de Creation Theatrales* ('International Centre for Theatre Creation'). He gathered together a group of performers from all over the world with the intention of fully researching the potential resources of the actor, and putting the results of this research to the test in performance.

As part of his work with the *Centre Internationale, Brook* embarked on the most ambitious project of his career. Accompanied by his performers, he set out to journey through Africa with a series of improvisations based on Farid Ud-din Attar's fable, *The Conference of the Birds*. *Brook*'s purpose in undertaking this work was broadly similar to *Grotowski*'s: the company was involved in a search for authenticity, wholeness and the self. And, as with *Grotowski*'s approach, much of the work had a real physical intensity, with rehearsals sometimes continuing for up to 19 hours.

Work on the fable continued throughout the journey, and performances were offered to different tribes along the way. As we noted above, one of *Brook*'s abiding concerns has been with simplicity and clarity. He was therefore anxious to perform to audiences who shared no common assumptions with his company. This meant that the company could not rely on the established conventions of Western theatre. Any barrier that stood in the way of communicating the meaning of the work had to be stripped away. This was *Brook*'s own version of *Grotowski*'s 'via negativa'.

But perhaps *Brook*'s greatest achievement is his mammoth, nine-hour long production of the Indian epic, *Le Mahabharata*. Fifteen times longer than the Bible, the Mahabharata consists of an intricate web of mythology, history, philosophy and politics. *Brook* spent nine years researching his material with Jean-Claude Carriere, who was responsible for producing the final text. Many would argue that this production represents *Brook*'s most concerted attempt to bring together the 'fragments of a theatre' into the *complete theatre* that has been the dream of so many theatre artists from ***Wagner*** onwards.

The importance of *Le Mahabharata*

The most striking feature of *Le Mahabharata* is not just the consummate interweaving of the many different stories contained in the epic, but the brilliant fusion of the various theatrical forms into one complex but coherent whole. ***Brook*'s production seems to move effortlessly between many different and diverse theatrical traditions:** simple storytelling sits comfortably side by side with epic scenes of combat; gods, demons and plain mortals present themselves simultaneously to the audience; realistic scenes blend harmoniously with highly stylised mime sequences; and character transformations occur smoothly and seamlessly. The author figure who appears in the production is called Vyasha, which derives from a Sanskrit word meaning 'to fit together'. Vyasha seems to serve as a symbol of *Brook*'s achievement in this work.

***Brook*'s work is often described as eclectic, drawing as it does on so many diverse influences and sources.** For some critics, he is more of an emulator than an innovator; someone who, lacking real originality, absorbs and recycles the ideas and techniques of others. A magpie, opportunistically and indiscriminately picking up bits and pieces from here, there and everywhere.

These same critics point to the lack of stylistic consistency in *Brook*'s work over the years – but this was never his aim. Instead, he was looking to develop performances that moved fluidly between different conventions – a modern production style, comparable with the works of ***Shakespeare***, which moves deftly from tragedy to comedy, in which a clown can be companion to a king. To maintain that *Brook* is inventive but not innovative one has to play down the immense significance of works like *Le Mahabharata*. Historians and critics will, no doubt, continue to debate and differ over the scope of *Brook*'s achievement; only history will reveal whether or not his contribution to theatre practice has enduring substance.

The influence of *Artaud's* ideas

We have attempted to identify and describe those directors who have, in some measure, either changed the course of twentieth-century theatre production, or pushed back the boundaries of performance practice. Such an undertaking has to be selective, and we have had to leave out some important figures. Perhaps the most striking omission is Antonin *Artaud*. We justify this on the grounds that, although *Artaud* was undoubtedly a visionary in terms of his thinking on the power and potential of theatre, his work as a practising director fell far short of the ground-breaking ideas that he put forward in his theoretical writings. Undoubtedly there are a multitude of reasons why this may have been the case: an inability to persuade the French theatre establishment to take him seriously; a failure to secure the necessary financial backing for his daring and scandalous experiments; psychological illness; or maybe he was just too many years ahead of his time. Whatever the truth, **it was left to *Grotowski* and *Brook* to partially realise *Artaud*'s vision.**

Others who are absent from our survey include Harley ***Granville Barker***, David ***Belasco***, Elia ***Kazan***, Joan ***Littlewood*** and Eugenio ***Barba***.

Task 2: What do we learn from the great directors?

The work of the great directors that we have described continues to affect the theatre of today. When you see plays or produce plays yourself you will find the influence of their ideas at work.

- **Write a paragraph on each of the directors in this chapter, which contains the key ideas associated with each. We have included some further research opportunities in the Webliography in the Resources section (Section Six). Keep these brief notes to refer to when you are producing or analysing performances.**

Conclusion

For every major twentieth century director who has broken new ground, there are thousands who have been quietly absorbed in the everyday business of bringing new plays to the stage, and breathing new life into the tried and tested texts of the past. Unspectacular though this work seems in comparison to the exciting innovation described above, it is the bread-and-butter work of the theatre director; and it is to this that we turn in the next chapter.

In this chapter we have provided you with a brief history of the emergence of the director as the new artist of the theatre. You will find further references to many of these artists scattered throughout the book.

Use the Index to find out more

You could build a practitioner file for directors who interest you by looking up all the references in the Index and then compiling a report on your chosen practitioner. You could add to this file by researching your chosen practitioner using the Webliography in Section Six. Or just type a name into your *search engine* and see what you find!

6

From Page to Stage

The Work of the Director

The partnership of *Stanislavski* and *Nemirovich-Danchenko*

We have already noted that ***Stanislavski*** was co-founder of the ***Moscow Art Theatre*** with Vladimir ***Nemirovich-Danchenko***. The two colleagues enjoyed a long and productive professional relationship. *Nemirovich-Danchenko* is often remembered as *Stanislavski*'s 'literary adviser', the man who brought the plays of ***Chekhov*** to the company. But this is only part of the story. *Nemirovich-Danchenko* was a practising director of some stature and, in point of fact, for the *Moscow Art Theatre*'s original production of *The Seagull* he directed more of the rehearsals than *Stanislavski* himself. The two men were credited as 'joint directors' for most of the company's productions.

So it is worth pausing for a moment to consider how their collaboration worked in practice. *Nemirovich-Danchenko*'s reputation as a 'literary man' is well deserved; his detailed study of the text provided the basis for the whole production. After this painstaking textual work, the two men would meet for long discussions during which *Nemirovich-Danchenko* would provide a basic interpretation of the work. *Stanislavski* took notes as his colleague spoke. These notes would then form the basis of the ***mise en scene*** that *Stanislavski* developed prior to beginning rehearsal. During the period of preparation, *Nemirovich-Danchenko* would try to ensure that *Stanislavski*'s flair for theatricality and stage effects did not overwhelm or obscure the basic interpretation that had been agreed upon.

In one sense we can think of *Nemirovich-Danchenko* as 'reining in' some of *Stanislavski*'s more extravagant flights of fancy. He was not always completely successful in this, since we know that *Chekhov* became increasingly irritated by the excessive number of special effects that *Stanislavski* insisted on adding to his plays.

Functions of the Director

Realising the vision based on interpretation

The division of labour that ***Stanislavski*** and ***Nemirovich-Danchenko*** had agreed upon is instructive for us as we try to tease out the role of the director in the process of production. Essentially, the director's role can be reduced to **two essential functions**: the first is to evolve a **vision** of the play which is consistent with the *interpretation*; the second, once this is successfully accomplished, is to help the designer, the actors and the technical team **bring the interpretation to life on the stage**.

We will begin by considering the first of these functions – the vision or *conception*. Later on, we will look in more detail at how the director works with actors in order to *realise* the interpretation.

In this chapter our primary focus is on the directing of text-based plays. However, we will not be concerned here with the kind of detailed analysis that engaged *Nemirovich-Danchenko* in the first stages of the ***Moscow Art Theatre*** process. Chapter 8 covers this ground. A good deal of contemporary theatre work is not text-based, and the whole area of devising for theatre is considered in Chapter 9.

Conception

Getting a feel for the play

Peter ***Brook***, in *The Shifting Point,* talks about how he begins his work as a director. He begins, '**with a deep, formless hunch which is like a smell, a color, a shadow**'. In other words, his first feeling about the play is a vague one; something, perhaps, which he is unable to put his finger on, but which nevertheless drives him to give shape and form to his 'hunch'. Something in the play text catches his imagination. This is the feeling that ***Nemirovich-Danchenko*** must have experienced when he first read *The Seagull.*

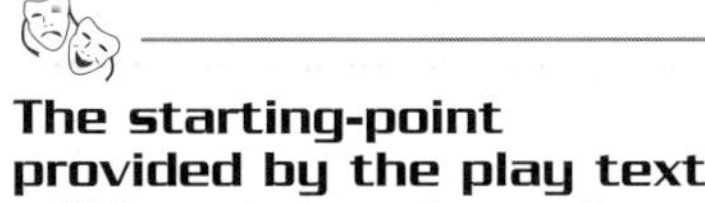

The starting-point provided by the play text will be returned to, time and time again

Whatever it is about the play that has caught the director's attention, the starting-point provided by the play text will be returned to, time and time again, in order that the director can gain a clearer sense of what it is about the play that has caught their eye. In the early stages of detailed textual work, the director will focus on what it is that the playwright is trying to say – the meanings which are embedded in the work.

The playwright's director

Some directors, *Nemirovich-Danchenko* and *Copeau* among them, see themselves as playwright's directors, who look deep into the heart of the text in an attempt to keep faith with what they believe to be the author's intentions. When working on a play, they try to empty themselves of any preconceptions they might have (perhaps from an earlier reading, or from having seen previous productions) in order that the play can speak to them afresh. The archetypal 'playwright's director' likes to be invisible, so that it seems as if the play speaks directly to the audience without them having any real sense that the play has been directed at all. Generally speaking, it would be true to say that the 'playwright's director' allows their own interpretation of what the playwright intended to shape the conception. This would roughly correspond to *Nemirovich-Danchenko*'s first stage of preparation.

As this work proceeds, a more fully formed idea about the play begins to develop as the director gains greater insight into the world of the play and a fuller understanding of the lives of the characters who inhabit that world. Slowly, a vision takes shape and thoughts turn to 'the look of the play'. At this point in the working methods of the ***Moscow Art Theatre***, ***Stanislavski***, under *Nemirovich-Danchenko*'s guidance, would develop his ***mise en scene***.

The *auteur* director

For the 'playwright's director', this vision will represent a fairly faithful attempt to make clear to the audience the playwright's intended meanings. **Other kinds of directors (*Craig* and *Meyerhold*, for example) may be somewhat more adventurous in their interpretations. Their concern is not so much with fidelity to the playwright's intentions, but rather with shedding new light on a classical or well-established text.** Where this is the case, the director will read and reread the play in an attempt to clarify whether their interpretation can really be supported by the playwright's text (if not, it's back to the drawing board). Having confirmed the viability of the new interpretation, the director will proceed.

The vision developed by this kind of director, which may involve a more or less radical departure from the original intentions of the playwright, can result in a complete transformation in how the audience views the play – a completely new 'perspective' that illuminates the text in previously unimagined ways. Sometimes, the interpretation is so far removed from the playwright's original version that it's possible to argue that the director has, in a very real sense, 'rewritten' the play: they become, alongside the playwright, its 'co-author'. **This kind of director is often referred to as an *auteur*** (*auteur* being the French word for 'author').

Interpretations of the classics

New interpretations of old, established or classical plays can come about in a number of different ways. Perhaps some of the most common are as follows:

- A realignment in the angle of vision, when a play is interpreted from the viewpoint of a particular character. In ***Shakespeare***'s day, the character of Shylock in *The Merchant of Venice* was presented very unflatteringly as a stereotypical Jew, until the great nineteenth century actor-manager, Henry ***Irving*** offered a much more sympathetic depiction.
- A new pattern is perceived in the structure of a play. In his book, *Shakespeare Our Contemporary*, the Polish critic Jan ***Kott*** offers a new interpretation of *King Lear* based on *Shakespeare*'s previously unnoticed repetition of negatives: 'no'; 'never'; 'nothing'; etc. – a pattern which, *Kott* claims, points to Lear's increasingly nihilistic view of the world.
- A new form is found for the presentation of a play. Peter *Brook*'s conception for his *A Midsummer Night's Dream* took shape after he and Sally Jacobs, the designer, saw a performance by a troupe of Chinese acrobats.
- A play takes on new significance because its themes speak powerfully of contemporary social and political events. At a time when civil wars are raging throughout the world, *Shakespeare*'s *Coriolanus*, or *Titus Andronicus*, or *Timon of Athens* seem to offer pertinent commentaries on events that are regularly reported in the news media.

Task 1: New interpretation of a classic play

Think back over the classic plays you have studied, or been involved in. Can you see how *one* of them might be reinterpreted? Perhaps you can imagine reconfiguring the play in order to present it from the point of view of one of the characters; or perceive a new pattern in the play's imagery, or, find a new form for presenting the play; or see new significance in the play because of recent events you have seen reported in the news.

- **Draw up a one-page outline of your new interpretation, offering some justifications for your original approach. Remember, you don't have to make it work in practice, so be as bold and ambitious as you like!**

Exceptions to the rule

Although we have suggested that, at the conceptual stage, there are two broad types of director (the **playwright's director** and the ***auteur***), we should not think of these as the only two possibilities. Neither type really exists in a pure form. It's entirely possible, for example, that a 'playwright's director' will, at times, find it necessary to become an *auteur* in order to make a particularly difficult scene work. Elia ***Kazan***, the great American director, is almost always described as a 'playwright's director', but found it necessary to revise a good deal of Tennessee ***Williams***' most famous play, *A Streetcar Named Desire,* and even redrafted two of the scenes completely. On the other hand, if the *auteur* were to totally 're-write' the play, then clearly it would cease to be the original author's work at all. This is what happened with Robert ***Lepage***'s version of *Shakespeare*'s *Hamlet* – so much so that it was renamed *Elsinore*. Between the two pure types then, there are many combinations of each.

The play must have an appeal for the director

Whether the director is an *auteur* or a playwright's director, something in the play must have caught their attention: it may be a desire to offer a new perspective on the play as a result of their having seen a new pattern of meanings (which may have emerged for any one, or a combination, of the reasons stated above); it may be a wish to clarify the meanings in the play; or it may be that the director has come across a new play which they feel *must* be brought before an audience.

We believe that it is useful to see the role of the director as standing between the playwright and the spectator, illuminating and clarifying the writer's text for the play's potential audience.

Below we have included a description of how a new interpretation of ***Lorca***'s *Yerma* evolved.

A production of *Yerma* by University of Northumbria students.

Conceiving *Yerma*: A Case Study

We have recently directed a student production of Federico Garcia ***Lorca***'s play, *Yerma*. In this section there are a number of exploratory tasks that we used in the early stages of our rehearsal process. In order to carry out the tasks it will be necessary for you to read and be familiar with *Lorca*'s play.

We had read some of *Lorca*'s other plays a while ago, and, as we recall, they left us fairly cold. Then, a colleague mounted a production of *Lorca*'s little-known play, *The Billy-Club Puppets*. We read the play, and subsequently we decided to re-visit his major works. It was *Yerma* that made the biggest impression on us. At the time we weren't sure why; but there was no mistaking the power of the play.

***Yerma*: the plot**

The story is a simple one. The central character, Yerma, longs for a child but is unable to conceive. As her repeated attempts to become pregnant fail, she becomes more and more frustrated, and, as her frustration turns to bitterness, her relationship with her husband, Juan, comes under increasing strain. Her prayers remain unanswered, and a pagan woman offers her the solution to her predicament. The pagan woman reveals to Yerma that the fault lies not with her, but with her husband; and she offers Yerma her youngest son as a lover. Yerma's sense of religious duty and honour prevent her from acceding to this, and, in the final scene, following another bitter quarrel with her husband, she kills him.

Great plays are great because they have the power to disturb. As the weeks following our reading of *Yerma* passed, we became aware of a sense of disturbance. We tried to work out what it was about the play that was creating this feeling. Yerma's anguish? A husband and wife tearing themselves apart because of circumstances over which they have no control? A woman increasingly alienated from the community in which she has grown up? But no. Compelling though these different possibilities are, we knew that they did not *fully* account for our disturbance. The question remained.

The director's 'hunch' begins to form

Some months later, we were visiting a university in Norway with a colleague. We were thinking about a workshop we were due to lead with some undergraduate students. Out of the blue, he suggested using a short piece of text from *Yerma*: the speech by the pagan woman in which she gives a brief flavour of the life she has led (the speech is on p. 110). After some introductory work, we invited the students to develop a series of scenes from the pagan woman's life based on the (somewhat sketchy) information contained in the speech. The scenes they produced were full of life, exuberance and humour. What struck us, on reflection, was the contrast between the experiences of the pagan woman as they were depicted in these improvisations and the sombre, troubled, oppressive life of Yerma herself. At the heart of *Lorca*'s play, it seemed to us, was a clash of two apparently incompatible worlds; and it was this that began to interest us.

Ideas based on the historical context

A few weeks before our visit to Norway we had seen a film, *Libertarias*, which examines the important role played by women in the early days of the Spanish Civil War. We were struck by the women's intensely passionate desire to see a new future for Spain, once the forces of fascism had been defeated. Their hopes and aspirations were given added poignancy following their betrayal by the men alongside whom they had been fighting. *Yerma* was written in 1934, two years before this savage civil war in which *Lorca* himself would become a victim of the fascists both for his politics and for his alleged homosexuality.

As we continued to think about *Lorca*'s play in its historical context, **Yerma's desperate desire for a child seemed to mirror the hopes of the women for the future of Spain**. It is often said that children represent hope for the future, and, as our formless hunch started to take shape, we began to see Yerma's unborn child as a symbol of the spark of revolution which was extinguished by the victory of General Franco's fascists in Spain. The treachery of the former male comrades of the women seemed to be akin to the sense of betrayal felt by Yerma when her husband dismisses her concerns, and tells her that their life together is better without children.

Ideas from other artisitc interpretations of the historical context

Libertarias triggered a memory of *Land and Freedom*, another film (by Ken Loach) which dealt with the Spanish Civil War. The scene that kept coming back to us was one in which a priest is executed by the revolutionaries for revealing to the fascists the names of members of left-wing organisations.

The collaboration between the Church and Franco's forces is well documented in histories of the period, and it was this discovery that brought us back, full circle, to **the clash between the two worlds which are present in *Lorca*'s play**: the suffocating world of Yerma's village, dominated by the reactionary forces of Church, convention and tradition; and the earthy, natural world of the pagan woman and her free-spirited, liberated outlook, unfettered by the bonds of custom.

Gradually, over a period of several months we came to understand what it was that had drawn us back to the play time and time again: the clashing forces of reaction and revolution, and the ways in which these powerful forces were symbolically present in Yerma's dilemma.

The director returns to the text to explore his or her interpretation

On returning to *Lorca's* play, **we had to convince ourselves that the text would support the interpretation that was beginning to take shape in our minds.** We wanted to begin by exploring the relationships between the three central characters. As you read the play, you undoubtedly became aware of the triangle of relationships between Yerma, Juan and Victor, which lies at the heart of the play.

Task 2: A triangle

1. Identify the scenes where any combination of Yerma, Juan and Victor appear together. In your group, reread them carefully.
2. When you have done this, make a *still-image* that captures the true essence of Yerma's relationship with both men **at the beginning of the play**.
3. Find the line of dialogue which you think most clearly expresses Yerma's feelings for each of the men. One member of the group should speak the line of dialogue aloud as the others recreate the image, so that you can see the effect of placing the line alongside the visual picture.

Towards the end of the second act, Victor reveals that he is leaving the village to be with his father, and comes to say goodbye to Yerma and to Juan.

4. Look again at this scene, and then repeat the same exercise (first the image, and then the accompanying line of dialogue). But this time show Yerma's feelings towards both men **at the moment of Victor's departure**.
5. Create a very simple movement sequence in which your first image from the beginning of the play changes into the second.
6. Talk about what these two images reveal about how Yerma's feelings have changed in the years that pass between Act 1 and Act 2.

Imagining Yerma's world

It was important for us to be sure that the atmosphere of Yerma's village was indeed as stifling and oppressive as we had remembered it. What struck us most forcefully was the scene by the river, in which a group of village washerwomen gossip as they wash their laundry. Their focus of attention is, of course, Yerma and her increasingly unconventional behaviour (for example, walking barefoot through the streets at night when she should be at home). The gossip, slyly malicious at the beginning of the scene, becomes positively menacing towards the end, as the early, naturalistic chatter gives way to an insistent and sinister chant, in which the more poetic lines are relentlessly hammered out to the work rhythm of the women. **One gets the sense of a puritanical and vengeful community sitting in judgement on an innocent victim of circumstance.**

Task 3: Yerma's World

In this task, we will be trying to develop a sense of the village community in which Yerma lives.

1. To begin with, look again at the first scene of the play. Reread the section where Maria, a friend of Yerma, brings the news that she is pregnant.

2. **Using improvisation**, rather than the script itself, try to find out how Maria breaks the news, and how Yerma receives it.

3. **Try the scene a number of different ways**, giving different people the chance to try out the roles.

- Discuss with your group which version seems to best capture the tone of Lorca's scene. How does Maria tell Yerma, and what are Yerma's *true* feelings when she hears Maria's news?

Exploring styles of performance and staging

In the next exploration, we will be experimenting with different stylistic conventions. Look again at the washerwomen's scene. **From the point of view of style**, what do you notice about it? The scene falls into two parts: the first, realistic; the second, more poetic and stylised.

4. In groups, try to create a version of the scene in which these two different styles are as sharply differentiated as you can make them. Discuss what effect the different styles have on the washerwomen's gossip.

5. Look again at the opening exchange between Yerma and Juan in the very first scene. Create a new piece of text, where you punctuate this scene with the washerwomen's gossip; and then perform it.

- Discuss the effect that is produced by juxtaposing the intimate conversation that takes place within the privacy of Yerma and Juan's home with the public condemnation and disapproval of the village washerwomen.

To add to Yerma's misery, Juan finally moves his two sisters into the house so that they can keep a close watch on his wayward wife; she literally becomes a prisoner in her own home.

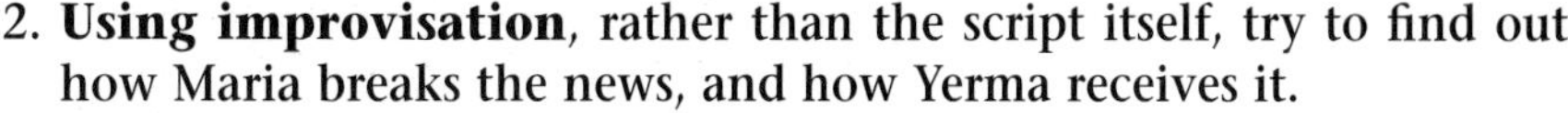

Task 4: Someone to watch over you

Think about the image of Juan's two sisters 'watching over' Yerma. They actually say very little, but look again at Act 2, Scene 2; despite their silence, they represent a very powerful presence. This task is designed to analyse the role of the sisters.

1. Visit the library to see if you can find a book containing the religious paintings of El Greco (a Greek-born artist who subsequently lived and worked in late sixteenth and early seventeenth century Spain). Look for images of angels in El Greco's paintings and study them. You can find some good examples at this website address:

   http://spanishculture.miningco.com/culture/cultureeurope/spanishculture/gi/dynamic/offsite.htm?site=http://members.aol.com/kerujo/greco/index.htm

2. Look at the opening image of the play where, in the early light of dawn, Yerma sits in a chair dozing and dreaming. In your group, see if you can create an image, *based on the paintings*, of two angels, compassionately and protectively watching over Yerma as she sleeps.

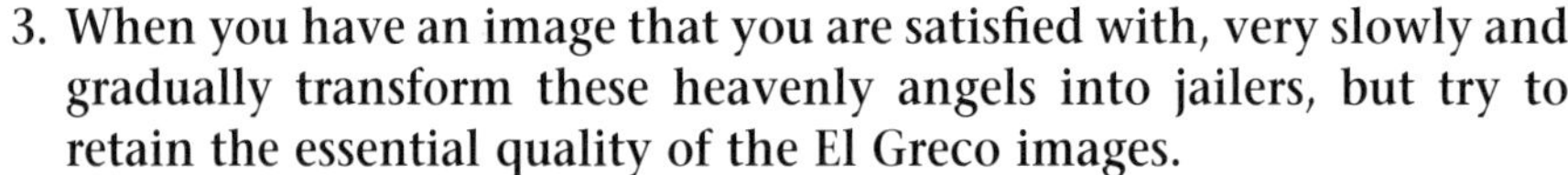

3. When you have an image that you are satisfied with, very slowly and gradually transform these heavenly angels into jailers, but try to retain the essential quality of the El Greco images.

- Does your transformation make it possible for you to see the sisters as guardians and jailers at the same time?
- Does one seem more appropriate than the other, and if so, why?

Interpreting the symbolism of the pagan woman

If Juan, his sisters and the village women embody the forces of reaction in the play, we felt that the revolutionary impulse was to be found in the philosophy of the pagan woman. Once again, we had to be sure that we could find justification in the play for this feeling, and so we began to analyse the character of the pagan woman.

Thoroughly sceptical of the Church and its teachings, she puts her faith in the world of nature. Her down-to-earth, common sense approach leads her to seek the solution to Yerma's problems in history and heredity. She tells her that it is no good offering up prayers to a non-existent god; rather, that she should understand that Juan's family has never been particularly fertile (his two sisters remain childless and his male relatives are 'made of spit'), whereas her own family has a long history of producing strong and healthy children.

The answer for Yerma lies in renouncing the stuffy, bigoted and repressive world represented by the village and embracing the pagan woman's way of life. In the last scene of the play, it seems that Yerma's religious convictions make it impossible for her to follow the advice of the pagan woman. But, having apparently rejected it, she then kills her husband (her oppressor) and the play ends with Yerma poised between the censure of the villagers and the escape route which has been offered to her.

Task 5: The Pagan World

Reread the pagan woman's speech in Act 1, scene 2.

Yerma: I am Enrique the Shepherd's daughter.

Pagan Woman: Enrique the Shepherd! I knew him. Good people. Get up sweat. Eat a few loaves of bread and die. No time for larking about. I could have married an uncle of yours, but there you are ... (*laughs*) ... I've chucked my skirts over my head in my time. Oh, yes, I've cut myself a good slice of the cake in my day, I can tell you. Many is the time in the night I've run to the door thinking I've heard the sound of guitars at the Fiesta, but it was only the wind. (*Laughs*) You may laugh but I've had two husbands and fourteen sons, five of whom died, and yet I'm not sad and I'd like to live a good while longer yet. But it's like I always say, look at the fig trees how long they last! And the houses! It's only us blessed women who go to rot.

1. Based on what she says about her past, try to imagine what her life was like as a girl and a young woman. In your group, develop five short scenes which depict this past.

2. When you have developed these scenes, condense each one into a *still-image*. When you have arrived at the *still-images*, give each a title that begins with the words 'The pagan woman learns . . .' (e.g. 'The pagan woman learns the pleasure of sex').

The pagan woman must be roughly the same age as Yerma's mother, the wife of Enrique the Shepherd. Although Yerma's mother never appears in the play, try to imagine what *her* life would have been like as a girl and a young woman (presumably she was brought up in the same village as Yerma, and it is probably fair to assume that the lives of the mother and the daughter would not be vastly dissimilar).

3. Return to the scene titles for the pagan woman still-images and try to come up with a new title that suggests the opposite of what the pagan woman had learned. When you have these five new titles, use them as a starting point for an equivalent scene describing the life of Yerma's mother (e.g. 'Yerma's mother learns that sex is sinful . . .').
4. Finally, play the five scenes describing the life of the pagan woman one after the other, and, straight away, play the five scenes showing the experience of Yerma's mother. What differences do you perceive between the lives of the two women?

From conception to realisation

By returning to *Lorca*'s play, rereading it with great care, and subjecting it to some rigorous textual analysis, we finally persuaded ourselves that our initial conception was viable and that our developing interpretation did not involve distorting the play beyond all recognition. Once the director has satisfied themselves that the conception is viable, they begin to work with the designer to develop the visual aspects of the production. **A good designer is able to highlight aspects of the director's conception by ensuring that visual motifs reinforce the themes which are foregrounded in the director's interpretation.**

At this point, the stage of conception gives way to the **stage of realisation**, where the director begins to work with their actors in order to explore, develop and give final form to the initial conception.

Realisation

Realisation = exploration + rehearsal

We can think of the process of realising a play as having two important aspects to it: an **exploratory** aspect and a **rehearsal** aspect. Some of the major directors we have already encountered were able to enjoy the luxury of prolonged exploration before embarking upon the rehearsal period leading up to the final production (Peter ***Brook***'s production of the *Marat/Sade* began life as an exploratory workshop on madness). It is our belief that 'exploration' has a vital role to play in the process of realisation.

Improvisation is an essential rehearsal aid

Joan ***Littlewood***, in her long career as director of *Theatre Workshop* and Stratford East's *Theatre Royal*, used **improvisation** as an essential rehearsal aid to:

- **improvise scenes that are implicit in the text**, but which the playwright 'forgot' to write (e.g. Macbeth hiring the assassins who are to kill Duncan);
- **find a parallel situation** that is closer to the actors' experience than the one in the play;

- **use contemporary language** to grasp the meaning and tone of classical verse.

Such exploratory improvisations help the actors gain a fuller understanding of context and background, the full weight and significance of individual scenes and the richness of the poetic language. Improvisation, of course, is not the only rehearsal aid. There are a wide range of conventions and exploratory techniques available to the creative director that not only serve to open up the world of the play for closer analysis and inspection, but also allow for a more thorough investigation into character and the network of relationships within the play. Most directors would, we think, agree that the more mechanical aspects of rehearsal will be considerably enriched by carefully considered, creative and imaginative explorations.

There does come a point, however, when the explorations have to stop. The demands of the schedule will require that decisions are made and certain aspects of the production are firmed-up and fixed. Now, the focus of the director's work begins to change. The more open, exploratory atmosphere of the early stages of realisation gives way to a period of consolidation in which the director's editorial and technical functions take over.

From exploration to rehearsal

At this point the director guides the actors to be more selective in what they are doing. In helping them decide what essentials must be preserved in their performances, the director eliminates any elements which serve to clutter and obscure. At the very end, the technical demands of the production become the main preoccupation. This is a time when the director ensures that all the technical elements (lighting, sound, scene changes, etc.) combine to create a clear, flowing, stylistically coherent whole which will hold the attention of the audience.

Unfortunately, however, for most professional directors, the combination of financial constraints and scheduling logistics means that productions have to be rehearsed and ready for performance within a period of four (sometimes three) weeks. Many directors would argue that their impossibly tight rehearsal schedules leave precious little time for the kind of enriching explorations that would fill out their actors' understandings of the play. It is inevitable that these pressures will affect how a production is realised and, although many directors seek to combine the process of creative exploration with the business of rehearsal, there is little doubt that many present-day productions come to the stage if not under-rehearsed then certainly inadequately 'filled out'.

The modern rehearsal process

Over the years, the pattern of the modern rehearsal process has become fairly firmly established. Typically, this is how it might look:

- On the first day, at the **read-through** of the play, the director and the designer will unveil their plans for the production. The actors and the production team will discover what the director's conception is, and how the designer has translated that conception into visual terms.
- Next, the director will work through the scenes of the play, giving the actor's their **blocking** (this is the term that refers to the patterns of the actors' movements on stage). Some directors like to set these patterns before the rehearsal process begins, while others prefer to work out the movements as they go from scene to scene.
- As rehearsals proceed, the director will find ways to help the actors explore **characterisation**, and the network of **relationships** within the play.
- The overall **style** of the play will need to be firmly established and refined in order that all the actors achieve some measure of consistency in their playing.
- As the whole play begins to come together, the director will give increasing attention to the **pacing** of the play, the **contrasts** between different elements

in the production, and the building of **tension** in those scenes where matters come to a head.

- Once this preliminary work has been done, the whole production team will want to see a complete run-through, from beginning to end, to make sure that the play hangs together as a **coherent whole.**
- The **technical rehearsal** is next, where all of the technical production elements are worked through in meticulous detail (smooth scene changes, lighting and sound cues, ensuring that any costume changes can be done in the time available, etc.).
- Then come the **dress rehearsals** in which actual performance conditions are replicated (sometimes 'dress rehearsals' may be public, or be described as 'previews').
- **First performance** (when the critics will be invited!).

These, then, are the vital components of the rehearsal process. Given that all of this has to be accomplished in a relatively short space of time it is easy to see why some directors feel that there is little time for wider exploration of the play's context, themes or characters. We would hold to the view that a broader exploration of key thematic, textual and character elements can actually save time because a carefully considered and well-structured exploration can have the effect of increasing the actors' understanding of the play and its meanings.

Task 6: Do you enjoy rehearsals?

How close is our model of the rehearsal process to your own experience of performing in plays? Which is your favourite/least favourite stage in the process?

- **Based on your own experiences, write a list of dos and don'ts for actors and directors for each of the stages of the rehearsal process. How practical is your list? Pass it to another group or student and see whether they would follow your advice!**

Realising *Yerma*

In directing *Yerma*, the early exploratory work was invaluable in helping the actors really come to terms with the conception already outlined. As a company we now embarked on the four-part exploration of the text that is outlined in the textual analysis questionnaire which follows Chapter 8. The four parts are:

1 an examination of the **triangle of relationships** at the heart of the play;
2 building **Yerma's world** (this also involved some attempts to experiment with different stylistic conventions);
3 building the contrasting **world of the pagan woman**;
4 examining the **role and function of Juan's sisters**.

What are Yerma's feelings for Victor? What is Victor's function in the play?

On a first reading of *Yerma*, the easy assumption is that Juan is the villain of the piece. But the other important central character is Victor. We know that Victor has known Yerma since childhood, and it appears that Juan and Victor, who are both shepherds, have also developed a close friendship. In her conversation with the pagan woman it becomes clear that Yerma has enormous affection for Victor and that, as her relationship with Juan deteriorates, her thoughts turn increasingly to the happy times she spent with Victor when she was a young girl. Although there are moments of real tenderness between Yerma and Victor in the brief scenes when they are alone together, ***Lorca*** gives no hint that anything improper has happened in their shared past; or, indeed, that anything is about to happen. Nevertheless, *Lorca* leaves us in no doubt that there is a certain 'chemistry' between them. However, the extent to which Juan is aware of his wife's feelings for Victor is never made wholly explicit.

In Task 2 you created two *still-images* that showed how Yerma felt towards Juan and Victor at two different points in the play. In watching the transition from the first image to the second, we were able to develop a clearer insight into how Yerma's feelings had changed during the years that elapse between the first two acts; and how the triangle of relationships at the core of the play have become much more intricate.

Given our interpretation, clearly the process of building Yerma's world, and a sense of the community in which she lives, was critically important. We attempted to do this by stages. First of all, we experimented with how Yerma's friend, Maria, breaks the news that she is pregnant. You tried out this improvisation for yourself as part of Task 3. In our work, Maria's excitement only served to highlight Yerma's own predicament, but we found that she, nevertheless, managed to put on a brave face and was genuinely happy for her friend. After trying the scene in a number of different ways it became clear to us that the most effective tone for the encounter was one of enthusiastic, girlish delight: Maria's authentic, bubbly exhilaration clashing somewhat with Yerma's slightly more forced enthusiasm.

This exercise served two important purposes for us: first, it highlighted the fact that, **at the beginning of the play, Yerma is still able to retain some of her youthful optimism** (which stands in stark contrast to her increasing sense of disillusion and despair as the play progresses); and second, **it clearly demonstrated the significance which the community attaches to the impending birth of a child** (and, equally, the extent to which Yerma feels her own failure to meet the community's expectations).

Our next exploration focused on the washerwomen's scene. As well as providing an opportunity to experiment with different stylistic conventions, this work proved to be crucial in building up the sense of oppression felt by Yerma as the full implications of her and Juan's inability to produce a child begin to dawn on her.

We have already mentioned the importance of the washerwomen's scene in developing our original conception into a workable proposition, and we decided that this was the scene that was integral to creating the whole atmosphere of moral censure surrounding Yerma. As you already know from your own practical work, the scene falls into two parts: the first, realistic; the second, poetic and stylised. We worked up a version of the scene in which the ***realism*** of the early part gave way to an elaborate choral recital, accompanied by appropriate work rhythms. We were forcibly struck by how the insistent, relentless rhythms of the second part created a truly menacing effect. **For us, this was an important exercise in terms of finding a suitable performance style for the 'chorus scenes' that *Lorca* has woven into the fabric of the play.**

When this was done, we returned to the opening scene of the play in which we first begin to sense the rift that exists between Yerma and Juan. We then played this scene side by side with the washerwomen's scene, as you did in Task 3. The effect of this juxtaposition between an intimate conversation taking place within the privacy of the marital home and the widespread public condemnation and disapproval, was startling. So compelling was this orchestration and rearrangement of *Lorca*'s original narrative, that it eventually found its way into the opening sequence of the production.

The repressive world of Yerma's village stands in stark contrast to the world of the pagan woman, and we felt that it was important to find a concrete way for us to understand what it means to live in each of these worlds. We began with the exercise our colleague had introduced to us in Norway, creating six scenes from the pagan woman's past. Each scene was then given a title that began with the words, 'The pagan woman learns ...' (e.g. 'The pagan woman learns the joys of love'). Subsequently, we contrasted the life of the pagan woman with the experience of Yerma's mother, as you did in Task 5 (e.g. 'Yerma's mother learns that love means sacrifice'). **By contrasting the life of the pagan woman with the experience of Yerma's mother, we were able to develop a real sense of the two worlds that coexist in the play.**

During the second act we discover that Juan has brought his two sisters to the house so that they can keep watch over his wayward wife. The double image of the sisters as, simultaneously, angels and jailers began to take root in our thinking. Like you, we created images, based on the religious paintings of El Greco, of angels compassionately and protectively watching over Yerma as she slept. These angels were then slowly transformed into vigilant jailers. **The effect was a subtle but powerful one, and convinced us that we could productively work with this 'double image' of the sisters as both guardians and jailers.**

Having completed these series of explorations, the student company was now in a position to begin working with a slightly adapted version of *Lorca*'s text. It is important to make the point that most of the textual modifications and adaptations were made as a result of these preliminary explorations.

The student actors were now ready to bring the understandings gained in their exploratory work to the rehearsal process itself. The explorations continued, but nowhere near as intensively, as we moved towards the production dates.

The next important consideration for the director is to decide how they will create the conditions in which the play's characters can most effectively be brought to life, so that they are able to fully inhabit the world of the play. Different directors have different ways of working with actors, and, in the final part of this chapter, we turn our attention to the different directorial approaches.

However, before reading the next section, we would like you to take a few minutes to consider the workshops and rehearsals that you have been involved in.

Task 7: The highs and lows of rehearsal

- **Think back over the times when you have been involved in group work, or in rehearsal, and try to remember those occasions when you felt that you had done your most creative work. Try to recall the *conditions* in which this creative work occurred. What were your own feelings? What was it about the group, or the rehearsal, that made the work so satisfying? What was the atmosphere like? Was there a leader/director? If so, how did they help/hinder?**

1. **Write a paragraph recalling as clearly as you can the conditions in which this work took place.**

- **Similarly, try to recall a time when you were frustrated by the whole rehearsal or group process. Once again, try to identify the conditions that produced this feeling. *Exactly* what was it that produced this frustration in you? What was the atmosphere like? Did the other group/cast members share your frustration? Were their reasons the same as, or different from, your own?**

2. **Write a second paragraph in which you identify some of the reasons why this work was so difficult for you.**

Having completed Task 7, your own past experiences of rehearsal, and of group work, should already be indicating to you the kinds of working conditions that you find most conducive to achieving your best and most creative work. Some actors respond well to a strong directorial lead, while others might find it too inhibiting, or intrusive, or stifling.

On the other hand, certain types of actor find that they do their best work with a more open, relaxed director, while others find this approach too free and easy, wishy-washy and lacking in leadership. This is why certain actors seem to do their best work with particular directors. Your reflections in Tasks 6 and 7 should already be indicating to you the directorial approach that suits you best; but additionally, it is also telling you something about the kind of actor you are.

Working with Actors

In a famous article, Tyrone ***Guthrie***, one of the early directors at Stratford-on-Avon's ***Shakespeare Memorial Theatre*** (in the days before the Stratford operation came to be called the *Royal Shakespeare Company*), wrote that the separate work of the director, designer and actor should 'grow together . . . and be the result of a productive exchange of ideas'.

Actors need to feel a sense of ownership

If you have already completed a GCSE drama course, this idea will not be totally alien to you. In creating group and class dramas, you will have discovered that it is important for everyone involved to feel that they have had the opportunity to contribute their own ideas to the creative process. If individuals know that their ideas are accepted and valued, they inevitably feel **a sense of ownership** of what is being created. Professional actors are not so very different. As the first night approaches, the director has to 'let go' of the work they have created; at this point, they have to put their faith in the performers who will go out, night after night, to realise their conception in front of an audience.

The actors' confidence in their ability to do so will be increased in direct proportion to the sense of ownership they feel of the production that they are a part of. The director, therefore, has a vested interest in ensuring that the actors are in tune with the interpretation that they have created together.

No two directors are alike in their work

The early autocrats (***Chronegk***, for example) would not necessarily have subscribed to *Guthrie*'s view, but few present-day directors would, we suspect, quarrel with it. However, while broad professional agreement probably exists on this ideal, the variety of methods employed to achieve its end can appear to be somewhat bewildering. Any actor will tell you that no two directors are alike, and it is sometimes said that for every different director working in the theatre there is a different approach.

It remains the case that no systematic codification of the art of directing has been firmly established. There are a number of reasons why this is so. First, as we have seen, the director, as a key figure in the making of theatre, only emerged towards the end of the last century. The 'job description' took shape gradually and progressively. Documented practice tends to be inconsistent in terms of outlining particular, detailed approaches. Second, theatre is a collaborative art, and the director's job is to coordinate the various contributions into a coherent, unified, whole; but, here again, the nature of the collaborative endeavour varies enormously from production to production. Finally, the process of conception and realisation takes place over a relatively long period, sometimes over many years (nine, as we have seen, in the case of ***Brook***'s *Le Mahabharata*). This means that **initial ideas become modified as a result of changing circumstances, scheduling logistics and production deadlines.**

All of these reasons, therefore, make it very difficult to separate out the essentials of the director's art when it comes to examining rehearsal-room practice. In the next section, we offer descriptions of five different types of director, and some analysis of the working methods associated with each type. In reading through this typology, you might like to bear in mind your own reflections on the approach that has helped you create your best work.

The Five Types of Director

1. The instructional director

The instructional director has its origins in the Greek playwright/director (or *didaskalos*) who, as we have seen, was referred to as a 'teacher'. Instructional directors tend to be very well-organised. Their conception (which they may, or may not, share with their acting company) is thoroughly worked out in advance of their arrival in the rehearsal room, and their efforts are all directed towards realising the strong vision that they have developed during the period of preparation.

The early stages of rehearsal tend to be dominated by 'blocking' the actors' entrances, movements and exits, and by composing the visual elements of the stage picture. Control is established from the read-through, and many aspects of the final production are fixed very early in the rehearsal process. Instructional directors do a lot of one-to-one work with actors, often providing extremely detailed character sketches, and they also tend to be avid note-givers. Ludwig ***Chronegk*** and the early ***Stanislavski*** would offer good examples of this type of director.

It is immediately obvious that this type of director is going to provide strong leadership and, in addition, can forge a real sense of unity in the acting company, as a clear sense of direction is evident to everyone from the outset. As a result of thorough preparation and preplanning, this type of director is also likely to produce results in a very short space of time – a distinct advantage in these days of strict financial control and tight rehearsal schedules.

The disadvantage of this kind of approach is that actors can begin to feel that they are little more than puppets in the hands of the puppet-master. Because the artistic vision is so well developed in advance of rehearsals, they may feel that there is minimal opportunity for them to make any kind of significant or meaningful input to the production. Consequently, they may be reluctant to offer suggestions for fear of obscuring or distorting the director's conception. The rehearsal process also tends to move very quickly, leaving actors with little time to experiment, or try things out, or become comfortable with the director's instructions. We have already noted how important it is that actors feel of a sense of ownership in their work, but the imposition of the strong vision and fast-moving rehearsal process of the instructional director can work against this.

2. The coaching director

Coaching directors usually tend to be 'actor's directors'. Rather than imposing their vision onto the acting company (in the manner of the 'instructional director') they work *with* the actors in order to realise it. The coaching director may still have a strong conception, but their means of realising it are more subtle than those of the instructional director. They tend to leave more room for the actors to make their own understandings and find their own ways with the interpretation.

The essence of the coaching director's work is simultaneously to draw out the character from the actor, and to lure the actor ever closer to the character. Coaching directors usually have a strong interest in, and understanding of, the process of acting and are therefore able to give actors very practical help and advice in the rehearsal room. For this reason, they tend to be very popular with performers. Like the instructional director, the coaching director may also spend a lot of time on one-to-one work with actors, but unlike the instructional director this will be a two-way process in which the emphasis will be on dialogue and interdependence. The later ***Stanislavski***, ***Brecht*** and Elia ***Kazan*** would be good examples of coaching directors.

We have seen how the approach of the instructional director can sometimes work against the actors feeling much of a sense of ownership, but the coaching director's methods will often produce the opposite effect. Because they feel they have been 'nursed' through the rehearsal process, actors tend to develop a real sense of enthusiasm and commitment to the production because they have been made to feel an integral part of it. The benefits of this level of dedication can often be seen in strong performances and a high-quality production.

As with any other directorial method, there are pitfalls as well as advantages. It is essential that the coaching director has a genuine, technical understanding of the process of acting. They have to know what works for actors in rehearsal. If they falter in this, actors can quickly become frustrated and disillusioned, and the whole process can grind to a halt. The coaching director generally tends to work fairly slowly anyway, setting things fairly late (simply as a consequence of their desire to give the actor plenty of time and space), and this can be another source of frustration for performers. **All in all, this can be a high-risk approach, unless the director is assured in their handling of the whole rehearsal process; and instinctively attuned to the needs of the actors.**

3. The input director

Adrian ***Noble***, one of the major *Royal Shakespeare Company* directors of the last decade, begins with a strong conception of the play he is directing, but believes in allowing his actors tremendous freedom within the framework he has created, placing great faith in the 'inspiration' of actors. **Provided that the actors' contributions to the rehearsal process do not massively distort the conception, the input director tends to be very receptive and responsive to their ideas.**

The characteristics of this type of director are: an inside-out knowledge of the play and its possibilities; a commitment to dialogue with actors and a willingness to listen; and adaptability and flexibility within the confines of the overall vision. Like the coaching director, the input director also tends to be popular with actors, especially those who enjoy the creative freedom that this type of director offers. In addition to Adrian *Noble*, Eugene ***Vakhtangov*** would be an example of the input director.

Because the input director has such a thorough knowledge of the play being produced, they tend to inspire confidence in the acting company. This confidence is, of course, vital because the kind of exploratory, 'inspirational' work that is encouraged by the input director requires an environment and atmosphere in which actors feel that they can work without inhibitions, and where they can take risks. The receptivity of this type of director is also beneficial in creating a feeling of 'ensemble' in the acting company – a willingness to work for each other to best serve the needs of the play.

One of the major drawbacks of this working method is that it can, if the director is not alive to the problem, quickly become a very intellectual process. Because so much time is spent listening to ideas, discussing their possibilities and evaluating their merits, the rehearsal can deteriorate into a 'talking shop'. It is inevitably the case that, if a director is open to suggestions, many more ideas will be generated than can actually be used in the production.

The input director therefore needs a range of strategies for sorting, sifting and testing the ideas that arise during rehearsal, and also needs to be able to justify why some suggestions are taken on board while others are rejected. Actors who feel that their ideas are constantly being neglected can become alienated by this working method.

4. The critical director

Like the input director, the critical director relies a great deal on the contributions of their actors. They will encourage experimentation in the rehearsal room, will evaluate its effects and then decide whether or not the results are worth holding onto.

In many respects, the critical director is the opposite of the coaching director; intervening less, but usually offering comments and observations after having seen rehearsal in action. They will often leave actors to their own devices, allowing plenty of time and space for them to make discoveries and come to their own understandings (the very opposite of the stop/start directorial approach), but will usually make extensive notes which will then be fed back to the actors.

Because of this non-interventionist style, the critical director will often get to the run-through stage very early in the rehearsal process. Despite the fact that Max ***Reinhardt*** came to the rehearsal room with a highly developed and thoroughly prepared conception, his rehearsal methods were very much those of the critical director. He saw his role as being a receptive, concentrated, critical sounding-board for the performers: in Tyrone ***Guthrie***'s famous phrase, 'an audience of one'.

Actors' attitudes to the critical director will vary according to the kind of performer they are. **Actors who enjoy creative freedom appreciate the amount of leeway that they are given, while others feel that the lack of intervention can leave them somewhat adrift and lacking in leadership.**

5. The empirical director

Deborah ***Warner***, who formed *Kick Theatre Company*, reflecting on her first *Royal Shakespeare Company* production *Titus Andronicus*, said, 'I think a director's role is to create the right environment and then step out of it for as long as possible and hope the actors will feel confident and brave enough to try to experiment'.

Experiment and discovery would be the watchwords of the empirical director. Sometimes, the empirical approach is thrust onto a director because of circumstances. Michael ***Bogdanov***, co-founder (with Michael *Pennington*) of the ***English Shakespeare Company*** in 1986, describes how, in his attempts to direct seven plays in a 13-week period, he was forced to set different groups of actors tasks which they had to complete without any sustained help. He likened this approach to playing 20 games of chess at the same time. *Bogdanov* claimed that, by discovering the plays *together* in this way, everyone has a stake in the productions.

It goes without saying that empirical directors must place great faith and trust in their actors. This belief in the creative abilities of the performers makes the empirical director very much the opposite of his instructional counterpart, who keeps a very tight rein on the actors. As with the critical director, the process leaves lots of room for the actors to make their own discoveries and this approach, which often generates fresh thinking about (and original insights into) the text, can result in highly creative and inventive productions.

Ironically, given Michael *Bogdanov*'s adoption of this approach to solve the problem of directing a number of productions at the same time, the empirical director's process can be very slow-moving, simply because the acting company's discoveries have to be evaluated before being moulded into the overall directorial conception. **Final production decisions are often taken very late on in the rehearsal process, and actors who like to fix aspects of their performance gradually during the course of rehearsal sometimes find this approach stressful.**

We have now considered the difference between a **playwright's director** and an ***auteur***, and we have identified **five** different types of approach that directors use when working with actors. We have already cautioned against thinking that the playwright's director and the *auteur* exist in a pure form, and we should also bear in mind that any *typology* of directorial approaches is only useful as a model that helps us understand the variety of methods open to any director. It would be an oversimplification to say that *Reinhardt always* used the critical approach. In his directing, there is a *tendency* towards this particular method, but a detailed study of his notebooks would indicate that he also made use of other approaches. Richard ***Eyre***, artistic director of the ***Royal National Theatre***, does not apply any particular method across the board; he observes that each play generates its own working process, and his approach will vary with the demands of the production in hand.

To close our examination of the director, you might like to complete one final task.

Task 8: Categorising directors

Copy the grid below and, working with a partner, try to assign particular directors to each of the empty boxes in the 'Playwright's director' and '*Auteur*' columns. For example, Max *Reinhardt* would sit quite comfortably alongside the critical director category in the '*Auteur*' column. Use your reading of this chapter and any additional research you have done, to place some of the better-known directors on the grid. It would also be useful to give reasons for the choices you have made.

	Playwright's director	***Auteur***
Instructional director		
Coaching director		
Input director		
Critical director		
Empirical director		

SECTION 4

Textual Analysis

7 Reading for Performance

Reading Texts

Reading different kinds of literary text is part of our everyday schoolwork. We have all studied poetry, short stories, novels and plays, and sometimes our tendency is to read each of these different kinds of text in much the same manner. But it is important to understand that each of these literary **genres** is quite distinctive, and each benefits from being read in a quite particular way. So, we want to spend a little time considering how we approach the reading of poems, novels and plays.

Task 1: Reading strategies exercise

1. **Think about your own ways of reading literary texts. Make three columns on a sheet of paper like this:**

Poetry	Stories and novels	Plays

2. **Under each heading, make a list of the things you think about and look for when you are reading each of these three types of text. Compare your own lists with those of others in the class.**

In the first part of this chapter we will be examining these different genres. We want to look, first of all, at what is distinctive about each one; but, more importantly for our purposes, we will want to see **how the various strategies we use in reading poetry and fiction can help us when it comes to analysing dramatic texts.**

Reading Poetry

Lyric poems convey feelings

A **lyric** (probably the most popular category of poem, which includes sonnets, odes and haikus) is a short, highly condensed poem which usually expresses the poet's innermost feelings. So, the reader has to pay particular attention to the **mood** which the poet is trying to create by means of the **rhythm** of the verse, the **tone** which the sound of the words helps create, and the visual **images** which are used to reinforce the emotional quality and content.

Narrative poems tell a story

Almost all modern plays are written in prose, but there is a strong tradition of dramatic poetry in European drama

Narrative poems (including ballads and epics) tend to be much longer, and more extended, because they tell a story which can be wide-ranging in terms of the timescale, the number of characters involved, and the various different locations in which the action takes place. So, close attention should be paid to how **time** is used and manipulated by the poet, the pattern of **relationships** between the different **characters**, and the ways in which the movement of the verse helps the reader follow the twists and turns of the **plot**.

Almost all modern plays are written in **prose**, but there is a strong tradition of **dramatic poetry** in European drama. Classical Greek and Roman drama, the medieval mysteries and moralities, Elizabethan and Jacobean drama in England and the plays of the classic French, Spanish and German dramatists (***Racine***, ***Corneille***, ***Lope De Vega***, ***Calderon***, ***Schiller***, ***Goethe***) were mostly written in verse. But, even where these playwrights use prose, they still employ more heightened forms of language than we are used to encountering in modern plays. In a sense, the dramatic poetry of ***Marlowe*** and ***Shakespeare*** combines both narrative and lyric sub-genres. The **narrative** elements in these plays are obvious enough: *The Merchant of Venice*, for example, tells the story of a financial bond struck between the merchant, Antonio, and the Jew, Shylock. The dramatic action involves 19 named characters, and extends over a period of three months, alternating between two locations – Venice and Belmont. But it is also important to note that within the narrative structure of these verse plays, we will also find **lyric** elements.

Task 2: Reading verse in a play

1. Read the following extract from ***Shakespeare***'s tragedy, *King Lear*. The lines are taken from Act 3, scene 2, which takes place on a wild and windswept heath, during a temporary lull in a violent storm.

The context of the extract is as follows. At the beginning of the play, the king has announced his intention to divide up his kingdom between his three daughters, Goneril, Regan and Cordelia. But first, the daughters are required to say how much they love him. Goneril and Regan play along with their father, professing their boundless love for him. But when it comes to Cordelia's turn, she refuses to follow the extravagant example of her two sisters, saying that she loves her father as a daughter's duty demands, 'nor more, nor less'. Upset by his youngest daughter's refusal to indulge him, Lear disowns and disinherits her. He divides the kingdom between Goneril and Regan. Before long, the sisters begin to show their true colours. Once they have secured their portion of the realm, they turn their father and his servants away, and he is left to wander the countryside – a deflated, disappointed and defeated old man.

Lear: Blow, winds, and crack your cheeks! Rage! blow!
You cataracts and hurricanoes, spout
Till you have drench'd our steeples, drown'd the cocks!
You sulphurous and thought-executing fires,
Vaunt-couriers of oak-cleaving thunderbolts,
Singe my white head! And thou, all-shaking thunder,
Strike flat the thick rotundity o' the world,

Crack nature's moulds, all germens spill at once
That make ingrateful man! . . .
. . . Rumble thy bellyful! Spit, fire! Spout, rain!
Nor rain, wind, thunder, fire are my daughters.
I tax not you, you elements, with unkindness;
I never gave you kingdom, call'd you children.
You owe me no subscription; then, let fall
Your horrible pleasure. Here I stand, your slave.
A poor, infirm, weak, and despis'd old man.
But yet I call you servile ministers,
That will with two pernicious daughters join'd
Your high-engender'd battles 'gainst a head
So old and white as this. O! O! 'tis foul.

We noted earlier that lyric poems express emotion. We are going to approach this piece of dramatic text in much the same manner as we might analyse a lyric poem.

- Examine Lear's speech and describe the feelings he is experiencing as he stands on the heath. What is the prevailing tone and mood that ***Shakespeare*** creates? Next, look carefully at the rhythm of the verse, noting particularly the punctuation, and how the lines are broken up. What clues to Lear's state of mind does the movement of the verse provide?

2. Make a list of the images that *Shakespeare* uses in this speech. Try to say how these images reinforce the emotional quality of the speech.
3. Take a little time to prepare a rehearsed reading of the speech, trying to capture as accurately as you can Lear's mood and state of mind. Paying particular attention to the rhythm of the verse, and pointing-up the images which *Shakespeare* uses will help you enhance the dramatic quality of the lines. This task could take the form of a prepared monologue, or you could work on the speech in a group to produce a choral reading, in which you use the different voices to heighten the effect of the lines, rhythms and images.

The plays of the great Elizabethan and Jacobean dramatists (not to mention the French, Spanish and German classical playwrights) often appear to be extremely difficult when we first encounter them. But if we remember to apply some of the strategies we use in our reading of poetry, the prospect of tackling a full-scale verse drama becomes a little less daunting.

Reading Novels

Both plays and novels have a plot

Reading novels (and short stories) requires a somewhat different approach to that of reading poetry. As in narrative poetry, the *plot* or storyline is probably the most important element in drawing-in the reader – we are keen to know 'what happens next'. If the plot is compelling, our interest is maintained and we continue to engage with the novel's themes as the narrative unfolds. Most of us, as we read, visualise the pictures which the action conjures up in our mind's eye and we try to link them together in an unbroken line, almost as if we have a movie running inside our heads as we read.

In common with novels and short stories, most (but not all) plays have a plot: a sequence of events carefully arranged to emphasise relationships between the different incidents that make up the storyline.

The well-made play

We have already seen that critical discussion about plot originates with *Aristotle* in the fourth century BC. However, in the nineteenth century, French dramatists developed a comic form, which was based on a formula initially recommended by ***Aristotle***. This formula enabled writers like Eugene ***Scribe*** and Victorien ***Sardou*** to produce a type of play which came to be known as *la piece bien faite* (or ***the well-made play***). There are five stages in this kind of play:

1 **exposition**, where we are introduced to the characters and the situation in which they find themselves (which often refers to events that took place before the play begins);
2 **conflict**, where a central problem is introduced which the protagonist must deal with;
3 **complication**, where the problems and difficulties become much more complex;
4 **climax**, where the tension builds towards a crisis which must be dealt with;
5 **denouement**, where the complications in the plot are finally resolved.

This formula was widely used in the late nineteenth century, and is still used in some plays, novels and many Hollywood movies today.

Task 3: Recognising a 'well-made play'

- **Can anyone in your group think of a play or film that seems to follows the structure of the well-made play? Listen to the suggestion and then use the list above to analyse the structure of the play or film to see if it really does fit the pattern.**

Although the plot is the engine which drives us to finish the story, the careful reader of fiction will also pay attention to a number of other factors, such as:

- characterisation;
- structure;
- function of the narrator.

Analysis of character

Analysis of character plays an important part in the reading of both novels and plays. We can begin by identifying three **character types**: the **stock character**; the **flat**, or **two-dimensional** character; and the **rounded** character.

Stock characters **are stereotypes**

Stock characters **are stereotypes, which are familiar and easily recognisable to us, simply because we have encountered them many times before.** Examples might include the country bumpkin, the damsel in distress, the old miser, the wicked stepmother, the absent-minded professor, and so on. **A number of theatrical styles rely on the use of *stock characters*.** Perhaps the best known are ***Commedia dell'Arte*** and Victorian ***melodrama***. In *Commedia dell'Arte*, the plot usually revolves around some kind of intrigue practised by lovers (Pierrot and Columbine), or servants, clowns and villains (Pulcinella, Harlequin and Scaramouche), against the rich father (Pantaloon). Many of the stock *Commedia dell'Arte* characters survived in other dramatic forms, like farce and pantomime. The stock characters of *melodrama*, an extremely popular form throughout the first half of the nineteenth century, usually include the black-cloaked villain, the pure, innocent, naive maiden, and the hero who invariably manages to save the maiden from the evil clutches of the villain.

The flat, or two-dimensional character

The flat, or two-dimensional character is a staple of the nineteenth century well-made play. Such characters are usually simple, straightforward and fairly predictable. They lack psychological depth and, perhaps most importantly, they almost always manage to stay the same in spite of the tide of events that engulfs them.

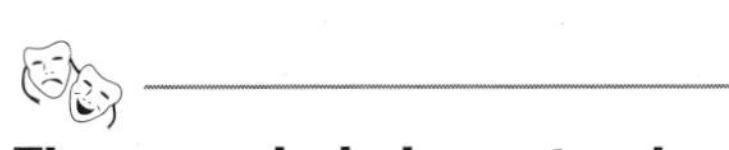

The rounded character is more fully developed

By contrast, the more rounded character that we usually encounter in the realist plays of the twentieth century (and the plays of ***Shakespeare*** and the classical European writers), **is much more fully developed and dynamic, with a complex psychological make-up** that changes in response to the dramatic circumstances in which they find themselves. It is not uncommon to find both flat and rounded characters in the same play. In the hands of a skilled playwright, the former tend to be found in the minor roles, while the more complex characters are usually the major players.

Structure

When we read fiction, we might find ourselves thinking about how the novel is structured: is there one main plot (supported and illuminated by sub-plots), or are a number of storylines woven together? How do the various storylines connect with each other? In the end, do the different narratives in the novel come together to make sense to the reader, or are there loose ends which the reader has to tie up for themselves?

Plots and sub-plots

According to ***Aristotle***'s recommendations, the plot of a play should consist of one **unified action**. The French classical playwrights followed *Aristotle*'s prescription to the letter: ***Racine***'s *Phedre* consists of a single action with no distracting sub-plot to divert our attention away from the plight of the central character. On the other hand, *Shakespeare* showed a healthy disregard for *Aristotle*'s advice, often choosing to augment his main plot with one or more sub-plots which are designed to shed light on the play's central action. In *King Lear*, for example, the sub-plot involving the Duke of Gloucester's relationships with his two sons is designed to provide a commentary on Lear's relationships with his daughters.

Although many playwrights do layer-in a sub-plot to support the main action, **as a general rule dramatic texts do not seek to juggle a number of different narratives in the way that some modern novels do. The main line of action is usually readily apparent.**

Narration

In reading a novel, we might ask the question: who is telling this story, and with what intention? And this could lead us to consider the function of the narrator: what is their relationship to the events being recounted? Are they disinterested and impartial, or do they have an axe to grind? Are they a reliable storyteller, or should we take what they have to say with a pinch of salt?

Whose story is it?

In fiction, the narrator functions as a guide who directs our attention to significant matters in the story. By doing this, the narrator often *manipulates* our view of events so that we see things from their *particular perspective*. Most plays do not rely on a narrator to guide us through the plot (although plays written in the ***Brechtian*** style will sometimes use a 'storyteller' or a 'singer' to comment on the action). Each of the characters provides us with a new perspective on the dramatic action, and this enables us to view the events from a number of different points of view. Inevitably, we will be more sympathetically inclined towards some viewpoints rather than others, but the good playwright always provides us with an *all-sided* perspective on the events they want us to consider.

When we read fiction, ultimately we will want to make our own assessment of what the novel amounts to – what its major themes and preoccupations are. The same is true when reading a play. **We are concerned to find out what connections we can make between the world of the fiction (whether it is a novel, or a dramatic fiction) and our own experience.**

It should be clear from the above that many of the strategies we employ when reading fiction are also useful in analysing play texts – the two genres share much in common. Therefore, it is perhaps not at all surprising that, over the last 20 years, there has been an explosion in the number of novels that have been adapted for the stage (Charles Dickens' *Nicholas Nickleby*, Jane Austen's *Pride and Prejudice* and Victor Hugo's *Les Miserables*, to name just three of the more successful adaptations).

Having considered some of the different reading strategies for poetry and fiction, many of which can be applied to the reading of dramatic texts, it is now time to turn our attention to the reading of plays.

Reading Plays

Plays are written to be performed

The reading of a play poses some problems that we do not encounter in the reading of other literary genres. This is because, with very few exceptions, plays are written to be performed, and in reading the play text we need to keep this very firmly in mind. If we read a play simply with the intention of finding out 'what happens next' (as we sometimes do with a novel, or short story), our focus will almost certainly be on the spoken dialogue, since this is the principal means by which the playwright advances the storyline. (Some modern plays, of course, have no plot to speak of – e.g. Samuel ***Beckett***'s *Not I* – and reading them on the basis of a 'what happens next' approach will quickly become an exercise in frustration.) **In concentrating on the dialogue alone, we are likely to miss other important details that the playwright wishes to convey to us.** It is important, therefore, to look beyond the spoken words and stage directions as we read a play text. In this section, we examine three additional elements:

1 the **visual**;
2 the **action**;
3 the **sub-textual**.

Mise en scene

When considering the visual elements of a play it is important at this point to introduce the French term, ***mise en scene***. This term refers to the staging, or visual arrangement, of the entire dramatic production. Included under this heading would be: setting and scenery, costume, lighting, properties, the movement of the actors and any other visual elements (e.g. slide projections, film clips, videotaped inserts).

Some playwrights are highly specific about the visual picture they wish to create. Henrik ***Ibsen***, in *A Doll's House*, after telling us that the action takes place in a small Norwegian town in 1879, calls for a tasteful, well-furnished room and goes on to detail the precise location of the doors leading into and out of the room, and the windows; he specifies the exact positioning of the piano, a round table, armchairs, sofa, a rocking chair, a small bookcase, a stove lined with porcelain tiles; moreover, he tells us that the floor is carpeted, that there are engravings on the wall, that the books in the bookcase are leatherbound, and that a fire burns in the stove (see Chapter 10, page 214 for an exercise based on this description). By contrast, Sarah *Kane*, at the beginning of *Phaedra's Love*, simply tells us that the action takes place in a royal palace.

The world of play

The playwright's descriptions of the physical environment in which the

dramatic events unfold provide important clues about the fictional world which the characters inhabit. They help us to form a picture of the world of the play.

In *A Doll's House, Ibsen*'s stage directions conjure up a very clear picture of a comfortable family home (see page 208). And, because his description of the Helmers' sitting-room immediately reminds us of the kind of *actual* room which we are used to seeing all the time, we can be fairly sure that the world of the play is going to be *true to life* – an accurate representation of the reality around us. Once we read the first lines of dialogue, our original impressions are reinforced as we begin to settle into a familiar, recognisable, domestic world (even though it is a nineteenth-century domestic world). The consistency of the setting (and costume, which the writer, by specifying the exact year in which the play is set, suggests should be in keeping with the historical period), the behaviour of the characters and the *realistic* dialogue is reassuring for the reader who can straight away see a correspondence between the world of the play and their own experience.

But this measure of consistency between the various dramatic elements is not always present at the beginning of a play. In *Phaedra's Love*, a man called Hippolytus inhabits Sarah *Kane's* royal palace. Hippolytus is a figure from classical tragedy, so we could be forgiven for thinking that this play is going to be set in ancient Greece. But such expectations are immediately confounded as we read that Hippolytus is sitting in a darkened room, watching television. We then learn that he is eating a hamburger! Clearly, the world of this play is a confusing mixture of dramatic elements, some of which suggest that the play is set in the present day, while others hint at a remote, historical past. It quickly becomes apparent that there is work to be done in making sense of these sharply conflicting dramatic elements. The world of Sarah *Kane's* play is nowhere near as easily recognisable as the domestic world of *A Doll's House*.

The world of the play can be represented or presented

Crudely speaking, we can say that in *Ibsen*'s ***realist*** play, the world of the Helmers is **represented** (it is an accurate *representation* of the world as we know it), whereas the world of Phaedra and Hippolytus is **presented** to us in somewhat unfamiliar, ***non-realist*** terms. We noticed this difference in the acting workshops. The world of *The Crucible* is represented to us, while the world of *Mother Courage* is presented.

Often, as in *Ibsen*'s *realist* plays, the playwright largely provides the world of the play. In such cases, the visual clues in the text enable the reader to piece together a coherent view of the world of the play. But, sometimes, the confusing assortment of clues provided in the text requires readers to make certain decisions about the visual quality of the play for themselves (e.g. will the royal palace in *Phaedra's Love* suggest ancient Greece as a conscious contrast to the contemporary figure of Hippolytus watching television, or will the palace be consistent with our contemporary view of how a modern prince lives?). In this case, the reader will, to a certain extent, be **constructing** the world of the play.

The text also gives the attentive reader a sense of the play's dramatic action

In addition to the visual clues, which help in constructing the *mise en scene*, the text also gives the attentive reader a sense of the play's **dramatic action**.

Sometimes this action is made explicit in the stage directions provided by the playwright. At the beginning of *A Doll's House*, we are told that, after tipping the porter who has carried the Christmas tree, Nora closes the door and that she laughs happily as she takes her coat off. After taking out a bag of macaroons from her pocket and eating a few, she walks towards the door of her husband's study and listens.

Explicit and implicit actions

When the text includes this kind of explicit direction it makes it relatively easy for the reader to visualise the action of the scene; but **sometimes important actions are implicit within the dialogue and these can be easily missed.** In the

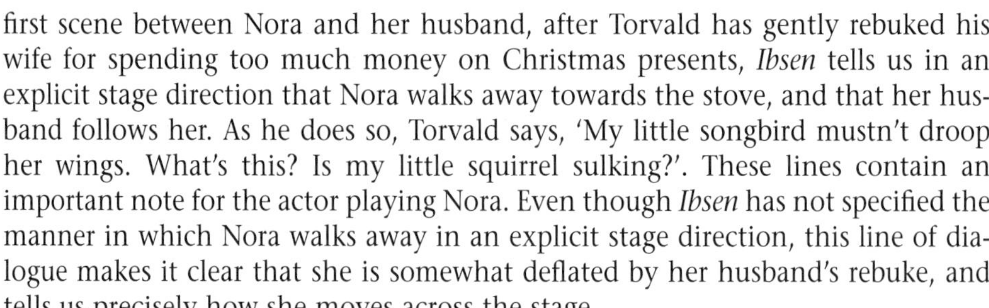

first scene between Nora and her husband, after Torvald has gently rebuked his wife for spending too much money on Christmas presents, *Ibsen* tells us in an explicit stage direction that Nora walks away towards the stove, and that her husband follows her. As he does so, Torvald says, 'My little songbird mustn't droop her wings. What's this? Is my little squirrel sulking?'. These lines contain an important note for the actor playing Nora. Even though *Ibsen* has not specified the manner in which Nora walks away in an explicit stage direction, this line of dialogue makes it clear that she is somewhat deflated by her husband's rebuke, and tells us precisely how she moves across the stage.

Clues in the dialogue

The more general behaviour of a character can also often be inferred from the dialogue. The opening scene of Sarah *Kane's Phaedra's Love* contains fairly detailed stage directions for the actor playing Hippolytus – so the reader has no trouble in visualising the dramatic action. But, at the beginning of the second scene, a doctor tells Phaedra that Hippolytus is depressed, and this piece of information, of course, will help the actor decide precisely *how* the actions in the opening scene are to be carried out.

Both of these examples highlight the importance of checking and rechecking the detail, which the playwright provides for us. **Constant reference back to earlier passages is essential if we are to build up a complete picture of the play's given circumstances, the characters and the developing action.**

It is much easier for a novelist to help the reader follow the action of the narrative, and indicate exactly how the characters behave (and what their innermost thoughts and feelings are), by means of descriptive passages. But reading a play text requires more of the reader. Action and behaviour often have to be inferred from scanty textual evidence. But, as we have discovered, important clues are to be found in the explicit stage directions provided by the playwright, and in the dialogue spoken by the characters themselves.

A good play will also have a *sub-text*

In addition to the words spoken in the play text, a good play will also have a *sub-text*. Perhaps the most important part of the playwright's text is the spoken dialogue, and it is perhaps best to think of the *sub-text* as the *unspoken* words of the characters.

This idea can be best explained if we think about our own behaviour in ordinary social situations. We can probably all remember times when what we said did not correspond with what we were thinking or feeling. Sometimes, we may have decided that what we are thinking is better left unsaid, perhaps because it would cause offence. So, instead of speaking out, we remain silent. The thoughts or feelings remain inside us (as a sub-text) but they are not spoken.

At other times, we may say something which is quite different to what we are thinking. If someone is upset, for instance, we may say 'the right thing' in the circumstances ('There was nothing you could do about it') when we really think that they were to blame in the first place ('Well, it was all your own fault'). 'There was nothing you could do about it' is the *text*, whereas 'Well, it was all your own fault' is the *sub-text*.

We can perhaps also think of times when we didn't quite say what we meant to say – somehow 'It all came out wrong'. This can happen when we find it difficult to tell someone exactly how we are feeling (feeling = sub-text); but the words that come out (text) don't properly express what we were trying to say. And sometimes, of course, words simply fail us. The 'text' may be a shrug of the shoulders while the sub-text is 'I'm not telling'.

As in real social life, so too in theatre

As in real social life, so too in theatre. The actual words the characters speak may or may not truly reflect their actual thoughts and feelings: what is *not said* may be more important than what is spoken out loud.

It has often been said that the plays of Anton ***Chekhov***, the great Russian playwright, are *all sub-text*, and what is actually spoken by the characters is simply intended to mask their real hopes and disappointments. What the reader must judge is whether the given dialogue is a genuine expression of the character's thoughts or feelings, or whether the words are veiling a deeper, unspoken emotional sub-text.

Task 4: Finding the sub-text

1. At the beginning of *A Doll's House*, Nora receives a visitor. It turns out to be an old school-friend, Christine Linde, who she has not seen for many years. It transpires that Mrs Linde has been living in a town many miles away from where she and Nora grew up together. After the initial pleasantries, the following exchange of dialogue takes place. When you have read the passage below, consider the questions that follow. They will help you to distinguish between those lines which are sincerely meant, and those which hide a sub-text. (Each sentence is numbered, and the question numbers correspond to the sentences, which have the same number.

Nora: (1) All that way in winter? (2) How brave of you.

Mrs Linde: (3) I arrived by the steamer this morning.

Nora: (4) Yes, of course, to enjoy yourself over Christmas. (5) Oh, how splendid. (6) We'll have to celebrate. (7) But take off your coat. You're not cold, are you? *(Nora helps her off with it.)* (8) There! Now, let's sit down here by the stove and be comfortable. (9) No, you take the armchair. (10) I'll sit here in the rocking chair. (11) *(Clasps Mrs Linde's hands.)* Yes, now you look like your old self. (12) Just at first I – you've got a little paler, Christine. And perhaps a bit thinner.

Mrs Linde: (13) And older, Nora. Much, much older.

Nora: (14) Yes, perhaps a little older. Just a tiny bit. (15) Not much. *(Checks herself suddenly and says earnestly.)* (16) Oh, but how thoughtless of me to sit here and chatter away like this! (17) Dear, sweet Christine, can you forgive me?

Mrs Linde: (18) What do you mean, Nora?

Nora: (19) Poor Christine, you've become a widow.

Mrs Linde: (20) Yes. Three years ago.

Nora: (21) I know, I know – I read it in the papers. (22) Oh, Christine, I meant to write to you so often, honestly. (23) But I always put it off, and something else always cropped up.

Mrs Linde: (24) I understand, Nora dear.

2. **Questions to consider:**

(1) Is this a genuine request for information, or just small talk? Does it disguise Nora's surprise, or disapproval?

(2) Does Nora mean 'brave' or in the sub-text, might she mean 'foolish'?

(3) Does this seem straightforward? Is Mrs Linde simply replying to Nora's first question, or is there more to it? An urgency, perhaps ('I couldn't wait until Christmas was over')?

(4) Does Nora *really* believe that this is a social visit, with no other motive? Or is there a sub-textual 'fishing' for more information?

(5) Is this expression genuine, or what social convention demands?

(6) Does she mean this?

(7) Is this a real show of concern, or has she just remembered her social obligations?

(8) Is Nora really anxious about Mrs Linde's comfort and well-being? Or is she 'softening her up' in order to get the full story of the past nine years out of her?

(9) A straightforward request? An order? Or is the sub-text, 'You really must stay for a while'?

(10) A simple statement of intent, or does the careful physical arrangement of the two women indicate some hidden sub-textual intention on Nora's part? If so, what?

(11) Does she mean this, or is she trying to lower Mrs Linde's defences?

(12) A straightforward observation, or a coaxing?

(13) A simple statement of fact, or a defensive manoeuvre?

(14) 'A little older', or, 'My God, you really have aged'?

(15) An honest response, or a dismissive response? Probably depending on the answer to question (14).

(16) Has she really been thoughtless? Or has she been working her way around to this subject?

(17) Is she really feeling guilty?

(18) Is this genuine naivety, or does she really know what Nora has just remembered and is simply forcing her hand?

(19) Remembering or fishing ('Tell me what happened')?

(20) Providing information, or making Nora feel more guilty?

(21) Did she read it in the papers, or was there talk and gossip?

(22) Did she mean to write, or has she just remembered that writing would have been the right thing to do?

(23) Is Nora really so busy that she couldn't find a minute to write?

(24) Does she understand, or has she seen through Nora's lie?

Of course, the sub-textual dimension to this whole exchange will depend upon the way that the relationship between Nora and Mrs Linde is being set up for the remainder of the play. The key question might be: are they genuinely trying to re-establish the terms of a former relationship? In which case much of the text might be taken at face value. Or is there a sense in which each of the women sees the other as being of some possible use to them in the future? In which case the sub-text would take on much greater significance. A director working on the text with a view to performance would need to pose these questions as part of the preparations for rehearsal. The answer will depend upon the interpretation the director wants to offer of *Ibsen*'s text.

Reading as a director

A director, of course, is a very particular kind of reader, but the ordinary reader of a dramatic text should approach the play with the same kind of attention as the director does when envisaging a production of the play. In reading the text, the director will be trying to build up a visual picture of the world they will create on the stage, and this will involve them having an eye for the action and sub-textual elements outlined above. All of these concerns help in constructing the world of the play which is contained within the text. (We will consider the director's whole approach in Chapter 8.)

Different texts = different reading strategies

Different kinds of text, then, require different **reading strategies** and we have suggested that in any reading of a dramatic text **visual**, **action** and **sub-textual** elements should *all* be taken into account. This is a useful way to begin thinking about how to read a play, but theatre professionals, of course, need to have a much more comprehensive method of analysing dramatic text. In the final part of this chapter, we suggest how you might go about making a thorough textual analysis of a play that you are either studying or working on. But first, we need to briefly consider the terms 'meaning' and 'interpretation', since any careful reading of a play is an attempt to distil meaning from the text, and any production of a play requires an act of interpretation by the director, designer, actors and technicians.

Meaning and Interpretation

Making connections to our own experience

As we try to make sense of a literary text, we try to establish some sense of connection between the events, experiences and feelings we read about and our own life experience. We have probably all read a poem, or a story, or a play, which seems to 'speak' directly to us because it somehow manages to express exactly how we were feeling at a particular moment in our lives. What this implies is that there is a strong connection between life as it is expressed artistically and life as it is lived. When we make this kind of connection, we are perceiving meaning in the text because the experience described there is similar to something that has happened to us.

Any work of art (not just literary works) carries *meaning*, but because our life experiences differ, the meanings that are perceived in the work of art will vary from person to person. As we revisit a work of art, we sometimes begin to see a larger pattern of meaning emerge. When this happens, the larger pattern begins to come together to form an **interpretation**. This is a vitally important concept in theatrical terms, because each production of a play represents the director's interpretation of the playwright's work. Once the director's work reaches the stage, the audience is then invited to make its own (secondary) interpretation of the (primary) interpretation offered by the director. It is this complex layering of interpretation on interpretation that creates a space in which multiple meanings can emerge from the performance.

In the next section, we try to tease out some further distinctions between the terms 'meaning' and 'interpretation'.

The Meaning not the Message

You will often hear people talking (and writing) about a play's 'message'. We prefer *not* to think in terms of 'messages' because the word 'message' implies something clear, explicit and unambiguous. For example, 'I'll come to your house at seven o'clock this evening' is a straightforward message that, provided we heard it right, is impossible to mistake. To suggest that a play has a clear message implies that, once it has been seen, the audience will all be able to agree on what the 'message' was. But theatre, in common with all other art-forms, doesn't quite work in this way.

Theatre consists of a system of signs and symbols

Signs and actions can be interpreted differently

Theatre consists of a system of signs and symbols, and these signs and symbols do not have *fixed* meanings. You will find a more detailed analysis of how the sign systems of theatre are used to make meanings in Chapter 10.

In *A Doll's House*, Helmer asks Nora to dance the tarantella at a fancy dress party. At the end of the second act, Nora rehearses the dance as her husband, Dr Rank and Mrs Linde look on; and, in the final act, Helmer describes Nora's performance to Mrs Linde. Clearly, the dancing of the tarantella carries symbolic meaning, but what are we meant to make of the dance?

For some observers, the dance is a symbol of Nora's rebellion, and in support of this they point to the fact that in the rehearsal at the end of Act 2, Nora refuses to listen to her husband as he tries to offer her advice about the dance steps. Furthermore, since she dances immediately before finally turning her back on her home, husband and children, the dance acts as a kind of springboard for her liberation. For others, the dance is a symbol of Nora's entrapment – she dances at the request of Helmer, and, as soon as the dance is over, he insists that she leave the party.

The picture is confused even further once we understand a little more about the origins of the tarantella. In southern Italy, where the dance originated, it functions as a kind of *catharsis* – crudely, a way of 'letting off steam', getting certain emotions out of the system. Its original purpose was to allow women a *temporary* escape from marriage and motherhood into a liberated, lawless world of uninhibited movement. At the dance's conclusion, the woman returns to her responsibilities and duties as a wife and mother, purified and cleansed of any feelings of resentment, restraint and rebelliousness.

That the dance operates symbolically within the play is not open to doubt, but the *precise meaning* we attribute to the dancing of the tarantella will depend on how we *interpret* it within the broader context of the play; and, as we now understand, the **meanings may vary** from one observer to another.

As we have already suggested, the whole question of meaning and interpretation, and their interrelationship, is complicated, but it is important to try to disentangle what the two words designate and how they are connected.

The story operates as a pretext for a bigger idea or a broader theme

When a playwright begins to write a play, they will have some sense of what they want the play to be about. By this, we mean much more than simply the story they want to tell. The story, if there is one, operates as a pretext, or particular example, for a bigger idea or a broader *theme*.

At one level, the story in ***Chekhov***'s play, *Three Sisters*, is about three women who yearn to escape from their rural backwater to the excitement of the big city. But, at a deeper level, it could be argued that the play is about the passing of an old, outdated social order. It is at this deeper level that we begin to sense something of the play's meaning. Usually, a playwright will set out with an intention to tackle some idea, or theme, that is important to, and significant for, them. They may want to explore a psychological conflict within an individual, a moral or ethical contradiction within a community, a pressing contemporary social issue, an unresolved historical question or a complicated philosophical or political argument.

In the process of writing, the playwright is undertaking an *investigation*, or *exploration*, of the subject matter; and the finished play will be shaped and formed to convey the playwright's overall perspective on the idea, or theme they have chosen. However, because the idea being explored is undoubtedly complex and contradictory, this perspective is unlikely to be firm, fixed and absolute. During the course of their exploration, the playwright will undoubtedly have discovered that different people hold different points of view about the subject matter under investigation. As we noted earlier in this chapter, these diverse points of view will usually be represented in the different outlooks of the various characters that appear in the play. At one level, therefore, the playwright's job can be seen as *orchestrating* these differing viewpoints.

Different characters offer different perspectives

Each particular viewpoint, embodied in one of the characters, offers the audience a different *angle of vision*, or perspective, on the subject matter that the playwright set out to explore. In *A Doll's House*, each of the characters offers a different angle of vision on the question of the role of women in late nineteenth century Norwegian society. For example, Mrs Linde believes that a woman can find fulfilment only in looking after and caring for her husband, whereas Nora comes to understand that only by standing on her own two feet will she be able to find the self-respect and sense of human dignity that have been denied to her as Torvald's doll-wife.

Simply put, in this play, your angle of vision on the role of women in society depends on where you are standing. Mrs Linde's more traditional view is reinforced by the experience of having been prevented from giving wholehearted support to her husband, because of the demands placed on her by a helpless, bedridden mother and two younger brothers. On the other hand, Nora's determination to seek a measure of independence is driven by the need to escape the stifling atmosphere of Torvald's unbending self-righteousness. In listening to the words of Mrs Linde and of Nora we become aware of the *shifting viewpoints* in ***Ibsen***'s play.

Of course, it is often the case that the playwright's own perspective coincides, more or less, with the particular viewpoint of one of the characters. The unsympathetic manner in which *Ibsen* has drawn the character of Torvald gives us a strong indication that his own position was much closer to Nora's than to her husband's.

But it is also interesting to speculate on what *Ibsen*'s attitude to Mrs Linde might have been. In offering to give herself to Krogstad, she makes him 'the happiest man in the whole wide world'; and we may feel some sense of pleasure because these two people, who were once in love, have found each other again and are embarking on a relationship rekindled by a new sense of hope and optimism.

Task 5: Playing the playwright's intentions

In this task we are going to explore a key scene between Mrs Linde and Krogstad, to see if we can pinpoint *Ibsen*'s attitude towards Mrs Linde.

1. In pairs, read the following scene between Krogstad and Mrs Linde which is taken from the beginning of Act 3 of *A Doll's House*.

1. *Mrs Linde (whispers)*: Come in. There's no one here.

2. *Krogstad (in the doorway)*: I found a note from you at my lodgings. What does this mean?

3. *Mrs Linde*: I must speak with you.

4. *Krogstad*: Oh? And must our conversation take place in this house?

5. *Mrs Linde*: We couldn't meet at my place; my room has no separate entrance. Come in. We're quite alone. The maid's asleep, and the Helmers are at the dance upstairs.
6. *Krogstad (comes into the room)*: Well, well! So the Helmers are dancing this evening? Are they indeed?
7. *Mrs Linde*: Yes, why not?
8. *Krogstad*: True enough. Why not?
9. *Mrs Linde*: Well, Krogstad. You and I must have a talk together.
10. *Krogstad*: Have we two anything further to discuss?
11. *Mrs Linde*: We have a great deal to discuss.
12. *Krogstad*: I wasn't aware of it.
13. *Mrs Linde*: That's because you've never really understood me.
14. *Krogstad*: Was there anything to understand? It's the old story, isn't it – a woman chucking a man because something better turns up?
15. *Mrs Linde*: Do you really think I'm so utterly heartless? You think it was easy for me to give you up?
16. *Krogstad*: Wasn't it?
17. *Mrs Linde*: Oh, Nils, did you really believe that?
18. *Krogstad*: Then why did you write to me the way you did?
19. *Mrs Linde*: I had to. Since I had to break with you, I thought it my duty to destroy all the feelings you had for me.
20. *Krogstad*: (*clenches his fists*): So that was it. And you did this for money!
21. *Mrs Linde*: You mustn't forget I had a helpless mother to take care of, and two little brothers. We couldn't wait for you, Nils. It would have been so long before you'd have had enough to support us.
22. *Krogstad*: Maybe. But you had no right to cast me off for someone else.
23. *Mrs Linde*: Perhaps not. I've often asked myself that.
24. *Krogstad*: (*more quietly*): When I lost you, it was just as though all solid ground had been swept from under my feet. Look at me. Now I'm a shipwrecked man, clinging to a spar.
25. *Mrs Linde*: Help may be near at hand.
26. *Krogstad*: It was near. But then you came, and stood between it and me.
27. *Mrs Linde*: I didn't know, Nils. No one told me till today that this job I'd found was yours.
28. *Krogstad*: I believe you, since you say so. But now you know, won't you give it up?
29. *Mrs Linde*: No – because it wouldn't help you even if I did.

30. *Krogstad*: Wouldn't it? I'd do it all the same.
31. *Mrs Linde*: I've learned to look at things practically. Life and poverty have taught me that.
32. *Krogstad*: And life has taught me to distrust fine words.
33. *Mrs Linde*: Then it has taught you a useful lesson. But surely you still believe in actions?
34. *Krogstad*: What do you mean?
35. *Mrs Linde*: You said you were like a shipwrecked man clinging to a spar.
36. *Krogstad*: I have good reason to say it.
37. *Mrs Linde*: I'm in the same position as you. No one to care about, no one to care for.
38. *Krogstad*: You made your own choice.
39. *Mrs Linde*: I had no choice – then.
40. *Krogstad*: Well?
41. *Mrs Linde*: Nils, suppose we two shipwrecked souls could join hands?
42. *Krogstad*: What are you saying?
43. *Mrs Linde*: Castaway's have a better chance of survival together than on their own.
44. *Krogstad*: Christine!
45. *Mrs Linde*: Why do you suppose I came to this town?
46. *Krogstad*: You mean – you came because of me?
47. *Mrs Linde*: I must work if I'm to find life worth living. I've always worked, for as long as I can remember. It's been the greatest joy of my life – my only joy. But now I'm alone in the world, and I feel so dreadfully lost and empty. There's no joy in working just for oneself. Oh, Nils, give me something – someone – to work for.
48. *Krogstad*: I don't believe all that. You're just being hysterical and romantic. You want to find an excuse for self-sacrifice.
49. *Mrs Linde*: Have you ever known me to be hysterical?
50. *Krogstad*: You mean you really – ? Is it possible? Tell me – you know all about my past?
51. *Mrs Linde*: Yes.
52. *Krogstad*: And you know what people think of me here?
53. *Mrs Linde*: You said just now that with me you might have become a different person.
54. *Krogstad:* I know I could have.
55. *Mrs Linde*: Couldn't it still happen?

56. *Krogstad:* Christine – do you really mean this? Yes – you do – I see it in your face. Have you really the courage – ?

57. *Mrs Linde*: I need someone to be a mother to; and your children need a mother. And you and I need each other. I believe in you, Nils. I am afraid of nothing – with you.

58. *Krogstad: (clasps her hands*): Thank you, Christine – thank you! Now I shall make the world believe in me as you do! Oh – but I'd forgotten –

59. *Mrs Linde (listens)*: Ssh! The tarantella! Go quickly, go!

60. *Krogstad*: Why? What is it?

61. *Mrs Linde*: You hear that dance? As soon as it's finished, they'll be coming down.

62. *Krogstad:* All right, I'll go. It's no good, Christine. I'd forgotten – you don't know what I've just done to the Helmers.

63. *Mrs Linde*: Yes, Nils. I know.

64. *Krogstad*: And yet you'd still have the courage to – ?

65. *Mrs Linde*: I know what despair can drive a man like you to.

66. *Krogstad*: Oh, if only I could undo this!

67. *Mrs Linde*: You can. Your letter is still lying in the box.

68. *Krogstad*: Are you sure?

69. *Mrs Linde*: Quite sure. But –

70. *Krogstad (looks searchingly at her)*: Is that why you're doing this? You want to save your friend at any price? Tell me the truth. Is that the reason?

71. *Mrs Linde*: Nils, a woman who has sold herself once for the sake of others doesn't make the same mistake again.

72. *Krogstad*: I shall demand my letter back.

73. *Mrs Linde*: No, no.

74. *Krogstad*: Of course I shall. I shall stay here till Helmer comes down. I'll tell him he must give me back my letter – I'll say it was only to do with my dismissal, and that I don't want him to read it –

75. *Mrs Linde:* No, Nils, you mustn't ask for the letter back.

76. *Krogstad*: But – tell me – wasn't that the real reason you asked me to come here?

77. *Mrs Linde*: Yes – at first, when I was frightened. But a day has passed since then, and in that time I've seen incredible things happen in this house. Helmer must know the truth. This unhappy secret of Nora's must be revealed. They must come to a full understanding. There must be an end of all these shiftings and evasions.

78. *Krogstad*: Very well. If you're prepared to risk it. But one thing I can do – and at once –

79. *Mrs Linde (listens):* Hurry! Go, go! The dance is over. We aren't safe here another moment.

80. *Krogstad*: I'll wait for you downstairs.

81. *Mrs Linde*: Yes, do. You can see me home.

82. *Krogstad*: I've never been so happy in my life before!

2. Decide with your partner how you think ***Ibsen*** intended this scene to be played. Should it be played with real sincerity? Or do you detect any note of expediency, suspicion or cynicism in either or both of the characters?
3. Mark those lines which you think contain a sub-text.
4. Give a reading of the extract to the rest of the group – can they detect your ideas about *Ibsen*'s intentions for the scene? Can you detect theirs?

While it is probably true to say that *Ibsen* is obviously unsympathetic towards Torvald's viewpoint, his view of Mrs Linde is, perhaps, more difficult to discern. If she is truly sincere in wanting to offer Krogstad the happiness she once denied him, then perhaps *Ibsen* intended her, along with Nora, to be an object of admiration. If her behaviour is at all calculating or opportunist, then perhaps he intended her to be an object of pity or scorn. **The important lesson here is to understand that it is not always wise to imagine that one particular character speaks for the playwright**; good writers, recognising the complex and contradictory nature of their subject matter, will usually offer a number of angles of vision in order that the play presents the audience with some sense of just how complicated the issue is.

The playwright has conscious and unconscious intentions

We have seen in Chapter 2 how Western theatre forms often developed out of a desire to explain, or challenge, the prevailing social conditions. Hence, the playwright's primary intention is to **communicate** her or his view of these conditions to a potential audience. These views are embedded in the play's meanings, but because, as we have seen, theatre consists of a system of signs and symbols which are always ambiguous, the audience may see more layers of meaning in the play than the playwright intended. If this happens, and we see some meaning that was never intended, it does not necessarily mean that we have 'got it wrong'. **The writer sets out with *conscious intentions* to communicate meanings; but any art-making is also susceptible to the artist's *unconscious mind*.**

Sometimes, unbeknown to the artist, the unconscious mind will layer in deeper levels of meaning than those which are consciously intended. Often, these unconscious meanings will only surface when the work of art is placed before a reader or spectator. The 'reader' sees beyond the artist's conscious intentions to the unconscious mind, which has also been at work in the making of the art-work. When the poet has completed a poem, it appears printed on the page, ready for the reader; similarly, when the sculptor's work is finished, it is offered for public view at an exhibition. In theatre, the process is more complicated. The playwright's work is never put before an audience until the written word has been transformed into the living, dynamic performance we see on the stage. And before the play reaches the stage, it must, of course, undergo a period of preparation and rehearsal.

The director must interpret the playwright's intentions

Preparing a play for public performance is the job of the director. The director's role is considered in full in Chapter 6, but it is worth making a few observations here about the *interpretative* function that the director fulfils. As you saw in Chapter 6, some directors see their job as being to interpret the playwright's intentions and create a production that is faithful to the original conception (in so far as this can be known). Others view their interpretative function more creatively, and see the playwright's work as a pretext for a bolder and more adventurous production. But, whatever the case, it is useful for us to view the director as the **primary interpreter** of the playwright's work.

Interpretation

We have already seen how the ambiguity of an art-work can give rise to different readings or interpretations. This is not to suggest that any old interpretation will do. For example, over the years, there have been a number of interesting interpretations of *King Lear*, but any interpretation designed with the intention of transforming ***Shakespeare***'s text into a comedy would, in the normal run of events, be rejected as unworkable and invalid.

Interpretations need to be logical and reasoned

Generally speaking then, interpretations will be valid within certain limits. A playwright's text will stand a variety of directors' interpretations, but an interpretation could only be considered valid if the director was able to provide a **reasoned justification** for it, and if the interpretation can be **supported by the text** itself.

As you develop more confidence in your own analytic skills, you will be able to offer your own original interpretations of the plays you read. But always remember that you need to argue your case patiently, rationally and carefully. You will have more chance of persuading others that your interpretation is valid if a body of supporting evidence backs it up.

The great classic plays achieve their eminence because they have something fundamental to say about the human condition. Because they touch on universal areas of experience, they are plays that we can return to time and time again. Each time we revisit them, we see something new. They teach us a little more about what it means to be human.

The classic plays are the ones that are open to the greatest number of interpretations

This is probably why the classic plays are the ones that are open to the greatest number of interpretations. And it is probably why, in the twentieth century, we are used to seeing new and bolder interpretations of the classics. It is not uncommon to see productions of *Shakespeare*'s plays set in eighteenth century period costume, or in Edwardian times, or in modern dress.

If a director decides to set, say, *The Tempest* in modern dress, then this is because his or her interpretation suggests that the themes of the play are relevant to contemporary society, as well as to the fictional and magical world of Prospero's island. Some might argue that to set *The Tempest* in modern dress is pushing the limits of interpretation. In support of their position, they might point to the fact that Prospero's magic is not believable within a twentieth-century context, or that the fantastical spirit figure of Ariel and the savage slave Caliban are out of place in a contemporary setting. **The bolder the director's vision, the more likely it is to provoke discussion and argument about the validity of the interpretation.**

Rehearsals begin from the director's interpretation

At the beginning of the rehearsal period, the director has to justify the validity of her or his interpretation to the actors who will have to make it work in performance. Assuming that the director is successful in this, the actors (who also have a creative and interpretative function to fulfil) will be keen to bring their own ideas to the process.

An essential part of the director's job is to find out which of his or her ideas are feasible, and which do not work. The director will be keen to harness the creativity and inventiveness of the actors in order to test out those ideas in practice. For example, the actor cast as Ariel in the modern dress version of *The Tempest* will have to discover (with the director's help) how the spirit can be played in such a way that it is compatible with the contemporary setting. As a result of the actors' input, the director's original conception will perhaps need to be modified as the production begins to take shape.

The acid test of the director's interpretation

The acid test of the director's interpretation comes on the first night when the production opens. This is why the work of the playwright, director and actor is not complete until it has been publicly performed. Indeed, the word '**performance**' is derived from the Old French verb *parfournir*, which means 'to complete', where 'completion' refers to the act of communication (with an audience).

Different spectators come to the theatre with diverse expectations. Some will come to our imaginary modern-dress production of *The Tempest* never having read or seen the play before; one or two may come having seen every British production of the play in the last 40 years. The former will undoubtedly have some expectations of a *Shakespeare* play, and may be pleasantly surprised to find that the modern setting helps them grasp part of the play's meaning. They may not be unduly bothered by the fact that the production is pushing the limits of interpretation. The latter might have seen Trevor ***Nunn***'s ***Royal Shakespeare Company*** 'white magic' production, and believe that this is the definitive *Tempest*. They may therefore feel that the contemporary setting makes a nonsense of *Shakespeare*'s play. The likelihood is that these spectators will reject the new interpretation as invalid because it is at odds with the range of possibilities they are prepared to accept as a result of their intimate acquaintance with the play.

Our first group of spectators may be happy to accept the director's new interpretation because it seems to make perfect sense. They perceive in the play the pattern of meanings that the director's interpretation has attempted to bring out, and are also able to see a significance beyond what the director intended. Their **secondary interpretation** builds on the primary interpretation *and* the playwright's original conception.

As a result of being exposed to the play in performance, spectators may begin to form their own interpretations of the work they have been watching. The play as written, and the performance as staged, are bound together in an **interdependent relationship** (the play needs the production just as much as the production needs the play). The director's 'reading' (even if it is a daring new interpretation) will inevitably shed light on the playwright's original conception. What the individual spectator takes away from the encounter with the play may be a vague sense of the play's rich fabric of meaning, or it may be a profound understanding of the director's insight into the intentions of the playwright.

We have now considered some of the ways in which plays and other literary texts can be read. In the next chapter we will set out a model for making a full-scale analysis of a dramatic text.

A Director's Model for Textual Analysis

Outline

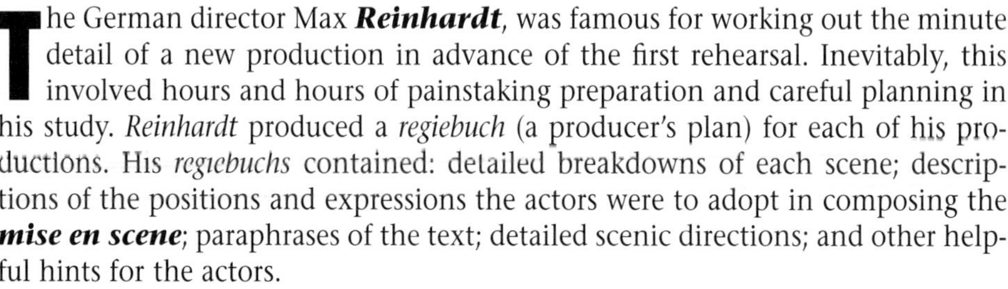

The German director Max ***Reinhardt***, was famous for working out the minute detail of a new production in advance of the first rehearsal. Inevitably, this involved hours and hours of painstaking preparation and careful planning in his study. *Reinhardt* produced a *regiebuch* (a producer's plan) for each of his productions. His *regiebuchs* contained: detailed breakdowns of each scene; descriptions of the positions and expressions the actors were to adopt in composing the ***mise en scene***; paraphrases of the text; detailed scenic directions; and other helpful hints for the actors.

Breaking down a play text

Not all directors are as methodical as *Reinhardt*, preferring instead to experiment with ideas and solve problems as they arise during the rehearsal process. But **every director who embarks on a new production of a play**, irrespective of their preferred rehearsal methods, **will have undertaken a thorough analysis of the play text prior to meeting the designer, actors and production team**. Different directors have their own particular methods of analysis, so there is no generally accepted way to proceed. Although the model we offer here is not the only way of undertaking an analysis, it does represent a comprehensive way of breaking down a play text into its constituent parts.

Directors, of course, are not the only theatre professionals who engage in this kind of detailed analysis. Set, costume, lighting and sound designers all have specific responsibilities in the production process, but each one needs to approach their own work with a thorough understanding of the whole play. The actor(s) who is to perform in the play also needs to subject the text to detailed study so that they understand how their part fits into the larger scheme of things. Some theatres employ a *dramaturge*, whose job it is to act as a literary adviser to the artistic director and/or the theatre management – the *dramaturge*, too, makes use of analytic skills in order to assess the suitability of plays for performance.

In addition to the professionals, of course, students taking A level and undergraduate theatre studies, performing arts and drama courses also need to be equipped with the tools of analysis!

We suggest that this chapter should be read in parallel with your study of a full length set text. At the end of the chapter you will find a textual analysis questionnaire, which you can use to help you organise your study of the text. As we go through the chapter we will suggest when to apply the questionnaire to your study of the set text. In this chapter we will explain the headings that we suggest you use for organising your analysis of the set text and give you examples drawn from different periods, styles and genres. You can read our advice and apply it by using the questionnaire.

We recommend looking at a play under five main headings:

1 the **given circumstances**;
2 the play's **language**;
3 the **dramatic action**;
4 the **characters**;
5 the playwright's **intention**, or **ruling idea**.

Each of these main headings is then broken down into a number of sub-headings.

Because the model seeks to cover all of the major aspects of a play's structure, as well as its content, it may well be the case that some of the sub-headings are not appropriate for *all* plays. For example, under the sub-heading 'Environmental facts' in the 'Given circumstances' section, the model suggests that the economic, political, social and religious environments should be taken into account. Clearly, when analysing ***Brecht***'s play, *Galileo*, the religious background will be of enormous significance, but this is unlikely to be the case in an analysis of *Brecht*'s *Resistible Rise of Arturo Ui*.

Our model is intended to be used by directors for the pre-rehearsal analysis of the text. It focuses on what the director needs to be aware of and think about so that they can begin work with the actors and designers. We have based our model on the work of the American teacher Frances Hodge in *Play Directing: Analysis, Communication and Style*.

The Given Circumstances

As we now know, this term is borrowed from the work of ***Stanislavski***, and we are already familiar with it from the acting workshop on *The Crucible*. It refers to the **essential information** about the past histories of the characters, their relationships, and the background against which these histories and relationships are set. For the purposes of analysis we can subdivide the given circumstances into three separate but complementary parts: the environmental facts and background; the previous action, or important events, that precede the opening of the play; and the principal polar attitudes (the protagonist/antagonist) that produce the tension and conflict in the play.

Environmental Facts and Background

Geographical location

As we have already noted, some playwrights are explicit about the location of their plays – for example, Sarah *Kane's* play, *Blasted*, takes place in an expensive hotel room in Leeds. The spacious, expensive, interior setting of *Blasted* suggests luxury, comfort and warmth, and these conditions will have a particular effect on the characters' behaviour (which would be different if they were in a cheap boarding house). At the end of the second scene there is a huge explosion, and, at the beginning of Scene 3, we learn that a mortar bomb has ripped away one of the walls. The intrusion of the brutal external world into the luxury of the expensive hotel significantly changes the way the characters behave.

Ibsen tells us that *An Enemy of the People* takes place in a coastal town in southern Norway. The geographical location of the play will give some indication as to the likely weather conditions, but other clues are to be found in the text. Mayor Stockmann enters his living-room wearing an overcoat, so we would be justified in assuming that the weather outside is cold. Cold weather affects people differently to warm weather, so we could generally expect the behaviour of *Ibsen*'s Scandinavian characters to be rather different from the behaviour of ***Lorca***'s Mediterranean characters in the hot, dusty setting of *Yerma*.

Where the location is not specified in the stage directions, or cannot be deduced from textual clues, it is usually safe to assume that the behaviour of the characters is not significantly affected by location or climate.

Date and time

Occasionally, a playwright will be quite specific about the **year** in which a play, or a scene from the play, is set. This is usually the case when the play deals with documented historical events: ***Brecht***'s *Galileo* takes place in the final years of Galielo's life, in the 1630s and 1640s, and, logically, Peter ***Weiss***' play, the *Marat/Sade*, has to be set during the years in which the Marquis de Sade was incarcerated in the asylum at Charenton. If a playwright tells you that their play is set 'today', or 'in the present', it poses something of a problem. Does the author want the play to be set in the year that it was written, or are they telling us that it should be updated to coincide with the new date of production? If we assume the latter we have to be convinced that the play will work in a modern setting.

On balance, it is probably safest to assume that the setting should approximately coincide with the year that the play was written.

In some plays, it is the **season** which is important, rather than the year. The action of *A Doll's House* takes place over the Christmas holiday period. *Ibsen* has chosen his season with particular care. In the West, Christmas is traditionally a time of year when families come together to celebrate, and the fact that Nora abandons her family at precisely this time is calculated to increase the sense of shock the audience should feel at the end of the play. ***Strindberg***'s *Miss Julie* takes place on midsummer's eve, and in his Author's Preface the playwright tells us that the festive and magical atmosphere of the midsummer celebrations is an important factor in *Miss Julie*, allowing her to be seduced by the servant, Jean.

Where the season is specified, it is usually worth asking: what is the dramatic effect of setting the play (or scene) at this particular time of year?

Sometimes the playwright will indicate that the action takes place at a particular **time of day**. The two acts of Samuel ***Beckett***'s *Waiting for Godot* take place in the evening. Estragon and Vladimir return to the same place each evening to wait for the mysterious figure of Godot, who never arrives. Because the second act has the same kind of circularity as the first, Beckett perhaps wants us to infer that they spend all of their evenings waiting, day after day. Evening precedes nightfall, and nightfall is often symbolically associated with death. If Godot represents death, then evening becomes significant because night (death) beckons; evening becomes a kind of 'chamber' in which the two men wait for death.

The significance of a particular time of day is always worth considering.

Timescale

In performance, plays usually last anything between an hour and a half and three hours. But the **timescale** which is covered in that short space of time varies enormously from play to play. At one extreme, the time it takes for a play to run in performance may coincide exactly with the amount of time it would take for those events to unfold in reality. For example, the running time of the *Marat/Sade* corresponds with the amount of time it would take for the events depicted there to actually happen.

At the other extreme, some plays span many years; David ***Hare***'s play, *Plenty*, covers three decades. And, in between, there are an infinite number of possibilities: from the four or five hours covered by ***Shakespeare***'s *Comedy of Errors*, through the few days over the Christmas holiday in *A Doll's House*, and the months it takes for Jimmy Porter and Alison to lose their unborn child in John ***Osborne***'s *Look Back in Anger*, to the years *Brecht* needs to chronicle the rise to power of *Arturo Ui*.

Economic environment

In any textual analysis, it is usually worth considering how the economic environment significantly impacts on the lives of the characters. All of the classical Greek and Roman tragedies, as well as many of the plays of the Elizabethan and Jacobean playwrights, deal with the lives of kings, princes and other high-born nobility, for whom money is rarely a factor. But in some plays, the economic environment has a very significant effect in determining the destinies of the characters. Many of *Shakespeare*'s plays include 'lower-class' characters (for example, in *Henry IV, Pt. 1*, Falstaff and his companions plan robberies in the tavern), and several seventeenth century comedies concern themselves with the whole economic spectrum. In Ben ***Jonson***'s *Bartholomew Fair* we see how the poorer characters try to earn a living by playing on the weaknesses, foibles and follies of the well-to-do. In a more modern context, many of Noel ***Coward***'s plays depict the somewhat decadent lifestyles of the 'upper classes', while at the other extreme, Jim ***Cartwright***'s *Road* shows his various characters grappling with the consequences of terrible poverty. In Arthur ***Miller***'s *Death of a Salesman*, it is Willie Loman's sense of professional failure and his inability to adequately provide for his family that leads ultimately to his suicide.

Social environment

Often the social and economic environments are intimately connected, and it is sometimes difficult to separate the two, simply because our social position (or class) is so closely tied in with our economic status. As we have suggested above, *Shakespeare* and many of his contemporaries were acutely aware of the class differences to be found in Elizabethan and Jacobean England and many of their plays reflect this social diversity. The social environment also provided a significant backdrop to the nineteenth-century drama, where class differences often determined the destinies of the characters. As the title of Tom ***Robertson***'s play suggests, *Caste* describes the obstacles that the wealthy George d'Alroy has to overcome before he can marry the woman he loves – the 'lower-class' actress, Esther. In analysing the characters who appear in a play, attention should always be paid to relative social status and background: try to work out which characters have the most social 'prestige', and which tend to be dismissed on account of their 'inferior' social status. In *Ibsen*'s *Hedda Gabler*, for example, Hedda's social standing as the daughter of the renowned General Gabler sets her head and shoulders above the profligate and dissolute Eilert Loevborg.

Political environment

The various 'political theatre' movements of the twentieth century have provided us with a number of plays in which the political background is by far the most significant factor in shaping the dramatic events. Trevor ***Griffiths***' play, *The Party*, offers a sustained analysis of the various factional groupings on the political left, and the plays of the Chilean playwright, Ariel ***Dorfman*** are mostly set against the backdrop of General Pinochet's ruthless, fascist regime.

Shakespeare wrote a number of plays in which political events are portrayed. Most obvious, perhaps, is *Coriolanus*, but in any textual analysis it would be unwise to ignore the political landscape of *Richard III*, or *Antony and Cleopatra*. In plays like this, the importance of the political environment is very obvious, but in many other plays the influence exerted by the political background is more subtle, but no less significant. The stuffy, political conservativism of late nineteenth-century Scandinavia is an important, but understated, feature of *Ibsen*'s work; and ***Chekhov*** was politically attuned to the changes which were about to happen in Russia at the turn of the nineteenth century.

The important lesson here is not to dismiss the political landscape simply because it does not present itself as immediately obvious. Clues can often be found by researching the significant real-world social and political events that coincided with the writing of the play.

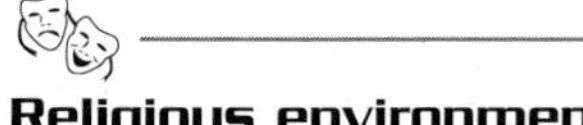

Religious environment

As with the political environment, the significance of the religious environment will be more or less evident from play to play, and in some historical dramas the religious and the political are closely connected. The religious background of Greek tragedy cannot be ignored: it is not uncommon for gods, or goddesses, to make an appearance, and we are constantly made aware, often by means of the chorus, of how the gods are at work, determining the destinies of the principal characters. Similarly, the religious environment of the medieval mystery and morality plays is difficult to ignore.

As the power of religious conviction and the strength of religious belief has declined somewhat in the twentieth century, the significance of the religious environment is less prominent in many modern plays. *Lorca* is a notable exception. His major works are set against the backdrop of Spanish Catholicism, and the behaviour of his characters is profoundly affected by the religious expectations of the rural peasantry. In T.S. ***Eliot***'s *Murder in the Cathedral*, a complex relationship exists between the religious background and the political situation surrounding Henry VIII's decision to divorce Catherine of Aragon. Substantial research would be necessary in order to get a firm grasp of these historical events.

Arthur ***Miller***'s *The Crucible* provides an even more complicated example of the relationship between religious and political factors. The repressive puritanism of seventeenth-century New England permeates the play, so a thorough analysis would require detailed research into the historical background of puritanism. But as we have already seen in the acting workshop on playing the given circumstances, *Miller* wrote the play intending to draw parallels between the proceedings of the House Committee on Un-American Activities. Research into the background surrounding the political witch-hunt of the 1950s would also be required to gain a full understanding of *Miller*'s play. Generally speaking, however, the religious influences working on the characters in contemporary plays are harder to discern and evaluate.

Careful character analysis will sometimes reveal how religious beliefs shape behaviour, but clues can be hard to find.

Previous Action

In classically constructed plays, the exposition usually comes in Act 1

We have already introduced the term ***exposition***, which refers in part to the events that took place before the action of the play begins. In classically constructed plays, the exposition usually comes in Act 1 and furnishes the audience with the necessary background for them to make sense of what is about to happen.

An obvious illustration of how a playwright immediately sketches in 'the story so far' is to be found in ***Shakespeare***'s *Comedy of Errors*. Here, the complete background to the play is revealed in the first 140 lines. The merchant from Syracuse, Egeon, under threat of execution, explains to the Duke of Ephesus how he came to be in the city. Essentially, he is looking for his twin sons. He explains that, on a sea voyage, he and his wife were separated during a fearful storm. Egeon is rescued, and ends up with one of the twins in Syracuse. He knows that his wife and the other twin were also rescued, but has no idea what became of them subsequently. He reports how his son became curious about his twin brother, and set out on a journey to find him. When his son fails to return, Egeon himself sets out on a journey to discover his whereabouts, and as part of these travels, he arrives in Ephesus, ignorant of the law which forbids any Syracusan merchant to set foot in the city. It quickly becomes clear that, unbeknown to Egeon, the son he is searching for has also just arrived in Ephesus where, unbeknown to both of them, the lost twin has been living for most of his life. Thus the scene is set for the series of 'errors' that are referred to in the play's title.

Sometimes, essential information referring to previous action is scattered throughout the play

It is not always the case, however, that the complete background is revealed at the very beginning of a play. Sometimes, essential information referring to previous action is scattered throughout. In ***Ibsen***'s *Hedda Gabler*, the full details of Hedda's past relationship with Eilert Loevborg are only revealed gradually, and the complete picture has to be pieced together, bit by bit. 'Scattered exposition' is very much a feature of ***Chekhov***'s plays.

Each scene of a play, therefore, has to be read very carefully for any clues that might indicate what has happened in the past lives of the characters. The amount of information available varies from writer to writer, and from play to play. Usually, *Ibsen* is kind to the reader, providing plenty of detailed background for his major characters, whereas in Harold ***Pinter***'s early plays (for example, *The Birthday Party* and *The Caretaker*), he is notoriously vague about the background and past histories of his characters.

As you read, keep a note of any background information that the playwright provides in relation to:

- the **past histories of the characters** (e.g. Hedda's relationship with Loevborg);
- **significant events that took place before the play begins** (e.g. details of Hedda and Tesman's honeymoon).

Sometimes it may appear, as you read, that a detail is incidental or too insignificant to be noteworthy; but remember that it is rare for a major playwright to include detail which is irrelevant to the action of the play.

Protagonist/Antagonist

Identify the opposing attitudes held by the principal characters in the play

Plays are full of: enemies who oppose each other in battle (e.g. *Richard III*); adversaries who argue over a burning issue (e.g. who has the right to bring up the child in ***Brecht***'s *Caucasian Chalk Circle*); families which tear themselves apart (e.g. *Death of a Salesman*); husbands and wives who constantly bicker and argue (e.g. Edward ***Albee***'s *Who's Afraid of Virginia Woolf?*); lovers betrayed (e.g. *Troilus and Cressida*); and friends who part company (e.g. Prince Hal and Falstaff in *Henry IV*, Pt. 2). At the heart of almost all plays is a tension which arises from a conflict in beliefs, values and attitudes. The sharpest expression of this conflict is usually to be found in the attitudes held by the ***protagonist*** and the ***antagonist***. So, it makes sense to look for and identify the opposing attitudes held by the principal characters in the play.

In *Shakespeare's Henry IV*, Pt. 1, the principal conflicting attitudes are to be found in Prince Hal and Hotspur. The comparison between them is drawn by the king in the very first scene of the play: he despairs of the prince, his son, saying that 'riot and dishonour stain the brow of my young Harry', while he views Hotspur as 'sweet fortune's minion and her pride'. However, the king is deceived by appearances, and it is quickly confirmed for the audience that Prince Hal and Hotspur are indeed 'opposites', but not in the way the king imagines. In the second scene, the prince tells us that his behaviour is carefully calculated, and, throughout the play we become aware of his true 'kingly' qualities: his courage and heroism, his modesty, his generosity and his versatility. By contrast, the king's view of Hotspur is also quickly dispelled, as we learn that he is hot-headed, boastful, arrogant and self-obsessed.

The *true* attitudes and qualities of the two characters are revealed during the course of the play, so that our first impressions (heavily influenced by the king's comparison) are gradually modified as we find out more about them. When we attempt to identify this conflict in the early stages of the play, we should always bear in mind that our view of these attitudes is liable to change as we make further discoveries about the characters; and the attitudes, at the end of the play, may have changed quite radically in response to the events that we have witnessed. We should, therefore, attempt to chart how these original conflicting attitudes change as the action of the play progresses. In a modern play like *Look Back in Anger*, Jimmy Porter, the central character, is outspoken, abrasive and explosive; but at the end of the play, after learning about his wife's miscarriage, he is altogether different.

Task 1: Identify the given circumstances

Turn to the textual analysis questionnaire and complete Section 1, The given circumstances for your set text. There are questions and prompts to help you. In order to complete this section you will need to read the whole play at least once.

Language

Language reveals character

It is usually the case that the play text consists mostly of dialogue. Hence, in any textual analysis we will do well to **pay particular attention to the spoken word.** The language used by each of the characters will usually have its own distinctive idiom, and careful study of the dialogue will tell us a great deal about the following.

Social class: does the character's language reveal their social status?	Compare, for example, the way Henry Higgins and Eliza Doolittle speak in ***Shaw***'s *Pygmalion.*
The character's image of self: what does the character say about him/herself?	Examine, for example, the self-important tones of Malvolio in ***Shakespeare***'s *Twelfth Night*, and Othello's address to the Senators in Act 1, Scene 3 of *Othello.* (See page 147).
The character's view of others: how does the character talk to others and what is said about other characters?	Look, for example, at the contemptuous way in which Caius Marcius speaks to the citizens of Rome in the opening scene of ***Shakespeare***'s *Coriolanus.*

It is useful to examine the language in a play under four headings:

- the characters' choice of words, or **vocabulary;**
- how the characters' phrases and sentences are put together (the **structure** of the language);
- how **imagery** is used; and
- any **peculiarities** in a character's speech.

Vocabulary

The actual words used by a character often convey a great deal of information about them. If we look carefully at the restricted vocabularies of the characters in Edward ***Bond***'s *Saved*, we immediately become aware of their working-class environment, and their somewhat limited educational backgrounds. In Arnold ***Wesker***'s *Roots*, we are quickly struck by the contrast between Beattie's more self-conscious, 'elevated' language (influenced, as it is, by her 'intellectual' boyfriend, Ronnie) and her mother's much more direct, down-to-earth choice of vocabulary. The university-educated Jimmy Porter in *Look Back in Anger* metaphorically batters all those around him with his carefully-chosen, intimidating barrage of sophisticated insults (at one point he refers to his wife as 'The Lady Pusillanimous').

Generally speaking, in looking at a character's choice of vocabulary, we might consider some or all of the following questions:

- Does the character use slang, everyday speech, or a more formal (or 'posh') vocabulary?
- Does the character use monosyllables?
- Does the character speak plainly and to the point, or does he or she 'beat about the bush'?
- Do words 'come easy', or does the character struggle to put thoughts and feelings into words?
- Is the character easy or awkward in conversation with others?
- Does the character speak to everyone in the same way, or does the character adjust his or her vocabulary according to who he or she is speaking to?
- What does the vocabulary tell us about the character's general level of education?
- Does the character use specialist vocabulary or jargon, and if so what does this tell us about him or her?
- Does the character use words to abuse and intimidate others, or to 'show off', or to 'put others down'?

Taken together, the answers to these questions can provide some real insight into the background and psychology of a character.

Structure

The way in which the vocabulary is strung together into phrases and sentences makes up the structure of a character's speech. Vocabulary and structure work very much in tandem, and we would normally expect someone who has a good command of language to also be fluent when it comes to putting the words together. The structure of Jimmy Porter's speeches varies enormously; he is equally at home with the punchy, one-line put-down and the more extended and elaborate sardonic diatribe. By contrast, the characters in *Saved* tend to speak in short, simple and direct sentences. Many of the questions we listed in the 'vocabulary' section would also apply to the structural aspects of a character's language.

Task 2: Stucture of language exercise

Look at the following speech. These are Othello's words, spoken to the Venetian Senate, in reply to Brabantio's accusation that his daughter, Desdemona, has been bewitched, and stolen away, by Othello.

1 *Othello*: Most potent, grave, and reverend signiors,
2 My very noble and approv'd good masters,
3 That I gave ta'en away this old man's daughter,
4 It is most true; true, I have married her:
5 The very head and front of my offending
6 Hath this extent, no more. Rude am I in my speech,
7 And little bless'd with the soft phrase of peace;
8 For since these arms of mine hath seven years pith,
9 Till now some nine moons wasted, they have us'd
10 Their dearest action in the tented field;
11 And little of this great world can I speak,
12 More than pertains to feats of broil and battle;
13 And therefore little shall I grace my cause
14 In speaking for myself. Yet, by your gracious patience,

I will a round unvarnish'd tale deliver
Of my whole course of love; what drugs, what charms,
What conjuration, and what mighty magic,
For such proceeding I am charg'd withal,
I won his daughter.

In line 6, Othello says that he is 'rude' (i.e. 'rough' or 'crude') in his speech. Let's see if we agree with him. To begin with, look at the structure of the 19-line speech:

1. **How many sentences are there?**
2. **Look at each of these sentences in turn: what do you notice about them?**
3. **Take the sentences in turn and try to determine what Othello's *intention* is in each. Put yourself in the position of one of the Venetian Senators: from these few lines, what impression do you form of him? Are you inclined to believe Brabantio's accusations, or Othello's account of events? Why?**

This brief examination of Othello's words should illustrate that there is a great deal to be learned about him simply from the way in which his sentences are structured. So careful attention to the structural aspects of a character's speeches will almost always repay study.

Structural features of the dialogue can also provide us with important clues about the rhythm and pace of a scene. Always look at the relative lengths of the speeches: where the lines are short (and aren't broken by 'pauses' or 'silences') we can usually assume that the scene should be played at a reasonable pace; longer speeches usually indicate that a more leisurely pace is appropriate. If one of the characters has longer speeches than anyone else, it is a fairly strong indication that this character dominates the scene, and controls the pace at which it should be played.

Imagery

In studying ***Shakespeare***'s plays in English courses, we have probably all learned about how **the pattern of imagery in the play provides important clues to the meaning.** In *The Merchant of Venice*, in keeping with the background of commerce and trade, we are struck by the number of references to gold, silver and other precious metals and stones. The blood imagery in *Macbeth* is appropriate in a play which deals with a ruthlessly ambitious couple who will, literally, stop at nothing to gain the throne. But it is not only *Shakespeare*, and the other Elizabethans and Jacobeans, who use imagery to such telling effect in their work. Based on the pattern of images he perceived in ***Ibsen***'s play, the celebrated Russian director, Vsevlod ***Meyerhold*** set out to create a cold, regal, autumnal *Hedda Gabler*. The animal imagery in *Look Back in Anger* (bears and squirrels) offers a telling commentary on the relationship between Jimmy and Alison.

So, the lesson is clear: **pay careful attention to the patterns of images that playwrights weave into their plays, and try to assess what clues the imagery provides to some of the deeper layers of meaning.**

Peculiarities of speech

Occasionally, you will find characters who have quite distinctive and peculiar speech patterns. Probably the most famous of all is Mrs Malaprop in ***Sheridan***'s eighteenth century play, *The Rivals*, who persistently confuses one word for another. She refers to another character in the play as 'the very **pineapple** of politeness', when she really means to say 'the very **pinnacle** of politeness'. Although this kind of mistake is now widely known as a 'malapropism', it was not invented by *Sheridan*. In *Shakespeare*'s play, *Much Ado About Nothing*, the constable, Dogberry, is prone to making the same kind of mistake.

Where a character is given this kind of peculiarity, we should try to judge what the effect is likely to be on the audience. Clearly, the effect of Mrs Malaprop's mistakes is to make the audience laugh by making her an object of ridicule. Often the effect of an exaggerated peculiarity is to irritate; and when an audience becomes irritated by a peculiarity of speech, then, by extension, they are also likely to quickly become irritated by the character. But some peculiarities of speech can have the opposite effect of endearing the character to the audience. As a conscious opposite to Jimmy Porter in *Look Back in Anger*, ***Osborne*** gives his friend Cliff a slightly old-fashioned, 'folksy' Welsh idiom when he tries to protect Alison from Jimmy's verbal onslaughts. This gentle, consoling tone makes him a character for whom we have enormous sympathy. Sarah *Kane* tells us that Cate, in *Blasted*, speaks with a stutter when she is under stress; hence the playwright wants us to know that this character is prone to feelings of anxiety.

Dialects and marked accents, either regional or foreign, can also be described as peculiarities. In *Roots*, ***Wesker*** makes it very clear in his writing that Beattie's mother, Mrs Bryant, should have a broad Norfolk accent, the effect of which is to reinforce her narrow-minded parochialism, but also to provide a contrast to Beattie who consciously 'parrots' Ronnie's ideas in an effort to sound more refined and worldly than she really is. Where a dialect, or accent, is indicated in a play text it is usually for a specific purpose, and we should try to work out why it is important for us to see this character as different. (Where the playwright indicates that *all* of the characters speak the same dialect, it is usually because she or he wishes to reinforce the importance of the regional setting.)

Task 3: *Hedda Gabler* exercise

We are going to look at a passage from *Ibsen*'s *Hedda Gabler*, and subject the language of Hedda and her husband, George Tesman, to some detailed scrutiny. (You do not need to know the play in order to complete this exercise.)

This is the section where we first meet Hedda. She and her husband have just returned from their honeymoon. Hearing that the newly-weds have arrived home, Juliana, Tesman's maiden aunt, has called to pay her respects. Prior to the section we are interested in, there has, first of all, been a short conversation between Tesman's aunt and Bertha, the maid; and then a brief exchange between Tesman and his aunt.

***Miss Tesman*:** **(*goes to greet her*) Good morning, Hedda dear! Good morning!**

***Hedda*:** **(*holds out her hand*) Good morning, dear Miss Tesman. What an early hour to call. So kind of you.**

***Miss Tesman*:** **(*seems somewhat embarrassed*) And has the young bride slept well in her new home?**

***Hedda*:** **Oh – thank you, yes. Passably well.**

***Tesman*:** **(*laughs*) Passably? I say. Hedda, that's good! When I jumped out of bed, you were sleeping like a top.**

***Hedda*:** **Yes. Fortunately. One has to accustom oneself to**

anything new, Miss Tesman. It takes time. (*Looks left.*) Oh, that maid's left the french windows open. This room's flooded with sun.

Miss Tesman: (*goes towards the windows*) Oh – let me close them.

Hedda: No, no, don't do that. Tesman dear, draw the curtains. This light's blinding me.

Tesman: (*at the windows*) Yes, yes, dear. There, Hedda, now you've got shade and fresh air.

Hedda: This room needs fresh air. All these flowers – ! But my dear Miss Tesman, won't you take a seat?

Miss Tesman: No, really not, thank you. I just wanted to make sure you have everything you need. I must see about getting back home. My poor dear sister will be waiting for me.

Tesman: Be sure to give her my love, won't you? Tell her I'll run over and see her later today.

Miss Tesman: Oh yes, I'll tell her that. Oh, George – (*Fumbles in the pocket of her skirt.*) I almost forgot. I've brought something for you.

Tesman: What's that, Auntie Juju? What?

Miss Tesman: (*pulls out a flat package, wrapped in newspaper and gives it to him*) Open and see, dear boy.

Tesman: (*opens the package*) Good heavens! Auntie Juju, you've kept them! Hedda, this is really very touching. What?

Hedda: (*by the what-nots, on the right*) What is it, Tesman?

Tesman: My old shoes! My slippers, Hedda!

Hedda: Oh, them. I remember you kept talking about them on our honeymoon.

Tesman: Yes, I missed them dreadfully. (*Goes over to her.*) Here, Hedda, take a look.

Hedda: (*goes away towards the stove*) Thanks, I won't bother.

Tesman: (*follows her*) Fancy, Hedda, Auntie Rena's embroidered them for me. Despite her being so ill. Oh, you can't imagine what memories they have for me.

Hedda: (*by the table*) Not for me.

Miss Tesman: No, Hedda's right there, George.

Tesman: Yes, but I thought since she's one of the family now –

Hedda: (*interrupts*) Tesman, we really can't go on keeping this maid.

Miss Tesman: Not keep Bertha?

Tesman: What makes you say that, dear? What?

Hedda: (*points*) Look at that! She's left her old hat lying on the chair.

Tesman: (*appalled, drops his slippers on the floor*) But, Hedda – !

Hedda: Suppose someone came in and saw it?

Tesman: But, Hedda – that's Auntie Juju's hat.

Hedda: Oh?

Miss Tesman: (*picks up the hat*) Indeed it's mine. And it doesn't happen to be old, Hedda dear.

Hedda: I didn't look at it very closely, Miss Tesman.

Miss Tesman: (*tying on the hat*) As a matter of fact, it's the first time I've worn it. As the good Lord is my witness.

Tesman: It's very pretty, too. Really smart.

Miss Tesman: Oh, I'm afraid it's nothing much really. (*Looks round.*) My parasol. Ah, there it is. (*Takes it.*) This is mine, too. (*Murmurs.*) Not Bertha's.

Tesman: A new hat and a new parasol! I say, Hedda, fancy that!

Hedda: Very pretty and charming.

Tesman: Yes, isn't it? What? But Auntie Juju, take a good look at Hedda before you go. Isn't she pretty and charming?

Miss Tesman: Dear boy, there's nothing new in that. Hedda's been a beauty ever since the day she was born. (*Nods and goes right.*)

Tesman: (*follows her*) Yes, but have you noticed how strong and healthy she's looking? And how she's filled out since we went away?

Miss Tesman: (*stops and turns*) Filled out?

Hedda: (*walks across the room*) Oh, can't we forget it.

Tesman: Yes, Auntie Juju – you can't see it so clearly with that dress on. But I've good reason to know –

Hedda: (*by the french windows, impatiently*) You haven't good reason to know anything.

Tesman: It must have been the mountain air up there in the Tyrol –

Hedda: (*curtly, interrupts him*) I'm exactly the same as when I went away.

Tesman: You keep on saying so. But you're not. I'm right, aren't I, Auntie Juju?

Miss Tesman: (*has folded her hands and is gazing at her*) She's beautiful – beautiful. Hedda is beautiful. (*Goes over to Hedda, takes her head between her hands, draws it down and kisses her hair.*) God bless and keep you, Hedda Tesman. For George's sake.

Hedda: (*frees herself politely*) Oh – let me go, please.

Miss Tesman: (*quietly, emotionally*) I shall come and see you both every day.

Tesman: Yes, Auntie Juju, please do. What?

Miss Tesman: Good-bye! Good-bye!

- **Look carefully at the language of Hedda and Tesman (since Miss Tesman is a minor character in the play, we will leave her out of our deliberations). You will need to read through the extract a number of times. When you have done so, fill in the chart below:**

Language		
Category	Hedda	Tesman
Vocabulary		
Structure		
Imagery		
Peculiarities of speech		

Task 4: Identify language features

- **Turn to the textual analysis questionnaire (page 161) and complete Section 2: Language – for your set text.**

Dramatic Action

In the first part of the model, we focused attention on the essential information relating to the environmental facts and background, including the past histories of the characters and the significant events which took place before the play begins. In this section we shall be concentrating on the *action* of the play itself. In the acting workshop on playing the given circumstances, you started to explore, from the **actor's point of view**, the significant action of a short scene from *The Crucible* between John Proctor and his wife, Elizabeth (see pages 57–58). Since you are, by now, very familiar with this scene, we will continue to work with it; but this time we will undertake a broader analysis under three headings: breaking the scene down into **units**; giving descriptive **titles** to the units; and finding a way to express the **sub-text** of each speech.

Break the scenes into units

Stanislavski recommended that, in order to understand the shape, rhythm and true significance of a play, each scene should be divided into its constituent parts; and he called each of these parts a 'unit' of meaning. (If you read some American accounts of the process of directing, you will often find that these units of meaning are referred to as 'beats'.) According to *Stanislavski*, each unit of meaning, or sequence of thought, can be logically marked off from the other parts of the scene as being relatively self-contained.

If we look again at the beginning of the scene between Proctor and Elizabeth, we might identify the first unit as beginning with Elizabeth's line, 'What keeps you so late?' and ending with Proctor's words, 'Aye, the farm is seeded'. In this section, the two characters are, on the surface, simply establishing the reasons for Proctor arriving home later than Elizabeth anticipated. At the simplest level, the unit deals with the demands of running the farm. The next part of Proctor's speech, 'The boys asleep?' represents a change in the line of thought; attention switches from issues relating to farm work to concerns about the family. Where do you think this next unit ends?

Task 5: Breaking a scene into units

Go through the rest of the scene with a partner. Divide it up into units and number them. Make sure that there is a logic to the way in which you have broken down the scene (in a way, the next task is a test of the logic you have brought to bear on your work). This will involve you and your partner agreeing that your breakdown makes good sense. Remember, though, that this is not rocket science. There are no definitive right and wrong answers; breaking down the dialogue in this manner is simply a way of seeing the mechanics of how the playwright has put the scene together. Different directors would probably break up the scene in different ways; the important thing is that you can give logical reasons for your own analysis.

Give each unit a descriptive title

The next stage in analysing the dramatic action is to go back over the units, giving each one a title. **Titles should be descriptive:** this ensures that the title really captures the essence of the unit. Vague or ambiguous titles can be unhelpful and, sometimes, misleading. Sometimes the title can be found in the dialogue itself. If we take the first unit of the scene between Proctor and his wife, we have already noted that it deals with the practical aspects of running the farm. We could borrow the title from words taken from Proctor's last line, 'Seeding the Farm'. Alternatively, we might choose to give it the title, 'A Farmer's Work'. The act of finding a descriptive title for the unit will usually tell us if we have been successful in isolating a single unit of meaning; if two very different, competing, titles suggest themselves, it probably makes sense to go back and look at the unit to make sure that it does not include two or more separate sequences of thought.

Task 6: Naming the units

- **With your partner, look at your breakdown of the Elizabeth/Proctor scene, and give each unit a descriptive title. Once again, try to make sure that you are both in agreement over the titles you select.**

Note how the sub-text should be played

In the previous chapter we distinguished between text and sub-text, and in Task 4 of that chapter you examined a short sequence from *A Doll's House* with a view to exploring the possible sub-textual elements in the exchange between Nora and Mrs Linde (see p. 129). It might be useful, briefly, to turn back to that exercise and remind yourself of the kinds of questions that we posed as a way of discovering what the sub-text might be.

In the analysis of the scene from *The Crucible*, in the acting workshop, you looked at the speeches in order to try and assess whether the spoken text disguises a deeper sub-text. Remember that the scene opens with a question from Elizabeth, 'What keeps you so late?'. If we take the line at face value, it appears that this is a straightforward enough question; but, once we know that Elizabeth is aware of the fact that her husband has had an affair with a much younger woman, then the question assumes much greater significance. We may think that there is an accusation lurking just below the surface. The words 'It's almost dark', seem to reinforce this impression.

In order to really pin down what lies beneath the surface, we could choose a suitable verb to express the sub-text for Elizabeth's opening speech. We might decide that the appropriate verb is 'accuses'. But, if we go a little further, we may think that Proctor's lateness suggests to his wife that he is still continuing the affair, in which case we might choose the verb 'fears' to most accurately convey Elizabeth's sub-text.

Task 7: Adding the sub-text verbs

- **With your partner, go through the scene one last time. Look at each speech in turn, and try to assign the verb that best expresses the sub-text for each of the speeches. Write the verb beside the speech, in the left-hand margin; this way the verb acts almost as a note to the actor who speaks the line.**

Task 8: Identify the dramatic action

- **Turn to the textual analysis questionnaire (p. 160) and complete Section 3: Dramatic action – for your set text or selected scenes from the set-text.**

Characters

We have already noted the important part that character analysis plays in the study of both novels and plays, and we have examined the different kinds of character types that are to be found in literary texts. In the acting workshop on *The Crucible*, we saw how defining objectives provides the character's through-line of action, and leads to the determination of an overall **super-objective**; a statement of what the character is trying to achieve and what is at stake if he or she fails. But, in a full-scale analysis, we can go further.

Super-objective = wants vs. will + moral stance

In order to build up a rounded-out picture of the major characters and their significance within the play, each super-objective can be broken down and studied under a number of sub-headings. We do this by trying to decide what the character's principal **want** is. We can then make some judgement about the strength of the character's **will** in trying to get what they 'want'. Finally, it is useful to assess the character's **moral stance** in relation to these 'wants' (for example, will the character stop at nothing, or are there limits to what they will do in order to achieve their ends?).

We might also find it useful to develop a sense of the **physical appearance** of the character. Having done all of this, our final task in our analysis of character is to draw up a summary list of adjectives that provide us with a full description of the character's qualities and attributes.

He/she wants to . . .

Broadly speaking, **the character's overriding 'want' is contained within the super-objective**. In ***Shakespeare***'s most famous play, Hamlet's want is straight-forward enough: to revenge his father's death. As the action of the play develops, we discover that a number of obstacles stand in the way of him achieving this end. We, therefore, have to examine each scene in which Hamlet appears in order to establish the want that is specific to that scene (for example, in Act 1, Scene 5, Hamlet wants confirmation from the ghost that the new king, Claudius, was responsible for the death of his father).

A careful reading will reveal that the **tension in a play results from the fact that the various characters have different (and sometimes competing) wants**, and one of the purposes of this kind of character analysis is to try to understand, first of all, how these varying wants bring the characters into conflict (the strongest wants are usually manifest in the competing objectives of the ***protagonist*** and ***antagonist***). As the play draws to its end, we may realise that some of these wants are irreconcil-able; Nora wants to escape from the stifling clutches of her husband, while Torvald wants Nora to remain his doll-wife. Clearly, in these circumstances, something has to give – her want prevails and she walks away from her family and her home.

Sometimes, the tension in a play is resolved by the characters reaching a point where their diverse wants have to be negotiated and modified. At the end of *Look Back in Anger*, Jimmy and Alison manage a kind of reconciliation after her miscarriage. Each scene then, has to be carefully examined in order that all of the specific wants are clearly understood. And how these subsidiary wants relate to the principal want is the super-objective that motivates and drives the charac-ter through the play.

But will he/she?

The next consideration is to judge the intensity of the characters' 'will' in achieving their wants. In making this judgement it is important to pay attention to the **actions** of the characters, rather than to their stated **intentions**; to what the characters actually *do*, not to what they *say* they will do.

As we read *Hamlet*, we may begin to question the central character's strength of will. He talks a great deal about his intention to kill Claudius in revenge for his father's death, but his actions betray hesitation, indecision and, at times, paraly-sis. It is not until the very end of the play that we glimpse Hamlet's real determi-nation and strength of will. By contrast, in *King Lear*, the king's youngest daughter, Cordelia, wants to have no part in her father's 'test of love', preferring instead to retain her dignity by speaking plainly and truthfully of her real feelings. She shows an unshakable determination and strength of will (some would say, remarkable foolishness) in her refusal to indulge her father's wishes; and, as a consequence, she is disowned, disinherited and effectively banished. At the heart of ***Ibsen***'s *Hedda Gabler* there is a fatal test of will between Hedda and Eilert Loevborg, the consequence of which is a double suicide.

Sometimes, strong-willed characters are presented as being full of integrity and wholly admirable (Portia in *Merchant of Venice*, for example; and Grusha in ***Brecht***'s *Caucasian Chalk Circle*). But, equally, the kind of iron-willed determi-nation shown by characters like Cordelia and Hedda produces tragic conse-quences. Many plays show us characters engaged in a struggle to overcome their indecision, faint-heartedness and lack of courage, and, here again, the outcomes can vary. In ***Chekhov***'s play, *The Three Sisters*, each is destined never to fulfil her dreams of escaping to Moscow, whereas in ***Strindberg***'s *Miss Julie*, the central character marches from the kitchen to her tragic fate. And, finally, there are those characters who are simply lacking altogether in will: Trigorin, in *Chekhov*'s *The Seagull*, tells Arkadina that he has no will of his own. Consequently, his dominant characteristic is his passivity.

In any thorough analysis, **it is important to try to establish the nature of the relationship between each character's principal want and the strength of will that drives them to achieve it.** However, a moral element often enters into this equation, and this element can present the character with a substantial barrier in getting what they want. We now turn our attentions to this third element in character analysis.

Moral stance: should he/she?

In our everyday lives, most people tend to live by a set of moral standards. Individually we may be more, or less, conscious of these standards and the way they shape our behaviour, and these moral standards anchor our behaviour in a strong sense of what is right and what is wrong. For some people, religious belief underpins their sense of morality, while for others it is a particular political conviction that provides them with their moral orientation. For the majority, perhaps, **our moral outlook comes from a combination of factors: parents, upbringing, education, experience, etc.** Most of us understand that you can't always have what you want: we may desperately want an expensive item of clothing but know we can't afford it; usually, our moral sense of what is right and wrong prevents us from walking into the shop and stealing it.

In general terms, then, we may say that **our moral stance acts as a kind of check, or curb, on our wants.** Some plays revolve around this conflict between want (and the will to pursue it) and moral stance. Macbeth, in his desire to be king, understands perfectly well that murder is morally wrong, but, driven by a sense of destiny (the prophecies of the witches) and his wife's ruthless ambition, he kills Duncan and spends the rest of the play wrestling with the consequences of his amoral action. Some characters seem to have no moral qualms about their actions: in *Othello*, Iago sets out to take his revenge on Othello and his lieutenant, Cassio, in the most cool and calculating manner; and Jacobean *revenge tragedy* is littered with similar Machiavellian types, who set aside all moral considerations in their desire for revenge.

The conflict between want/will and moral stance is often to be found at the heart of a play. In John ***Ford***'s *'Tis Pity She's a Whore*, Giovanni and his sister, Annabella, driven by overwhelming desire, defy the moral taboos surrounding incest and become lovers. In *Brecht*'s *Good Person of Setzuan*, the good-hearted Shen-Te has to transform herself into the morally corrupt Shui-Ta simply in order to survive. In both of these cases, morality is cast aside, and we witness the triumph of want.

This is not always the case – morality can also win the day. In *Shakespeare*'s *Measure for Measure*, Isabella's moral stance, backed up by an iron will, is implacable. Her icy resolve to spurn the advances of Angelo almost brings about her brother's death. In *Ibsen*'s play, *The Wild Duck*, the character of Gregers Werle, driven by his own moral crusade, is responsible for a chain of events that brings tragedy to the Ekdal family.

These examples illustrate how **the interrelations between want, will and moral stance offer playwrights a rich seam to work.** A complete analysis has to take account of all three elements in coming to terms with the complexities of the main characters.

Physical appearance: how does he/she look?

A playwright's text will occasionally determine a character's physical appearance. In *Shakespeare*'s play, Othello is described as a 'Moor', and this tells us that he is black. It would make no sense to ignore this fact, and play Othello as a Caucasian, because, by doing so, a good deal of the text would then be ridiculous. In point of fact, the whole plot revolves around Othello's 'blackness'. In this play, at least, there is no room for doubt: Othello has to be black. (Of course, this has not stopped most of the 'star' actors throughout history 'blacking-up' in order to take on the role, but in the last few years this tendency has almost become obsolete.)

The case of Othello is extremely clear-cut, but textual requirements often provide strong hints about a character's physical appearance: in *Twelfth Night*, Viola's physical appearance is such that she has to be able to pass for a boy when she disguises herself as Cesario; and in *Romeo and Juliet* the lovers are quite definitely teenagers, so it makes sense to cast actors who look fairly young (once again, the history of theatre is full of 'star' actors coming to these roles in middle-age, and Peter ***Brook***'s 1948 production, in which he cast young actors as the lovers, was considered ground-breaking).

It is not uncommon for a playwright to give a fairly detailed description of a character. *Ibsen* tells us not only that Hedda Gabbler is 29 years old, and distinguished, with an aristocratic face and figure, but also that she has a pale complexion, steel-grey eyes and auburn hair.

Textual evidence will also give strong hints about physical appearance. ***Lorca*** never describes the physical characteristics of Yerma and Juan in a stage direction, but we can assume that Yerma is strikingly attractive, since the text tells us that she is capable of turning heads in the street, and we know that Juan is pale and thin, as a result of a conversation he has with Yerma in the very first scene. *Lorca* clearly wants to convey a real physical contrast between the two.

When the playwright gives clues as to the physical appearance of the characters, it is always important to think about what these details add to our general understanding of them.

Who shall we cast?

Sometimes, as we read a text, we will begin to form a picture in our mind's eye of the character whose words we are reading. And, while there may not be any definite clues available to us in the text, our intuition may suggest to us how a particular character might look. An interesting exercise is to try to think of a famous stage, screen or TV actor who you could imagine playing the part.

Summary adjectives: what makes him/her tick?

The final task in building up a rounded picture of the character is to review our findings in relation to want, will, moral stance and physical appearance, and to draw up a list of adjectives which give as full a description as possible.

Task 9: Identify characters

- **Turn to the textual analysis questionnaire (p. 160) and complete Section 4: Characters – for no more that three of the characters in your set text.**

Variations in characterisation

The headings we have used above are intended to help you arrive at as comprehensive a character analysis as possible. However, within the limits imposed by the character's overall consistency, complex characters do tend to vary from scene to scene. A good playwright will show us the many different sides and moods of the characters, and we should **examine each scene carefully in order to try to chart the different moods and intensities of the characters.**

In *The Seagull*, the difference between Konstantin and Trigorin in Act 1 is striking. When we first meet Konstantin he is in a state of tremendous excitement at the prospect of Nina performing the play he has written. His intense excitement shows itself in restlessness, high energy and extreme agitation. In reality, this emotional state would be accompanied by certain bodily sensations: an inability to be still; a faster heart rate; perspiration; and 'butterflies' in the stomach. The contrast with Trigorin, the other writer, is remarkable: he enters unobtrusively, in a group of six which includes Arkadina, and does not speak until the performance is over. Trigorin's mood is relaxed, almost to the point of boredom, so that his bodily sensations will be almost the exact opposite of Konstantin's.

If we then compare Konstantin's mood in Act 4, we find it is very different. He has become disillusioned with his career as a writer and has lost Nina, who ran away and became involved in an affair with Trigorin. After his final encounter with Nina, we see Konstantin standing grim-faced and motionless. He then proceeds deliberately to destroy all of his manuscripts prior to committing suicide. His bodily sensations, following Nina's final departure, will be very different from those which attended his sense of anticipation at the play's beginning: absolute stillness; the 'butterflies' replaced by a knot in the stomach; an overall feeling of tension in the muscles.

In attempting to assess the mood of a character at the beginning of a scene it is important to bear in mind the general characteristics that your overall analysis has revealed. In real life, most people behave with a certain degree of consistency from situation to situation, but within the limits of this consistency we can also be contradictory and unpredictable. We should **pay particular attention whenever a character's behaviour departs significantly from what we have come to expect** (for example, Nora's unexpected departure). **This normally indicates a vital turning-point in the play's action.**

The Playwright's Intention

We are already familiar, from Chapter 2, with the idea that plays can be viewed as having a social function, and this function can range from the didactic plays of ***Brecht***'s earlier years to the pure entertainment value of the Whitehall farce. Playwrights, of course, are acutely aware of the social function their work is designed to fulfil. An important consideration, therefore, in analysing the playwright's intention, or ruling idea, is to assess the play's intended **social function**: What is the play designed to do? And to whom? Looking carefully at the play's form, genre and style will help us work out the answers to these two questions.

We can then move on to examine the content and action of the play under four headings:

- the **title**;
- any **philosophical statements** *drawn* from the text itself;
- an overall **synopsis** (or summary) of the play's action; and
- the particular **significance of individual scenes** within the play's overall structure.

The title gives clues

An important clue to the playwright's intention is often to be found in the title. Some titles are purely literal (for example, *The Three Sisters* is a play, as you would expect, about three sisters): if a playwright names his play after one of the characters, we can be reasonably certain that the play's principal focus will be on that character (for example, *Miss Julie*).

But titles can also be more metaphorical. ***Chekhov*** did not name his play *Nina*; instead he gave it the title *The Seagull*. On a number of occasions, during the course of the play, Nina refers to herself as a seagull. This metaphor works on several different levels. At the simplest level, Nina sees herself as a seagull soaring away to escape from the confines of her limited, provincial existence (she longs to become an actress). In Act 2, Konstantin enters with a dead seagull, and sets it on a bench. It is possible to see the dead bird as a symbol for the doomed relationship between Nina and Konstantin, but the writer, Trigorin, on seeing the dead bird, makes the association with a girl (Nina?), and immediately begins to formulate a story: a man comes along, sees her, and – just for the fun of it – destroys her, like the seagull lying on the bench. This outline, of course, foreshadows the story of the affair between Nina and Trigorin which happens in the two years that pass between Acts 3 and 4. The symbol of the seagull in *Chekhov*'s play is so multi-layered that it gives an important insight into the playwright's intentions in writing the play.

Playwrights will occasionally choose a title which is intriguing, mysterious, or enigmatic. It is interesting to speculate on the significance of titles like ***Strindberg***'s *The Ghost Sonata*; ***Beckett***'s *Endgame*; Edward ***Bond***'s *Saved*; David ***Hare***'s *Plenty*; C.P. Taylor's *Bandits*; and Mark ***Ravenhall***'s *Shopping and F***ing*.

Philosophical statements

A careful textual analysis will often reveal a line of dialogue that seems to encapsulate the playwright's intention, or the play's major theme. It is often useful to go back over a play to see if such a line presents itself.

In *The Seagull*, Masha, one of the more minor characters, replies when asked why she always wears black that she is in mourning for her life. *Chekhov*'s play deals with the various characters' inabilities to find the happiness that they seek. Masha is in love with Konstantin, but she understands that her affections will never be returned because Konstantin is obsessed with Nina. Consequently, she is doomed to unhappiness, and is, therefore, in mourning for the life she can never have as Konstantin's wife. Gradually, as the play unfolds, we discover that all of the main characters are in much the same situation: each longs for a sense of emotional fulfilment which is never forthcoming. In this sense, we could view all of them as being 'in mourning for their lives'.

A careful reading should always yield at least one quotation that helps crystallise the playwright's intention: in *The Merchant of Venice*, we could argue that the famous phrase 'the quality of mercy' adequately captures ***Shakespeare***'s ruling idea; the line 'I don't believe in miracles any more' neatly sums up Nora's journey of self-discovery in *A Doll's House*; and, in *Waiting for Godot*, the oft-repeated line 'Nothing to be done' seems apposite in relation to the lives of Estragon and Vlaidmir.

Synopsis

Having considered the significance of the title of the play and after pinning down the playwright's intention, or ruling idea, the next step is to draw up a full synopsis of the action of the play. This helps us see how the playwright's overall intentions are realised, and how the ruling idea develops as the play progresses towards its conclusion. As we make our synopsis, we begin to get a much firmer sense of the play's shape and structure. We should begin to see the main plot in sharper relief, and we should also perceive what the relationships are between the main action of the play and any sub-plots.

The significance of individual scenes

Each scene must be examined in order to establish its precise **function** and **purpose** within the overall structure of the play. Generally speaking, in a ***realist*** text where the narrative is linear, we will find that each of the scenes develops organically from those that have gone before. Although there may be varying lengths of time between the events depicted in the play, it is usually possible to discern a sense of continuity and a logical relationship between the scenes. In more episodic plays, written in the manner of *Brecht*, we may have to work harder to discover how the scenes work together to create a coherent whole.

Task 10: Identify writer's intentions

- **Turn to the textual analysis questionnaire (p. 160) and complete Section 5: Writer's intentions – for your set text.**

Conclusion in Seclusion

The practice of analysing texts usually suggests a solitary individual, deep in concentrated thought, studiously poring over books and papers. And this is certainly the image that springs to mind when we imagine ***Stanislavski***, in the summer of 1898, closeted for six weeks in a tower overlooking the grain fields of his brother's farm, analysing *The Seagull*, and preparing his ***mise en scene*** for the forthcoming ***Moscow Art Theatre*** production. And certainly, the model we have offered in the preceding pages requires, for the most part, just such a quiet, desk-bound approach.

However, we should also bear in mind that analysis can also be an active as well as a passive process. Some directors, who are able to enjoy the luxury of a series of exploratory workshops prior to the beginning of the rehearsal period proper, engage in a practical analysis of the text in order to deepen the acting company's understandings of the play they are working on. In Chapter 6 there was a study of a student production of ***Lorca***'s play, *Yerma*. The case study consists of a number of practical activities which formed the early stages of the rehearsal process.

After reading this chapter and the case study on *Yerma* in Chapter 6, you now have **two ways of analysing a play text: the first, a detailed model for desk work; the second, a practical workshop method**. Each can be used to great effect on its own and both can, of course, be used in tandem. This kind of detailed analysis is essential preliminary work for anyone who is preparing to direct a play, and a more detailed discussion of the work of the director can be found in chapters 5 and 6.

Textual Analysis Questionnaire

The textual analysis questionnaire is designed to help you make a detailed analysis of a play text from a director's point of view. It is the level of analysis which a director needs to apply prior to rehearsals so that they can offer an interpretation of the play and ideas about the ***mise en scene*** to the actors and designers. The previous pages give a detailed breakdown of each of the sections in the questionnaire and offer illustrations from a wide range of plays as examples for you to follow, or as the basis for comparisons between different kinds of plays.

		Environmental Facts and Background
The given circumstances	Geographical location	Where is the play set? What is significant about the locations used in the play?
	Date and time	Are there any specific references to time of day, season, year? How will the time or season effect the characters?
	Timescale	How much time passes during the play? How will the 'passage of time' be played/represented?
	Economic environment	What is the economic environment of the characters? How are they affected by their economic environment?
	Social environment	Is the social and economic environment the same? What differences are there in the social environment of the characters? How will this affect how characters interact?

The given circumstances	Political environment	Are there any references to political events? What was the political environment of the writer? How will the political context be played/represented?
	Religious environment	Are any of the characters influenced by their own religious beliefs, or by the beliefs of others? What effect does religion have on the way characters behave?
		Previous Action
	Past histories of characters	What clues are there to the biographies of the main characters? How will the characters' future actions be affected by their biographies?
	Events prior to play	Are there references to key events prior to the play? Do any of the characters carry scars or memories from these events? How will the characters be affected by these events?
		Protagonist/Antagonist
	Protagonist's attitude and how it changes	Which character is the protagonist – who initiates the play's central action? What is their attitude? How does it develop or change during the play?
	Antagonist's attitude and how it changes	Which character is the antagonist – who opposes the protagonist's objectives? What is their attitude? How does it develop or change during the play?
Language	Vocabulary	How formal/informal is each character's language? Are there any clues to levels of education or background in the words used by characters? Do any of the characters use language to bully, or to impress, or to promote themselves to others? Do words come easily or are they struggled over? What does the vocabulary used tell us about the personalities of the characters? How do you imagine them based on the words they use?
	Structure	How are speeches structured? Are they elaborate and long or short phrases, for instance? What does the structure of each character's speech tell us about the character and their relationship to others? Does the structure change according to who the character is talking to? Are there any clues to the pace and rhythm of the scenes in the structure of the speeches?
	Imagery	Are there any patterns in the imagery used? Are these patterns scattered across the play or restricted to certain characters? Does the imagery relate to setting? Ideas? Mood? Atmosphere? Character traits? How can the imagery be pointed out so that an audience is aware of its pattern? How will the design of the play reflect the imagery?

Dramatic action	Peculiarities of speech	Do any of the characters have accents, dialects, speech problems? If so what does this *add* to the character?
	Scene units	How many identifiable 'units' are there in each scene? What is the logic of your choice of unit breaks? How should each unit be played?
	Labelling the units	What word or phrase best describes the action, or objectives, in each unit? Do the unit titles accurately summarise the scenes?
	Playing the sub-text	What is the sub-text of action in each scene? What is *really* going on? Which verbs accurately describe for the actors how the speeches should be played so that the sub-text becomes visible to an audience?
Characters	Wants	What are the super-objectives of the main character/s? What do the main characters *want* to happen in the scenes they appear in? Are there conflicts or tensions between what different characters want? Do the main characters wants significantly change or create contradictions during the play?
	Will	Is there a difference between what characters say they will do and what they *actually* do? What is the intensity or strength of the main characters' resolve or determination? Do they really want their super-objectives to be realised?
	Moral stance	How do culture, morality and upbringing shape the main characters behaviours? How does the main characters moral stance encourage, justify or constrain the fulfilment of their wants?
	Physical appearance	Are there direct references to the physical appearance of characters? Are there any other clues or inferences about physical appearance? Are there any implications for casting? What significant connections are there between how a character looks and how they behave?
	Summary adjectives	Which sets of adjectives best describe the characters? How will these adjectives be played? What are the design and costume implications?
	Variations in characterisation	Are there any significant changes or variations in the way that characters behave in different scenes? Are there any inconsistencies in how characters react to situations or other characters? How will the 'inconsistencies' be either smoothed out or exaggerated in the playing of the characters?
The playwright's intention	Title	What is the significance of the title? Is the title metaphoric or literal? What sub-title or alternative title might be given to clarify the writer's own title?
	Philosophical statements	Are there any key lines or speeches which seem to encapsulate the writer's view or which summarise and capture the ideas or mood of the play? Where are these lines positioned in the play and who speaks them? Is there anything significant in this?

The playwright's intention	Synopsis	What is the main plot of the play and how does it develop? What sub-plots are there and how do they relate to the main plot? How are the writer's ideas developed over the play? How can the shape of the play be best described and represented? As a story? As episodes? As a journey? As a diagram or map?
	Significance of individual scenes	What is the function and purpose of each scene within the overall structure of the play? Which scenes are the most important and which the least? What is the logic of the relationship between scenes? Is it cause and effect? ***Brechtian*** knots? Contrasts in mood, atmosphere, location?

SECTION 5

Devising and Analysing Performances

9 Devising Theatre

The Ten-Stage Devising Process: An overview

In this chapter we are going to suggest a ten-stage process for devising a theatrical performance. First, we will begin by identifying the recent history of devised theatre and the influences that have made it such a popular genre of theatre for a wide range of social functions and artistic intentions. Then we will guide you through a detailed account of each of the ten stages of the devising process. Finally there is a devising process questionnaire to help keep you on track during your own devising. The questionnaire asks you key questions at each stage of the process. These questions are based on the notes and ideas contained in the detailed description for each stage.

As we have often said, theatre is a lot more messy than the idea of a ten-stage devising process suggests! **The ten-stage devising process is there to provide you with a framework for devising, but not every devising process will be the same.** The framework is there to support you, but don't allow it to be used mechanically so that it blocks your creativity or stops you from finding your own characteristic style for devising. In particular, you may find that you need to change the order of the stages to reflect your particular project.

Starting From Scratch

The other practical chapters in this book have assumed a relationship between acting and directing styles and a play text of some kind. In Chapter 6 we learnt that different directors have seen the relationship between a play text and the performance text in different ways. We suggested that a useful distinction can be made between the *playwright's director* who faithfully represents the play text according to the author's intentions and the ***auteur*** who seeks to interpret, comment on and modify the original play text so that the performance text is as much the work of the *auteur* and the performers as it is of the playwright's.

In most productions the modern actor can expect to be involved in some devising even where there is a play text. Most modern directors will involve the actors in devising stage movement and gesture, 'business' and even aspects of character.

Again, some playwrights will leave sections of the play to be worked out by the actors. ***Ibsen*** and ***Beckett*** are examples of playwrights who strictly determine the way the play text should be played, but other writers such as Caryl ***Churchill*** and Jim ***Cartwright*** are often quite open about directions and leave the detail to be creatively devised by the performers and director.

Devised theatre goes one step further. There is no pre-existing playtext. There is no anchor or fixed point for the performance to grow from. Alison Oddey describes devised theatre in these terms:

The Berliner Ensemble

Brecht's company was generously funded by the East German State. Together with *Brecht* the company spent long periods in workshop and study developing their *ensemble* style of performance and the acting skills required for *Brecht*'s *epic theatre*. The company performed in London in 1956 and had a profound effect on the new wave of English directors and writers, which included Peter *Brook*, Edward ***Bond***, Harold ***Pinter***, Joan ***Littlewood*** and William Gaskill. The *Berliner* offered an example of *Brecht's* ***presentational*** style of theatre, and the sparse stage design and tightly worked ensemble performances influenced new styles of performance at the *Royal Shakespeare Company* and a new wave of writers interested in developing *Brecht*'s socially committed, potentially popular, *presentational* style of theatre.

The Group Theatre and the Actors Studio

Lee ***Strasberg*** modelled the Group Theatre and the Actors Studio on the *Moscow Art Theatre*. It was a collective of actors and directors who experimented with the games, exercises and improvisation techniques that became known as the *method*. In 1965, *Strasberg*'s highly controversial production of *The Three Sisters* played in London.

Joan Littlewood and Ewan McColl

Littlewood and her partner, the folk singer Ewan McColl, were committed socialists whose work was influenced by the Russian *Blue Blouse* workers' theatre of the 1920s, the German *Agit-Prop* theatre of ***Piscator***, and the leftist *Federal Theatre Project* in America, particularly the *Living Newspaper* project and the writing of Clifford *Odets*. They formed a radical touring collective – *Theatre Union* – which combined sketches, songs and satire in devised performances for working people. Later, *Littlewood* developed her collaborative and ensemble style of theatre with the *Theatre Workshop* collective at the *Stratford East* theatre. The 1963 production of *Oh! What a Lovely War* is remembered as a landmark in socialist and popular devised theatre. *Littlewood* encouraged a generation of young writers who sought a more collaborative relationship with actors and directors as part of the writing process. These writers and plays included Brendan Behan's *The Quare Fellow*, Shelagh Delaney's *A Taste of Honey* and Frank Norman and Lionel Bart's *Fings Aint What They Used T'Be*.

Beck and the Living Theatre

Founded by Julian ***Beck*** in New York in 1948, *Living Theatre* sought to mix political and aesthetic radicalism in their work. The social function of this new theatre was to advocate anarchist-pacifist ideas through theatre. The company organised themselves as a socialist 'collective' committed to their own political education and campaigning as well as to developing new forms of socially committed theatre. At first the company produced interpretations of plays by ***Lorca***, *Cocteau* and *Brecht*. In the 1950s the company began to devise their own performances based on exercises and improvisations. Between 1964 and 1968, the collective remained in Europe and provided a model for the establishment of similar collectives based on radical political and aesthetic ideals and committed to group devising.

Guerrilla Theatre

Guerrilla Theatre is the term used by Ron Davis, the founder of the *San Francisco Mime Troupe* to describe the popular political theatre of his own collective and *Bread and Puppet Theatre* in the 1960s and 1970s. Both these companies used carnival and *Commedia dell'Arte* conventions to produce highly political and spectacular performances which were often enacted as part of larger political demonstrations and protest gatherings. The use of *Commedia dell'Arte* conventions together with the visual splendour of the masks and huge puppets meant that both collectives could devise material very quickly and have a big impact on large audiences.

New writers, new funding, new theatres

The relationship between writers and other producers was becoming more collaborative. During the 1960s and 1970s the Arts Council was generous to companies and theatres that encouraged new writing. The bountiful level of subsidy allowed for longer rehearsal periods in which writers could develop the final drafts of their plays. These final drafts would include the results of improvisations and the suggestions of actors and directors. In 1956, the English Stage Company founded by George ***Devine*** to promote new writing took over the ***Royal Court Theatre*** and the season included John ***Osborne***'s *Look Back in Anger*, which is often regarded as the beginning of the modern revival of English drama. George *Devine* also encouraged new writing at the *Royal Court* by Arnold ***Wesker***, John Arden and Anne Jellicoe, and staged the first English performances of works by Samuel ***Beckett*** and Eugene Ionesco. During the 1970s and 1980s the *Royal Court* became a centre both for new writing and for new styles of collaborative rehearsal and performance.

The Influence of Joint Stock and Mike Leigh

The directors Max **Stafford-Clarke** and William Gaskill (both of whom have worked as artistic directors at the ***Royal Court***) and the writer David ***Hare*** founded *Joint Stock* in 1974 as a loose collective of *fringe* actors, directors and writers. The idea was to create a new form of collaborative and *ensemble* theatre in which the eventual performance would be forged through workshops and other forms of theatrical and social research.

The Joint Stock Method

Joint Stock **developed a method for producing plays that has had an important influence on the working methods in alternative and *avant-garde* theatre today.** The method was based on a ten-week production period in which the first six weeks were spent in identifying themes and content through research, physical training and improvisation involving the whole company and a writer. There would then be a 'gap' while the writer prepared a script based on the devising process, which was followed by a four-week rehearsal period. The 'play' that emerged from this process was a reflection of the collaborations between the actors, writers, directors and designers involved. The *Joint Stock* style was based on extraordinarily detailed and effective ensemble acting, minimalist sets and a predominantly ***Brechtian presentational*** style of performance.

Among the many important plays produced through the *Joint Stock* method were Caryl ***Churchill***'s *Light Shining in Buckinghamshire, Fen* and *Cloud Nine*, David *Hare*'s *Fanshen* and Hanif *Kureshi's Borderline*.

The workshop period involved the collective in activities that are now familiar tools in devised forms of theatre. Improvisation, games and physical work were interspersed with lectures from experts, reading and study periods, interviews with character models, living and working among the subjects of the plays (living in the Fens, for *Fen* for instance), discussion and political analysis. The 'truth quiz' in which company members had to answer direct questions not just about their characters but also about their personal politics and relationships with other members of the company from other company members ensured that there was no distinction between the actor as social being and as performer. Commitment was total!

In 1975 the collective began work on an adaptation of William Hinton's book *Fanshen*, which would become the play of the same name written by David *Hare*. The book detailed the changes that rural culture in China went through after the Communist Revolution replaced the old feudalism with a new socialist society. This production would have a profound effect on the company who decided that they should organise themselves on the same egalitarian principles as the villagers

Joint Stock's production of *Fanshen*, 1975.

of China. Equal status, equal pay and equal voices in every aspect of the collective's business became enshrined in the collective's policy.

During the 1970s and 1980s *Joint Stock* became a model for many of the leftist experimental theatre companies that were formed in their wake. The idea of a collective organised on the principles of equality for all members and of an equal say in both the devising process and the management of business, together with a emphasis on *Brechtian presentational* and political theatre was shared by *7:84, Gay Sweatshop, Red Ladder* and many *Theatre in Education* companies.

Mike Leigh was developing a different form of devising in his 'improvised plays'

During this period Mike ***Leigh*** was developing a different form of devising in his 'improvised plays'. *Leigh* was more influenced by the new forms of ***realism*** based on improvisation and character research emerging from ***Strasberg***'s *Group Theatre* than by the revolutionary politics and aesthetics of *Brecht*. For this reason, we might say that *Joint Stock* represented a development of *Brechtian presentational* theatre whereas *Leigh*'s work is in the *realist* and ***representational*** tradition of ***Stanislavski*** and *Strasberg*. *Leigh* was impressed by the authenticity and detail of character which came from the case study research done by actors in Joan ***Littlewood***'s production of *The Quare Fellow*, which was based on real-life interviews with Borstal boys. ***Brook*** had used the same method of using real case studies to create characters in his production of *Marat/Sade*. Leigh was also influenced by the realist acting, forged in improvisation, in John Cassavetes movies such as *Shadows*.

Leigh* developed a method of devising highly realist representations of the extraordinariness of ordinary lives.** In plays like *Abigail's Party* and TV dramas like *Nuts in May*, *Leigh* exposes the minute details of ordinary suburban characters in a tradition of realism that includes ***Ibsen and the ***tragi-comedies*** of ***Chekhov***. The detailed realism of the work made it best suited to the small screen and *Leigh* is now best known for his TV dramas.

Leigh's devising method begins with the selection of a group of actors who are

Abigail's Party by Mike ***Leigh***, Hampstead Theatre 1977.

chosen for their potential for interesting ensemble work. *Leigh* has said that he looks for four qualities in his actors: a sense of humour; a keen eye for habits and physical mannerisms; a good ear for dialects; and an ability to turn their ideas into microscopically defined and unique characters.

Through a long workshop process the actors identify a group of characters based on people that they know or have experienced. The character development and scenarios that follow are based on highly detailed research. *Leigh* divides the processes of devising a character into **narrative work** and **behaviour work**. Through narrative work the content, or biography, of a character's life is established in detail through improvisation and discussion. This includes their relationships and conflicts, and the major events of their lives. In the behaviour work, the characters ideas, culture and consciousness are established as well as their physical mannerisms – the way they walk, the way they talk.

The Social Functions and Artistic Intentions of Today's Devised Theatre

Actor-Audience relationships

Towards the end of the nineteenth century the theatrical ideas of ***Antoine***, ***Strindberg***, ***Chekhov***, ***Wagner*** and ***Stanislavski*** produced a theatre for middle-class educated audiences. These artists also developed a ***representational*** style of performance which clearly separated the world of the performance from the actual world of the audience. *Wagner* called this distance the *Mystiche Abgrund* or 'mysterious gulf'. ***Artaud*** would later describe the audience in this form of theatre as 'peeping toms' rather than witnesses or participants in what was happening.

Throughout the twentieth century, practitioners worked against this tradition of theatre by seeking out new audiences (particularly working-class audiences) in new venues, like pubs, factories and working men's clubs as well as in streets, parks and abandoned buildings. ***Meyerhold***, ***Piscator***, ***Brecht***, ***Brook*** and others have all worked to develop new styles of ***presentational*** performance which seek to include the audience in the live experience of theatre. Sometimes, as with ***Grotowski*** and *Brook* the social function has been to try and recreate the spiritual, quasi-religious feel of ritual. For *Meyerhold* and *Brecht* the purpose was political: they sought to create a public forum in which the theatre played a similar role as a mirror and debating ground for society as it did for the fifth century Greeks.

In recent years, devised theatre has become a useful means of responding to particular situations in theatre.

Community plays

The tradition of locally produced devised theatre goes back to medieval times and the travelling *morality* players. In Africa, the ancient *Alarinjo* tradition was based on local community play-making.

In the 1960s the playwright John Arden, author of *Sergeant Musgrave's Dance*, and his partner Margeretta D'Arcy began to devise plays like *Ars Longa, Vita Brevis* with the people of Kirkbymoorside in Cumbria, as a radical alternative to the West End theatre. The plays were intended to be by, for and about the local community who were involved in every aspect of the devising. Anne Jellicoe began writing plays like *The Knack* and *The Sport of My Mad Mother* before turning to devising community plays with local people in Dorset. Community plays such as *The Reckoning* in Lyme Regis used over 150 local people to tell the local history of the town. These performances, which depended on local stories shaped by professional writers, performed by local people for their family, friends and neighbours, proved to be a popular form of entertainment and local community plays are now an established genre of popular theatre.

Issue-based

Devised theatre is a particularly useful response to the need for local theatre – theatre that is immediately concerned with the needs and interests of local communities.

The political potential of devised local theatre dealing with local, or broader, political issues from a local perspective has been exploited by Augusto *Boal* who began work with the *Arena* Theatre in Brazil before developing, *arena theatre, newspaper theatre* and *forum theatre* as the means of involving local people in devising and developing work based on relevant political issues. *Boal*'s ideas and methods of devising political theatre have been developed by groups in many countries as a means of offering oppressed groups a voice and as a means of debating the sources of their oppression and freedom. In India such companies deal with the oppression of women and the tyranny of the landlords; in North America, companies like *Teatro Campesino* work with Chicano communities and migrant workers from Mexico.

Therapy and education

Professional theatre work for young people with explicit educational aims is often produced for local audiences through a devising process that ensures that the performance will be both educationally and theatrically relevant.

Theatre-in-Education (TiE) has its roots in the work of Joan ***Littlewood***, *Brecht* and Brian Way. The first TiE company was formed in America in the 1930s as part of the *Federal Theatre Project*, but it was soon closed down for being too radical in its content. The first company in England was the *Belgrade TiE Company* in Coventry, which devised shows for local school audiences like *Pow-Wow* in 1968, which uses the context of a 'cowboy and indian' story to introduce issues of prejudice and the study of aboriginal cultures.

More recently, TiE companies have become involved in devising health education projects focusing on drugs, AIDS and other related issues. Health education theatre is also a popular and effective means of education in many rural areas of the African and Asian continents.

Site-specific

Carnival and *Mardi Gras* are good examples of the tradition of devised performances in a particular *space*: the streets and open spaces of a town or neighbourhood. In England, this tradition was given a radical political edge in the early work of ***Welfare State International*** who devised large-scale open air performances using giant puppets, masks, mechanical constructions, fire, lanterns and music.

Eugenio ***Barba***'s company, *Odin Teatret* have also revived the popular

Mediterranean tradition of outdoor *fiestas* and carnivals to produce devised work that uses the local buildings and spaces as an integral part of the performance. Again, because the work is outdoors and with huge crowds there is an emphasis on the visual rather than the oral elements of performance.

Performances that are devised for outdoors, or non-theatre spaces, are sometimes referred to as *environmental theatre*, after the work of Richard Schechner and ***The Performance Group***.

Welfare State International, *'Last Ferry'*, Belfast 1991, Youth Theatre project on the docks.

Task 2: What devised work have you done?

Have you ever seen or been involved in any of these examples of devised theatre? Have you been in a 'community play'; seen a TiE programme; taken part in a carnival or outdoor performance?

Discuss your experiences with the group. What are the key differences between these performances and others?

The Stages in Detail

1 Identify

Working as an ensemble

A devised theatre product is work that has emerged from and been generated by a group of people working in collaboration. The key here is: a group of people working in collaboration! Unlike a poem, picture or even a musical composition a devised piece of theatre is always a collective achievement.

At the heart of the work of both *Joint Stock* and Mike ***Leigh*** is the idea of ensemble. Ensemble is used to refer both to a grouping of objects and to a group of performers. In both cases the definition of the word includes the idea that it is the sum of the parts rather than the individual elements that create the 'ensemble' effect. In performance this means that **the result of the whole group playing and interacting together is greater than the individual performances in the group.**

If you look at the play texts produced by the *Joint Stock* method you will see that they are also ensemble pieces in the sense that there tend not to be major and subsidiary roles: each character is given equal weight. Both David ***Hare***'s *Fanshen* and Stephen Lowe's *Ragged Trousered Philanthropist* would be examples of ensemble characterisation.

In other cases – in Caryl ***Churchill***'s *Top Girls* and *Fen* for instance, the characters are shared out among the group of actors involved in the devising. It is a very democratic system, which doesn't suit star players or loners!

In order to play as an effective ensemble, you have first to become one! Both *Joint Stock* and Mike *Leigh* (like many other devising companies) rely on a stable group of actors who come to know each other and each other's work very well. This knowledge creates trust and allows a group to work off each other's strengths. It also allows a group to develop a shared vision of the social function and artistic intentions of the work – they develop a 'house style'.

In order to be an effective devising group, you must begin by becoming an effective group. This may involve discussion, hanging out, playing games and physical exercises together. But it may also involve working out some ground rules for your work together as a group prior to beginning the devising process.

Warm-ups and physical work

It is a good idea to begin every session with some physical work or warm-up games. Inevitably, you will spend some time on your bottoms trying to thrash out ideas. Starting with physical work helps to energise you and stop you from getting lethargic during the discussion. This physical work is also a good opportunity to just play and have some fun together.

Taking it in turns to lead the warm-up session is a good way of sharing out the responsibility for the work. Agree before each session who will lead the next session's warm-up. If it's your responsibility to lead, don't let the others off the hook, however tired or 'not in the mood' they say they are!

Keep a running list of all the games and exercises that you know as a group – some may be from your drama experience, others from childhood or other group activities you have been involved in. **Keep adding to this list as you go so that there is plenty to choose from when planning a warm-up.**

Ground rules

You may remember the idea of a **contract** from your earlier drama work in school. Drama teachers often negotiate certain ground rules for their classes which govern behaviour and how the space is used, but also offer protection to the class.

Remember the kinds of contract or rules that were laid down in your drama class. Which rules were for the teacher and which for the protection of individuals in the class? How well did the contract work?

It will certainly help you later on in the process if you begin by establishing some ground rules for your group work together. Once these ground rules have been established and agreed on by you all they will take the heat out of any disagreements you might have later. They will also help to make any conflicts less personal. The rules belong to the group, not to individuals, so if *you* need to refer back to them or question whether they are being properly observed, you are doing so on behalf of the *group*, who decided on them in the first place!

The following ground rules are taken from a selection used by three devising groups working on *TiE* projects. Look closely at the list below. **Discuss and then place the ground rules in order of importance.** What kind of situation or problem is each of the ground rules designed to cover or prevent? Which ground rules will be the hardest to keep?

We collectively agree to:

- Be prepared for each session and complete agreed tasks
- Regular attendance and punctuality

- Make an active contribution during sessions
- Compromise, be flexible, and listen to others
- Sustain responsibility for the production in chosen areas
- Take an appropriate share of responsibilities for the work
- Offer and receive constructive criticism
- Be willing to commit to tasks and explore possibilities
- Make an equal input/responsibility for the devising process

Discuss and decide on your own ground rules for this devising project. This is a chance to voice any concerns, fears, hopes and desires that you have for the project and to listen to others. Try and work out a set of ground rules that will help you all to feel safe, committed and focused on the work to come.

Keep your ground rules to hand and turn to them every now and again so that you can check on the health of the group and reassess the ground rules if necessary.

It can also be helpful to sometimes use a neutral 'chair' or 'process observer' in your discussions. This means that one member of the group sits out and observes how the discussion goes and helps to point out when people have been ignored, or not listened to, when someone's enthusiasm gets out of hand, when someone seems to be blocking or taking the group off task. The 'process observer' may also be the one who suggests getting off the floor and trying something out instead of talking about it!

Decide what kind of 'blocks' get in the way of creative work – being tired, fed up, no ideas, too worried about other things – and think of what strategies you will use to get past these 'blocks' should they get in the way of the work.

Roles and responsibilities

Although devised theatre is a collective and democratic form of work it is still important to make sure that all the roles needed for the production of theatre will be covered. It is worth allocating responsibility for these roles early on in the devising process; then people can be thinking about their responsibilities as the devising develops. Allocating the roles will also avoid discovering too late that some aspect of the production has not been considered.

The allocation of roles should reflect the strengths and interests of the group members. Taking responsibility for a role doesn't mean taking over. It means that you are responsible and answerable to the group for that dimension of the work – you may well call on others to help you and part of your responsibility is to listen to and include other people's ideas.

Identify the strengths in your group. These may be associated with drama – acting, directing and design, for instance. Or they may be related strengths like singing, dancing, writing poetry, visual art, sewing and technical or computer skills. The devised work **emerges** from the group, so it makes sense to try and use as many of the individual strenghts and skills as you can.

Allocate responsibility for:

- Design
- Technical aspects including sound and video
- Recording the process, keeping the notes from one session to the next
- Directing
- Writing
- Props and costumes

Content: identifying the theme and/or finding a particular starting point

You may have the freedom to choose your own area of content or you may have been offered a stimulus to work with in the form of a picture, poem or idea. In both cases you need to **identify the theme that you will work on. Themes describe broad areas of human experience, such as love, or childhood, or war.**

If you are offered a starting point it will be because it is a *particular* example of a broader theme. The picture, song, story or other stimulus will have been chosen for its potential to open up themes for dramatic enquiry. In the same way, the plays that you have studied are 'particular' examples of a theme. *King Lear* is a particular story about the lives of a king and his daughters, but it is told in order to reveal the themes of family ties and love, kingship, age and madness. In devising we *begin* with a human theme of some importance and then devise the particular lives, situations and dilemmas which will best reveal the theme to an audience.

We are going to use a particular example of a starting point and the themes it generates to illustrate how you move from stimulus to drama. If you have the time you may want to follow our example as a training exercise. If you have already begun work on your own theme, then follow the same instructions but use your own ideas rather than ours.

Working from a stimulus – an example in practice

Look at the picture below. It is of a particular woman and two children. The title of the picture is *The Migrant Mother 5*. The photographer, Dorothea Lange, took it in a camp for migrant farm workers in America during the 1930s. It comes from the same historical experience as John Steinbeck's novels *The Grapes of Wrath* and *Of Mice and Men*. Lange wrote:

She told me her age, that she was 32. She said that they had been living on frozen vegetables from the surrounding fields, and birds that the children killed. She had just sold the tyres from her car to buy food. . .

The Migrant Mother 5 by Dorothea Lange 1936.

So, we know that this particular woman is a mother, poor, and alone with two children. These are the particular circumstances of the picture. But as you gaze at the mother and her two children, what are the **broader themes** that the picture might be a starting point for? Motherhood? Poverty? Make a list of all the broad areas of experience that might be suggested or touched upon by this picture.

- Which theme interests your group the most?
- Which theme could you commit yourself to exploring further?
- Which theme do you, yourself, care most about?

It is always worth using drama conventions to help you get inside the stimulus so that you can **explore the material from the inside and discover its potential themes through dramatic exploration**.

If you want to work on the characters in a visual stimulus like *The Migrant Mother 5*, then begin by asking questions about the **human experience and relationships** represented in the picture, and then use the following ideas to help you explore possible answers:

- Physically model the characters. Pay attention to the exact physical position of the figure/s.
- What does the character think at this moment?
- What does the character feel at this moment?
- Are there any clues in the stimulus about the given circumstances?

- What lies *beyond* the picture or other stimulus? What is the landscape? Are there other people present? Are there any significant 'props' that relate to the character? What can you hear as well as see? Try to physically represent these ideas by adding figures, or props, or *soundscapes* to the sculpted figures.
- What might have happened, or been said, immediately after or before the picture was taken?
- Make a series of four images (two before, two after) which show what might be happening. If you are interested in the results, try to improvise the scenes, keeping your attention on how the central character acts and reacts.

This initial exploration of the particulars in the stimulus (the characters, settings, possible dramatic tensions or conflicts) should quickly move you to identifying the broader themes touched on by the stimulus. **It will be these broader themes that you will develop in devising rather than the narrow particulars in the stimulus.** This process of selecting the theme is vital – you must care about the theme yourself; it must inspire you if you are to inspire others.

Managing the theme: perspective and focus

The selection of a theme for devising will tend to suggest a perspective or angle for the devising process. **Themes can be organised under different headings**, which will prompt different kinds of approach to the rest of the devising process. In terms of *The Migrant Mother 5*, these headings might include:

- **Sociological theme** (emphasises social roles and relationships): e.g. the role of women in society, or the relationships between mothers and children.
- **Cultural theme** (emphasises attitudes, values and morality): e.g. what is our responsibility to the poor, unemployed and homeless?
- **Psychological theme** (emphasises the effects on the individual): e.g. the stresses and strains of motherhood and poverty, or the life and character of this particular woman.
- **Historical theme** (emphasises the events in a particular period): e.g. the years of the Great Depression in North America and the experiences of those who lived through this time, or how the lived experience of poverty has changed over time.
- **Artistic theme** (emphasises the role of the artist, and styles and techniques used): e.g. the role of the artist in times of social hardship, or images of women in photography.

Listing themes under thematic headings helps you to begin to narrow down or focus the theme that you have selected. A broad theme like '*the experience of poverty*' will need to be focused more precisely so that it can be adequately explored during the devising process. You can't cover every possible element of a broad theme. This focusing will also help members of the group to find commitment and to clarify their own interests in the devising.

Either choose one of *The Migrant Mother 5* themes you listed earlier, or one of the themes from your own stimulus. Draw a large circle and divide it into segments like slices of a cake. The circle represents the whole theme. Each segment represents a narrower aspect of the theme. If we draw a circle for the theme we've chosen – *the experience of poverty* – we might now sub-divide the theme into the following segments: causes of poverty; the effects on relationships and family life; society's responsibilities to the poor; the relationship between poverty and crime. Fill in the segments for your chosen theme and through discussion, decide which segment your group will now focus on.

Key question to guide the devising

The devising process is always an exploration of the human experiences suggested by the theme. It is a journey towards first understanding and delving into the experiences yourself through to organising your discoveries and ideas into a communicable form for others. **It helps to have a key question that will guide the exploration.** A question helps to remind you that you are not presenting an audience with answers. One question leads to another; each question raises new possibilities or prompts further thinking about the theme. A guiding question also helps you to focus on what it is that you are exploring and looking for in the devising process.

For our chosen segment, or aspect, of the broad theme of 'poverty' we might select '*the relationship between crime and poverty*'. For our key question for the devising process we might borrow the key question ***Brecht*** used when writing *Mother Courage*: 'Is it possible to be both poor and good?' This question opens up the possibility of exploring the extent to which 'being honest' and 'doing the right thing' may be easier if you have money than if you and your children are starving. We are already beginning to think about the question in relation to *The Migrant Mother 5* – did she steal the frozen vegetables from the field? Did her children have a right to kill birds? Were these decisions driven by poverty?

Choose a key question for your segment. Brainstorm the possibilities in a spider diagram stretching out from the key question. You can see that our own brainstorming began with the questions first raised by our key question.

Style and Genre

Your initial ideas about the styles and genres that you will use in the devised performance do not have to follow the selection of theme. In some cases you might be given a style or genre that you must use in your devising and the style or genre will suggest a suitable theme or area of content that is appropriate for the style and genre you have been given.

Or, it may be that when you were offered a free choice in your devising you first were drawn to working in a particular style or genre rather than to a theme. You may begin the devising process wanting to produce a ***realist*** piece in the genre of ***tragi-comedy*** or performed in a ***Stanislavskian*** *psycho-realist* style. You may have already decided, like Mike ***Leigh***, to do a piece of hard *realism* in a ***representational*** style in which you will create closely observed characters locked in their daily struggles. Or, like ***Brecht***, you may have decided on a ***presentational*** piece that addresses the audience directly and includes songs, slides, poems and a ***non-realist*** setting.

What does the migrant mother picture, or your chosen stimulus, suggest in terms of style? Which practitioners or playwrights are associated with these styles?

If your devising is led by a choice of genre and/or style you will need to research the history and characteristics of the chosen genre and style in the research stage of the devising process.

Means and Meanings

The choice of style and genre will determine the treatment of the theme. Remember that the 'means' (form) and the 'meanings' (interpretations of theme) of a performance are inseparable. The 'means' used will become part of the 'meanings' produced and received in performance. **The 'means' will tend to emphasise certain kinds of 'meanings' rather than others** – a comedy produces different meanings and effects on the audience from a tragedy, for instance, even if the content and theme are the same.

The Migrant Mother 5 picture might be a useful resource for exploring a wide range of styles and genres.

Naturalism developed as a 'means' of describing the relationship between poverty, environment and character. A devised piece in the genre of *naturalism* might focus on the struggle of the mother to keep her family together and to protect her children from the appalling poverty and potential violence in her environment. It might stress that a woman in this situation has no choice but to suffer the consequences of her environment. The structure of the piece will stress the relationship between 'cause and effect' in a series of events presented in chronological sequence.

If you have chosen a theme under the psychological heading, then a realist and representational style may be the most suitable 'means' for developing the theme.

Brecht devised *epic theatre* as a 'means' of describing the relationships between history, class and poverty. A *Brechtian* piece would focus on the mother as a 'type' rather than as a unique individual. The migrant mother represents the class of dispossessed farmers who roamed America looking for work in the 1930s as the result of the failure of capitalism and the greed of banks. Through her encounters, in the form of *episodes* (with bankers, rich farmers and other migrant workers) we would not come to empathise with her but would become angry at the causes of her poverty and understand who is really to blame. The structure of the piece will be *episodic*. Each episode will tell a complete story, or the story of a particular incident, and be linked by what *Brecht* called 'knots' – in other words, the links may not be immediately clear to an audience; they will have to think about the meaning of the order and sequence of the episodes.

If you have chosen a theme under the sociological or historical headings then *Brecht*'s style of political and presentational theatre may be the most suitable 'means' for developing the theme.

One can even imagine the mother as the main character in a Greek *tragedy* with a chorus that comments on her plight and how she found herself in her present situation. The chorus may move between the *representational* (questioning the mother and the moral choices and actions she takes) and the *presentational* (reminding the audience of their moral responsibility for the poor, or urging them not to make the same mistakes).

If you have chosen a theme under the cultural or sociological headings then using the style, or adapting the genre, of Greek tragedy may be the most suitable 'means' for developing the theme.

Look at your chosen theme, or the theme you chose in relation to *The Migrant Mother 5* picture, and the thematic heading it is under. **Which styles and genres do you think will be the most appropriate 'means' for exploring the chosen theme?** Discuss the possibilities, choose the most appropriate style/s and/or genre and keep a record of your reasons for the choice.

As the work develops your ideas about style and genre may well change. You may also need to use a wider range of 'means' during the devising and rehearsal process, but it helps to have some idea now about which 'means' you think will prove to be the most appropriate to the 'meanings' that you are interested in exploring.

Audience

Who will be your audience? It is likely that you will have very little control over choosing an audience for your work. The audience may have to be your classmates or another teaching group. They may also include a teacher or examiner who will grade your work. Even so, thinking about to whom you will communicate in performance is an important stage in the devising process.

So far you have defined your own focus and interest in the theme. You have also made a first selection of the genres and styles which you are interested in using. So what about the audience? What will be interesting for them? What social function or purpose do you want the performance to have – to amuse, to stir people to take some sort of social action? What previous experience will the audience have of the theme, the styles and genres that you are focusing on?

Even if your classmates and an examiner will be the audience its still important to **identify the target audience. Look at and discuss the questions relating to** audience in the devising process questionnaire. Keep returning to these questions about audience during the devising process to remind you that your performance must *communicate* with, and be understood by, the chosen audience

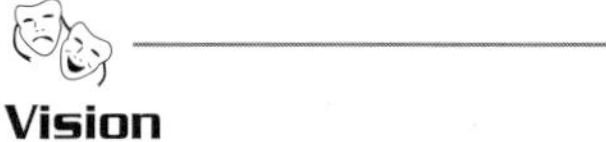

Vision

Finally, treat yourself to a daydream! **What vision do you have of the performance itself?** You have a lot of work to do, but it may help you through the bad times if you have a clear sense of what your ideal vision is. Imagine the sounds, the characterisation and settings, the design, the audience response, the effect and how that might all come together in the 'perfect' performance at the end of the devising process.

2 Research

Identify sources of information

One reason for encouraging you to find an aspect of your chosen theme that you feel committed to is because you will need to totally immerse yourself in researching and discovering as much as you can. Devising carries the responsibility of seeking out the 'truth'.

At one level, the 'truth' means ensuring that the information that you use is based on accurate sources of information. The audience expects you to have done a lot of detective work and collating of evidence. They expect your performance to be based on more than your existing hunches and understandings of the theme.

In your play text-based work you may already be familiar with the idea that the period of the play and the context in which it was written will need to be researched. You may also research other plays by the same author or of the same period. You may read critical commentaries written about the play and you will, of course, research the character that you will play.

In devised work you have to go further and do the same initial research that the playwright might do before producing a play text. It is important to ensure that the material you use in your devised piece is based on fact as well as on your own imaginative impulses. Characters, settings, plot, even the language and gestures should be 'true' to the real-life experiences that you are dramatising. In terms of the poverty theme we are working with here, we owe it both to our audience and to those who suffer poverty in their lives to give an honest and 'true' account in our devising.

What kinds of information will you be seeking? Research in theatre draws on a wide range of factual, artistic, personal and literary sources. We will suggest what these sources might be, but before you start there are some precautions!

Make a list of all the possible sources of information that you think it would be useful to look at in relation to your chosen aspect or theme and divide the work up between the group.

Use a critical eye

Always be alert to bias and distorted information, particularly when you look at statistics or official reports. When you look at the information given, ask who has produced it, for whom and for what purpose.

- **Does the information given tell the whole story**, or is it carefully selected to give a particular perspective?
- **Look for alternative accounts**. Never rely on a single source for your information – check it out against other sources.
- **Pay particular attention to sources that seem to contradict each other**, or which give very different accounts of the same experience or information. These may well provide you with useful tensions and conflicts of opinion to develop later.
- **Be careful to ensure that your research includes different 'voices'**. How is poverty differently experienced by the old or young? By men or women, min-

ority ethnic groups, the disabled, etc. Again you may find striking contrasts between the accounts given by different voices which may be usefully developed later in the process of devising.

- **Challenge your own values and attitudes.** Closely examine your own attitudes and beliefs and try to think out how you learnt them. If you want to challenge your audience to take a fresh look at a theme such as poverty, you need to challenge yourself first!

Sources: WWW and CD-ROM

We live in a world in which there is more information available than ever before. This information is increasingly visual as well as textual, which is very useful when devising theatre.

Electronic encyclopaedias on CD-ROMs such as *Encarta* are a very useful starting point for researching historical information. You could call up the 1930s in North America, for instance, and find out about the Great Depression and the effect it had on poor farmers like the migrant mother. You could then compare her experiences with what was happening in Europe at that time.

The WWW provides an increasingly important source of information for you. While we were writing this section, we needed to find the photograph of the migrant mother. You might like to follow our journey yourself, so get connected!

1 We opened the *search engine* on our web browser and typed in 'The Migrant Mother 5, Dorothea Lange' because we already knew the title of the picture and the name of the photographer. The results gave us a list which included: http://www.fotomuseum.ch/ENG/9804SHOW1/Pix_01_Zoom.html, which is a perfect copy of the original migrant mother photograph held in the Library of Congress in America. We copied the picture and pasted it straight into this chapter.
2 We also checked this site: http://www.loc.gov/rr/print/128_migm.html and found out more about the series of pictures Lange took of the migrant mother and the context of the pictures. This is where we found the contextual information about the picture that we gave you.
3 Next we decided to look and see what kind of styles and genres of theatre were popular in America at the time that the photo was taken. We went to a very useful site which gives links to other theatre-related sites: http://www.brookes.ac.uk/VL/theatre/images.htm
4 There we found a link to an American site which was recommended and were taken to: http://rs6.loc.gov/ammem/amtitle.new.html
5 In the list of topics, we found a reference to the *Federal Theatre Project* 1935–1939, and as this was the right period we clicked the link to discover more and were taken to: http://memory.loc.gov/ammem/fedtp/fthome.html which contained pages of interesting information and images.
6 Finally, we decided to look for social history information about the Great Depression and used the Go menu on our browser to go back to the same site we used in Step 3 and were taken to: http://memory.loc.gov/ammem/afctshtml/tshome.html which again had all the information that we might need.

Choose the keywords carefully when you make a search. If we had just typed in 'poverty' we would have received thousands of sites. Narrow down your search for what you are really looking for: 'poverty, children, pictures' for instance, or 'poverty, statistics, England'.

Media and bibliographic research

Keep an eye on the newspapers and TV schedules. You may well find articles and documentaries that are relevant to your chosen theme. While researching our theme, we came across an article in the *Guardian* titled: 'Britain Lagging on Child

Health'. In this article we discovered that low birth weights in England (an indication of poverty) are on a par with Albania and that by another poverty indicator we have a worse rate of infant mortality than Slovenia. An expert is quoted as saying:

> **We should ask ourselves why we are now below countries like Slovenia . . . and why the gap has widened between the health of rich children and poor over the last 20 years.**

But do remember to think about where this information is coming from – whose opinion does it represent? The *Guardian* is a liberal paper that represents the left of centre in politics. They may well tell a different story from a right-wing newspaper such as the *Daily Telegraph*.

Finding books on the subject you're interested in is more difficult. However, many libraries now have a search facility on computer terminals in the library. If you are connected to the Internet at home, you can sometimes find what you want by visiting a university website and getting into the library pages. Most universities have simple addresses like www.Warwick.ac.uk and allow visitors to search for book titles held in the library. You could also search a site that sells books, like www.Amazon.co.uk and find out titles, which you could then borrow from the library.

Art-works

How have other artists treated the same theme? Art-works, pictures, sculptures, prose, poetry and plays all offer a different kind of information for your research. The art-work itself is likely to be based on research and is helpful in that respect.

Art-works will tend to try and get inside the human dimension of the experience – how it might feel, the struggles, the hopes and the lost dreams. An effective art-work may well provoke strong feelings in you, like the feelings that you will want your audience to experience.

The artist also demonstrates how the broad experience and theme might be turned into something particular – a story with characters, a symbol or image.

The Migrant Mother 5 is a particular image of the misery and pain that affected thousands of people living at that time. The artist, Dorothea Lange, selected this particular image to stand for all that suffering. Go back to the picture again. Why do you think it has become one of the most reproduced photographs in the world?

Two of the most poignant pieces of writing that we found when researching *The Migrant Mother 5* were a poem by W.B. ***Yeats*** (the Irish poet and playwright) and an extract from John Steinbeck's *The Grapes of Wrath*. Steinbeck wrote:

> **And the dispossessed, the migrants, flowed into California, two hundred and fifty thousand, and three hundred thousand . . . and new waves were on the way, new waves of the dispossessed and homeless, hardened, intent and dangerous. . . .**
>
> **And a homeless hungry man, driving the roads with his wife beside him and his thin children in the back seat, could look at the fallow fields which might produce food but not profit, and that man could know how a fallow field is a sin and the unused land a crime against the thin children . . .**
>
> **. . . and in the South he saw the golden oranges hanging on the trees, the little golden oranges on the dark green trees; and guards with shotguns patrolling the lines so a man might not pick an orange for a thin child, oranges to be dumped if the price was low.**

Yeats wrote: 'He wishes for the cloths of heaven':

> **Had I the heaven's embroidered cloths,**
> **Enwrought with golden and silver light,**
> **The blue and the dim and the dark cloths**
> **Of night and light and the half-light,**
> **I would spread the cloths under your feet:**
> **But I, being poor, have only my dreams;**
> **I have spread my dreams under your feet;**
> **Tread softly because you tread on my dreams.**

Your search for art-works should include the popular arts and entertainment as well. The migrant mother may not have read *Yeats*, but she probably would have heard popular songs of the time on the radio. Songs like 'Brother Can You Spare a Dime?' sung by Bing Crosby, or Shirley Temple's 'The Good Ship Lollipop'. Popular songs, sayings, jokes, literature and other forms of entertainment provide a good source of information about the cultural attitudes and experiences of people living at the time. They can also be usefully developed into the devised piece to set the context, or to contrast with more formal and ***non-realist*** material.

Workshop: Turning ideas into actions

You are not writers or photographers; you are theatre artists. The theme that you have chosen will not be turned into words on a page or a photograph, but into drama and theatre.

The practitioner, Augusto *Boal*, offers a useful reminder of what you are looking for in your research when he says: 'There is no such thing as love. There are only ACTS of love'. By that he means that 'love' is a concept, an idea, but ACTS of love are something more concrete. In theatre there are only ACTIONS, so at **some early stage you need to begin to research into which actions you will use in your devising.**

The information that you collect in the research stage can be used to begin this process. You are just trying out dramatic ideas at present, using drama as a means of research. Some of these ideas may come back in later stages but they may also lead you on to new lines of enquiry and development.

You may, for instance, find a statistic, or statement, which you find surprising, shocking or disturbing. In order to make use of what you have found it will need translating into drama – as an image, or as a character who lives the experience, or as scenes which represent the 'truth' or given circumstances of the context or situation. You have to ask yourself **how is this information actually experienced by people in their lives?** Not as numbers or as statistics but as flesh and blood experience.

Take the opinion of the expert on child health that we referred to earlier. He claimed that the gap between the poorest and richest children has widened over the last 20 years. What does that actually mean? How do children themselves experience the 'gap'? Can we see the 'gap'? How are we all affected by the consequences of this widening 'gap'?

Make two sets of *still-images* which can be linked together (one for a child born in poverty and one for an economically privileged child) with the following captions as a means of beginning to see how these questions might be explored in drama:

- The baby is born
- The infant child sees his mother cry
- The first day of school
- The family treat
- The two children meet in the park

Fictional sources of information can usefully be explored through improvisation and role-play. The writer selects and describes a situation, but it takes drama to bring it 'alive'. Try out the following suggestions for a role-play sequence based on the Steinbeck extract:

Task 3: Bringing it alive

1. Make tableaux to represent each of the three paragraphs in the extract. You might use three titles:
   a Dispossessed, homeless, hard, intent and dangerous.
   b A fallow field is a sin and the unused land a crime against the children.
   c So a man might not pick an orange for a thin child.
2. Divide the space into two with a 'fence' dividing the orchard from the road on which the migrants travel. Half the group improvise the guards patrolling the orchard. The rest of the group should help them to find the physical actions by asking questions like: How would they behave? How do they do their job? What do they talk about as they work? Why are they necessary? Why was the decision taken to employ them? What are their instructions? Have they ever fired their guns in anger?
3. A second group represents a migrant family with hungry children standing the other side of the fence. Improvise what happens when they ask the guards for oranges for their children.
4. Let the family continue to put pressure on the guards. What would happen if one of the children made a run for the oranges? As you improvise this scene, agree that one of you will improvise the child who will suddenly make a dash for the fruit during the improvisation – how will the migrants and guards react? Don't plan the reactions, just see what happens. You could also agree that when the 'child' makes the dash this is a cue to drop into extreme slow motion so that the split second reactions of the others can be closely followed.

3 Focus

What is important to you and your audience?

Research may continue throughout the devising process. As you become more involved in developing your piece, your own interest will keep leading you to new sources and ideas. But at this stage you have collected together enough research material to begin the process of selecting that which will be important in your own devising and that which now needs discarding.

Remember to keep your theme manageable. Keep reminding yourself of the *aspect* of the theme that you are committed to, the *key question* that guides you, and the needs of the target *audience*. Use these 'anchors' to help you decide what to keep and what to 'throw away'.

Bring together all the material from the research, including a written record of any drama work done. Ask group members to take the first responsibility for selecting from the information that they were responsible for collecting, so that each individual only brings that which is relevant and important to the aspects of theme, key question and target audience. Lay the materials out in a large space and spend time looking closely at everything that is there. It's best not to talk too much at this stage – don't explain what's there, just let the group move around quietly, absorbing the material as they might do in a museum or gallery.

When everyone is familiar with the material you should begin trying to group the 'bits' together under appropriate headings which might include:

- Ideas for characters and roles
- Ideas for situations and possible dilemmas
- Facts and figures
- Background information on the theme

Now take two large sheets of paper and write down the following questions (one on each sheet):

- What is the importance of this theme for us?
- Why should our target audience care about this theme?

You could discuss your responses to these questions and note down the points made, but this is often a messy and noisy stage where individuals will disagree or push their own perspective. You could try having a 'silent argument': once the questions are down the group has 20 minutes of silence to argue in *writing*. If someone writes down 'because the theme is important to everyone' someone else might add 'who says so, it wouldn't be to my father' etc.

Finally, use a sheet of paper to brainstorm your responses to the question:

- What MUST we see and hear?

This is an important list, which represents your personal stake or interest in the devising. It is like saying, whatever may be thrown out or added, these images and these voices must be part of the final piece.

When this list is complete it will give you a clearer sense of the *mood* and *tone* that the devised piece is likely to have.

Focus on the social function

Does this process of focusing and getting a 'feel' for the material you have selected begin to suggest the social function of your devised piece? Any theme can be focused for an audience in quite different ways.

In Chapter 2 we noted that performances can have a broad range of social functions from the *didactic* with its emphasis on educating the audience and teaching a particular lesson, through to the stirring up of public debate on issues, through to the purely entertaining and pleasurable.

What social effect do you want to achieve? Remember that there can be a mix of social functions – a performance that seeks to change the world or the audience in some way is unlikely to produce this effect unless it is also entertaining. ***Brecht*** reminds us that: 'Theatre consists in this: in making live representations of reported or invented happenings between human beings and doing so with a view to entertainment'.

In the same way, a piece which is full of fun and pleasure for the audience can also have an edge of social comment or a challenge to the audience's attitudes. Dario ***Fo***, for instance, reminds us that theatre is 'a great machine, which makes people laugh at dramatic things. . . In the laughter there remains a sediment of anger'. *Fo* produces savage social satires using clowning, tumbling, mime, song and stand-up comedy as his means in plays like *Mistero Buffo* and *The Accidental Death of an Anarchist.*

Focus on the artistic intention

You also need to focus on the styles and genres that you think will be useful to you and decide on whether the play is likely to mix ***realist*** and ***non-realist*** elements and ***presentational*** and ***representational*** theatre.

Go back to our discussion of these topics in Chapter 2. Remind yourself of the distinctive characteristics of both *realist* and *non-realist* styles. Look at the materials you have selected to use in the devising process and make some initial decisions as to how you think the material should be handled.

Now consider the relationship between the performance and the audience. Will it tend towards a *representational* style that seeks to represent a powerful fictional world for the audience, or will it tend towards a *presentational* style that presents characters and situations to the audience directly? Again, you may well decide on a mix of the two styles, depending on the material that you have selected.

Remember the strengths in the group as well. If you can sing, choreograph, use computers to generate music, or create video images then make sure that one of your artistic intentions it to use these skills effectively in your piece!

Modify your vision

Go back and look at the vision you described in Stage 1. Modify and redraft the vision on the basis of the work and decisions taken since.

4 Collect and Develop

The bits not the whole

Your vision is of the final performance, but you must begin with the 'bits' that will make up that performance. **Be careful not to start with a story or plot.** Start by creating the characters, scenes, situations and other dramatic ideas which you might use in your final product. Thinking up a story and then dramatising it closes your mind to the exploration and discovery of dramatic ideas. Drama is not the same as storytelling. Be patient.

Think of this stage of the process as being like making a collage or montage. Before you can begin you have to collect together all the scraps of material or images that you might want to use. Then you play around with them looking for what shapes, patterns and textures might work together to create the effect you want. Then, and only then, do you begin to stitch or paste the bits together to make your collage or montage.

Characters

As we have suggested, **characters are living flesh and blood examples of the chosen theme.** The migrant mother is a real woman living through the experience of poverty, which is our theme. Character is at the heart of this stage of the process. Sometimes the idea for a character, or characters, will be suggested by the stimulus, like the migrant mother. But If you are building characters from scratch then:

- Remember that a dramatic theme is always rooted in actual human experience. So what kind of a person, or people would *live out* your theme? How can the theme be *embodied* in a character? Identify the kind of person, or people, that you want to base your characters on.
- Are there any useful ideas for character from your previous research?
- Use the work on given circumstances in Chapters 3 and 8 to flesh out your characters.
- Use the 'Circle of Life' exercise below to develop character.
- Use *role on the wall* or some other form of notation to keep a record of the characters' given circumstances and circle of life. Refer back to this information, particularly if you are creating ***Stanislavskian*** characters who are expected to behave in ways that are consistent with their given circumstances.

The 'Circle of Life' exercise

Divide a large sheet of paper into five sections with a circle in the centre of the page where the name and age of a character are written. The surrounding paper is then divided into four sections that will represent areas of that character's life and the people they interact with at those times. These sections are labelled: 'Home', 'Family', 'Play', and 'Day'. The heading '**Home**' indicates where the central character normally lives, while '**Family**' indicates any immediate or extended family and may include estranged family members we might otherwise expect to find at home. '**Play**' indicates any type of social life and '**Day**' indicates the character's workplace, if appropriate, or otherwise encompasses their daily routine – for example, if they are too young to work or unemployed.

Now brainstorm ideas about the character and enter these into the appropriate section. Divide into four groups, take a different section each and create a short dialogue between the central character and one other character selected from the chosen section of the diagram.

Scenes and settings

The previous exercise has begun to give you ideas for scenes and settings which might be usefully developed. But keep your mind open to new possibilities. Remember that what you are trying to do is to identify events, times and places which your characters might be involved in, which will *illuminate* the theme and your key question.

Remember that our key question for the migrant mother work was: 'Is it possible to be poor and good?' Two scenes suggest themselves. In the first a farmer who has plenty of food threatens to throw the mother off his land if he catches the children stealing vegetables again – how will she react? In the second a money-lender offers her cash for her wedding ring – will she sell it and what will she tell her husband?

Use separate pieces of paper or card to brainstorm other possibilities for scenes. Write down the essential information for each scene under these headings:

- The ACT (what happens)
- The SETTING (where and when it happens)
- The AGENTS (who makes it happen)
- The AGENCY (how the action is carried out)
- The PURPOSE (why does it happen)

Once you have a selection to choose from discuss the dramatic possibilities of each – which is the most revealing, or which might reveal the most through improvisation? Which are most closely related to your key question? **Select two or three scenes to work on**, keep the others for future reference and make a note of your choices. Carefully and slowly improvise the scenes with observers. The observers should note and interrupt the work if necessary to point out:

- Moments of real tension
- Significant gestures or movements
- That which is 'true' and not 'true' to the given circumstances
- 'What-if' developments to the scene

The observers should also '*hot-seat*' the actors in character about their motives, feelings, and reactions to what is going on.

If appropriate, the improvisations can be interspersed with other dramatic conventions like *sculpting, thought-tracking, alter ego, shape shifting* and *flashbacks*. The purpose here is to step back from the realism of improvisation and work on finding depth and honesty in the characterisation. **Using these conventions can also avoid heated discussion.** If there are differences of opinion in the group try to find ways for these differences to be tried out or dramatically explained rather than argued about.

Scenarios and scripting

The previous exercise has given you three or more *anchor scenes*. Not the whole plot but some key moments, or the *scenario*, which is a summary or précis of the plot. Do you have ideas about the ordering of these anchor scenes? Remember that they don't have to be organised chronologically – you can move backwards and forwards in time using the most appropriate scene as your starting point.

Place your anchor scenes in order. How close together are these scenes in terms of time and setting? Arrange the scenes on the floor to show the 'gaps' in between the anchor scenes. Do the 'gaps' need filling in with additional scenes, which lead up to, or link, or follow on from the anchors? Use additional sheets of paper with your ideas on to fill in the 'gaps'.

Remember that the links between the anchor scenes don't have to be more scenes in a realist style that 'fill in' the plot. You could use songs, monologues, images, dance, storytelling and video as links, which would stress the theme, mood or context rather than the storyline. If your anchor scenes are ***representational*** then these kinds of link will add a ***presentational*** dimension to your work.

The anchor scenes are crucial to establishing your piece. You may not want to leave these scenes to chance and to improvisation. Scripting the anchor scenes will fix them for the actors.

Rehearsal strategies

Use all the notes made during the improvisation and during discussion to **prepare a draft script for the anchor scenes** at least. Refer back to the advice we gave on language and character in Chapter 8.

You now have a set of anchor scenes and some ideas about links between these scenes. The next stage of the work moves from exploration to the problems of communicating your intentions to an audience. The anchor scenes and links need to be extensively rehearsed so that characters have a chance to develop and the playing of scenes can be shaped and focused towards performance.

Throughout this book there are examples of rehearsal strategies that you might use at this stage:

- Use the textual analysis questionnaire in Chapter 8 to identify the **wants**, **will**, **moral stance**, **physical appearance** and **summary adjectives** for characters.
- Use the exercises for playing **objectives**, **strategies** and **obstacles** in Chapter 3.
- Identify the units in each scene using the exercises in Chapter 8.
- Use the ***Brechtian*** rehearsal techniques described in Chapter 4.
- Identify and fix a rehearsal schedule based on the example given in Chapter 6.

5 Building the Performance Text

The montage of attractions

The performance text refers to everything that will be seen, heard and experienced in the performance itself. It refers to the weaving together of all that is present in a performance into a coherent and well crafted text. The performance text is not the same as the plot or the ***mise en scene***, although it includes both. It refers to the ordering and sequencing, in space and time, of *all* that is seen and heard in the performance. In this sense the performance text is a composition like a play text, musical score or novel. It is a construction according to artistic principles and intentions. In the previous section you developed the 'bits and pieces' for the performance text like collecting together the scraps of material for a collage or montage; now these pieces need to be woven together and prepared for performance.

Montage is a synonym for collage and this term was first used by the director and film-maker Sergei Eisenstein in the 1920s to describe the principles of composition in ***non-realist*** theatre. In the previous stage we compared the process to collecting together the bits to be used in a collage. This next stage of building the montage is like the process of putting together the bits of the collage and stitching them into the pattern or shape that you decide on as being the most effective for bringing the bits together into a new meaningful relationship – a performance text.

Montage comes after the first stages of rehearsal, which are used to develop the characters and scenes. **Now the earlier work must be woven together so that it becomes a textured, layered and coherent whole for the audience.**

It is the director's responsibility to organise the building of the montage. All of the theatrical elements needed to create a performance text need to be combined to create a clear, flowing, stylistically coherent whole, which will hold the attention of the audience.

Eisenstein talked of the 'montage of attractions' to remind us that what we are seeking to do is to *attract* the audience's attention, senses, thinking and feeling. ***Meyerhold*** first used the term 'attraction' because he realised that effective moments in the theatre are not always driven by the twists and turns of the plot and character. Changes in light, a dramatic use of space, clever design, a striking physical image, a dramatic change of tempo or mood, colours and textures in costume and setting; all of these may provide strong moments of 'attraction' for an audience. But they must be planned for!

Decide where the moments of 'attraction' are going to be in your performance text and how they will be achieved. What will the audience need to see and hear in order for each moment of 'attraction' to be effective?

The sign systems of theatre

How will the sign system of theatre be used? In Chapter 10 we identify the multiple systems that theatre uses to communicate its meanings to an audience and in the performance analysis questionnaire we list the sign systems. Whoever is taking directorial responsibility for your work should familiarise themselves with these sections and the ideas in them.

Acting styles

Is the whole performance based on one style of acting or is there a mix of styles? In other words, do you find that you have a mix of ***representational*** scenes in which the characters are totally locked in their world and ***presentational*** scenes in which the actors are directly showing the audience what happens, or happened? If so, how will the audience accept this mix? What conventions of design, or light, or use of space will you use to help the audience recognise that there are different acting styles being used for a clear purpose?

Design

How can the 'look of the play' be established through design features? What props or setting will be used and how will an appropriate theme be established through the choice of shapes, colours and textures? The design should offer a commentary on the plot and characters rather than merely provide a realistic landscape. Your ideas about the relationship between the theme that you have chosen and the particulars of your plot and characters (the overall intention) can be expressed through your choices concerning the design of the performance.

Technical theatre

How will technical effects be used to create 'attractions' for the audience? Remember that lighting, sound, video images and other technical devices can be used to offer an interpretation or commentary on the plot and characters. In the modern theatre these effects are rarely used to faithfully recreate realistic settings. Cinema does that better. Lighting and sound can be used to describe moods, feelings and portents of what will happen next as well as to signal night/day and the sounds of birds! But again, remember that if you are using technical effects to express ideas and the theme you need to be sure that the audience will accept your combining of ***realist*** and ***non-realist*** elements in performance. If some of the *realist* scenes are lit using strong colours to express the mood but others are not, the audience will question why this is and look for the 'logic' of your choices – why certain scenes are lit this way and not others. So again be consistent in whatever choices you make.

Actor/audience

The relationship between the world of the performance and the audience's world is partly established through your choice between a *representational* style which creates a distance between the performance and the audience, and a *presentational* style which seeks to involve the audience directly in the world of the performance. But it is the use of space which does most to establish the actor-audience relationship.

How will the space be divided between the performance space and the audience space? Think creatively about the possibilities for fresh and interesting ways of establishing the use of space. Even if the space seems inflexible – a proscenium arch stage for instance – you can build extra staging or perform scenes in different locations, each of which creates a different actor-audience relationship.

Draw a ground plan for your performance showing the division between audience and performance space. Locate the scenes in the performance space – where *exactly* will each scene be played? Now ask yourselves why you have made these decisions and whether you could find a more original or interesting arrangement. Consider the following:

- How physically close to the audience do you want your actors to be?
- Will the audience stay in a fixed position, or might they be asked to move, as in a *promenade* performance?
- How will the audience be arranged? Front-on? In the round? Around three sides? In groups within the performance space?
- How can exits and entrances be used to effect? Might the actors move through the audience, for instance?
- Will there be a consistent use of space for particular locations? Will family scenes always be played in one place and street scenes in another? How will the logic of your choice be made clear to an audience?
- How can the stage architecture and lighting be used to clearly guide the audiences' awareness of how space is being used in your performance – use of levels, staging, spotting, colour codes, etc?

Finally, remember that the use of space will need signalling to the audience. How might lighting, colour or props be used to help clearly distinguish between space used for performance and audience space? How might these signs be used creatively – to lead the audience in or to blur the boundaries between audience and performance space, for instance?

Rhythm and pace

The rhythm and pace of individual scenes should have been established via the rehearsal process in which you worked to establishing the units of each scene and how the objectives and strategies should be played. The use of linking material between your anchor scenes should also have produced a rhythm and pace in the structure of you piece. Now the *overall* rhythm and pace needs establishing.

Make a list of the scenes. Connect this list to a second list of the 'attractions'. Are the 'attractions' evenly distributed, or **does a rhythm need establishing which builds up and down from the core attractions of the piece?**

Draw a flow diagram based on the example given in the performance analysis questionnaire. Divide the performance up into units (possibly the act/scene structure or time elapsed). Make a simple flow chart to show the rhythms and pace of the performance – the bottom of the chart to represent 'slow/quiet' and the top 'fast/loud'.

6 Refocus I

Fixing the overall intention

By now you have spent a lot of time as a group experimenting and developing your ideas. If you have done this with an open mind you may well have drifted by now from your original intentions and focus. **You may have become so absorbed both in the theme and in the drama work that you have forgotten that the audience will be coming to this material much as you first did.** You may also have forgotten what you first decided it was important to communicate to an audience.

Now the montage is nearing completion – it will be completed in performance – it is useful to go back and reconsider the choices you made in Stages 1 and 3 ('Identify' and 'Focus'). Are they still relevant? Do they now need modifying? Does the montage need further development or modifications to bring it back into line with your intentions?

7 First Sharing

Critical feedback

It is a common problem in devising for the work to become obscure to anyone who has not been a part of the devising itself. You have worked intensely in your group and you will have had hours and hours of discussion about your ideas and the emerging montage or collage for performance. The montage may make perfect sense to you, but it may not communicate as clearly and coherently to an audience of strangers.

It is important, then, at this stage in your work to share all or some of the work in performance conditions. You need to choose your audience carefully. If you have a particular target audience (children, for instance) it would make sense to ensure that they are represented. You need an audience that can offer honest, critical feedback on your work. It doesn't help to have friends who just say its great!

Check intentions and effects

Before the first sharing, think through the montage and list the questions that you want to put to your trial audience. You may want to focus these general questions on specific characters or scenes in your piece.

Don't prepare the audience by giving a full account of your ideas and intentions; only tell them as much as they need to know in order to follow and understand the performance. When the performance is finished, give the audience a few moments to share their responses and the effect of the performance with each other before putting your questions to them. Give someone the job of carefully recording *everything* the audience offers.

If the audience is critical of your work, if the gap between intention and effect is wider than you had hoped for, if they failed to understand some aspects, don't be defensive – don't argue or justify yourself. Instead, just listen and record the comments for later analysis.

The proof of the performance is, as ***Brecht*** constantly remarked, in the pudding! If it doesn't work in performance, you need to go back and fix it. Don't blame the audience! Remember Noel ***Coward***'s advice: 'Do what pleases you, and if it doesn't please the public, get out of show business!'

8 Refocus II

Mind the gap!

You should leave some rehearsal time between the first sharing and the assessed performance. There are several considerations for you:

- How can the gap between your intentions and the effects experienced by your trial audience be closed?
- Can anything be lost and or added to make the performance tight and coherent?
- What additional work needs to be done on character and setting to clarify the intentions?
- What changes of rhythm and pace need to be made (did the trial audience comment on the work being a 'little slow' or 'boring in parts')?

Go through the analysis of performance questionnaire and apply it to your

own work. The questionnaire sets out what a critical member of the audience might be looking for in your performance. Analysing your devised piece against the questionnaire will help you to see the work from a critical perspective as well as from your own perspective as deviser/performer.

9 Performing

Where does it begin and end?

When does a performance begin? Is it when the lights go up? Or is it, for the actors, in the quiet period of preparation that might begin hours before the performance? During this pre-performance period the actor needs to prepare physically and mentally. Focusing on your character and the relationships with other characters; focusing on key speeches or difficult moments of physical work; and focusing on intentions are all-important prior to performance. Familiar warm-ups and exercises can help to prepare the body and voice, and to calm nerves!

When does the performance begin for an audience? How will their expectations be prepared through the marketing of your performance in posters and flyers? How can you 'dress' the lobby and entrances to create the right impression and mood for your piece? How can this pre-performance information be used as part of the performance by giving essential information about the characters, plot, style and theme in programme notes and images? You might even play with starting your performance in the lobby by organising 'happenings' between characters and audience or through song and visual images in the lobby or in the performance space as the audience is led in.

How will you measure your success?

Before the first performance, establish how you will judge the success of your work. Identify the effects you want to achieve at different points in the performance – are you expecting laughter, or fear, or pity at certain points? If so, what will be the signs from the audience that you will be looking out for? Laughter is fairly obvious, but in quieter, more intense moments how will you recognise the signals of interest/disinterest in the audience?

Between the idea and the act: were your intentions realised?

T.S. ***Eliot*** reminds us of the gap that often exists in creative work between the idea and the execution of the idea. He said: 'Between the idea and the act falls the shadow'. In the case of devising the 'shadow' can take many forms! Look again at your vision of the performance that you described in Stage 3. How much of this vision were you able to realise? What reasons would you now give for any differences between the vision and the actual performance?

10 Evaluation and Writing Up

The process
- **Collect**
- **Summarise**
- **Select and emphasise**
- **Headings and paragraphs**

We have encouraged you to keep a detailed record and collection of all the materials, ideas and developments during the devising process. This collection and record now serves as the basis for your written account of the process you have been through.

In writing your evaluation you will need to describe how you moved from Stage 1 in which you first identified your theme, styles and genres, and target audience. You will then need to describe how you focused the theme and identified the social and artistic functions and intentions together with appropriate styles of theatre. The middle section of the evaluation will describe the working methods you used to devise a piece of theatre that realised the decisions you took in Stages 1 and 3. Finally, you will need to assess the extent to which your performance realised your intentions.

It might be useful to begin by making summary notes, on separate pages, of what happened at each stage in the process under the appropriate headings. These notes form the basis for your written evaluation. The way in which you now assemble your notes into a written evaluation will depend on the assessment focus for the evaluation.

In other words, there are ten stages in this devising process. It is not a simple question of giving equal weight to all ten stages. If you are asked to comment on the research that you did, or to describe your intentions, or to comment on your role as an actor, you will emphasise, or give more room to, certain stages of the devising process rather than others.

When you know the focus for the evaluation, go through your summary notes and highlight the relevant information: Decide which stages should be given emphasis and add any additional information that you might have overlooked or which needs to be stretched out.

Draft a series of headings to use. These headings might be based on the headings used for the stages of the devising process, or they might reflect the focus of the evaluation.

Think also about the different text types that you will use to **recount, explain, persuade and discuss** in your evaluation and remind yourself how these different types need to be structured and written. Remember that you should keep recounting – telling the story of your devising process – to a minimum. The bulk of your evaluation should be written in the other three text types to ensure that your evaluation has more **analysis** than **description** in it.

Once you are confident that the headings and balance of text types will give you a structure for the evaluation, assemble the relevant notes into paragraphs and prepare your first draft!

The Kissing Dance – or She Stoops to Conquer, The National Youth Music Theatre/Linbury Studio Theatre, Royal Opera House, December 1999.

Devising Process Questionnaire

The devising process questionnaire is designed to provide you with a set of key questions to guide your work in each of the ten stages of the devising process. The questions suggest what you might look for and do in each stage and they also provide a checklist of what you should have done in order to complete the stage successfully. Remember that any devising process is messier and more complicated than our simple framework suggests. While we believe that all of these stages form part of an effective devising process it is inevitable that the order of the stages may be different and the questions here may not all prove to be relevant to your particular project. Remember, also, that it is vital that you collect and keep detailed notes, drawings and other forms of record from the first meeting to the final performance. These records will form the basis for your detailed evaluations of the project.

Stage	Questions
1 Identify	Have you agreed and established the ground rules for your work together? Have you decided on the 'blocks' that might get in your way as you devise together? What strategies will you use when you get 'blocked'? Have you allocated production roles and responsibilities? What stimulates you about the 'stimulus'? What questions and curiosities does it raise? Would using drama conventions like still-images, thought-tracking and hot-seating help you to make an initial exploration? What human themes and experiences are touched on by the stimulus? Have you narrowed down a theme so that it is focused clearly? Have you agreed on a key question that will guide your devising decisions? Does the stimulus suggest a particular performance style or genre? Does the chosen theme and/or key question suggest a style or genre? Have you identified the mix of genres and styles that you will use? Who will be your audience? Who would be most interested in this theme? How much experience will the audience have of the styles and genres you are thinking of using – will they recognise the conventions? What effect are you hoping to have on the audience: what do you want them to think and feel? How inclusive do you want to be – how broad an age and cultural background do you want to appeal to? Why would this audience be interested in your product? How will the audience's interests and expectations be remembered and included in the shaping of the work? Have you dreamt a vision of the performance that excites and encourages you?
2 Research	Which sources of information are you going to use? Who is going to collect the information? Have you included a balance of views and voices? Are you making full use of the WWW? Can you find inspiration in other art-works that relate to the stimulus or theme? Have you used a full range of drama conventions and workshop strategies to explore the research materials? Have you identified and researched the work of other practitioners associated with the styles and genres of your own work?

3 Focus	What will you choose to keep from your research and what will you now put on one side? What is the logic behind your selection? Have you considered the audience in making this selection? What should the social function of the performance be: should it educate and/or should it entertain? Will the performance include both ***realist*** and ***non-realist*** styles? Will it include ***presentational*** and ***representational*** theatre? What is the logic of your choices?
4 Collect and Develop	Will you use any of the characters from the stimulus or research? What are their given circumstances? What other characters might you develop to bring the themes alive? Which methods and styles of characterisation will you use (e.g. ***Stanislavskian***, ***Brechtian***, physical)? Have you explored characters *practically* by using improvisation and other conventions? What are the key scenes that will best illustrate and develop your chosen theme and key question? Have you established your framework of anchor scenes? What is important about each of these scenes from the point of view of the chosen theme? How will the anchor scenes be sequenced? Is this sequence: cause and effect (narrative); episodic; thematic development? What links between the anchor scenes are needed and what form will these links take: scenes, songs, storytelling, video clips or other images? Which rehearsal strategies will best suit your work? Will the ideas and methods of particular practitioners be used? Is too much discussion and too little action beginning to bog you down? Have you used drama conventions rather than discussion to resolve differences of opinion or problems with character development and structure?
5 Building the Performance Test	What will be the key 'attractions' in the performance? How will these 'attractions' be realised? How will space, design, light, contrasts of style and other theatrical elements be used to add power to your scenes? Who will take responsibility for coordinating and directing the performance text? Which type of director will best suit the performers and the need to ensure that the performance text is effective and completed on time? What conventions will you need to establish so that the audience will understand the mix of styles and genres in the work? How can the 'look', or the 'world', of the play be established through design? How can technical effects be used to create 'attractions', moods and atmosphere for the audience? How will the space be divided between performance and audience? Have you established the rhythm and pace of the performance? How will the audience's attention be held for the duration of the performance? Is the balance between highly active scenes and more moody and quiet scenes right? Is there enough variation in pace, mood and style to keep an audience engaged or might there be flat spots that need attention? Have you checked that the logic of the performance will be clear for an audience in terms of everything that happens, that is seen and that is heard during the performance?

6 Refocus I	How far have you drifted from your original intentions identified in Stages 1 and 3? Do you need to modify, or correct, the performance text so that the relationship with your chosen theme and key question is re-strengthened? Do you need to modify, or correct, your original intentions in the light of the new discoveries made during the devising process? Will the relationship between your intentions and the performance text be clear for an audience?
7 First sharing	Which audience will offer you the most useful feedback? How will this feedback be collected? Does the characterisation work? Does the plot, if there is one, seem credible and logical? Is the progression and rhythm of the performance effective? Are the setting and other design features clear enough for the audience? Are the performers' skills good enough – is further targeted rehearsal needed? What range of effects does the audience describe?
8 Refocus II	What is the 'gap' between your intentions and the effects the audience experienced? How can this 'gap' be closed? Does the performance text need editing, or adding to? What additional work will need to be done on characters, scenes and technical effects? What changes in rhythm and pace might need to be further explored and tested before the next performance?
9 Performing	How will the performance space be prepared? Where, when and how does the performance begin and end for both performers and audience? What criteria will you use to judge the success and effectiveness of your performance? Have you realised the initial vision that you had for the performance? Were some of your initial ideas unrealisable? Were some ideas technically too difficult to realise? Were there problems with people, time, space, technical support? Might the performance have worked better with a different audience in a different space? Would you want to repeat or continue to develop the ideas and themes in your performance?
10 Evaluation and Writing up	Have you collected together all the evidence from the first nine stages? Have you summarised the main points from each stage? Which stages will you emphasise in your evaluation? Have you drafted a series of headings which will keep you focused on the main point of the evaluation? Does your evaluation make sense to an 'outsider'? Someone who has not been intimately involved in the process? Which text types will you use in your evaluation? Is the balance between recounting, explaining, persuading and discussing ideas appropriate?

10 Reading the Signs of Performance

Evaluating Performance

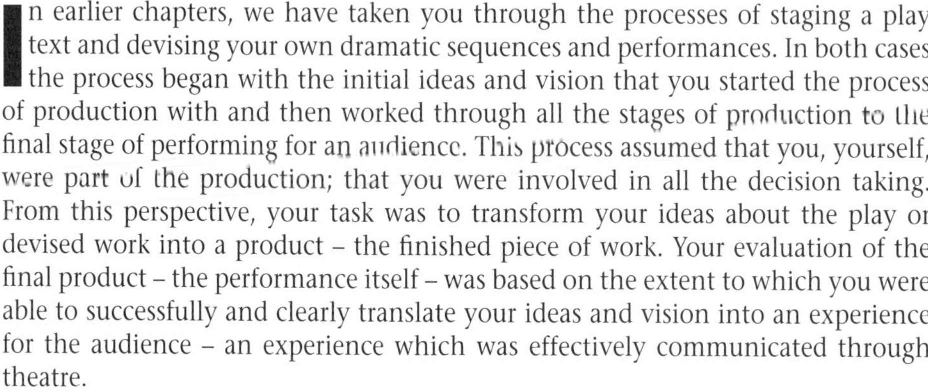
In earlier chapters, we have taken you through the processes of staging a play text and devising your own dramatic sequences and performances. In both cases the process began with the initial ideas and vision that you started the process of production with and then worked through all the stages of production to the final stage of performing for an audience. This process assumed that you, yourself, were part of the production; that you were involved in all the decision taking. From this perspective, your task was to transform your ideas about the play or devised work into a product – the finished piece of work. Your evaluation of the final product – the performance itself – was based on the extent to which you were able to successfully and clearly translate your ideas and vision into an experience for the audience – an experience which was effectively communicated through theatre.

The performance must speak for itself

The evaluation of your own performance, the product of the rehearsal/devising processes, rests on the extent to which the performance was able to 'speak for itself'. In other words, the extent to which all your intentions and ideas were successfully translated into what the audience actually *saw*, *heard* and *experienced* during the performance. In this sense, however hard and long you may have worked, it is the performance itself that counts. The audience were not there during rehearsals, they did not hear all the discussions or know about all the choices you made. The only part of the work that they share with you is the product of all your work – the performance.

Although one of the unique characteristics of theatre, as opposed to sculpture or poetry, is that the artists (performers) and the audience both need to be present in the same place and time, it is not usual for the artists to speak to the audience beyond the performance itself. It is not usual, for instance, for artists to hold a discussion with the audience where they explain all their intentions or tell the audience what they *should* have seen, heard or experienced. Either the performance speaks for itself or it doesn't!

Your evaluation of a performance by another group places you firmly in the position of the audience. In a sense, what you have to do is to reverse the process of evaluation. Instead of starting with the initial ideas and tracking them through to the performance, you now need to start with the effect of the performance itself and try to track backwards to discover what kinds of ideas, visions, rehearsal processes and interpretations might have been made and used during the invisible processes of production that led to the performance.

In evaluating your own work, you move from *production* to *reception* – how the work is received by an audience. **In evaluating the work of others, you move from *reception* – the effect the performance had on you – to *production* – how this effect might have been constructed during the process of production.** What you see and hear and experience during the performance forms the basis for this detective work.

Task 1: What the critics say

The most commonly available form of performance evaluation or criticism is to be found in the **reviews** of recent performances in the media. These reviews are based on how a performance was experienced by a specialist member of the audience – a critic. The critic's job is to give an accurate account of the performance – what was seen and heard – and to offer an opinion on the performance based on their prior experiences and knowledge.

1. Find two or more reviews of the same performance in the newspapers.
2. Make copies of the reviews.
3. Use different colour highlighters to mark: information that appears in both reviews; any differences of opinion or differences in factual information.

- Do the reviews include any additional information about the actors or director, other performances of the same play or the venue?
- What are the reviewers' opinions, or judgements, based on? What aspects or moments of the performance do the reviewers use as examples to justify their opinion of the play (these might include acting, directing, design or interpretation of a play text).

If possible, try to see the performance yourself. Is your experience different? In what ways? Can you understand the performance from the reviewer's point of view? Write your own review based on what was the same or different in your experience of the performance.

The Role and Power of the Critic

You may have had the experience of having a 'critic in the house'. Someone who was sent to review your performance for a local newspaper for instance. Often, a great deal of attention will be paid to the critic – to where they sit, how they seem to be responding during the performance, anything they might have said before they left. **The critic is powerful!**

You as the critic

Part of this power is based on the critic publishing a review that may well influence whether people come to see the show or not. But, part of this power is also based on the *knowledge* that a critic has and the *value* that is placed on the critic's taste and preferences. In many ways your own study of theatre has begun to give you the same power. You no longer experience a performance in quite the same way as you once did. You know something of the history and traditions of theatre. You know what to look for in a performance. You have some sense of the difference between 'good' and 'bad' acting. You may have studied and worked with the play that you are going to see and that will have given you certain expectations. You have devised and rehearsed and produced your own work. You know what it is like to be a performer in performance.

For these reasons, you are becoming a 'special' member of the audience too. You will experience the performance differently from other members of the audience who have not studied theatre, or taken the same interest as you have. **Your experi-**

ence of the performance will be coloured by your prior learning and experiences in drama.

Between Intention and Effect

Different individuals are affected differently

The prior experience and learning that we bring to a performance goes beyond our specialised knowledge of theatre and drama. All forms of theatre offer a commentary on the human condition. So, **who you are and what you have already learnt about the human condition will also influence your experience of the performance** and the effect that the performance has on you. Each of us experiences the world in different ways – we have our own stories, our own journeys, our own bodies and our own place in the world. For this reason, no two members of the audience will have quite the same human experience of the performance.

The differences between individual responses to a performance might be based on:

- Gender
- Age or generation
- Physical appearance (or how we imagine others see us!)
- Culture
- Ethnicity
- Class or social and economic status
- Beliefs
- Political views
- Key life experiences similar to those represented in the performance
- Prior knowledge and experience of performance

Task 2: Different audiences, different effects

Go back to the scene from *The Crucible* that was used in Chapter 3.

Imagine and describe the different ways that this scene might be experienced by:

- **a middle-aged woman whose husband has had an affair with a younger woman;**
- **a middle-aged man who has strong religious beliefs but who also feels trapped in a 'loveless' marriage;**
- **a young girl who has been harassed at work by a male employer;**
- **a young man or woman whose parents divorced because of infidelity.**

Because there will be so many different responses to a performance, it is important to be aware that what you experience during a performance and what you have to say about a particular performance will depend on where you are coming from as a person. **Any review of a performance is, therefore, a mixture of the *subjective* – your particular and personal response – and the *objective* – factual information based on what was actually seen and heard by everyone who was there.**

Test out your opinions in discussion

The trick is to establish a relationship between the two: to understand and explain your own response by referring to what it was that you actually saw and heard during the performance, and in the same way to look and listen carefully during a performance and try to work out what the playwright, performers and directors *intend* you to experience. It is also important to try and talk with other members of the audience after a show. How are their responses the same or different from your own? What did they see and hear? If they saw and heard things differently from you, try to understand why that might be – *where* are *they* coming from?

Producers have intentions that affect the audience

It is always important for you to bear in mind, both as a performer and as a critic, that *intention* and *effect* are not the same. Sometimes performers and directors will speak of their work having a certain kind of effect for an audience. But for the reasons we have given they cannot know what effect the work will have on the individuals who make up an audience. They can only have the intention that the work should effect the audience in a certain way. One important job for the critic is to make this distinction between intention and effect. The director may intend a certain line to be funny, for instance, but the effect may be to make you cringe! You can work out the intention, to be funny, and then work out why it failed to have that effect on you.

There is, if you like, a triangular relationship between:

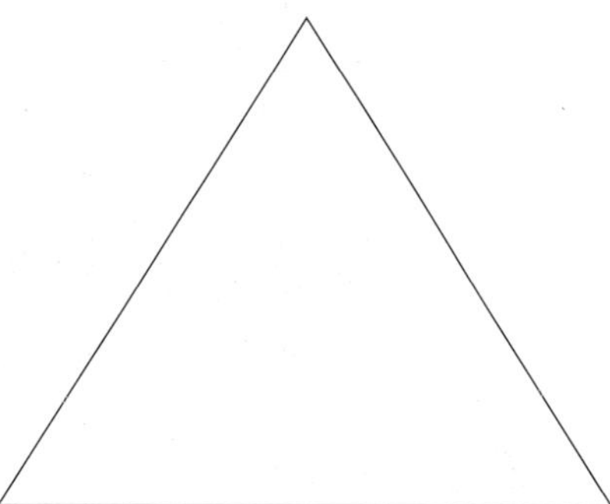

What was intended?

What was the effect on you?

Task 3: Testing the subjective within the objective

Try and remember a performance that you were part of, or watched with others in your class, which either didn't 'work' (the audience didn't respond as you expected) or which aroused very different responses from your classmates in the audience. Use the triangle above to try to work out why.

- **Begin with the facts – the words spoken, the number of actors, the set, the images created on stage.**
- **Then consider what your intentions were, or what you imagine the intentions might have been in a performance you watched.**
- **Then consider the responses of the audience, or the effect on you.**

Because there will be so many different subjective responses to a performance it is very difficult to write or talk about a particular performance in general terms, without making the false assumption that everyone was affected by what they saw and heard in the same way. In the past, it was often assumed that what was seen and heard on stage would be the same for everyone. People still sometimes talk about the play's *effect* as if there could only be one effect.

A Short History of Signs and Meanings

***Semiotics*: a science of signs and their meanings**

There have been many attempts to try and produce a stable, reliable and completely objective method for analysing performances. Many of these attempts belong to a form of literary criticism known as ***semiotics***. The first *semiotician* was Ferdinand de Saussure who proposed semiotics to be **the science of the life of signs in a society.** Saussure's theory was that meanings in society are tied to the signs that are commonly used or understood. This is how we communicate – the words that we use in speech and writing are 'signs' for certain meanings. Words as speech and as writing are the most obvious signs. Languages are made up of sounds and symbols (writing) that have particular meanings, or *sign*ificance, for those who use the language. A sign, in language, is made of two elements, the word itself, which is known as a *signifier*, and the idea or concept that it is a sign-post for, which is known as the *signified*.

$$\text{Sign} = \frac{\text{Signifier (the word 'cat' for instance)}}{\text{Signified (the idea, or image, of a cat)}}$$

Language is a system based on the difference between signs used

In Saussure's theory, a language is always a system based on *difference*. In other words, different sounds and written words mean different things. If a language user makes the sign 'dog' in speech or writing it is intended to *mean* something different from 'cat'. People communicate by building up signs to indicate what they mean by establishing 'differences' between their intended meaning and other possible meanings – a *fat* cat establishes that the cat is different from a *thin* cat! But I might respond by asking, 'What do you mean 'fat?' or, 'How fat?'. I am asking for more signs to help me understand what is *different*, or particular, about this cat.

Saussure made a distinction between language as a system and language as speech. Language as a system refers to the conventions of language use – the grammar if you like – of sentence construction, paragraphs etc. Language as speech refers to how the language is actually used to communicate meanings. What Saussure hoped was that it would be possible to develop a science of meanings in which we could accurately and certainly know what is meant by looking at how the system of signs is used and the relationship between signifiers and signifieds.

This assumes that everyone means the same thing when they use a common *signifier* such as 'cat'. But of course, life isn't like that! We may have quite different pictures in our heads even when we hear a simple *signifier* like 'cat'. The idea that comes into your head will depend, as we have suggested, on *where* you are coming from! If you have a dread fear of cats, you will have a different idea from someone who loves them!

People don't always *mean* what they *say*

And of course, people don't always mean what they say! In Chapter 7, there is an exercise based on the opening dialogue of *A Doll's House*, on page 129. In that exercise we discover that there are different ways of understanding the meaning of the words spoken by the characters. This is particularly important. Artists often play with the relationship between the *signifier* (what is seen or heard) and the *signified* (what is actually meant) in order to be ironic, or to create ambiguity and uncertainty, or to create *sub-text,* or to disturb and challenge the audience. A famous example of a playwright using words to mean the opposite of their usual meaning is to be found in the closing lines of *Waiting for Godot* by Samuel ***Beckett***:

Vladimir: Well? Shall we go?
Estragon: Yes, Let's go.
(*They do not move*)

CURTAIN

Theatre is Physical, Visual and Aural

Signs, of course, come in all shapes and sizes. Saussure was concerned with language but we use all kinds of other visual and gestural signs in our daily lives. Traffic lights, for example: the red light is the *signifier* which signifies 'stop!' In some cultures, shaking hands is a *signifier* that signifies a welcome or introduction. As we will find out in this chapter, **theatre also communicates its meanings through sign systems based on difference**. If the stage is bathed in blood-red light it will mean something different from if it is lit by natural light or by purple light.

Signs in theatre are physical, visual and aural

Saussure's mistake was to try and isolate language from the other systems that might be used together with language. A simple *signifier* in language like 'hello' becomes more complicated when it combines with the physical signs of body language! Rather than simply meaning a welcome it might be a threat, an insult or a put-down according to the body language of the speaker. Unlike written forms of communication, theatre uses a combination of physical, visual and aural (what is heard) signs as well as the signs of spoken language.

The full meaning of the dialogue in a play may come from the other physical and visual signs at work. In other words, in order to understand the dialogue it has to be put into the context of the actor's physical signs and any other visual or aural signs that are being made. In theatre then, as in life, we respond to the ways in which the physical, visual and aural signs *combine* to make a meaning for us.

Task 4: How close is drama to living?

The drama in education practitioner, Dorothy Heathcote, claims that:

'Actual living and theatre, which is the depiction of living conditions, both use the same network of signs as their medium of communication; namely the human being signalling across space, in immediate time, to and with others, each reading and signalling simultaneously within the action of each passing moment . . .'

- **From your experience of both actual living, and drama and theatre, how true would you say this claim is?**
- **Is 'signing' in life the same as 'signing' in the theatre?**
- **If there are differences what are they?**
- **Is this claim more true of certain styles of theatre than others?**

Iconic signs are pictures of the real thing. Symbolic signs are symbols of the real thing

The physical, visual and aural signs used in theatre tend to fall into two categories, the **iconic** and the **symbolic**. In an iconic sign the *signifier* is literally a 'picture' of the idea, or concept, that is *signified*. For example, the male and female signs on toilet doors are iconic signs. The sign is made up of a literal picture (*signifier*) which directly represents 'man' or 'woman' (the *signified* meaning). In most forms of Western theatre, the actor is often an iconic sign because the actor literally 'signifies' a character: one human being (the actor) signifies another (the character). In the same way, set designs in a ***realist*** style are often iconic – the real furniture that is used signifies the imaginary room or place that is represented in the play. If a director and designer decide to use real, useable objects on stage to represent the playwright's directions then they are using iconic, or literal signs. ***Brecht***, for instance, insisted that the tools, clothing and other props should look as if they had really been used in life.

In a **symbolic sign** there is no obvious or direct connection between the appearance or sound of the *signifier* and the idea or concept that is *signified*. Spoken language is made up of symbolic signs – there is, usually, no obvious connection between the meaning and the sound, or look, of a word. A change in lighting that signifies a change in mood in the play rather than a change of time or place is a symbolic *signifier*. The music in ***melodrama*** that accompanies the entry of the villain is a symbolic *signifier*. The use of a rose to signify love or romance is also a symbolic signifier.

Signs only communicate among people who share the same understanding of their meanings. The signs used to communicate in English are only understood by those who speak the language. Both iconic and symbolic signs often depend on a shared cultural understanding of the sign and its intended meaning. A rose signifying love is recognisable in those cultures that make an association between the *signifier* 'rose' and the *signified* 'romantic love'. The same is true in a performance – the signs that are used will only make sense to an audience if they are familiar from either their own cultural experience or from their knowledge and understanding of the Western theatre tradition. If I go to watch ***Kathakali*** and ***Kabuki*** performances, I often fail to understand many of the signs used because I don't have enough knowledge or experience to understand them.

All Signs in Theatre have a Symbolic Intention

Modern performances mix iconic and symbolic signs

It is useful to make a distinction between the iconic and symbolic signs used in performance. Iconic signs are often used to create a ***realist*** style and symbolic signs are often used to create a ***non-realist*** style.

It is also likely that you will find a mix of iconic and *symbolic* signs in a modern performance which reflects the trend in theatre towards mixing *realist* and *non-realist* styles. Part of ***Brecht***'s *verfrumdungseffekt*, for instance, was achieved by combining iconic signs for tools and other useable props with symbolic signs such as distorted or oversized furniture and doorways or two-dimensional sets in order to emphasise the true social relationships between the characters.

Every sign in performance has a symbolic intention and a symbolic effect

But always remember that every sign in performance has a symbolic intention and a symbolic effect. It is part of the magic of theatre that every sign, whether it is iconic or symbolic in form, is taken to have a symbolic value; is taken to mean something important. Anything that is seen, heard or experienced in the performance is taken to have a special value far in excess of its value outside the performance. Imagine an empty stage with a single chair on it. The chair may

be an iconic sign (a real useable chair) but its value will be symbolic. In other words, we don't just think 'Oh, there's a chair'. We will look and wonder what it represents – absence perhaps, or loneliness, or a particular period of history, or the character of the chair's owner or maker.

Imagine that your own bedroom, or the mantelpiece in your front room, was a 'set' for a performance. How would each of the objects be 'read' by an audience? What clues of character would they find in the selection and arrangement of the objects? What symbolic value would be given to that old teddy, the bits and pieces on your shelves? Once your bedroom, or front room, is treated as if it was the setting for a character, then everything that is placed in it becomes a potential symbol of that character in the same way that ***Ibsen***'s long list of furniture and other objects in the opening stage directions for *A Doll's House* were intended to be read as symbols of Nora and Torvald's character and class (see page 208).

The Italian semiotician Umberto ***Eco*** made a distinction between 'involuntary' and 'intended' signs. Involuntary signs are natural signs over which we have no control – smoke signifying fire, clouds signifying stormy weather – but also sneezing, or other 'involuntary' human signs that are not intended to have meaning for others. Intended signs are made with the intention of communicating a meaning. **It is an important principle in theatre that every sign, everything that is seen and heard as part of the performance, is intentional**. There is no such thing as an involuntary use of sign in performance – everything that is seen and heard will be 'read' by the audience as an intentional sign which is meaningful.

We once saw a production of *Macbeth* in which some electrical work needed doing on stage during the first interval. When the audience returned there was a ladder and screwdriver on the set that had not been there before. Our first reaction was not to dismiss these objects as 'unintentional' but instead to think about their symbolism in the play – is the ladder a symbol of the Macbeth's ambition? Does the screwdriver symbolise Macbeth's and Lady Macbeth's intentions towards Duncan? In other words, we assumed these objects had been **deliberately placed with meaningful intentions**. This is why in your own work you need to be very disciplined in your signing – everything, even the accidents, will be read as being intended by you.

Task 5: Space of intentionality exercise

In most performance traditions, the performance space is divided in some way so that some section of the space is reserved as a 'stage' or the place in which the fiction will be created. The audience understands that whatever happens in this space is *intended* to be read as part of the performance rather than as part of the everyday world. In the Chinese tradition, the performers would draw a circle with chalk to mark the performance space, or what we shall call the '*space of intentionality*'.

1. **Draw a chalk circle on the floor and agree with the rest of the group that anything that is placed or done inside the circle is to be read as an intentional *signifier* which will *signify* something to the audience.**
2. **Collect together the following objects and place them outside the chalk circle:**
   - **Wooden chair**
   - **Religious book**

- Candle
- Flower
- Baby's shoe
- Family photo torn in two

3. Take it in turns to place the chair in the circle. How do you read the chair each time it is placed? If the chair is turned on its side in the middle what does it suggest? If the chair is turned away from the audience, what does it suggest? The game is to play with the 'suggestiveness' of the sign in the space. Play with the group's imagination by choosing unusual, or 'loaded' ways of placing the chair in the space and see what the audience make of it.
4. Now begin to add in the other objects, one at a time. What is suggested when you begin to combine the signs – when you place the religious book next to, or further away from, the overturned chair, for instance? Gradually introduce more and more of the objects and notice how much we tend to read in to their arrangement in the *space of intentionality*. You may find that you are developing a whole story and imagined world around the objects in the circle! What role does the 'space' itself play? As you move objects around and change the distance between the objects, how much of what is suggested is a result of the use of the space? The space between; the space surrounding; the space between the audience and the chalk circle? In the *space of intentionality*, the space marked out in chalk becomes one of the 'objects' that you work with.
5. Finally, you can add an actor in whatever position you choose. You may also use a single spotlight with a choice of blue, red or gold gels – how can you light the objects to make further suggestions to the audience?

The Sign Systems of Theatre

Semiotics has had a considerable influence on literary criticism. The idea is that we can understand what a text such as a novel or poem 'means' by analysing the 'signs' used in the text. We can refer to the 'words on the page' and what they signify as a way of explaining our responses to the text and discussing the writer's intentions. But of course a performance is not like a book or a poem.

The differences between analysing performance and literature

The words on the page are printed and permanent. We can close the book, put it under the pillow and go to sleep. When we wake, the words are still in the same place. A performance, however, leaves no permanent record that can be referred back to or looked at over and over again. **The morning after a performance there is nothing left save our memories of what we saw and heard the night before.** Even if we go to the next performance of the same play it will no longer be the same as the first. This difference helps to explain why the records of performances, in the Western theatre tradition, tend to be in the form of literature – the play text. The play text is a permanent record of what was said and the stage directions, but the text of the performance is more than the words and the directions – it is literally everything that is seen and heard during the performance itself.

Theatre uses multiple sign systems simultaneously

In literature, there is only one sign system at work – language. In theatre, there are not only many different sign systems used (language, physical gesture, costume, lighting etc.) but they are also used simultaneously. The French semiotician Roland ***Barthes*** in his *Critical Essays* described the performance text as a 'cybernetic machine' rather than as a passive text like a novel:

> What is theatre? A sort of cybernetic machine. When not working, this machine is hidden behind a curtain; but as soon as it is revealed it begins to transmit a certain number of messages in your direction. These messages are distinctive in that they are simultaneous and yet have different rhythms. At every point in a performance you are receiving (at the same second) six or seven items of information (from the scenery, the costuming, the lighting, the position of the actors, their gestures, their mode of playing etc), but some of these items remain fixed (this is true of scenery) while others change (speech and gestures) . . . We have therefore a density of signs.

So, there are two further problems when it comes to making a semiotic analysis of a performance. First, there are **multiple sign systems at work** and as we have seen, our response in performance may be the result of several signs (physical, visual and aural) combining together. Second, we cannot sequence, or order, the signs in performance like we can when we read a sentence in a book. You can't read all the words on a page simultaneously – you have to read the words (the signs) in the order that they appear on the page. But in performance, when several signs may occur in the same moment, different members of the audience will 'read' the signs in a different order. Was the sense of gloom generated from the lighting? From the change in costume? From the change in the tone of the actor's voice? Which did I notice first? Peter ***Brook*** suggests that:

> What's the difference between a poor play and a good one? I think there's a very simple way of comparing them. A play in performance is a series of impressions; little dabs, one after another, fragments of information or feeling in a sequence, which stirs the audience's perceptions. A good play sends many such messages, often several at a time, often crowding, jostling, overlapping one another . . . in a poor play the impressions are well spaced out, they lope along in single file, and in the gaps the heart can sleep while the mind wanders to the day's annoyances and thoughts of dinner.

Task 6: Identifying the sign systems of theatre

What are the different sign systems used in theatre?

1. Make a list using slips of paper with one system on each slip. Use the sign systems mentioned in the ***Barthes*** quotation and add any that you think are missing. Indicate whether the system is visual, physical or aural (including language). When you are sure you have thought of every sign system that might be used, lay the slips in front of you.
2. Try and place the systems in a vertical order so that the most important, or significant, sign system is at the top and the least at the bottom. It is the process that is important here – what decisions did you take? What issues did the process raise? How can you decide whether lighting is more significant than make-up for instance?
3. Is there another way of grouping the systems? *Technical* (sound and lighting effects)?; *Physical* (movement and gesture, for instance)? Or in terms of the *elements* of *drama* (space, time, physical action)?

Performance Text: the Sum Total of the Signs Used

Signs in theatre are always actions

In literature, the *text* refers to all the signs of language which taken together make a complete or coherent intended message. **In performance the *text* refers to all the signs of 'action' that take place during the performance** – every sign in theatre is an action in the sense that it makes something happen. Theatre's mode of language is speech, which is language as it is *used* in the world, language in action. When a character says that he is leaving, he does, and even if he doesn't it's still an action! Lighting changes are signs of action too – dimming the lights makes evening happen, makes the mood change. Even objects are actions in performance, in the sense that every object on the stage changes the stage, making it a different place.

When we produce theatre we often ask the question 'How do we make that happen?' meaning how do we turn the idea we have into something that happens (takes place) on stage. In the same way, the critic asks: 'How did they make that happen?' meaning what signs were used to make a response happen – what took place, or is taking place, that effects the critic in this way?

Text = *textus* + *texere*

The origin of the word 'text' is derived from the Latin words *textus* meaning tissue and *texere* meaning weaving. The text in both literature and performance refers to the 'tissue' or 'fabric' of signs/actions, which together make a complete or coherent message. It also refers to the 'weave' – how the actions/signs are woven together into one piece; how all the signs in the performance are organised. This is the job of the critic and the reviewer – to try and see and comment on the effectiveness of the weave; to see how and why the actions that make up the performance are being used and interlinked. To see, for instance, the relationships between costume, lighting, colour theming, gesture, acting style and the theme or interpretation of the play.

The Framework of Sign Systems

Kowzan's sign systems of theatre

The first detailed attempt to analyse the sign systems used in performance was made by the Czech, Tadeuz Kowzan, in the 1940s. Although Kowzan's original ideas about the sign systems of theatre are now outdated, his work still has an influence on how we understand the use of signs in a performance and the relationship between the signs of a performance and the sense that an audience makes of it.

Kowzan identified 13 sign systems in use. Of these, the first eight belong to the actor and the remaining five to the set and technical effects. Kowzan also distinguished between 'auditive signs' (what we hear) and 'visual signs' (what we see). Finally he identified which signs happen in space and time (the actor's gesture, for instance) which signs happen in time only (sound effects, for instance) and which happen in space only (props, for instance).

Kowzan believed that his framework would allow scenes or moments in the performance to be *deconstructed*; that the weave of the text could be unpicked into its separate strands. The framework provides a series of headings for critics to use in understanding how the performance has been made – what was actually seen and heard.

Kowzan's 13 sign systems:

<table>
<tr><td>1 WORD
2 TONE</td><td>SPOKEN TEXT</td><td rowspan="3">ACTOR</td><td>AUDITIVE SIGNS</td><td>TIME</td><td>AUDITIVE SIGNS – ACTOR</td></tr>
<tr><td>3 MIME
4 GESTURE
5 MOVEMENT</td><td>EXPRESSION OF THE BODY</td><td rowspan="3">VISUAL SIGNS</td><td>SPACE and TIME</td><td rowspan="2">VISUAL SIGNS – ACTOR</td></tr>
<tr><td>6 MAKE-UP
7 HAIRSTYLE
8 COSTUME</td><td>ACTOR'S EXTERNAL APPEARANCE</td><td>SPACE</td></tr>
<tr><td>9 PROPS
10 DECOR
11 LIGHTING</td><td>APPEARANCE OF THE STAGE</td><td rowspan="2">OUTSIDE THE ACTOR</td><td>SPACE and TIME</td><td>VISUAL SIGNS – OUTSIDE THE ACTOR</td></tr>
<tr><td>12 MUSIC
13 SOUND EFFECTS</td><td>INARTICULATE SOUNDS</td><td>AUDITIVE SIGNS</td><td>TIME</td><td>AUDITIVE SIGNS – OUTSIDE THE ACTOR</td></tr>
</table>

Task 7: Using Kowzan's system

You will need to have access to a video extract of a live performance, filmed as theatre, for this task. Ideally, the production should be traditional and based on a *realist* play, or a classical play staged in a realist style – *Shakespeare*, *Ibsen*, *Chekhov* or *Miller*, for instance. For the purposes of this exercise you do not need to know the whole story of the play or to see the whole play first.

1. Choose a one-minute extract to study.
2. Divide the sign systems up among the members of your group so that you have no more than three each to concentrate on.
3. Watch the extract very closely and only make a note of the signs that belong to your chosen group of sign systems.
4. After the extract has finished complete your notes and try to work out what was intended by these signs. If there were differences in the quality of the costumes worn by different characters what might this indicate? If there were differences in the way that characters moved, what might this be showing about the characters?
5. Now go around the group and listen to each other's findings. You may be surprised by how much information has been gathered and by the different interpretations in the group.
6. Finally, discuss the overall effect of the signs used in your chosen extract. Is there a theme running through them? What is the effect of the weave, as a whole?

Kowzan's list works best with realist performances

Despite the detail of Kowzan's framework, it still does not take into account all of the sign systems used in performance today, and it also assumes a certain tradition in theatre which is less popular today than it was in Kowzan's time.

The framework works best when it is applied to productions of ***realist*** plays, in the ***Stanislavskian*** directing tradition, which are intended to be a faithful interpretation of a playwright's work. In this tradition, all the sign systems tend to be used to support the written text; to tell the playwright's story. In other words, the signs are organised to reinforce the words and directions in the play text. In this tradition of realism, the playwright is often very specific about the signs required. The job of the production team (actors, directors, designers and technical staff) is to follow the playwright's instructions.

Here, for instance, is the opening stage direction from ***Ibsen***'s *A Doll's House*:

A comfortably and tastefully, but not expensively furnished room. Backstage right a door leads to the hall; backstage left, another door to Helmer's study. Between these two doors stands a piano. In the middle of the left-hand wall is a door, with a window downstage of it. Near the window, a round table with armchairs and a small sofa. In the right-hand wall, slightly upstage, is a door; downstage of this, against the same wall, a stove lined with porcelain tiles, with a couple of armchairs and a rocking chair in front of it. Between the stove and the side door is a small table. Engravings on the wall. A what-not with china and other bric-a-brac; a small bookcase with leather bound books. A carpet on the floor; a fire in the stove. A winter day.

(A bell rings in the hall outside, and a moment later the door is heard to open. NORA comes into the room, humming happily. She is in outdoor clothes, and is carrying an armful of parcels)

Task 8: Working with Kowzan's framework

1. **Use Kowzan's list to identify the 'signs' that will be needed to realise *Ibsen*'s stage directions. You can also add any other 'signs' that you think will assist. You may want to think of additional sound effects, lighting etc.**
2. **Make a diagram, or drawing, of the stage with all that *Ibsen* required in exactly the positions he describes.**
3. **Use the diagram and your list as the basis for the following role-play with two partners. Decide on your roles and get started!**

   A = the director

   B = the designer

   C = the actor cast as Nora

The director is holding a design meeting with the designer; they have to decide on the set, props and costumes that will be used. The designer is anxious to get enough detail from the director to be able to start looking for the props and building the set. The designer might want to discuss, for instance, how to design the room so that it is comfortable and tasteful but not expensively furnished. The actor is also taking part in the discussion because they think that talking about the details of Nora's apartment will help them to understand the character. The actor is is also thinking about how

their costume will look and hoping that the director will give them some advice on how to play their entrance – how will their first 'signs' be chosen to complement the work of the designer?

In the role-play you may have discovered that there was not much room for the director, designer and actor to talk about their own ideas and vision for the play; to make their own creative choices. The meeting is about how to understand and then realise *Ibsen*'s own intentions for the play in performance. Playwrights in the *realist* tradition aim to offer a 'slice of life' or the 'illusion of reality'. One level of the evaluation of a *realist* play is to do with the extent to which the performance is 'real', lifelike' or 'true to life'.

Signs can be used to create the illusion of reality

In this form of theatre, the sign systems are often organised by the director to tell the story and to create a consistent and realistic setting for it. The first eight of Kowzan's systems, those that belong to the actor, are used to create a 'living example' of the playwright's character. The actor playing Nora will use all eight to play a 'convincing' performance of *Ibsen*'s imaginary character. The remaining five systems are all then used to create the 'living illusion' of Nora and her husband Helmer's apartment.

The review of a conventional production of *A Doll's House* will tend to dwell on the play text in performance, rather than on the performance text. A judgement may be made about how effectively the sign systems have been used and woven together to present the play text: whether characters were 'convincing', whether the set is 'true' to the period and the social setting of the play.

New Directions in Twentieth Century Theatre

Although many performances are still based on this conventional model of theatre there were important changes in theatre during the twentieth century which often make the task of analysing a performance more complex and which require a more sophisticated model for analysis than that offered by Kowzan.

The status of directors, actors and designers has changed since Kowzan

The status of directors, actors and designers has changed so that **this group of artists are now seen as being responsible for doing more than merely 'telling' the playwright's story**. They are now seen as artists in their own right rather than as servants to the playwright. There is an expectation that these artists will offer their own 'interpretation' of the playwright's work. Directors and designers may play with the sign systems in order to offer their own idea of the play or to introduce themes that may not have been suggested by the playwright. ***Meyerhold***, ***Artaud***, ***Grotowski***, ***Brook***, ***Lepage*** and ***Mnouchkine*** are all examples of twentieth century directors, or ***auteurs***, who have tended to adapt and transform original works into quite new pieces that are as much an expression of the director's imagination as the writer's. A good example is *Brook*'s production of *A Midsummer Night's Dream*.

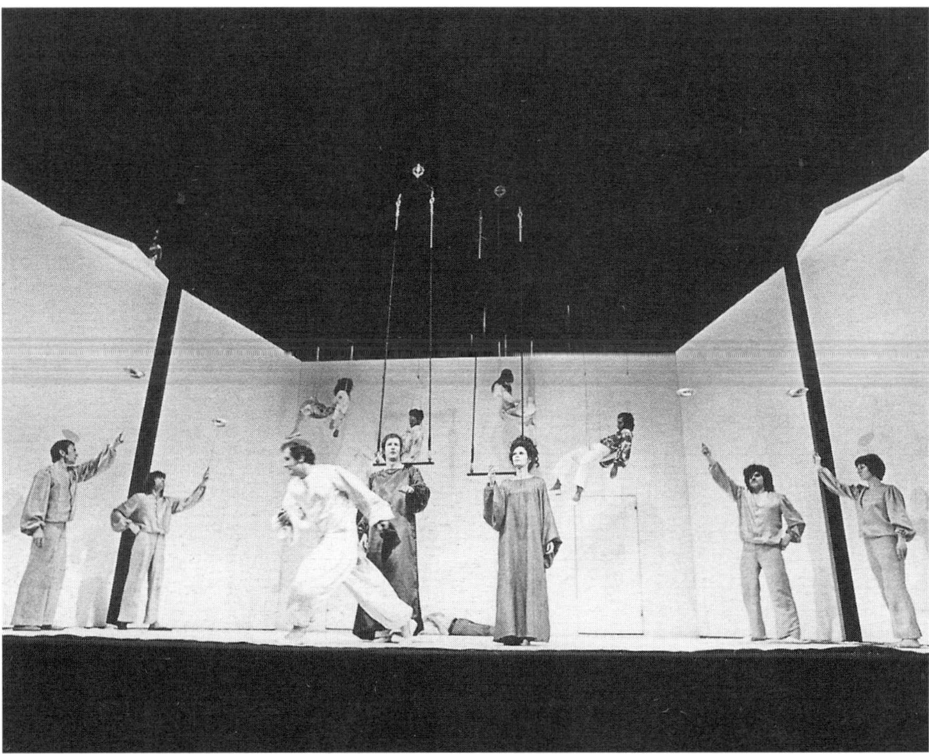
A Midsummer Night's Dream, directed by ***Brook***, Royal Shakespeare Company 1970.

This form of interpretation is often evident in 'revivals' and in productions of classic plays like those of ***Shakespeare***. We discussed the whole issue of creative interpretations of play texts in Chapter 8. If a director chooses to set *Macbeth* in present-day Bosnia for instance there would be two kinds of information flowing through the sign systems: *Shakespeare*'s original story and characters and the director's own commentary on the play's theme. The director, not *Shakespeare*, is suggesting that new meanings can be found in the play by setting it among the conflicts in Bosnia. If Macbeth is costumed as a Bosnian warlord, we will have the experience of some signs (the words) belonging to the playwright and some signs (the costume) belonging to the director's interpretation. Now the audience has a more complex task: to make sense of the 'difference' between the original play of *Macbeth* and why and how the director has chosen to *add* an additional layer of information through changing the settings, costumes and maybe even the physical style of acting.

Kenneth Branagh's film of *Much Ado About Nothing*, 1993.

The status of actors has changed

The status of actors has also changed, so that **we think of actors as artists in their own right rather than as 'mouthpieces' for the playwright's words.** Part of our interest in the modern theatre is in the actor as a performer as well as in the actor's performance of a classic role. The director Eugenio ***Barba*** puts it this way: 'Why is it that when I watch two actors playing the same character, only one of them interests me?' In Kowzan's framework, there is no mention of the distinctive contribution that the actor as performer makes to the 'meaning' of the performance. In modern theatre the performer is recognised to be the principle *signifier*.

A skilled performer, or a performer with a very strong stage presence, will bring 'life' to a character in ways that an amateur, or less skilled actor, cannot. It is not simply a question of *which* signs the actor makes; it is *how* the actor makes a sign which affects us in performance. So, **part of the analysis of the performance will be the analysis of the performer** – the way in which the performer works on stage and the extent to which your response to what happens in the performance comes from the personality and skill of the performer, rather than from the character and what happens to the character in the story. When this happens we become as interested in the *signifier* (the actor) as we are in the *signified* (the character). In Kowzan's framework the identity of the performers and the director is made invisible; it could be anyone making the signs rather than someone who signs in their own particular way.

Certain performers are able to bring something so special and different to a role that we speak of the role 'belonging' to the performer; ***Olivier***'s Othello, ***McKellan***'s Richard III. Certain performances become legendary or are referred to as the benchmark for other performers to match. Helene ***Weigel***'s performances of ***Brecht***'s female characters are a benchmark for all actors taking on these roles now. In the same way, certain TV and film actors are expected to bring something extra special to a performance – can you imagine anyone else playing Inspector Morse or Del boy? Or think of the problems when a new actor takes on an established role in a long-running soap or drama series. We never can quite forget the original performer. We are also conscious, sometimes, of the other roles that certain actors have played before and this affects our response to how the same performer creates the character in the performance we are experiencing now.

Task 9: Same character, different actors

Have you seen the same character played by two different performers?

- **If so, what were the *differences* in the performance?**
- **Which differences were of style, of intention, or from different direction?**
- **Which differences do you think were because of the different ways in which the performers played their character?**

If you have difficulty finding an example from you own experience, look at different video versions of a *Shakespeare* play such as *Macbeth* or *Romeo and Juliet*. You could also visit the *King Lear* website where different performers talk about how they approached the role of King Lear: http://www.bbc.co.uk/education/archive/lear/

There is no mention of the audience in Kowzan's framework

There is no mention of audiences in Kowzan's framework; no mention of the interaction between actors and audiences; how the space between the performers and the audience is arranged; the 'signs' made by the audience – laughing, crying, applauding; no mention of how the performance 'signs' to the audience how to respond.

The audience as a part of the performance, and the nature of the spatial relationship between the actors and the audience, became an increasingly important consideration in twentieth century theatre. In the ***realist*** tradition of ***representational*** theatre, there is very little contact between the actors and the audience. The high *proscenium* stage which was introduced in the nineteenth century – brightly lit, with all of its 'tricks' like lighting, music and other effects hidden away – isolated the performance from the dark auditorium and the silent faces of the audience. The advent of film and TV has increased the theatre's interest in involving the audience more, ensuring that there is something special in the **live and shared experience** of performance.

From a commercial point of view, the theatre needs to offer an experience which is different from the experience of watching drama on film and TV. There is often an emphasis on making the audience feel included in the performance in some way rather than having the performers totally ignore the audience as they did at the end of the nineteenth century.

The use and division of space is important

The way in which the performance space is organised will have an important effect on our response to the performance and the performers. Since ***Brecht*** it has become usual to reveal all the 'tricks' in the performance: the lights are visible, entrances are not hidden from us, the musicians can be seen, props and scenery are often moved before us. The *cybernetic machine* is no longer hidden from us, and the experience of a performance – the effect of the signs – will include both the proximity of the actors and any other signs which are not a part of the performance itself but which contribute to it. If an actor is in a state of great distress only a few feet from you in the audience, it will have a powerfully different effect to your being further away. In some cases the 'performance' may include events in the foyer before entering the auditorium: actors sitting or walking among the audience, specially chosen music, the pictures and posters of the show, or maybe from the period of the play to set the context.

Task 10: What does an audience *contribute* to the performance?

- **Make a list of the different ways in which an audience's contributions might affect the performance and the performers: applause, silence, laughter etc.**
- **How would the following methods of staging affect the audience? Consider the differences between:**
  - **A proscenium stage**
  - **A thrust stage**
  - **Theatre in the round**
  - **Promenade (where the audience moves around the space with the actors)**
  - **Street theatre**
  - **Environmental space (outdoor, or in museums and old buildings)**

The mix of styles and genres

There is no consideration of style and genre in Kowzan's framework. The way in which the actor signs, for instance, may be in a certain style or in a mixture of styles (e.g. ***representational/Stanislavskian***, or ***presentational/Brechtian***). The signs in the performance may be organised in order to reflect or correspond to a particular genre of theatre (e.g. tragedy or comedy). During the twentieth century it became quite common to mix genres and styles so that a single performance might include elements of tragedy and comedy; a broad range of acting styles; dance, mime and realistic acting; elements of storytelling, ritual, games, clowning or stand-up comedy. In performances that mix styles and genres **it is important to comment on the effect of this mix** as well as to recognise what is signified by the individual signs themselves.

Technical theatre and other media influences

During the twentieth century, directors used new media to add to the performance. ***Meyerhold***, ***Piscator*** and *Brecht* are examples of directors who were quick to use new technologies in their work to reflect the increasing importance of technological progress in society. They used slides, captions, film and mechanical constructions in their work. **A modern performance may include technological media such as slides, film strips or video**. It may also 'borrow' from other art-forms such as sculpture, puppets and electronic music soundtracks. The boundaries between art-forms and different styles and genres of theatre are not as clear-cut as they might have been in Kowzan's time.

Task 11: Adding to Kowzan's framework

What criticisms would you now make of Kowzan's framework?

- **In what ways is it perhaps no longer a useful tool for analysing contemporary performance?**

- **Use the list of sign systems that you made in Task 6 and *Kowzan's* original list to create a new framework of sign systems that you could use to analyse the next performance that you see. Ideally, you should try your framework out several times with different kinds of performance and keep modifying it with experience.**

Signing in the Twentieth Century: Economy of Presentation

These developments in theatre during the twentieth century resulted in important changes in the way that the sign systems of theatre are used and understood. In the example from *A Doll's House* we noticed how *all* 13 of Kowzan's sign systems were used to do the same job – to faithfully tell the playwright's story in a realistic setting.

Using less to do more!

The English stage designer Gordon ***Craig*** asked a question early in the twentieth century that brought about profound changes in the way that sign systems are used. The question was: 'How much is it essential to put on the stage to convey a forest?'

Craig was challenging the myth that every tree, branch and leaf needed to be represented – why not a single piece of wood on a bare stage? There were two important consequences of *Craig*'s question that would lead to innovative uses of sign systems in the new *post-realist* (i.e. ***non-realist***) theatres of the twentieth century.

Craig led other practitioners to value economy of presentation in their use of signs; to only use that which is *essential* to presenting a forest or any other setting; to use a single *signifier* to signify forest rather than multiple *signifiers*. Later, ***Grotowski*** would refer to the economy of presentation as a 'poverty of means' in defining his idea of a *poor theatre*.

Task 12: Re-designing *A Doll's House*

Go back to the opening stage directions from *A Doll's House* on page 208.

1. **Look at the list of signs that you made in Task 6. How many are *essential* rather than merely duplicating or reinforcing what is already there? Reduce the list as far as you can to a few essential signs – no more than three or four, which will *symbolise* the room and its relationship to the characters and themes of the play rather than literally representing every detail of a 'real' room.**
2. **Now that you have cleared the stage and freed up some of the sign systems that were all used just to represent the room, what might you *add*? Add signs of mood, theme, period or portents of events to come.**

The difference between iconic and symbolic signs

This paring down of the signs on stage to a few essentials has had two important effects. First, it increases the **symbolic value** of the sign used. A hundred 'trees' on stage is an *iconic* or literal sign – a picture of a forest standing for a real forest. One dead branch hanging, or even lying, in the empty space becomes a *symbolic* sign in the sense that the immediate connection between the *signifier* (the dead branch) and the *signified* (a real forest) may not be obvious. The audience has to work harder to make the connection. They are forced to see the branch as *symbolising* the forest rather than imitating the forest. Because there is only one sign for the audience to consider they can spend longer dwelling on what is suggested. The difference between using a dead branch as opposed to a living one will suggest something, or symbolise some aspect, of the forest that is being represented. Is the 'fallen' branch a symbol of the main character's situation in the play? Is a 'dead' branch a symbol of that character giving up, or failing to take action? The imagination is triggered; the audience is made conscious that this is an *interpretation* of reality, not the *illusion* of reality that we associate with the ***realist*** tradition of ***Ibsen***.

The effect will be to make the audience think about the *signifier* as much as the forest that is *signified*; to make them conscious of the artistic interpretation offered on stage. In the same way that we suggested that the actor (the *signifier*) is of interest to us as well as the character that the actor is playing (the *signified*), now all the *signifiers* (objects, set and space for instance) become of interest in and of themselves.

When signs are used sparingly and with the intention of increasing the symbolic value, or resonances, of the signs we become conscious of the image that is made in the *space of intentionality*. We dwell on the signs and their arrangement in the space just as you did in Task 5 and we consider the 'stage picture' as we might a painted picture or sculpture. **The signs are more than a mere 'setting' for the other actions – they become important symbols, or artistic statements in their own right.**

Samuel ***Beckett*** took this idea furthest in plays like *Breath* and *Act Without Words II*, which presented the audience with *signifiers* but no *signifieds*. *Beckett* argued that life was, in reality, meaningless and chaotic and that we *impose* meanings on the world. By stripping his signifiers of any intended meaning he hoped to force the audience to realise that it was making its own meanings – creating its own *signifieds* for the *signifiers* present on stage; imposing meanings on the stage signifiers that were not intended by the playwright, but suggested by the audience's imagination.

Task 13: Waiting for Godot exercise

Compare the opening stage directions of *A Doll's House* with the opening directions to *Beckett's Waiting for Godot*. Is there any 'meaning' to *Beckett's* directions? In addition to the opening directions, we have also added the directions from the beginning of Act 2.

Waiting for Godot	
Act 1 *A country road. A tree. Evening.*	*Act 2* *Next day. Same Time. Same Place.*
Estragon, sitting on a low mound, is trying to take off his boot. He pulls at it with both hands, panting. He gives up, exhausted, rests, and tries again. *As before.* *Enter Vladimir.*	*Estragon's boots front centre, heels together, toes splayed. . . The tree has four or five leaves.* *Enter Vladimir agitatedly. He halts and looks long at the tree, then suddenly begins to move feverishly about the stage. He halts before the boots, picks one up, examines it, sniffs it, manifests disgust, puts it back carefully. Comes and goes. Halts extreme right and gazes into the distance off, shading his eyes with his hands. Comes and goes. Halts extreme left, as before. Comes and goes. Halts Suddenly and begins to sing loudly.*

1. Try to enact Estragon and Vladimir's actions as they appear in the text. As you rehearse these actions, and watch each other, what is suggested? The two roles are often performed using a clowning style and clowning techniques – does this help you to understand *Beckett's* intentions?
2. Now work both sets of actions simultaneously with one of you as Estragon and the other Vladimir. Focus on the directions that indicate the pace and rhythm of the actions – fast/slow, stop/start. Exaggerate these contrasts as you work. When you are ready, show the two sequences simultaneously, repeating the actions three times – what is the effect?

As we saw in Chapter 4, ***Brecht*** went further and suggest that economy of presentation was also the key to characterisation and the signs made by the actor. The basis of ***gestic*** acting lies in the same principle – if a character is old, does it really take all eight of the actor's sign systems to make the same point? Isn't one simple sign sufficient? *Brecht's* rehearsal techniques were about stripping away everything that proved to be inessential to the characterisation, reducing the character to a bare outline of simple *gestes*, or physical actions. In the *Couragemodell* he writes:

> **Positions should be retained as long as there is no compelling reason for changing them; and a desire for variety is not a compelling reason. If one gives in to a desire for variety, the consequence is a devaluation of all movement on the stage; the spectator ceases to look for a specific meaning behind each movement, he stops taking movement seriously.**

Simple means can produce complex meanings

The idea of using signs sparingly and with ***symbolic*** rather than *iconic* intention also allowed for the development of *epic* theatrical presentations, or large-scale productions spanning many locations and spread over a wide timescale. The use of a few simple signs to indicate places or times was a feature of ***Shakespeare***'s theatre as well. *Shakespeare* could move the action very rapidly from one time and place to another because the stage was not crowded with visual signs that would need changing every time he shifted scene. His words described the fictional place and he saw no reason why the other sign systems were needed to repeat the effect of the words.

In *Henry V* (Act 5, Scene 1) there is a good example of *Shakespeare* explaining, via the words of an actor, directly to the audience the conventions that will be used in the performance:

> Vouchsafe to those that have not read the story,
> That I may prompt them: and of such as have,
> I humbly pray them to admit th' excuse
> Of time, of numbers, and due course of things,
> Which cannot in their huge and proper life
> Be here presented. Now bear we the king
> Towards Calais: grant him there; there seen
> Heave him away upon your winged thoughts
> Athwart the sea . . .

Brecht would reclaim this tradition of large-scale *epic* historical plays in the twentieth century, which spanned across time and space in a single performance, without using elaborate settings. But it is Peter ***Brook*** who has gone furthest in using very simple but very carefully chosen symbolic signs to create *epic* performances. Colin Counsell writes:

> In the *Mahabharata* simple bamboo sticks represented bows and arrows, and a chariot by two warehouse pallets laid end to end. Forest undergrowth was figured with coils of wire in a *Midsummer Night's Dream* and in Brooks' . . . *Ubu aux Bouffes* an industrial cable spool became a war machine on which Ubu rode crushing his enemies before him . . . In *Ubu* three bricks arranged in a hearth-shape successfully implied an entire dwelling whilst in *The Mahabharata* a (second) chariot was suggested with a single wheel held up by an actor . . . Locations may be indicated very succinctly, a carpet and some cushions representing the luxury of a king's court . . . In *The Conference of the Birds* the hawk was evoked by two bent fingers forming a beak like hook, the parrot with head movements and a wicker grid held before the actor's face as a cage . . .

Brook's skill lies in his ability to use symbolic rather than iconic signs to represent both the setting and the ideas in the performance. But the success of his symbolic signs rests on there being a sufficient resemblance to the real objects that are depicted for the audience to understand the connection that is being made.

Signs *combine* to make meaning

For instance, in *Brook*'s *A Midsummer Night's Dream* the magic flowers referred to in the text of the play were symbolised by spinning plates on top of long sticks. There is no obvious connection between the *signifier* (the spinning plates and sticks) and the *signified* (the magic flowers). But on reflection there are sufficient connections between the *signifier* and the *signified* to make sense. There is a **physical resemblance** between a stick and a plate and the flower-head and stem of a flower. There is also a **functional resemblance** between the *magic* flower and the *magic* trick of spinning plates. However, the audience has to think more about the connection than if *Brook* had used an *iconic* sign – a prop flower.

Task 14: Symbolic signing exercise

Look at the extracts from Angela Carter's writing that we used in the story theatre exercise in Chapter 2. In that exercise, you focused on creating physical and vocal signs for the extracts. Now we are going to use the examples from *Brook* to create the stage design and props.

1. Divide the extracts up among the group; refresh your memories of the work by recalling the mood and atmosphere that you tried to create in your physical and vocal work.
2. As a whole class discuss what will be **fixed** and present for every extract and what will be **changed** (added and taken away) either between or during each extract. Draw (or make if you have the time and resources) the fixed stage design – the set and the props that will be constant.
3. Each group should now work out ideas for **symbolic** signs, in the form of objects, props and costume, for use in their extract. Begin by highlighting the text to identify the things and ideas that you want to provide signs for: the leg of a pig; a hard life; the ominous if brilliant look of blood on snow; the red shawl; the forest; the starving wolves; the scabby coat. Now, let your imaginations loose and begin to sketch and think about how you would use your ideas in performance.

Signing in the Twentieth Century: Multiple Signs, Multiple Messages

Using signs to comment on the story that is being told

In Task 12 you discovered that the second effect of economy of presentation in performance is to free up the sign systems for other purposes and intentions. If, instead of using all 13 of Kowzan's suggested sign systems to recreate the playwright's character, to re-tell the story and to represent the setting, a director only uses the simplest and fewest of signs, then there are still systems and space available that can do other kinds of work. We have already noticed examples of directors using signs to provide a simultaneous commentary on the story or central action on the stage. ***Meyerhold*** began the tradition of including headlines from the newspapers as backdrops to his stage story so that audiences were made to think about the relationship between events in the world and events on the stage. ***Brecht*** then developed the theory and practice of a form of *epic* theatrical presentation in which the purpose of the sign systems was to both *tell* the story and also *comment* on it; to *create* and also *destroy* the illusion of his characters and settings being real or consistent.

Remixing the original

Some of the sign systems can be used to offer interpretations or themes in the performance text that may not be present in the original play text. Alternatively, a performance can be built up out of fragments, images and physical ideas, rather like what happens in dance music and hip-hop. The DJ or producer may take an old song or sample an existing track and then add break-beats, raps, and other samples in order to make a new 'mix' which is based on fragments – samples of the old rearranged in order to make a new product which reflects the recording artist's own identity and vision.

The recording artist has multiple channels of sound to play with and use. Some channels will carry the original material and some will be used to carry the recording artist's interpretation, which may be a style such as trance or techno, or a rap. The original material is like the play text to which the artist adds his own performance text.

Task 15: The same new song

1. **Bring in some current examples of 'remixes' of old R&B or soul songs or special remixes of current tunes. Try and get hold of copies of the originals as well.**
2. **Play the old and new versions and consider what the new remix adds to the original and how this in turn has changed the effect of the original.**

Performance: text and sub-text

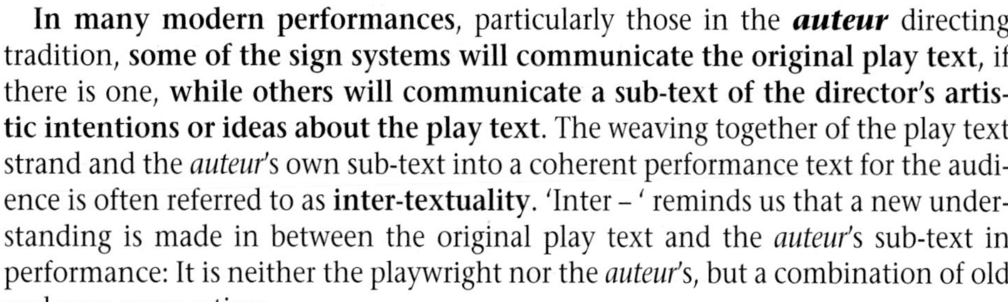

In many modern performances, particularly those in the ***auteur*** directing tradition, **some of the sign systems will communicate the original play text**, if there is one, **while others will communicate a sub-text of the director's artistic intentions or ideas about the play text**. The weaving together of the play text strand and the *auteur*'s own sub-text into a coherent performance text for the audience is often referred to as **inter-textuality**. 'Inter – ' reminds us that a new understanding is made in between the original play text and the *auteur*'s sub-text in performance: It is neither the playwright nor the *auteur*'s, but a combination of old and new perspectives.

In *Brecht*'s case, the sub-text is always political; but there other kinds of intentions for creating a sub-text in performance, and some examples follow.

Social criticism

There may be signs that indicate a feminist, or post-colonialist perspective. Here, the sub-text is provided in order to make the audience think about the play from a new or challenging perspective. In 1997, the physical theatre actor Kathryn Hunter played *King Lear*, directed by Helena Kaut-Howson, although both rejected the idea that it was a feminist perspective. However, a woman playing Lear is bound to cause us to question the extent to which Lear's character and plight are particular to old men rather than universal for both men and women. Hunter claimed that 'there's a Lear in all of us' and Kaut-Howson spoke of 'the meeting between the character of Lear and Kathryn'. (You can read about this production and the views of the director and actor at: http://www.bbc.co.uk/education/archive/lear (p. 212)).

Inter-culturalism

There may be a deliberate 'borrowing' from different cultures in terms of performance styles or setting in order to draw attention to, or *de-familiarise* the cultural context of the original play. The intention in using a diverse range of cultural traditions may also be to draw attention to the effect of mixing different kinds of performance.

During the 1980s Jatinder *Verma* and his company ***Tara Arts*** produced a number of classic plays from the Western tradition using a variety of Asian forms of performance such as ***Kathakali***, masks and Asian settings. ***Moliere***'s *Tartuffe* was staged in the context of an eighteenth century Mogul emperor's court in India.

Peter ***Brook*** frequently refers to and uses a variety of non-European performance traditions in his work. The 'tricks' in his famous production of *A Midsummer Night's Dream* (the spinning plates on sticks to represent the magic flowers, the trapezes from which Oberon and Titania swung, and the stilt-walking of Puck. See p. 210 for a photo of this performance.) were all borrowed from the Chinese State Circus. In the *Mahabharat* he used a number of techniques from different Asian theatre traditions.

Beckett, as we have seen, often referred to clowns and clowning in his work.

Joan ***Littlewood***'s *Oh! What a Lovely War* borrowed from *music-hall*, ***vaudeville*** and end-of-the-pier performances as a setting for her dramatic exploration of the First World War.

A theatrical language

There may be an emphasis in the performance text on movement, non-human sound and visual images in order to increase the live experience of the performance for the audience and/or to try and suggest a language of the theatre in addition to words. Many twentieth century practitioners were fascinated by ***Artaud***'s quest for an alternative 'language' of gestures, movement and strong visceral images.

The sources of these attempts to define such a language often 'borrow' from Asian performance with its highly stylised gestures which are 'read' by the audience like a language system. *Artaud* was drawn to Balinese and Cambodian performances; *Grotowski* to *Kathakali*; *Brook* and *Brecht* to Chinese circus and opera techniques.

Other practitioners have been interested in the actor-audience interaction as the heart of performance and have deliberately blurred the boundaries between the signs of performance and those of non-performance; between the performance and audience spaces; between different kinds of performance (dance, carnival, ritual). Again, both *Artaud* and *Grotowski* were interested in this dimension of performance, and more recently both *Brook* and ***Barba***'s *Odin Teatret* have experimented with space and performer-actor interactions beyond the conventional.

The American director Robert ***Wilson*** has influenced a new generation of *performance artists* with his idea of a *theatre of visions* which offers the audience a series of apparently random and unconnected visual and physical images as a means of trying to capture the randomness and free associations of the unconscious mind. His *Einstein on the Beach* was a collaboration with the composer Phillip Glass, which lasted five hours and used giant TV and film projections, carefully integrated into the musical score.

Conventions are *still* the Key!

In the first chapter we included a section entitled 'Conventions are the Key!' in which we stressed that communication in theatre is made possible through its conventions. The conventions of the performance are a kind of agreement between the performers and the audience about the possibilities of dramatic representation.

Complex conventions make the audience work harder to understand

In the twentieth century, practitioners constantly sought to stretch the boundaries of theatre; to invent new conventions as the 'means' for representing increasingly complex 'meanings' about the human condition. This led, as we have seen, to increasingly complex uses of the sign systems of theatre. For a performance to communicate to its audience there has to be some logic or key that helps and guides the audience to understand everything that is seen and heard. The conventions (the agreements between performers and audiences about how the 'means' of theatrical communication are being used) have become increasingly complex and demanding for the audience.

One of the attractions of the nineteenth and early twentieth century ***realist*** tradition in theatre (which is still dominant in popular theatre, film and TV) is to do with the simplicity of its logic. It tells a story in a realistic setting; it is often based on ordinary, recognisable characters, who use everyday language to communicate. Performances in this style of theatre are easy for an audience to follow.

Everything on the stage, including the characters, has the comforting familiarity of 'everyday life'. ***Stanislavski*** famously said:

> **these characters become your real friends. 'Let's go see the Prozorov's' or 'Let's go see Uncle Vanya'. You are not going to see the *Three Sisters* or *Uncle Vanya* as plays, you are really going to call on old friends.**

Stories, of any kind, often have the simple logic of a beginning, middle and end. When there is a strong story, simply told, the logic of a play's performance is clear to the audience from their own familiarity with the structure of stories. If the characters on stage behave 'realistically' and their behaviour is based on the given circumstances of the situations in the story, again it is easy for the audience to understand the logic of what's happening on stage. It is a cultural logic based on an understanding of how humans are likely to behave in certain social situations. Plays in the *realist* tradition seek to be 'truthful' to life and to establish their 'truth' through the lifelike nature of the acting and setting and the credibility of the story being told. The signs that are used tend to be *iconic*; 'pictures' of the real thing.

Since the beginning of the twentieth century, however, practitioners have questioned both the comfortable familiarity of *realism* and also its claim to be 'truthful'. Many of the signing practices we have described in the previous section have been attempts to go beyond *realism*; to break the familiarity and comfort of *realism*; to question how truthful lifelike representations are by emphasising ***symbolic*** rather than *iconic* signs.

Linear and non-linear structures

These modern forms of ***non-realist*** theatre have sought, as ***Brecht*** described it, to 'make strange' rather than make familiar; to break the cosy intimacy of story and plot. This has often meant abandoning the logic of story and replacing it with other kinds of structure – *Brecht's episodic* theatre, for instance. In some cases the performance may not have any story at all, or the happenings on stage may not occur in the order that they would in a story. A story is a **linear** structure; the events are connected together across a timeline; one event causes the next. Performances which are not based on a story structure are often termed as having a **non-linear** (or **alinear**) structure. These performances can be much more difficult and unsettling for an audience to follow.

The difference between a *linear realist* piece with a strong story, lifelike representations of character and *iconic* signs, and a *non-linear* performance with no story, stylised characterisations (if there are characters at all) and *symbolic* signs is like the difference between a landscape or portrait and a conceptual or abstract painting. When we see a realistic painting we know how to understand it – we consider the relationship between the painting and the object or person that it represents. When we look at conceptual or abstract painting we are presented with a greater puzzle. The lifelike likeness isn't there to guide us, so instead we have to look at colour, tone, shape, and pattern to try and make our sense of the picture.

The same effect is true in a *non-linear* performance. Instead of following the story and recognising the characters and situations we are forced to consider how the *signifiers* of theatre are being used – if they're not being used to tell a story, what are they being used for?

Non-linear performances often make us more aware of the 'live experience' – we can't follow or get lost and absorbed in a story, or comfortably recognise what's going on, so our attention is focused on 'what's happening to me/us'. There may be nothing to 'follow' in such a performance; there may be no distinction between performance and audience space, or any clues as to how to understand what's going on.

A Cornfield with Cypresses, Vincent van Gogh 1889.

The White Horse, John Constable 1819.

In such circumstances, we often become more self-conscious. More aware of our discomfort at not knowing what's going on, we may feel the heat of embarrassment, the physical disturbance of frustration, the shock of something unexpected happening. We become intensely aware of experiencing something. In the 1960s and 1970s many practitioners deliberately sought to create this discomfort and sense of experience for their audiences. Sometimes these performances would be called 'happenings' or 'events' rather than performances. Julian ***Beck*** and the *Living Theatre*, Allan ***Kaprow***, the painter Claes ***Oldenburg***, Tadeuz ***Kantor***, Richard Schechner and ***The Performance Group*** were all active in creating 'happenings'. More recently, practitioners such as Pina ***Bausch***, ***Welfare State International***, Elizabeth ***LeCompte*** and *The Wooster Group*, and Yvonne ***Rainer*** have continued the tradition of experimental, *non-linear* performance in all kinds of spaces for radical and challenging purposes.

There are certain guidelines which might help you to understand a *non-linear* performance:

Making sense of non-linear performance

- The less the performance emphasises time (the events of the plot), the less important the question 'What will happen next?' becomes. Instead, space, how it is used and what is in it becomes more important. The question becomes 'What is happening here?' or 'What is happening to me?' (physically and emotionally).
- If there is no clear story or characterisation to follow, we begin to pay more attention to concepts like the *rhythm* and *contrasts* between stillness and movement, sound and silence, light and dark.
- If we are not sure what the *signifiers* are *signifying* we become more aware of the *signifiers* themselves – the performers' physicality, the use of space and time, sounds, lights, objects. There may be connotative associations for us – we may be reminded of a resemblance to something in our lives or experience, or we may respond to the technique, or sensory effect, or the aesthetics of the *signifiers*. The performance becomes more like a dance or a piece of sculpture in which there are *non-realist* ideas and forms of representation at work.

Conclusion

Between the two extremes of **linear** realist performances and **non-linear** stylised happenings there lies the possibility of combining elements of ***realism*** and ***non-realism*** in one piece. Most contemporary performances will be of this kind. It is unusual to find a strictly realist performance even when it is based on a classic of *realism* such as *A Doll's House*. The tendency for directors and performers to make their own mark on a performance is likely to lead, as we have seen in this chapter, to some stylising in order to offer an interpretation – stylised costume or lighting perhaps.

Increasingly, the conventions used in performance require an educated audience, which is aware of the history and contemporary use of the sign systems of theatre. This is one purpose for your own study of theatre, so that you can make and enjoy theatre as a subtle, effective and powerful means of communicating ideas about the human condition. As you complete your course of study, you are now prepared to enter into the infinite variety of theatre with which we introduced this book.

The Lion King, Lyceum Theatre, London 1999.

Performance Analysis Questionnaire

In the pages that follow, we have created a detailed questionnaire to help you collect your impressions, responses and understandings of a live performance. The analysis of performance is an increasingly complex activity for the reasons that we have outlined in Chapter 10.

This complexity requires great detail in the questionnaire. There is so much that one might respond to both before, during and after a performance, and performance in today's theatre takes many different forms and has many social functions. The questionnaire is designed to include every sign of performance and to include both the analysis of devised performances and performances based on an existing play text.

The questionnaire is in six sections, as follows:

1 **Expectations**. We seldom go to a performance cold. More usually we have a set of expectations of the play, of the director and the venue among other sources of information that create a certain expectation of the performance itself.
2 **Summarise expectations**. In this section you are asked to gather together your expectations prior to the performance itself.
3 **Pre-performance**. Once you arrive at the venue, you encounter other sources of information about the performance from the venue itself and from the visual and spatial arrangements in the auditorium prior to the opening of the show.
4 **Text in Performance**. If the performance is based on an existing play text, you will need to consider how effectively the play text has been translated into performance. This section will be particularly important when you watch the performance of one of your set texts or of a play text you are studying or know well.
5 **Performance Text**. In this section you make an analysis of the actors' technical and interpretative skills in performance. You also consider the use of technical theatre and the dynamics, or flow, of the performance.
6 **Post-performance**. Finally, we help you to collect together your first impressions into a framework for group discussion so that you can share your responses and gain from the views of others in your group.

Each section makes use of some of the terms that we have introduced in this book and asks a number of key questions about the performance.

At some point in your studies it would be valuable to try and complete the entire questionnaire for a live performance so that you can become aware of all that is involved in making, performing and responding to performance. If you experience the performance in a group then you could divide up the various sections of the questionnaire so that individuals take responsibility for making a complete response to one section only.

In other situations, you may want to select from the questionnaire according to the type of performance that you are going to see and your own purposes for making an analysis. There are parts of the questionnaire which will be irrelevant if you go to see a devised performance rather than a performance of a play text, for instance. You may want to focus on a particular aspect of the performance such as the acting or the use of technical theatre, in which case you would focus on those sections rather than trying to keep a record of all the sections.

The questionnaire will also be useful to you in the final stages of your own performance work. It provides you with a checklist of all that you will need to consider in polishing your work for public performance.

1 Expectations

Play text	Play text	Title? Is it: a new play, revival, classic, translation, adaptation?
	Author (if applicable)	Is this a new or established author? What else has she or he written? Is the author's cultural background relevant in terms of gender, culture/ethnicity, social class?
	Period (if applicable)	In what historical period was the play written? What historical period is the play set in? What do you know about these periods?
	Genre	Is the play in a particular genre? What other plays have you seen and studied that are in the same genre? What do you expect from plays in this genre?
Style	Director	Does the director have a reputation? If so for what kind of work? (e.g. playwright's director/***auteur***)
	Company	Is it a permanent company (e.g. RSC/Rep/nationally known)? Are there any 'stars'? If so what previous work have they done?
	Venue	What type of venue is it? What else have you seen there? What do you expect from shows at this venue?
Extra	Reviews	Has this performance been reviewed? If so what were the opinions and points raised in the reviews?
	Publicity	How and where has the show been marketed? What images and text are used in the marketing? Does the publicity target a particular audience?
	Friends	Do you know anyone who has already seen the show? What's the word?

2 Summarise Expectations

Based on your pre-performance research: What do you expect the performance to be like, in terms of style and effect? What problems might there be in the staging of this play? If you have already studied the play what will you be looking for in the performance? Are there any interesting differences in the reviews to note? What do you expect to enjoy/not enjoy in this performance?

3 Pre-performance

Venue	Ambience at venue	What is the 'feel' of the venue? What is the age/economic/cultural profile of the audience? How welcoming is the venue?
	Visuals/graphics	Are there any posters? Are there any images from the production? Scenes, costumes, set? Are there any photos of the actors as themselves/in character? Are there posters and photos from previous shows?
	Programme notes	What information is given: About the play? About the interpretation? About the producers (bioraphies etc.)?

Venue	Pre-performance events Music/sound	Does the performance extend into the lobby, in terms of: Displays or material directly related to the performance? Actors mingling or calling the audience into the theatre? Sound or music to signal the performance is starting?
Staging	Performance space	When you enter the theatre/performance space, how is it organised? Sketch the space, paying careful attention to how it is divided into acting/audience space and any fixed objects or scenery present. How do you expect the space to be used? Will there be a close relationship between performers and audience for instance?
	Audience space	How will the seating affect the audience's response?
	Set	Are there any ambient sounds/lights?
Use of Acting/Audience Space	(Sketch of the space).	

4 Text in Performance

Consider and comment on:	• Casting • Spoken text • Characterisation • Genre and/or style • Period • Setting
Is it a literal presentation of the play, with few changes to the original text and directions? Is it an interpretation of the original play text based on the director's ideas and themes? If so, what changes have been made to the original text? Are the signs used to tell the story in its period and setting mainly realist or non-realist? Did this performance teach you anything new about the plot, language, characters, setting or themes of the play text? Did you have a problem with, or not like/understand, any aspect of the staging of this play?	

5 Performance Text

Actors use of:

	Literal	Interpretative	Realist	Non-Realist
Space				
Voice				
Body				
Movement				
Timing				
Interactions				

Use the tick boxes to decide whether the actors' signing is: literal (according to the original directions) or interpretative (commenting on or 'making strange' the original directions); mainly ***realist*** (iconic or 'lifelike') or mainly non-realist (***symbolic***).
Was there a dominant acting style: '***representational***' actors 'being' characters (**Stanislavskian**) or '***presentational***' actors 'showing' characters (***Brechtian***)?
Were there any significant changes, or contrasts, in the acting style during the performance? If so, what was the intention and effect do you think?
How conscious were you of the actors as actors rather than as characters?
What effect did the performance of the actors have on your understanding of the play and/or your experience during the performance?
How did the actors use each other and how much direct notice did they take of the audience?
Were there any outstanding/weak performances? If so, what distinguished these actors from others in terms of their signing?

Technical Theatre

	Fixed	Change	Realist	Non-realist	On	Off
Props						
Costumes						
Scenery						
Music						
Sound						
Other technical						

Use the tick boxes to decide which technical theatre effects were: fixed throughout or changed during the performance; realist or stylised in their appearance or effect; mostly 'switched on' (used) or 'switched off' (not used).
Which effects were you most conscious of during performance?
Were there any significant changes in the use of an effects system – e.g. sudden music, or dramatic lighting changes – if so, what was the intention and effect?
Did the effects blend in with the other signs in performance, or were they in contrast with other signs – i.e. realist acting with a stylised set or lighting?
Were there any design themes, such as colour, textures, shapes?

Dynamics

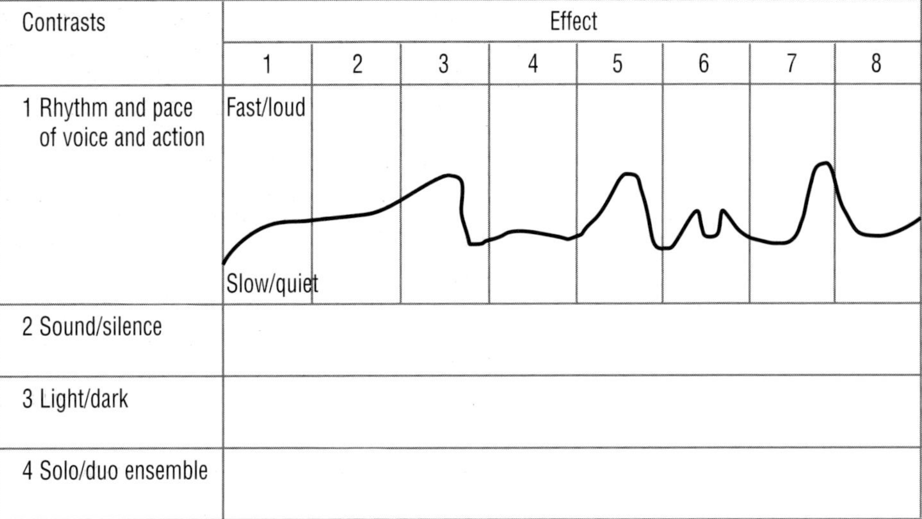

Contrasts	Effect							
	1	2	3	4	5	6	7	8
1 Rhythm and pace of voice and action	Fast/loud Slow/quiet							
2 Sound/silence								
3 Light/dark								
4 Solo/duo ensemble								

	Sound	Movement	Participation	Applause
5 Audience response				

Divide the performance up into units (see diagram above) – possibly the act/scene structure or time elapsed. Make a simple flow chart to show the rhythms and pace of the performance. The bottom of the chart represents 'slow/quiet' and the top is 'fast/loud'
Make a note of any significant moments of contrast between sound/silence and light/dark. What was the intention and effect of these moments?
What was the mix of solo/duologue and ensemble playing in the performance? Were there any obvious contrasts – e.g. an intimate duologue followed by a busy crowd or ensemble scene?
What did the audience contribute to the performance and how conscious were you of other audience members?

6 Post-performance

Use the information that you have gathered in Stages 1–5 to prepare the following notes as a basis for group discussion. Refer back to the evidence that you have collected during the discussion.

Personal Notes for:		
	Images retained	When you close your eyes and think back to the performance, how many moments can you *clearly* visualise in you head? Why are these the images that *you* have retained?
	Strongest moment	What for you was the strongest moment in the performance? A moment of tension, sadness, anger, beauty or truth, perhaps? A particular scene which affected you the most? One of the images that you retained?
	Weakest moment	Which moment was the weakest for you? A scene or use of sign that really didn't work for you? How might that moment have been 'rescued' or done differently?
	Inconsistencies	Were there any problems with the logic or coherence of the signs in performance? Anything that jarred or seemed out of place with the rest of the performance?
	Didn't understand	Were there any points in the performance that confused you, or where you couldn't work out the intentions?
	Strong points overall	Did the performance have a particular strength? The acting or design for instance?
	Weak points overall	Did the performance have a particular weakness? The pace or director's interpretation, for instance?
	Personal response	Finally, make a list of issues or points that you really would like raised and shared in the discussion.

SECTION 6

Resources

Appendix 1: Glossary of practitioners, stylistic, technical and historical terms

Abbey Theatre Founded in 1904 by the Fay brothers, Yeats, Lady Gregory and Synge in order to encourage and introduce the work of new Irish playwrights onto the stage. Such writers have included Sean O'Casey, Lennox Robinson, T.C. Murray and George Shiels. Contemporary artists include Brian Friel, Tom Kilroy, Hugh Leonard, Tom MacIntyre and Graham Reid.

Aeschylus (525/4–456/5BC) Greek dramatist. Aeschylus wrote over 90 plays, which include *Persians* (472), *Seven against Thebes* (467), and *Prometheus Bound* (exact date unknown). Aeschylus introduced plays that reduced chorus numbers, and also had more than one main actor. This formation is said to have shaped European theatre.

Albee, Edward Franklin (1928–) American playwright. His plays include *The American Dream* (1961); *Who's Afraid of Virginia Woolf?* (1962); *A Delicate Balance* (1966); and *The Lady from Dubuque* (1977). His most recent play, *Three Tall Women* (1991) won the Pulitzer Prize in 1994.

Alfreds, Mike (Contemporary) British director of Method and Madness Company and formerly of Shared Experience. Alfreds works in the Naturalist tradition with a strong emphasis on narrative conventions. Productions include *The Black Dahlia* and *The Cherry Orchard.*

Anouilh, Jean-Marie-Lucien-Pierre (1910–87) French dramatist who achieved critical acclaim and popularity in both France and Britain. Among his many achievements, his adaptation of *Antigone* (1944) (controversial because of the Second World War), acted as a commentary on the decline of fascism.

Antagonist The character who opposes the protagonist. Their clash of objectives is what makes a play dramatic.

Antoine, Andre (1858–1943) French actor, director and theatre manager, who gained much of his inspiration from the Meiningen Theatre Company. As a pioneer of modern naturalistic theatre, Antoine founded the Theatre Libre in 1887. The introduction of a naturalistic style of acting was accompanied by three-dimensional sets, in place of flats. In 1890 he founded Theatre Antoine, which in 1896 was used as a creative centre for young artists. Finally, in 1906 in recognition of his work, Antoine was appointed director of the Odeon, where he remained until retirement in 1916.

Appia, Adolphe (1862–1928) Swiss artist and director. Appia is considered to be the first stage lighting designer. He abandoned flat sets in order to create a more atmospheric scene, using mood-evoking lighting and music.

Aristophanes (448?–385BC) Influential Athenian playwright of satircal comedy. His plays include *The Acharnians* (425), *The Clouds* (423), *Lysistrata* (411), *The Frogs* (405), and *Plutis* (388).

Aristotle (384–322BC) Ancient Greek philosopher. Aristotle's theories that have shaped theatre were written in the 320s and the 330s BC, in his *Poetics*, he divided elements of poetry into a hierarchical system, placing 'tragedy' as the highest. Aristotle's *Poetics* was applied to world theatre, after its translation into Latin in 1498.

Artaud, Antonin (1896–1948) French actor, director and poet. Artaud began work as an actor employed by Lugne-Poe, in Theatre D'Oeuvre. In 1927 Artaud and Roger Vitrac formed the Alfred Jarry Theatre, in order to explore surrealism, believing that realism was a betrayal of theatre's purpose. Between 1929–35, Artaud formulated his 'Theatre of Cruelty', which was greatly influenced by the Balinese dancers, whose art was structured around very specific gestures. Artaud's only attempt to realise his idea, in a production of Shelley's *The Cenci* in 1935, failed. However he is now regarded as a highly influential force in the theatre.

auteur French word meaning 'author'. *Auteur* refers to a director who is considered a 'co-author' in the respect that they significantly revise the original play, and produce a final product which is very much their own creation.

avant-garde French term which is associated with the pioneering artistic period of modernism, dating from the late nineteenth century. Avant-garde drama was first produced across Europe at theatres such as Theatre Libre, Theatre de l'Oeuvre, Die Freie Buhne, The Abbey Theatre and the Moscow Art Theatre.

Bancrofts The, Sir Squire (1841–1926), Marie Effie Wilton (1839–1921) Actors and theatre managers, who owned the Prince of Wales theatre. The Bancrofts introduced naturalistic plays by dramatists such as Tom Robertson onto the stage, in place of popular melodramas.

Barba, Eugenio (1936–) Italian director. Time spent at Grotowski's laboratory theatre in 1961 encouraged Barba to found the Odin Teatret in Denmark, where he developed his idea of 'the third theatre'. His research allowed Barba to introduce drama into artistically starved communities. In 1979 Barba concentrated his work into a larger centre for research, the International School of Theatre Anthropology.

Barthes, Roland (1915–1980) French literary critic, and theorist. Barthes studied the semiotics of different cultures, and how they are expressed in written texts.

Bausch, Pina (1940–) German dancer, choreographer and actor. In 1973 Bausch founded the modern dance company, Tanztheater Wupperatal, in Germany.

Beck, Julian (1925–85) Founder of the experimental New York theatre company, Living Theatre.

Beckett, Samuel (1906–89) Irish playwright. Beckett was not recognised as a playwright until 1953 with Blin's production of *Waiting for Godot* (1947). Further successes include *Endgame* (1957), *Krapp's Last Tape* (1958) and *Happy Days* (1961). Beckett was heavily inspired by his Irish upbringing, and much of his comedy is based on this. In all of Beckett's plays he manages to engage the audience in a play that is relatively non-eventful, but invites the audience to share in a character's experience of waiting or reminiscing. Beckett's later work *Breath* (1969), *Not I* (1971), and *Footfalls* (1975), conveys his utter detachment from conventional theatre.

Behn, Aphra (1640–89) First female English playwright. Behn's satirical comedies and farces include *The Emperor of the Moon* (1687), *The Roundheads* (1681), and *The Lucky Chance* (1686). Her most famous play is *The Rover* (1677).

Belasco, David (1853–1931) American director and resident dramatist and manager at several theatres including the Baldwin Theatre in San Francisco, the Madison Square Theatre in New York (1882), and the Lyceum Theatre in London. Belasco worked closely with Henry C. DeMille, collaborating on many celebrated productions such as *The Wife* (1887). His individual work includes *The Darling of the Gods* (1902), *The Girl of the Golden West* (1905) and *The Governor's Lady* (1912). Belasco is also known for the Belasco Theatre which he opened in 1907.

Bely, Andrei (1880–1934) Russian novelist and dramatist. Of his Russian contemporaries Bely was much in favour of the innovative work of Meyerhold, and rejected the realist work of Stanislavski. Bely's symbolist plays include *He Who Has Come* (1903), *The Jaws of Night* (1907), and *The Death of a Senator* (1925).

Bennett, Alan (1934–) British actor and dramatist. Bennett was a member of the popular theatre group *Beyond the Fringe*. Satirical in both his acting and writing, Bennett exposed the hypocrisy and corruption in British politics in plays such as *Forty Years On* (1968). Later plays explored the issue of class in Britain, including *Habeas Corpus* (1973), and *Enjoy* (1980).

Bernhardt, Sarah (1844–1923) French actress. In 1862 Bernhardt gave her first performance at the Comedie-Franciase. During the early 1880s Bernhardt toured America, Russia and Australia, which gave her international recognition, publicity and stardom. Bernhardt's greatest performance was given in 1884, in *The Lady of the Camellias*. In 1899 Bernhardt joined the Theatre des Nations, which was later renamed in her recognition as the Theatre Sarah Bernhardt.

Blok, Aleksander Aleksandrovich (1880–1921) Russian poet and dramatist. Blok's *Lyrical Dramas* (completed in 1908), consisting of *The Puppet Show, The King on the Square,* and *The Unknown Woman*, experimented with Commedia dell'Arte and theatre of the grotesque. His innovative style was greatly admired by the pioneering director Meyerhold, who consequently produced several of his plays. Blok's later works include *The Miracle of Theophile* (1908) and *The Rose and the Cross* (1913).

Bogdanov, Michael (1938–) British director. After his work for various companies, including the Royal Shakespeare Company, Bogdanov was appointed associate director of the National Theatre in 1980. His productions include Brenton's *The Roman in Britain* (1980), Calderon's *The Mayor of Zalamea* (1981), and Kyd's *The Spanish Tragedy* (1982). In 1986 Bogdanov co-founded the English Shakespeare Company.

Bond, Edward (1935–) British dramatist. Bond's second play *Saved,* first performed at the Royal Court Theatre, caused uproar. Bond wanted to express the cruelty and self-crucifixion of the contemporary age, which was symbolised by a baby in a pram being stoned to death. Bond is a writer who is able to express his overtly left-wing views in a variety of genres. His plays staged at the Royal Court, the National Theatre and fringe theatres include *Early Morning* (1968), *Lear* (1972), and *War Plays* (1985).

Boucicault, Dion (1820–90) Irish born actor and playwright of over 250 plays, including *London Assurance* (1841).

Brahm, Otto (1856–1912) German director and literary critic, who, inspired by Antoine's Theatre Libre, opened the German equivalent, the 'Freie Buhne', in Berlin in 1889. After ten years training actors at the Deutsches Theater, Brahm took over the Lessing Theater in Berlin, where he worked until his death.

Braun, Edward (1936–) British author of several books about the theatre. His works include *The Theatre of Meyerhold, The Director and the Stage,* and *Meyerhold A Revolution in Theatre.*

Brecht, Bertolt (1898–1956) German poet, playwright and theorist. Brecht's theatre is often referred to as the 'Theatre of Intellect', engaging the audience to form a critical viewpoint. Undoubtedly Brecht was influenced by Piscator's Agit-Prop, multi-media theatre, in the creation of his own form of theatre, 'epic', which is founded upon emotional detachment. This distancing technique is called the *verfrumdungseffekt.* Brecht had early success particularly with productions such as *The Threepenny Opera,* written in collaboration with Elisabeth Hauptmann. While Hitler was in power, Brecht went into exile, and here wrote what are considered to be his greatest plays, including *Mother Courage and Her Children* (1941), and *The Good Person of Setzuan* (1943).

Brenton, Howard (1942–) British dramatist. Brenton's full-length political plays, including *Magnificence* (1973) and *The Churchill Play* (1974), were written to enlighten and shock the British public. *The Romans in Britain* (1980) included a violent scene of homosexual rape. Brenton's plays have established him as a pioneer of modern British drama, with major productions at the Royal National Theatre and the Royal Court.

Brook, Peter Stephen Paul (1925–) English director influenced by the contrasting styles of Artaud and Brecht. Brook achieved success at the Birmingham Repertory Theatre the Shakespeare Memorial Theatre and the Stratford Company with productions such as *Titus Andronicus* (1955), which starred Lawrence Olivier. In 1962 Brook was appointed co-director at the Royal Shakespeare Company. Productions here included Weiss' *Marat/Sade* (1964), and *A Midsummer Night's Dream* (1970). During the 1970s Brook broke away from the confines of traditional theatre and founded the International Centre for Theatre Research in Paris. He invited performers from a variety of cultures and countries to join his company in order to assemble a theatre that could dissolve cultural barriers. The company toured nationally to both commercial cities and remote villages, with productions such as *The Conference of Birds* (1976), *The Ik* (1975) and the hugely successful *The Mahabharata* (1985).

Brown, William Henry (fl. 1820s) African-American theatre manager, and playwright. In 1821 founded the first African-American theatre, which was based in New York. Brown did much for the emergence of black actors such as James Hewlett and Ira Aldridge in the Western world.

Buchner, Georg (1813–37) German dramatist. Buchner was the leader of an anti-revolutionist group. His first play, *Danton's Death* (1835) condemns the French Revolution. Due to the strong political statements Buchner made in his plays, they were not performed until years after his death: *Leonce and Lena* (1836), first produced in 1895; *Danton's Death* (1835), first produced in 1903. *Woyzeck* (1837), which was never completed, was first performed in 1913. Buchner dramatically differed to his romantic contemporaries, and is now recognised as a forerunner of naturalism.

Burbage, Richard (1530–97) English actor. Burbage was encouraged into the theatre by his acting father James Burbage, and began his own acting career with the Strange's Men. In 1594 Burbage became a founder member of the Lord Chamberlain's Men. With this company Burbage created many of Shakespeare's original roles, including Hamlet, Othello, Lear and Richard III.

Calderon De La Barca, Pedro (1600–81) Spanish playwright of the Golden Age. Calderon gained success and reputation, establishing himself by 1629 with his plays *The Phantom Lady* and *The House with Two Doors.* He wrote hundreds of grand scale plays, both comic and tragic, and is most renowned for his play *Life is a Dream* (1635).

Carter, Angela (1940–) Controversial British writer. Her novels include *Shadow Dance* (1965), *The Magic Toy Shop* (1967), *Several Perceptions* (1968), *The Infernal Desire Machines of Dr Hoffman* (1972) and *Nights at the Circus* (1984). Carter has also written several collections of short stories such as *The Bloody Chamber* (1979). Her poetry includes the collection *Nothing Sacred* (1982).

Cartwright, Jim (1958–) British playwright, known for his plays *Road, Bed, Two* and *The Rise and Fall of Little Voice.*

Chaikin, Joseph (1935–) American director, actor and producer. Chaikin first performed in New York in 1958 in *Dark of the Moon*. He established himself as a dramatist by founding The Open Theatre in 1964, a company which performed new innovative scripts. Successes that followed included *America Hurrah* (1966), *Terminal* and *The Serpent* (both 1970).

Chekhov, Anton Pavlovich (1860–1904) Great Russian dramatist. Chekhov's plays did not gain success on a grand scale until they were staged by the Moscow Arts Theatre, directed by Stanislavski and Nemirovich-Danchenko. Although Chekhov did not always agree with Stanislavski's interpretation, productions such as *Three Sisters, The Seagull* and *The Cherry Orchard* were hugely successful.

Chronegk, Ludwig (1837–91) Director and disciplinarian of the Meiningen Theatre Company.

Churchill, Caryl (1938–) English dramatist, who began her career as a writer of radio plays. Churchill's first stage play, *Owners* made its debut at the Royal Court in 1972. She is most famous for her feminist plays during the 1980s, including *Top Girls* (1982), and *Fen* (1983).

Commedia dell'Arte Comedy developed in Italy in the sixteenth and seventeenth centuries. Commedia is recognised primarily because of its stock characters, identified by their costume and mask. Often improvised performances were combined with rehearsed comical 'routines' called *lazzi*. Famous commedia companies include the I Gelosi, which performed from the 1570s to 1604. Commedia gave equal status to action as to verbal dialogue and narrative, which meant that Italian commedia could be understood in other countries, overcoming language barriers.

Congreve, William (1670–1729) English playwright. Congreve's plays include *The Old Bachelor* (1689), *Love for Love* (1695) and *The Way of the World* (1700).

Copeau, Jacques (1879–1949) French actor, director and playwright. In 1913 Copeau founded the Vieux-Colombier theatre company. Copeau's theatre strove to achieve non-realist powerful performances on minimalist sets. Copeau's later work includes productions performed at the Comedie Francaise, and his inspirational essay *Le Theatre Populaire* (1941).

Corneille, Pierre (1606–84) French dramatist. Corneille received critical acclaim in Paris with his comedies *The Window* (1631/2), *The Palace Gallery* (1632), *The Maidservant* (1633) and *La Palace Royale* (1633). Corneille is most renowned however for his tragedies, which include *Horace* (1640), *Cinna* (1641), *The Death of Popee* (1645), and *Heraclius* (1646). He dominated the tragedian stage in Paris until the rise of the young talented writer Racine during the 1660s. The competition of Racine overshadowed Corneille's later plays, which included *Tite et Berenice* (1670).

Coward, Noel (1899–1973) British playwright and actor. Most successful works include his comedies *Fallen Angels* (1925), *Design for Living* (1933), *Blithe Spirit* (1941), and *Present Laughter* (1942).

Craig, Edward Gordon (1872–1966) British director and set designer. Craig's early work includes designing and directing productions such as the opera *Masque of Love* (1901) and Ibsen's *The Vikings* (1903). In 1905 Craig published an essay *The Art of Theatre* which expressed his view that theatre should be a serious art-form equivalent to music. Craig also expressed his belief that theatre should have one controlling force, an *Uber-marionette,* which would make redundant the actor, designer and composer. Although this idea was never truly realised it did highlight the importance, and raised the profile of, the director, in place of the actor-manager.

Decroux, Etienne (1899–1991) French mime artist who trained at the School of Dramatic Arts in Paris.

Devine, George (1910–65) British actor and director. In 1934, Devine joined Gielgud's company at the New Theatre. During his time at the New Theatre he met the French director Michel Saint-Denis. Together the pair worked for many years as innovators of the theatre, experimenting with new forms. In 1954 he collaborated with the playwright Ronald Duncan, to found the English Stage Company, which was specifically designed to stage new innovative modern plays. The first season proved a success, opening with John Osborne's *Look Back In Anger* at the Royal Court.

dialectics Dialectics is the term used to describe the clash of opposites, and the resulting conflicts. Brecht particularly strove to achieve dialectical theatre.

Dorfman, Ariel (1942–) Chilean playwright, who now lives and works in the USA. He is known for his plays such as *Reader* (1995), *Death and the Maiden* (1996) and *Widows* (1997), which indirectly reflects the fascist regimes of General Pinochet.

Drury Lane, Theatre Royal First built in 1663. Famous performances at Drury Lane include those of David Garrick (who also managed the theatre) in Otway's *The Orphan*, Charles Macklin as Shylock, and Robert Elliston as Hamlet. After Garrick's retirement in 1777, Sheridan replaced him as manager. Sheridan had initial success with his production of his own play *The School for Scandal* (1777). During the 1920s Alfred Butt introduced musicals to Drury Lane, and today it is one of the key musical theatres in London's West End.

Duncan, Isadora (1877–1927) American dancer. Duncan was influenced by images from ancient Greek theatre. She broke away from the formalism of ballet, creating a new style, which became the foundation of modern dance.

DV8 Contemporary dance and physical theatre company, formed in 1986. Performances include *My Sex Our Dance, Deep End, My Body Your Body,* and *Dead Dreams of Monochrome Men.*

Eco, Umberto (1932–) Italian writer and semiotician. His novels include *The Name of the Rose* (1983). Eco is renowned for his work in semiotics, which is the study of symbols and signs. See *Semiotics and the Philosophy of Language* (1984).

Eisler, Hanns (1898–1962) German composer for theatre and film. Eisler composed the German national anthem, and was a close collaborator with Brecht.

Eliot, Thomas Stearns (1888–1965) American born English poet, critic and dramatist. His poetry includes *The Love Song of J. Alfred Prufrock* (1915) and *The Waste Land* (1922). Eliot is renowned in the theatre for his verse play *Murder in the Cathedral* (1955).

English Shakespeare Company Founded by director Michael Boganov in 1986. The English Shakespeare Company was designed as a touring company that would take classic Shakespeare productions to areas relatively untouched by and deprived of drama.

Euripides (?485/4–407/6BC) Ancient Greek playwright. Although he was criticised during his life by Sophecles and Aristotle, he is now regarded as the most highly influential tragedian. Euripides wrote approximately 90 plays during his life, which include *Alexander, The Trojan Women, Cyclops, Hippolytus, Hecabe,* and *Electra.*

exposition The exposition of a play usually occurs at the beginning. It gives the audience background information of previous events that are relevant to the play.

Eyre, Richard (1943–) British director, known for his pioneering contemporary productions. Eyre's experience at the Royal Lyceum Theatre (1967–72) led to his innovative work at the Nottingham Playhouse. Here he produced plays of fresh, new, talented playwrights such as Brenton and Hare. Eyre later went on to work at the National Theatre, with productions such as *The Beggars Opera* and *Guys and Dolls.* His television and film work include the BBC's *Play for Today* (from 1978), and two films, *The Ploughman's Lunch* and *Loose Connections.*

Fo, Dario (1926–) Italian actor, director and dramatist. Fo was a satirical writer who ridiculed and exposed the hypocrisy of the Italian government. During the late 1960s Fo formed a touring company, La Nuova Scena, which performed political theatre under the patronage of the Communist Party. Productions included *The Worker Knows 300 Words, the Boss 1,000; That's Why He's the Boss* (1968). During the 1970s Fo abandoned the orthodox left wing, and formed a new company La Commune, which served in support of the 'New Left Wing'. Fo's productions during the 1970s and 1980s attracted attention across Europe. They include *Accidental Death of an Anarchist* (1970), and *Can't Pay, Won't Pay* (1974).

Ford, John (1586–1639) English dramatist. Ford's later plays are considered his finest. They include *Love's Sacrifice* (1630), *Tis a Pity She's a Whore* (1633), *Perkin Warbeck* (1634), *The Lady's Trial* (1638) and *The Witch of Edmonton* (1658).

Franz, Ellen (1839–1923) Actress (married to the Duke of Saxe-Meiningen) who managed the group of actors at the Meiningen Theatre Company.

Friel, Brian (1929–) Playwright, whose work includes *Dancing at Lughnasa, Translations,* and *Molly Sweeney.*

Garrick, David (1717–79) English actor, theatre manager and playwright. As well as making regular performances at Drury Lane Theatre, Garrick's first play *Lethe* made its debut there in 1740. In 1747 Garrick became the manager at Drury Lane, producing and starring in spectacular Shakespearean productions. Garrick gave his final performance in Mrs Centlivre's *The Wonder* in 1776, after giving way to Sheridan as manager of the theatre.

Gay, John (1685–1732) English dramatist, who established himself in 1715 with *The What D'ye Call It*. Gay tasted real success with his ballad-opera *The Beggar's Opera* in 1728. This production was innovative in its style, genre and plot. It was later adapted by Brecht as the immensely successful *The Threepenny Opera*.

gestus Gestus is a major foundation of Bertolt Brecht's epic theatre. Gestus refers to physical actions which expose an underlying main social theme of a play.

Globe Theatre Built in London in 1599 by Cuthbert Burbage. The Globe Theatre was heavily associated with Shakespeare, and the company of the 'Chamberlain's Men', led by Richard Burbage.

Goethe, Johann Wolfgang von (1749–1832) German playwright, and director. Goethe worked closley with Schiller from 1791 to 1817, as director of the Court Theatre in Weimar, and here conceived the 'Rules for Actors' in his 'Weimar School of Acting'. This had a great impact on German tragedian performance. Goethe's most praised works are *Faust, Part 1* and *Part 2* (1808 and 1832 respectively). Both parts are commended for their depth and range of style and dramatic possibility.

Gogol, Nikolai Vasilievich (1809–52) Russian playwright. Gogol's unique style of grotesque comedy was the product of a variety of inspirational sources such as Tolstoi, Turgenev and Chekhov. Perhaps Gogol's most celebrated play is *The Inspector General* (1836), which was famously produced by Meyerhold in 1926.

Goldsmith, Oliver (1728–74) Irish playwright, who after training in medicine began writing in 1757. Goldsmith wrote two plays, which were satirical attacks, mocking the middle class of London. *The Good Natured Man* (1768) and *She Stoops to Conquer* (1773) were both performed at Covent Garden, however only the latter had any success.

Gorki, Maxim (1868–1936) Soviet writer, dramatist and critic. In both Russian revolutions, Gorki played an active role as a member of the Bolshevik party, and his political stance is conveyed in his plays. In 1902, the Moscow Art Theatre produced Gorki's first play *The Petty Bourgeoisie* (1902). Further successes include *The Lower Depths* (1902) which is considered a dangerous yet ingenious pro-revolutionist realist play. Gorki's career concluded with a trilogy of autobiographical plays, *My Childhood* (1914), *In the World* (1916) and *My Universities* (1924).

Granville Barker, Harley (1877–1946) British actor, director and playwright. In 1900, after several years as an actor, Barker wrote and directed his own play *The Marrying of Ann Lette*. As a director Barker was most highly acclaimed for his productions of *A Winter's Tale, Twelfth Night* (both 1912) and *A Midsummer Night's Dream* (1914).

Griffiths, Trevor (1935–) British dramatist. Griffiths' plays convey his Marxist viewpoint, and empathy for working-class lives. His plays include *Occupations* (1970), *Sam, Sam* (1972), *The Party* (1973) and *Comedians* (1975). Griffiths' television dramas include the series *Bill Brand* (1976).

Grotowski, Jerzy (1933–1998) Polish director, who studied at the Moscow State Institute of Theatre Arts. Grotowski had been trained in the methods of Stanislavski, and hence believed that if an actor committed themselves completely both mentally and physically, they could work without unnecessary lighting, scenery and costume. Grotowski published his ideas in *Towards a Poor Theatre*. During the 1960s he toured nationally with his Laboratory Theatre Company, achieving success with productions such as Wyspianski's *Akropolis*.

Guthrie, Tyrone (1900–71) Irish director. Guthrie worked mainly in Britain, the USA and Canada. He is praised for his avant-garde productions, including *Hamlet* (1937), *Henry V* (1937), and *Peer Gynt* (1944). In recognition of his work, the Gutherie Theatre in Minneapolis was built in 1963.

Hallam, Lewis (1714–55) English actor, belonging to a family of actors, who in 1752 travelled to the USA to become the first English professionals ever to have performed in the theatrically starved states of North America.

Hare, David (1947–) British dramatist and director. Hare's first plays were written for the Portable Theatre, which he co-founded in 1968. These early productions include *Slag* (1970) and *The Great Exhibition* (1972). Hare became resident dramatist at the Royal Court in 1970, and at the Nottingham Playhouse in 1973. After several successful plays written for the Royal National Theatre, which included *Plenty* (1978), *A Map of the World* (1983) and *Pravda* (1985), Hare was appointed associate director.

Hauptmann, Elisabeth (1897–1973) Hauptmann was Brecht's lifelong collaborator. She translated Gay's *The Beggar's Opera*, to produce the hugely successful *The Threepenny Opera*. Hauptmann kept valuable diaries of Brecht's work.

Hauser, Arnold (1892–1978) Hungarian art and society critic who studied at universities throughout Europe. His work includes *The Social History of Art* (1951).

Holcroft, Thomas (1745–1809) English playwright. In 1778, Holcroft's first major work, a comical opera *The Crisis*, opened at Drury Lane. This was followed by a series of successes including *The Follies of a Day* (1784), *Seduction* (1787) and *The School for Arrogance* (1791). Holcroft's most famous play is the comedy *The Road to Ruin* (1792).

Hugo, Victor (1802–85) French poet, dramatist and novelist. Many of Hugo's early plays were forbidden production because of his political opinions. However, in 1828 Hugo's play *Amy Robstart* made its debut at the Odeon. Many of Hugo's later plays were not performed until years after his death because of censorship. These include *100 Francs Reward*, which was not produced until 1961.

Ibsen, Henrik (1828–1906) Norwegian dramatist. In 1851 Ibsen went to the Bergen Theatre as an assistant. He was later appointed resident dramatist and stage director. Ibsen's move to Rome in 1864 saw a significant change in the mood of his plays. They tore away from the popular trend of romanticism and showed Ibsen to be a pioneering dramatist. The first of these plays were *Brand* (1865) and *Peer Gynt* (1867), which both convey a mood of inner turmoil. Ibsen's plays screamed messages of social reform, which emerged in the sub-text of plays such as *A Doll's House* (1879) and *Ghosts* (1881). During the 1880s and 1890s Ibsen's plays were symbolist; these include *The Wild Duck* (1884) and *Hedda Gabler* (1890).

Irving, Sir Henry (1838–1905) English actor-manager. Irving joined the Royal Lyceum Theatre in 1856 and worked as a professional actor until 1859. From then on he established himself as the most famous actor on the London stage. Irving's fresh interpretation of plays led to his appointment as manager at the Lyceum in 1878.

Jarry, Alfred (1873–1907) French author and dramatist. Jarry was the creator of the demonic puppet character King Ubu. His play *Ubu Roi* (1896) was shocking for its period. Jarry died of alcoholism at the young age of 34, however he was the source of inspiration for the Theatre of the Absurd, and Artaud's Theatre of Cruelty.

Jerrold, Douglas (1803–57) English actor and playwright, who also worked as a journalist for the comical journal *Punch*. Jerrold's melodramatic plays included *Black-ey'd Susan* (1829).

Jones, Inigo (1573–1652) English architect and set designer. Jones worked for King James I, as designer for masques, which were staged at the court. Productions included Jonson's *The Masque of Blackness* (1605). Jones is responsible for introducing the proscenium arch onto the English stage. He later developed ideas which would create a sense of perspective and depth on stage, such as backcloths and painted shutters and flats, which moved on turntables and grooves.

Jonson, Benjamin (1572–1637) English playwright. Jonson began his career during the 1590s as both an actor and a writer with the Henslowe's men. Jonson gained fame as a writer with the hugely successful *Every Man in His Humour* (1598). *Sejanus, His Fall* (1603) was a highly controversial Roman historical play, which angered King James I because of Jonson's overtly Catholic stance. He is most praised for his for his intelligent witty comedies *Volpone* (1605), *The Silent Woman* (1609), *The Alchemist* (1610) and *Bartholomew Fair* (1614).

Jouvet, Louis (1887–1951) French actor and director, who began his career with Copeau's company at the Vieux-Colombier theatre. Jouvet established himself as an actor with his performance in *Dr Knock or the Triumph of Medicine* at the Comedie des Champs Elysees in 1923. As a director Jouvet produced many of Giraudoux's plays including his final play *The Madwoman of Chaillot* (1945).

Kabuki Traditional Japanese drama, which evolved during the seventeenth century. Kabuki was originally regarded as a rowdy prostitutes' entertainment, however it eventually developed into a highly skilled melodramatic form. Kabuki actors move with puppet-like gestures and deliver the text in a staccato chant. Kabuki performances are often very elaborate. Lavish costumes, make-up and music collectively create an enchanting atmosphere.

Kaiser, Georg (1878–1945) German expressionist playwright. Kaiser is most famous for his trilogy of plays: *Die Koralle* (1917), *Gas I* (1918), and *Gas II* (1920).

Kantor, Tadeuz (1915–) Polish stage designer and director. During the Second World War Kantor founded the Independent Theatre. In 1956 he created the avant-garde Cricot II company, which was a collaborative company of performers and painters. Kantor developed his 'Theatre of Death' during the 1970s in productions such as *The Green Pill* (1973) and *The Dead Class* (1975).

Kaprow, Allan (1927–) American art theorist who was responsible for an artistic movement during the 1950s regarded as 'the happening', which gave rise to the movement of 'performance art'.

Kathakali (Story Play) Hindu dance and drama form, which depicts tales of the Mahabharata and Ramayana. Kathakali dates from the seventeenth century. The strong focus on facial, eye and hand gestures suggest that it was inspired by Kuttiyattam. A Kathakali performance is a lively, spontaneous and energetic event with a carnival atmosphere.

Kazan, Elia (1909–) American director. Kazan was co-founder of The Actor's Studio, which promoted a naturalistic style of acting, based on Stanislavski's system and Lee Strasberg's method. Kazan's stage productions include *A Streetcar Named Desire* (1947), *Death of a Salesman* (1949), *Cat on a Hot Tin Roof* (1955) and *Sweet Bird of Youth* (1959). His films include *Streetcar* (1951), *On the Waterfront* (1954) and *East of Eden* (1955).

Kean, Charles (1811–68) English actor and theatre manager. Son of the actor Edmund Kean. In 1950 Charles took up management at the Princess's Theatre. Kean's productions were noted for their historical accuracy and the great care and meticulous eye for detail in the lighting of sets. Kean was the first person to accurately focus limelight.

Kean, Edmund (1789–1833) English actor. Kean developed his talent as the Shakespearean villain, injecting characters such as Richard III with a volatile, monstrous energy. Although extremely talented and successful, Kean's scandalous personal life interfered with his work, and by March 1833 he was exhausted, giving his final performance as Othello, aged 44.

Kemble, John Phillip (1757–1823) English actor and theatre manager. In 1788 Kemble became manager of the Drury Lane Theatre, where he had a series of successes with productions such as *Henry VIII* and *Coriolanus*. By 1796 ill health caused Kemble to leave Drury Lane and continue work at the Covent Garden Theatre, which he managed until it was destroyed by fire in 1808.

Komissarzhevskaya, Vera Fedorovna (1864–1910) Russian actress and theatre manager. In 1896 Komissarzhevskaya joined the Alexandrinsky Theatre, and enjoyed success there in roles such as Nora in Ibsen's *A Doll's House*. In 1904 Komissarzhevskaya formed her own company that would explore new kinds of theatre, inviting Meyerhold to be artistic director. The company produced symbolist plays by dramatists such as Maxim Gorki.

Kott, Jan (1914–) Influential Polish theatre critic and Shakespeare expert whose works include *Shakespeare, Our Contemporary* (1964).

Kuttiyattam Ancient religious Indian art-form, originating in the Indian state of Kerala. Actors perform in a code of gesture and rhythmic chants in Kuttiyattam theatres, such as the vast and impressive Vatukumnathan Temple of Trichun. Main temples stage about one Kutiyattam performance per year, each lasting several days. Costumes are lavish; the brightly coloured headwear symbolises Indian gods and demons.

Laughton, Charles (1899–1962) English actor. Laughton made his debut in 1926 in *The Inspector General*. This was followed by several performances at the Old Vic in productions including *The Cherry Orchard* and *Macbeth*. The predominant remainder of his career was spent in America, where he continued to act in productions such as Brecht's *Galileo* and Shaw's *Don Juan in Hell* (1951).

Lecoq, Jaques (1921–) French mime artist, who trained at the School of Dramatic Arts in Paris. The highly disciplined Lecoq School in Paris now trains mime artists from all over the world.

LeCompte, Elizabeth (1944–) American director and playwright. In 1979 she became artistic director of the Wooster Group, in which she co-wrote and directed productions such as *Sakonnet Point* (1975), *Rumstick Road* (1977) and *Nayatt School* (1978). In 1984 LeCompte became Associate Director of the American National Theatre.

Leigh, Mike (1943–) British director best known for his film work based in realism which includes *Bleak Moments* (1970), *Nuts in May* (1975), *Home Sweet Home* (1982), *High Hopes* (1988), *Life is Sweet* (1991), and *Secrets and Lies* (1996).

Lepage, Robert (1920–) Lepage is the leading Canadian director of his generation and is considered an *auteur* director. He is known for his production of *Hamlet*, which was altered so dramatically it was renamed *Elsinore*.

Lillo, George (?1691–1739) English playwright. Lillo is known to have written two major tragedies, *The London Merchant* (1731) and *Fatal Curiosity* (1736).

Littlewood, Joan (1914–) English director who studied at the Royal Academy of Dramatic Arts. After training Littlewood moved to Manchester, with a desire to explore theatre outside traditional conventions. She founded her own amateur company 'Theatre Union', which after the Second World War reformed as 'Theatre Workshop'. The company, based at the Stratford East Theatre in London, gained huge success, with productions including *Oh! What A Lovely War* in 1963.

Lope De Vega (1562–1635) Spanish dramatist and poet of Spain's Golden Age. Lope's three-act verse commedia plays set a standard style for other Spanish playwrights to follow. His comedies include *The Idiot Lady* (1613) and *The Dog in the Manger* (1613–15). Among Lope's greatest works are his plays which focus on the theme of adultery. These include the sharp, dark comedy *The Wise Man's Punishment* (1598–1601) and the deeply tragic *Punishment Without Revenge* (1631).

Lorca, Federico Garcia (1898–1936) Spanish poet and dramatist. Lorca's early works include the unsuccessful symbolist play *The Butterfly's Evil Spell,* and the more popular revolutionary play *Mariana Pineda.* In 1932 Lorca founded a student touring theatre group, named La Barraca, which proved a great success in the rural areas of Spain. Lorca's final works, *Blood Wedding* (1933), *Yerma* (1934) and *The House of Bernada Alba* (1936) angered Spanish fascists due to their revolutionary subtext. This resulted in Lorca's murder, aged only 38.

Lugne-Poe, Aurelien-Francoise (1869–1940) French actor, director and theatre manager. In 1893 Lugne-Poe took over Paul Fort's Theatre d'Art, and renamed it Theatre de l'Oeuvre, producing symbolist plays such as Maeterlinck's *Pelleas et Mellisande.*

Maeterlinck, Maurice (1862–1949) Belgian symbolist poet and playwright who in 1911 won the Nobel Prize for literature. As a predecessor of the *Theatre of Silence,* Maeterlinck believed in the use of dramatic pauses, which encourage the audience to use their own imaginations to fill in perhaps verbally inexpressible emotions. Maeterlinck's plays include the famous *Pelleas and Melisande* (1893).

Marlowe, Christopher (1564–93) English playwright and poet. His first plays, such as *Tamburlane the Great* (c. 1587) were extremely popular because of their fresh and often controversial approach. Marlowe's plays, which include *The Jew of Malta* (c. 1589) *The Mascacre at Paris* (c. 1589), and *Edward II* (c. 1592), were most commonly produced by the Admiral's Men. The last of Marlowe's plays, *Dr Faustus,* a demonic play about the seven deadly sins; is perhaps his most famous and widely produced play.

McKellen, Ian (Murray) (1939–) British actor. McKellen developed his reputation as a classical and enterprising actor with the Prospect Theatre Company. He performed at the National Theatre in plays such as *A Lily in Little India* (1966). McKellen's work with the Royal Shakespeare Company from 1974 includes performances as Macbeth, and in touring productions such as *The Three Sisters* and *Twelfth Night.*

Meckler, Nancy (Contemporary) British director of Shared Experience her productions include *Anna Karenina.* Meckler's film work tackles taboo social issues such as homosexuality and AIDS, it includes *Sister My Sister,* and *Alive and Kicking.*

Meiningen Theatre Company The Meiningen Theatre Company at the court of George II was directed by the Duke of Saxe Meiningen and his wife Ellen Franz. The Duke's assistant Ludwig Chronegk, had tremendous influence on the company. The Meiningen Theatre promoted the idea of an ensemble company who worked closely together. Both Antoine and Stanislavski were inspired by the company when developing their naturalistic styles of acting.

melodrama Style of drama which descends from the medieval morality plays. It was begun in France in 1800 by the writer Guilbert Pixercourt. In England melodrama began later in 1852 with Dion Boucicault. Melodrama uses stock characters and always portrays a tale of good triumphing over evil. It was an extremely popular form of middle-class entertainment throughout the nineteenth century.

Meyerhold, Vsevold Emilievich (1874–1940) Pioneering Russian director who dedicated his life and career to revolutionising theatre. Meyerhold trained as an actor from 1898 at the Moscow Art Theatre. After leaving the Moscow Art Theatre in 1902, his early attempts at introducing symbolist drama to the provinces of Russia were not successful. Innovative work at Stanislavski's experimental studio theatre also proved unpopular. In 1906, Meyerhold was invited by the famous Russian actress Vera Komissarzhevskaya to become artistic director for her new exploratory theatre. Productions with Komissarzhevskaya included Ibsen's *Hedda Gabler* and Maeterlinck's *Sister Beatrice.* In 1908, Meyerhold was appointed director of St Petersberg's Imperial Opera and Drama Theatres. During his time there Meyerhold developed his theory of the actor-*cabotin,* based on Commedia dell'Arte, in which a performer would be multi-skilled in singing, dancing and juggling, and would have a mask-like appearance. In developing this theory Meyerhold hoped to embrace the theatre of past, combined with contemporary forms. He also injected political opinion and particularly Bolshevism into his theatre of revolution, which led to his appointment as head of the Theatre Division of the People's Commissariat for Education in 1920. During the 1920s Meyerhold developed his theory of biomechanics, which was a system of movement derived from the circus, with athletic movements working as a 'machine' for acting. His later productions included Sukhovo-Kobylin's *Tarelkin's Death*, Gogol's *The Inspector General* and Mayakovsky's Soviet play *Mystery-Bouffe*. They introduced a shift from symbolism to Theatre of the Grotesque, in which Meyerhold would use more than one contrasting genre.

Middleton, Thomas (c. 1580–1627) English playwright. Middleton's early works, including *A Trick to Catch the Old One* (c. 1604) and *A Mad World, My Masters* (c. 1605) were comedies written for the Boys of St Paul's. Middelton also wrote for the Henslowe's Men and the Admirals Men. He collaborated with other writers such as Deker to produce plays including *The Honest Whore* (1604), and with William Rowley to produce *A Fair Quarrel* (c. 1616) and *The Changeling* (1633). Middelton's last play, *Women Beware Women* (c. 1625) is perhaps his finest.

Miller, Arthur (1915–) American playwright. Perhaps Miller's most famous plays are *Death of a Salesman* (1949) and his tale of witchcraft trials, *The Crucible* (1953). During his brief marriage to Marilyn Monroe in 1955, Miller retired from writing, and did not return until 1964, after their divorce. Miller's marriage to the famous film star was the subject of his comeback play *After the Fall* (1964). He went on to produce two more successful plays, which were emotional works of modern tragedy: *Incident at Vichy* (1964) and *The Price* (1968).

mimesis The Greek word meaning to mimic or impersonate. The ancient theories of Plato questioned 'to what extent does art imitate life?'. Examples of art imitating life are the realist plays of the late nineteenth century. The work of the modernist, avant-gardes in the early twentieth century rejected art as an imitation of reality, which gave rise to several artistic movements including symbolism and surrealism.

mise en scene French term which refers to what is in the scene. It refers to how the director, designer and performer have interpreted the playwright's original vision.

Mnouchkine, Ariane (1934–) French director. Mnouchkine founded her own collective theatre group, Theatre du Soleil, which was successful with productions such as *The Golden Age* (1975). Breaking away from theatre for a short period, Mnouchkine sought inspiration from her father's experience in film by making a film based on Moliere. Returning to theatre in the 1980s Mnouchkine worked mainly on Shakespearean productions, such as *Richard II* (1981) and *Twelfth Night* (1982). Mnouchkine has collaborated with the feminist writer Helen Cixous on plays like *Norodom Sihanouk* (1985). Her work is characterised by the influence of oriental performance traditions.

Moliere, Jean-Baptiste Poquelin (1622–73) French actor-manager and dramatist. Moliere's comic talent was inspired by the Italian *commedia*. His early plays include *The Blunderer* (1653) and *Lover's Quarrel* (1656). The comedy of Moliere's plays relied heavily on the skill of the actor, rather than technical and artificial resources. His plays such as *The Affected Ladies* (1659) *School for Wives* (1662) and *The Magnificent Lovers* (1670) were a resounding success with the Parisian audience. However, they were heavily criticised by the church.

monologue A lengthy speech for one person. Often actors are required to prepare a monologue for an audition.

Moore, Sonia Author of *Stanislavski Revealed: The Actor's Guide to Spontaneity on Stage* and *Training an Actor: The Stanislavski System in Class.*

Moscow Art Theatre Founded in 1897 by Konstantin Stanislavski and Vladimir Nemirovich-Danchenko. Heavily inspired by the Meiningen Theatre Company, the Moscow Art Theatre was designed to achieve a new style of realist performance. The company premiered in October in 1898 with Tolstoi's *Tsar Fyodor Ioannonvich* at the Hermitage Theatre. It then went on to produce the opening performances of Chekhov's most successful plays. The Moscow Art Theatre also proved itself to be pioneering in its experimentation, over 30 years, with symbolist plays by writers including Gorki, Ibsen, Hauptmann and Maeterlinck.

naturalism Naturalism is a theory of human psychology. A naturalist play requires the actor to identify with the psychology and consequent behaviour of their character. Naturalism was a modernist movement born out of Darwin's *Origin of Species by Means of Natural Selection* (1859), and the ideas of Zola. The naturalist plays of writers such as Ibsen and Chekhov provided the fundamental building blocks for Stanislavski's system for acting. Today naturalism is most commonly used in television.

Neher, Casper German artist who collaborated with Brecht. Neher was very much invloved with the visual aspect of Brecht's epic theatre. He was very sensitive to the designs of theatre, and his main concern was the use of dramatic space.

Nemirovich-Danchenko, Vladimir Ivanovich (1859–1943) Russian director who worked as an acting teacher at the Moscow Philharmonic Society. However, in 1897 he left and collaborated with Stanislavski to found the *Moscow Art Theatre*, taking with him some of his best students, including Meyerhold and Olga Knipper. Nemirovich-Danchenko was a close companion of the great Russian writer Chekhov, and consequently the *Moscow Art Theatre* became the home of Chekhov's plays.

neo-classicism An artistic movement during the Italian Renaissance which recaptured rules from ancient Greek and Roman drama. Neo-classicism in the theatre refers particularly to Aristotle's *Poetics*.

Nietzsche, Friedrich (1844–1900) German philosopher. Nietzsche's influential theories of theatre were expressed in his essay *The Birth of Tragedy*.

Noble, Adrian (1950–) British director. Noble worked for several prestigious British theatre companies including Bristol Old Vic, the Royal Exchange Theatre and the Royal Shakespeare Company. His famous productions include *The Duchess of Malfi* (1980), *A Doll's House* (1981), *King Lear* (1982), *Henry V* (1982) and *As You Like It* (1985).

Noh Noh, meaning 'talent', is a Japanese form of ritual theatre which heavily focuses on gesture. Noh evolved in the fourteenth century and was originally performed by priests in Buddhist temples. Noh is made up of a variety of contrasting voices, music and movements, which express the Japanese theory that the world is in a constant state of change, and also the dialectic theory, 'yin and yang'.

Nunn, Trevor Robert (1940–) British director. Nunn joined the Royal Shakespeare Company in 1965 as artistic director, and later became chief executive. Nunn has had a series of successes with the company, which have included *The Reveger's Tragedy* (1966), *The Comedy of Errors* (1976), *Macbeth* (1976), and *All's Well That Ends Well* (1981). Outside of the Royal Shakespeare Company Nunn is also responsible for staging the West End hit musicals *Cats* (1981) and *Starlight Express* (1984).

O'Neill, Eugene Gladstone (1888–1953) The earliest successful US playwright. From 1916 O'Neill belonged to a group of writers called the Provincetown Players. He produced his first play, *Beyond the Horizon*, in 1918. O'Neill was a writer of multiple genres, and his many works include *Anna Christie* (1920), *Lazarus Laughed* (1925–6) and *The Iceman Cometh* (1939).

Oldenburg, Claes Thure (1929–) American sculptor, whose innovative pop-art work came to fame during the 1960s.

Oldfield, Anne (1683–1730) English actress. Oldfield's first professional performance was in 1692, at Drury Lane. However, she established herself as an actress in 1703, in a performance of *The Careless Husband*. Oldfield was successful in various roles, which included Silvia in *The Recruiting Officer* (1706), Anromache in *The Distrest Mother* (1712) and Lady Townly in *The Provoked Husband* (1728).

Olivier, Lawrence (1907–89) British actor and director. After establishing himself as a great theatrical actor at the Birmingham Rep and the Old Vic theatres, Olivier became an international film star in films such as *Wuthering Heights*. In 1941 Olivier returned to Britain to direct and star in *The Demi-Paradise* (1943) and *Henry V* (1944). In 1944 Olivier became director of the Old Vic Company, and here gave what are considered to be his finest performances as Richard III and Oedipus. In 1963 Olivier became director at the newly formed National Theatre, creating highly acclaimed productions such as *Othello* (1964) and *The Dance of Death* (1971). The remainder of Olivier's career was devoted to film roles, the most remarkable of which was as King Lear in 1984.

Osborne, John (1929–94) British dramatist and actor. His third play *Look Back in Anger* premiered in 1956 at the Royal Court and was a huge success. Osborne's major plays represent a break away from the conventions of realism. They include *The Entertainer* (1957), *Inadmissible Evidence* (1964) and *A Patriot for Me* (1965).

Pinter, Harold (1930–) British dramatist. Pinter's early plays include *The Birthday Party* (1958), *Slight Ache* (1959), *The Caretaker* (1960) and *The Homecoming* (1965). His play *Landscape and Silence* (1969) marked a change in Pinter's style; he began to experiment with the concept of time. His plays that followed (*Old Times* in 1971, *No Man's Land* in 1975 and *A Kind of Alaska* in 1982) were staged by the Royal Shakespeare Company. In 1975 Pinter became associate director of the Royal National Theatre, working extensively with Peter Hall.

Pirandello, Luigi (1867–1936) Italian dramatist and novelist. Pirandello's first plays were written during the First World War and include *Liola* (1916), *The Pleasure of Honesty* (1918) and *The Rules of the Game* (1918). Pirandello wrote three plays which are considered to be his 'theatre in theatre' plays, the first of which, *Six Characters in Search of an Author* (1921) was his most famous. Many of Pirandello's later work, including *To Dress Naked* (1922), *Bellavita* (1927) and *The Mountain Giants* (1937) were written for his own touring theatre company, Teatro d'Arte.

Piscator, Erwin Friedrich Max (1893–1966) German director. Piscator was a heavily influential force in political theatre. After founding the Tribune in 1919, he became director of the Proletarian Theatre, and there went on to develop his agit-prop theatre in *Despite All* (1925), which encapsulated in a range of media devices including film footage of events such as the outbreak of the First World War. Piscator's spectacular productions include Toller's *Hurrah We Live!* (1927), which took place on a four-storey stage. Piscator has been a great influence on many directors, particularly Bertolt Brecht, who applied many of Piscator's ideas to his own epic theatre.

presentational theatre The terms 'presentational theatre' and 'representational theatre' describe the relationship between the world of the performance and the audience's world. In representational forms of theatre, such as realism and naturalism, there is no direct contact between the performers, the performance and the audience. The performers create a parallel reality on stage and ignore the presence of the audience. In presentational theatre, such as Brecht's *epic theatre*, there is direct communication between the performers and the audience and the events of the performance are presented directly to the audience as if these events were a part of the audience's 'here-and-now' experience.

proscenium stage The most common stage used in Western theatres. The audience sit away from the stage and view the action as if looking through a picture frame.

protagonist A Greek term which refers to the main character of a play.

Psycho-realism The term that is sometimes used to describe the performance effects of Stanislavski's system of acting which sought to produce 'realism' in characterisation through creating a balance between the actor's 'inner experiencing' of the role and its precisely crafted physical and vocal expression.

Racine, Jean (1639–99) French poet and dramatist. Racine gained popularity and success with the Parisian audience with productions such as *Andromaque* (1667), which were staged by Moliere at the Hotel de Bourgogne. He is most famous for his tragedies which include *Britannicus* (1668), *Berenice* (1670), *Mithridate* (1673) and *Phedre* (1667).

Rainer, Yvonne (1934–) American dancer. Rainer is known for her innovative pioneering breakthroughs in dance during the 1960s. Rebelling against the traditional conventions of dance, Rainer often made use of multi-media resources, such as film clips and projected images.

Ravenhall, Mark (Contemporary) British playwright who is known for his shocking contemporary play *Shopping and F***ing.*

realism Realism is based on the notion of direct mimesis (art impersonating life). Realist theatre is traditionally performed on a proscenium arch stage.

Reinhardt, Max (1873–1943) Austrian actor and director. Reinhardt began his career as an actor at the Deutsches Theatre in Berlin, where he was tutored and influenced by Brahm. Here Reinhardt gained successful experience directing the plays of Gorki, Strindberg and Wedekind. After his appointment as director of the Deutsches Theatre, Reinhardt opened an intimate attaching theatre called the 'Kammerspiele', which introduced new modern plays. His later achievements include founding the Salzberg Festival, where he directed Hofmannstahl's *Jedermann* in 1920.

representational theatre See presentational theatre.

restoration drama A period in English drama, similar to the French neo-classical era, which dated from 1660 to the early 1700s. Plays of the restoration period include Dryden's *Indian Queen* (1664) and George Villiers *The Rehearsal* (1617).

review A short critical response to a play or film. A review has an impact on a prospective audience, which has a knock-on effect on the financial profit of the play or film. A review creates expectations, which can be good or bad, and hence has the power to influence viewpoint.

Robertson, Thomas William (1829–71) English playwright. Robertson introduced a style of realist farce onto the English stage. He is most renowned for his plays *Caste* (1867), *Play* (1868), *School* (1869) and *M.P.* (1870), which show Robertson to be a forerunner of naturalism.

romanticism Romanticism was the predominant artistic movement of the late eighteenth century and most of the nineteenth century, up to 1875. The movement began in Europe during the Age of Enlightenment with the philosopher Kant, whose ideas were dramatically realised in the plays of writers such as Rousseau, Nietzche and Schpenhauer.

Rose Theatre Built in London on the south bank of the Thames in 1587. The Rose was owned and managed by Philip Henslowe, and produced plays mainly by Christopher Marlowe. The Rose was the home to companies such as the Strange's Men, and the Admiral's Men.

Rousseau, Jean-Jaques (1712–78) French philosopher who condemned the theatre, stating it was an unnecessary extravagance. Rousseau did however write operatic pieces, which include *The Village Soothsayer* (1753) and *Pymalion* (1770), as well as a comedy, *Narcisse* (1752).

Royal Court Theatre From 1904 the Royal Court Theatre was managed by J.E. Vedrenne and Harley Granville Barker. It was during these years that the theatre introduced and established the huge influential talent of Shaw. From 1956, George Devine used the theatre to present plays of the English Stage Company. The company was responsible for introducing talents such as John Osborne, Arnold Wesker and John Arden into British theatre. In the seventies the Royal Court Theatre introduced the innovative talent of writers such as David Storey and Edward Bond, and the plays of Joint Stock.

Royal National Theatre After the Second World War, £1 million of public funds was given to build a National Theatre for Britain on the banks of the Thames. The first appointed Director of the National Theatre was Lawrence Olivier, who enabled the company to perform at the Old Vic Theatre until building was completed. Olivier retired as director in 1973, after success with productions such as *Hamlet* and Peter Shaffer's *The Royal Hunt of the Sun*. Today the National Theatre is highly acclaimed as one of Britain's most prestigious companies.

Sardou, Victorien (1831–1908) French dramatist. Sardou, along with Eugene Scribe, created the 'well made play'. Sardou's plays include *Madame Devil-May-Care* (1893), *Robespierre* (1899), *Fedora* (1882), and *La Tosca* (1887).

Sartre, Jean-Paul (1905–80) French philosopher, novelist and playwright. Sartre said that his theatre was a 'theatre of situations', in which characters are distinguished by the choices they make about the situations they face. Sartre's first play was *The Flies* (1943). Several comedies followed including *Dirty Hands* (1948) and *The Devil and the Good Lord* (1951). Sartre's later plays include the tragedy *The Condemned of Altona* (1959).

satyr play Developed in ancient Greece, satyr plays were parodies of historical myths and legends. The only remaining original satyr is Euripides' *Cyclops*. These original satyrs gave rise to a style of drama we now recognise as farce.

Schiller, Friedrich (1759–1805) German playwright. Schiller worked closely with Goethe at the Court Theatre in Weimar. His plays include *Robbers* (1781), *Love and Intrigue* (1782–3), *Don Carlos* (1787) and his trilogy *Wallenstein's Camp, The Piccolomini,* and *Wallenstein's Death* (all 1799). Schiller is greatly praised for his final play *Wilhelm Tell*, written in 1804.

Scribe, Eugene (1791–1861) French playwright who created the 'well made play' along with Sardou. Scribe wrote over 400 plays including *Un Verre D'eau* (*A Glass of Water*) (1850).

semiotics Semiotics is the study of signs. In the theatre semiotics applies to the meanings within a play, which are decoded by the audience. Semiotics in theatre can be present in the actual written text, sub-text, or in costume, setting, lighting or the actions of a character. Codes in different productions of the same play can alter due to individual interpretation.

Seneca, Lucius Annacieus (4?BC–AD 65) Roman philosopher and dramatist. Seneca is known to have adapted nine plays from Greek tragedies: *Hercules Furens, Medea, Hippolytus, Troades, Agamemnon, Oedipus, Phoenissae, Hercules Oeataeus* and *Thyestes*. These tragedies were profoundly influential across Europe. Seneca's use of rhetoric is a style which was often used by Shakespeare.

Shaffer, Peter (1926–) British dramatist. In 1958 Gielgud directed Shaffer's first success, *Five Finger Exercise*. Perhaps Shaffer's most famous drama is *The Royal Hunt of the Sun* (1964), which was a great success for the National Theatre. Shaffer also brought success to the National Theatre with his entertaining farce *Black Comedy* (1965). Two of his later works *Equus* (1973) and *Amedeus* (1979), were verbally and visually spectacular, and considered contemporary masterpieces.

Shakespeare Memorial Theatre Built in honour of the prolific playwright. The theatre opened on 23 April 1879, on the anniversary of Shakespeare's birth.

Shakespeare, William (1564–1616) Prolific English playwright, born in Stratford-upon-Avon. In 1594 Shakespeare became a member of a company of actors called The Lord Chamberlain's Men. Shakespeare's early works, which include *The Comedy of Errors, Two Gentlemen of Verona, The Taming of the Shrew, Titus Andronicus* and *Richard III,* were produced by the Lord Chamberlain's Men, and gave Shakespeare recognition and popularity on the London stage. This led to further successes which include *Love's Labour's Lost, A Midsummer Night's Dream, The Merchant of Venice, Romeo and Juliet* and *Richard II*. From 1598 The Lord Chamberlain's Men, renaming themselves as The Kings Men, performed at the Globe Theatre. During this time Shakespeare wrote what are considered to be his finest plays: *Much Ado About Nothing, As You Like It, Twelfth Night, All's Well That Ends Well, Measure for Measure, The Merry Wives of Windsor, Julius Caesar, Hamlet, Othello, King Lear, Macbeth, Antony and Cleopatra* and *Coriolanus.* Late works include *Pericles, Prince of Tyre, Cymbeline, The Winter's Tale* and *The Tempest.* Shakespeare has a timeless quality which appeals to a contemporary audience. His plays are still widely produced today in both the theatre and in film.

Shared Experience Company Theatre Company founded in 1975, which tours fringe theatres in Britain, particularly in London. The company is renowned for their fresh energetic approach and minimalist sets in productions of British classical plays and adaptations of literary classics such as *Anna Karenina.*

Shaw, George Bernard (1856–1950) Irish playwright and critic. Shaw's first play *Widowers' Houses* (1892) conveyed his political opinions on the greed-driven ruling bourgeois and aristocracy. Shaw was also heavily critical of his contemporary British theatre, and did much for the promotion of the director in replacement of the actor-manager. Shaw's greatest success, *Pygmalion* (1914), led critics to hail him as Britain's leading playwright.

Shchepkin, Mikhail Semenovich (1788–1863) Russian actor. In 1822 Shchepkin was invited to join the Maly Theatre Company in Moscow. Shchepkin was a great realist actor in the plays of Gogol, Chekhov and Gorki, and was greatly admired by Russia's creator of naturalistic acting, Konstantin Stanislavski.

Sheridan, Richard Brinsley (1751–1816) Irish playwright and theatre manager. In 1776 Sheridan was appointed manager of the financially struggling Drury Lane Theatre, where he remained until 1809. Sheridan is best known for his satirical comedy *The School for Scandal* (1777), which is a mocking portrayal of gossip and scandal among the upper class.

Shirley, James (1596–1666) English playwright. Shirely's sharp comedies include *The Witty Fair One* (1628), *Hyde Park* (1632), *The Lady of Pleasure* (1635) and *The Sisters* (1642). His tragedies include *The Traitor* (1631), *The Politician* (c. 1639) and *The Cardinal* (1641).

Siddons, Sarah (1755–1831) English actress. Siddons' skill developed when she worked with a Manchester-based touring company. Perhaps her greatest performance was at Drury Lane in 1785, as Lady Macbeth. Siddons was a dignified and elegant actress, whose success only grew when she left Drury Lane for Covent Garden in 1801.

soliloquy A speech delivered by one actor when no other actors are present on stage. A soliloquy is often an intimate speech during which a character expresses his or her true emotions and thoughts.

Stafford-Clarke, Max (1941–) British director who has worked for several prestigious theatre companies such as *Traverse Theatre, Joint Stock Theatre* (of which he is founder), and the *Royal Court Theatre.*

Stanislavski, Konstantin Sergeivich (1863–1938) Russian actor, director and acting trainer. In 1898, Stanislavski founded the *Moscow Art Theatre* with Nemirovich-Danchenko. They addressed the major problems that theatre of that period was facing. Dramatists were increasingly writing realist plays, rather than popular melodramas, and hence demanded a realist style of acting. Influenced by the Meiningen Theatre Company and the great actor Tomarso Salvini, Stanislavski devised a system of acting. This system was broken down into ten elements.

Stanislavski is noted for his success in directing and acting in the plays of Chekhov, such as *The Seagull* and *The Cherry Orchard,* which relied on the skill of the actor to communicate the subtle sub-text.

Steele, Richard (1672–1729) Irish dramatist. Steele's first play *The Christian Hero* (1701) was written whilst he was a soldier. The main influence Steele had on the theatre was his promotion of new genres and styles. In 1715 Steele was knighted and was later appointed manager at the Drury Lane Theatre.

Strasberg, Lee (1901–82) American director and acting trainer. Strasberg was a great believer in Stanislavski's system for acting, and from this he created the 'method', which he introduced during the 1950s at the Actor's Studio. Strasberg went on to train many great 'method' actors in both film and stage. These included Marlon Brando, Montgomery Clift, Ann Bancroft, Shelley Winters, Paul Newman and Joanne Woodward. Strasberg's method is still widely used today by many actors whom we see on our screens. Examples include Meryl Streepe, Al Pacino, Robert De Niro and Dustin Hoffman.

Strindberg, August (1849–1912) Swedish writer. Strindberg's most famous naturalist play is *Miss Julie* (1888), however elements of Strindberg's pioneering break to symbolism are also evident in this play. Strindberg's later symbolist plays have received immense praise and include *The Great Highway* (1909) and *The Dream Play* (1902). In 1907 Strindberg worked with August Falk, running the

Intimate Theatre, which was modelled on Reinhardt's Kammerspielhaus. The chamber plays he wrote for the theatre include *Storm Weather* (1907), *The Burned House* (1907), *The Ghost Sonata* (1907) and *The Pelican* (1907). These are all related by the theme of death. Strindberg's highly stylised theatre influenced and helped to shape the twentieth century modernist movements such as surrealism, expressionism and absurdism.

symbolism Modernist movement which began with the French poets during the 1870s. Symbolism was a rejection of realism and naturalism. Ibsen was one of the first symbolist dramatists, with plays such as *The Wild Duck*. The most famous symbolist dramatist was Maurice Maeterlinck. His plays include *The Intruder, The Blind* (both 1890) and *Pelleas and Melisande* (1892).

Symons, Arthur (1865–1945) British symbolist poet, playwright and critic. His poetry includes *Days and Nights* (1899) and *London Nights* (1895). Symons' critical work includes *The Symbolist Movement in Literature* (1899).

Synge, John Millington (1871–1909) Irish playwright. Synge produced his most acclaimed works in his final years. These plays include *In Shadow of the Glen* (1903), *Riders to the Sea* (1904) and *The Well of the Saints* (1905). Many of these later plays were controversial in the respect that they questioned Irish morality, and were the cause of some disturbance and rioting in Ireland. From 1905 Synge played an active role in the Abbey Theatre in Dublin, which introduced the plays of new writers onto the stage.

tableau French word, meaning 'living picture'. Actors form a still-image on stage, which is often used to create dramatic impact, and can give the audience an opportunity to reflect. Tableaus were very popular in late eighteenth and nineteenth century drama, observed particularly in plays such as *Caste* by Tom Robertson.

Tara Arts Company Founded by Jatinder Verma. During the 1980s the company produced a number of Western classic plays, using Asian styles of performance, such as Kathakali.

Teatre de Complicite British theatre group founded by Annabel Arden, Marcello Magni and Simon McBurney in 1983. Complicite are known for their highly physical and visual performance style which is influenced by the work of Jacques Lecoq. International productions include *The Streets of Crocodiles, The Three Lives of Lucie Cabrol, The Caucasian Chalk Circle* and *Mnemonic*.

Terry, Ellen (1847–1928) English actress. Terry performed for 25 years at Irving's Lyceum Theatre in leading roles such as Ophelia (1878), Lady Macbeth (1888), and Volumina (1901). After Irving's death Terry attempted management at the Imperial Theatre, employing her son Edward Gordon Craig as set designer in a production of Ibsen's *The Vikings* (1903).

The Performance Group Innovative theatre company founded by Richard Schechner in New York in 1967. The company performed at the Performing Garage in Wooster Street. Schechner's style of theatre was recognised as environmental theatre; it detached itself from the binding reins of traditional theatre, and was applied to productions such as *Commune* (1970) and *The Balcony* (1979). In 1980 the group was renamed the Wooster Group, after the departure of Schechner and the appointment of Elizabeth LeCompte.

the well made play (*la piece bien faite*) A formula for writing plays, invented by Eugene Scribe and Victorien Sardou. The well made play, is made up of a series of building blocks. Initially an exposition is provided, which gives the audience the circumstances and history they will need to know. Next the playwright introduces a conflict, which consequently turns into a complication and then a crisis. Finally the crisis will be resolved, and this is called the denouement. This formula was widely used throughout Europe during the nineteenth and twentieth centuries.

Thespis Thespis was a Greek actor whose idea it was to create a main character who was detached from the chorus. The word 'thespian' is still used today to describe actors.

Toller, Ernst (1893–1939) German expressionist poet and dramatist. Toller's first play *Die Wandlung* (1919) is an plea to end all wars. His career came to an abrupt ending when in 1939 he committed suicide at the announcement of the Second World War.

Tolstoi, Leo Nikolaivich (1828–1910) Great Russian writer who is most renowned for his novels *Resurrection, Anna Karenina* and *War and Peace*, all of which were dramatised by the Moscow Art Theatre. However, Tolstoi is also remembered for several successful plays, which include *The Power of Darkness* (1886) and *The Fruits of Enlightenment* (1891).

Tourneur, Cyril (c. 1575–1626) Little known writer who is famous for only one play, *The Revenger's Tragedy* (c. 1606).

Tragi-comedy Throughout history playwrights have tried to synthesise the genres of comedy and tragedy into a new hybrid genre. The Elizabethan dramatists often mixed comic and tragic elements in their plays. *Measure for Measure* is tragedy with a happy ending. The Fool in *King Lear* is an example of a comic character in a tragedy. Chekhov was the first modern writer to exploit tragi-comedy in plays like *The Cherry Orchard* in which a helpless and introverted group of characters are unable to see the comedy and tragedy of their lives. In tragi-comedy it is only the audience who sympathise with characters whilst appreciating their ludicrous behaviour.

Vakhtangov, Eugene (1883–1922) Russian actor and director. Vakhtangov began his career at the Moscow Art Theatre, as an actor in 1911. His symbolist and expressionist work gave momentum to the Moscow Art Theatre's Studio Theatre. Vakhtangov's achievements within the Studio Theatre led to it being renamed after his death: the Vakhtangov Theatre.

vaudeville French musical farce. During the nineteenth century vaudeville became very popular in America, existing as a loud and boisterous entertainment form for the working class.

Verhaeren, Emile Belgian poet and dramatist. Verhaeren was a revolutionary symbolist. His most famous play is *The Dawn*.

Vieux-Colombier Theatre Built in Paris during the nineteenth century. In 1913 Copeau founded his theatre company at the Vieux-Colombier. Other companies such as Compagnie des Quinze have based themselves at the Vieux-Colombier. It is also associated with Artaud, Sartre and T.S. Eliot.

Wagner (Wilhelm) Richard (1813–83) German composer of musical drama. Wagner is renowned for his opera's, which include *Rienzi* (1838–40), *The Flying Dutchman* (1841), *Siegfried* (1856) and *The Twilight of the Gods* (1869–74). Wagner believed that dramatic art should exist as a unity of expressive elements, in his idea of total artwork (*Gesamtkunstwerk*). These ideas, as well as others, were expressed in his essays *Art and Revolution* (1849), *The Art Work of the Future* (1849) and *Opera and Drama* (1851).

Warner, Deborah (Contemporary) British director, who has worked for prestigious companies such as the Royal Shakespeare Company, and was also the founder of the *Kick Theatre Company*.

Wedekind, Frank (1864–1918) German playwright. Wedekind differed dramatically to his romantic contemporaries. His plays were non-realist, almost symbolic works, and have caused many people to hail Wedekind as a very early forerunner of expressionism. Wedekind shocked audiences by exploring taboo issues in his plays, such as *Spring Awakening* (1891).

Wegman, Mary (1888–1973) Essentially a dancer. However, Wegman's work was often described as 'dance theatre' because it traversed the boundaries of the two art-forms.

Weigel, Helene (1900–71) Austrian actress and theatre manger. Weigel was married to the great theatre practioner and playwright Bertolt Brecht. She led the Berliner Ensemble Company, which produced Brecht's plays.

Weill, Kurt (1900–1950) German composer whose work ranged from the music for Brecht's *The Threepenny Opera* to Broadway musicals. Weill was married to Lotte Lenya, who was a famous Brechtian actress.

Weimar Court Theatre Founded in 1784, in Weimar town, Germany. In 1791 Goethe was appointed artistic director. The company performed plays by Goethe, Schiller, Lessing, Shakespeare, Calderon and Voltaire.

Weiss, Peter (1916–82) German dramatist, heavily inspired by the two contrasting forces of both Brecht's political theatre and the surrealism of Artaud. Weiss' most famous play is the *Marat/Sade* (1964). Other works include *The Investigation* (1965), *The Song of the Lusitanian Bogey* (1967) and *Vietnam Discourse* (1968), which all portray his revolutionary Marxist stance.

Welfare State International British Theatre Company founded in 1968. Welfare State is recognised for its high energy and bright festival-like atmosphere, which encourages input from the local community. Often grand-scale effects such as fireworks accompany the dramatic action.

Wertenbaker, Timberlake Anglo-American dramatist. Resident writer at the Royal Court Theatre, 1984–5. Her plays include *Case to Answer, Abel's Sister, The Grace of Mary Traverse* and *Our Country's Good*.

Wesker, Arnold (1932–) British dramatist. Wesker's first plays, *Chicken Soup with Barley* (1958), *Roots* (1959) and *I'm Talking about Jerusalem* (1960), strongly voiced his communist attitude. Wesker's working-class plays *The Kitchen* (1959) and *Chips with Everything* (1962) saw a distinct break away from naturalism. His most recent plays have been epic large-scale productions, which centre around major world themes. These include *The Wedding Feast* (1974), *The Journalists* (1975) and *The Merchant* (1976).

Williams, Tennessee (1911–83) Highly influential American playwright. Williams wrote his first play, *The Glass Menagerie*, in 1945. His most highly acclaimed play is the classic drama *A Streetcar Named Desire* (1947). Other well-known works include *Cat on a Hot Tin Roof* (1955), *Orpheus Descending* (1957) and *Sweet Bird of Youth* (1959).

Wilson, Robert (1550–1605) Elizabethan actor and dramatist, renowned for his wit. His career as an actor began in the Leicester's Men, and in 1583 he joined the Queen's Men. When the company dissolved in 1592, Wilson devoted his talent entirely to writing, particularly for the Henslowe's Admiral's Men.

Wilson, Robert (1941–) American director. Wilson worked extensively with brain-damaged children, and by studying the difficulty of perspective in autistic children he created performance pieces such as *A Letter to Queen Victoria* (1974). Wilson's productions are 'epic' in terms of their grand-scale lighting and scenery. During the 1980s Wilson worked solely in Europe gaining success with productions including *The Man in the Raincoat* (1981), *Great Day in the Morning* (1982) and *The Civil Wars* (1983).

Wycherley, William (1641–1715) English playwright. Wycherley had few successes, but is renowned as a satirical genius for his plays *The Country Wife* (1675) and *Plain Dealer* (1676).

Yeats, William Butler (1865–1939) Irish playwright and poet. Yeats' verse drama was expressed in the form of music accompanied by dance. Early plays include *The Countess Cathleen* (1899) and *The King's Threshold* (1903). In 1904 Yeats part founded and became manager of the Abbey Theatre, which encouraged and introduced new writing talent into the theatre. Yeats' later plays were heavily symbolist. They include *At the Hawk's Well* (1916) *The Dreaming of the Bones* (1931) and *Purgatory* (1938).

Zakhava, Boris Russian director. Zakhava became the successor of the innovative director at the Moscow Art Theatre, Eugene Vakhtangov. He adapted Vakhtangov's vision into working practice.

Zola, Émile (1840–1902) French novelist and playwright. Zola was the leading innovator of naturalism. His plays include *Therese Raquin* (1873). They contain believable characters which have a personal psychology. This approach broke away from the two-dimensional characters of melodrama. Zola's ideas were the main inspiration for Antoine's Theatre Libre, and later Stanislavski's Method and Moscow Art Theatre.

Appendix 2: Theatre timeline

In the charts that follow we have created a timeline from 600BC to AD1910. This timeline maps out the major developments in Western theatre as well as the intoduction of major non-European performance traditions. The majority of references to non-European traditions are to be found towards the beginning of our timeline. This is because many of these traditions, which are still alive and regularly performed, have changed less radically over time than the European traditions.

The timeline is divided into historical artistic periods from the *Classical* to *Realism* and *Naturalism*. **These period headings are only a very rough guide to the diversity of work to be found in any one period**. In the period of late romanticism (1800–1850), for instance, there were already artists working in ways that would become associated with the later periods of *Realism* and *Naturalism*. You may want to turn to the discussion of periods, styles and genres in the Chapter 1 to help guide your reading of these charts.

We do not intend you to try and go through all that is in these charts. They are, perhaps, best used when you want to place a play or practitioner in a historical context. If you are studying *Hedda Gabler*, for instance, and know that it was written in 1890, you can look at what else was happening in this period of *Realism* and *Naturalism* from 1850 to 1910. You can also look at the earlier work of Ibsen, *Brand*, written in 1865, in the context of the period of late Romanticism, 1800–1850. In each period we have given the titles of key play texts of the time so that you can read other works belonging to the period you are interested in. It is also important to remember that theatre doesn't exist in a vacuum. You can learn about the social and historical context of a play, playwright or practitioner through other art-works of the period – paintings, music, literature – and from reading about social, philosophical and political ideas of the period.

This brief history gives you a 'thumbnail' sketch of different periods in theatre history. You may want to flesh out what is here by doing your own research and sharing it with the rest of the group. You could:

- Take a period and research it more fully by looking at one of the plays that are mentioned as an example of the period and by using history books or a CD-ROM like *Encarta* to give a presentation on the period to the group. Alternatively you might do an exchange with the history A level group. They can fill you in on the most important events and ideas of a period and you can give them a presentation on the theatre of the time. You might also do an exchange with groups doing other arts subjects.
- Take a genre and/or performance tradition and research it further. Look at dictionary definitions for example. A powerful way of getting information and illustrations is to use the search engine on your Internet browser. Try typing in 'Kabuki, pictures' for instance, and see what you can find. All of the major practitioners, periods and genres will have web pages out there in cyberspace! We have included a **webliography** in Appendix 3 to get you started. Use this information to do a class presentation including visuals where appropriate.

	European theatre	Non-European theatre
600BC–600AD	**Classical** The 'golden' age of Greek theatre and the development of the classic genres of *comedy* and *tragedy*. The Greeks also developed the ***satyr play***, which was performed after a *tragedy*. The *satyr plays* were more informal, often crude, with phallic imagery. The plays satirised, or were parodies of, myths, legends, historical heroes and even the *tragedies* that would have been performed before the *satyr play*. *Satyr plays* combined songs, dances and sketches and laid the basis for the later development of both modern *farce* and *burlesque*. The Roman theatre was particularly influenced by the *satyr plays* as well as by Greek *tragedy* and literary *comedies*. The Romans developed new forms of theatre which are still popular today. These forms include: • **Mime**: vulgar, often improvised episodes performed without words by unmasked actors. • **Farce**: masked clowns in improvised slapstick routines based on simple plots; would later emerge again in the form of ***Commedia dell'Arte***. • **Pantomime**: a single masked dancer miming to a song performed by the chorus. The dancer would change masks as new characters were introduced. • **Spectacles**: the Romans were very fond of lavish spectacles including gladiatorial contests and mock sea-battles enacted in flooded amphitheatres. In 692 AD the Roman Church forbade any more theatrical performances thus ending the European Classical period.	The birth of Sanskrit drama in India based on episodes from the Hindu legends of the *Mahabharata* and the *Ramayana*. The *Natyasastra* (A treatise on theatre) is the first and most detailed account of the theory and practice of performance (rather than playwriting) written in the ancient world. Classic Sanskrit plays of the period include Sudraka's *The Little Clay Cart* and Kalidasa's *Sakuntala*, which are both love stories borrowed from the *Mahabharata*.
600–1500	**Medieval** At first, certain parts of the Catholic mass were enacted in church, particularly in the Easter liturgy. These enactments were developed in the monasteries and later spread to other churches. The 'plays' were performed by the community in Latin. Three principle forms of drama developed from the liturgical dramas: • *Mystery plays*: based on episodes from the Bible. • *Miracle plays*: based on the lives and deaths of saints and martyrs. • *Morality plays*: in which virtues like goodness and truth and vices like greed and sloth became characters in simple 'good triumphs over evil' stories. The plays became increasingly political and appealed to the socially oppressed peasant class. The *morality plays* influenced subsequent genres such as ***melodrama*** and ***Brecht***'s *Lehrstucke*, or learning plays. *Mummer's plays* were also popular. These plays were performed by local groups of amateurs in disguise on special occasions such as Christmas and would include songs, folk and sword dances and a ritual drama often involving St. George. The tradition of *Mummers* was revived in Victorian times and can still be seen in some rural areas at Christmas.	The birth of drama in China when music, dance and storytelling became woven into single performances played in a circle marked by chalk. ***Noh*** Drama develops in Japan. Masked and unmasked male actors used highly stylised costumes and gestures to tell simple stories of ghosts, greed and revenge. Although the origins of *Noh* are in simple peasant performances it developed into an aristocratic form of theatre. There was a more comical and satirical form of *Noh* called *Kyogen*, which played to a wider audience. The ***non-realist*** and ***representational*** style of both performances would appeal to twentieth century European practitioners trying to escape the dominance of ***realism***. The 'Golden Age' of *Khmer* dance-dramas in S.E. Asia. These dance-dramas were developed from harvest and thanksgiving rituals into elaborate masked performances. Both male and female dancers wore richly patterned and embroidered costumes. The movements of the dancers and the patterns their feet make on the stage all have special meanings. The movements were based on the movement of puppets in the earlier *shadow plays*. These dance-dramas are still performed today and the performance style hasn't changed over the last 500 years. The development of *Alarinjo* theatre in the Oyo Yoruba empire in what is now known as Nigeria. This form of travelling storytelling theatre using elaborate costumes and masks evolved out of the *egungun* masquerades of dancers, masked performers

	European theatre	Non-European theatre
600–1500	Two German nuns, *Hroswitha* and *Hildegard*, revived the art of playwrighting, which had disappeared in the West since the Roman writers *Terence*, and *Plautus*. Their plays followed the models of *Miracle* and *Morality* plays.	drummers and large-scale puppets. The *Ozidi* saga is still performed. It takes six years to prepare and three days and nights to perform. The Balinese *Gumbuh* form develops and becomes the traditional source for subsequent Balinese performance genres such as *topeng* and *legong*. The plays, based on Japanese legends, were performed in temple courtyards and a performance would last all day or night. The performance mixed stylised costumes and dance, clowning and music. The *Gumbuh* would have a profound effect on Antonin ***Artaud***'s *Theatre of Cruelty*.
1500–1650	**Renaissance** The Golden Age of English drama. Elizabeth I banned the performance of *morality plays*, which had begun to comment on and criticise the monarchy and the unjust laws of the land. The travelling groups of actors who performed the plays were persecuted and executed when caught. The new secular theatre that developed in London mixed new humanist ideas with elements of the old *morality plays* (e.g. Christopher ***Marlowe***'s *Dr Faustus*). Ben ***Jonson*** wrote his savagely biting comedies during this period, including *Volpone*. The plays of ***Shakespeare*** dominate the Renaissance period in England, but *revenge tragedy* was also popularised by writers such as *Tourneur*, *Webster*, ***Middleton*** and *Shirley*. As a genre, the plays were based on the Greek *tragedy* but followed the model for *tragedy* established by the Roman theorist ***Seneca***. The plays often began with the appearance of a ghost to the main character who would ask for vengeance. The audience is placed on the side of the avenger, and the ensuing story is often graphically violent. The story of *Hamlet* follows this model. The Roman's fondness for elaborate spectacles was revived in the English court *masques*. With some of their origins in the *mummer's plays* of medieval times, these were hugely expensive, lavish and elaborate forms of ritual entertainment, or pageants, often performed to observe Twelfth Night, Christmas and Midsummer as well as to impress foreign dignitaries and important guests at court. Writers like Ben ***Jonson*** collaborated with architects like Inigo *Jones*. *Masques* were often participatory and combined mime, music, dance and visual effects. The development of ***Commedia dell'Arte*** in Italy which kept alive the popular travelling theatre tradition in Europe. This improvised form was based on simple scenarios and stock characters. The professional actors would specialise in a particular character and develop skilful physical, juggling or slapstick *lazzi* or tricks to amuse the audience. The plays would be built around the same stock characters such as *Pantalone*, *Arlechino* and *Columbino* and be interspersed with the *lazzi*. The hero and heroine characters were unmasked, whilst the middle-class and servant characters (*zanni*) wore caricature masks. The *Commedia dell'Arte* has had an important effect on European ***non-realist*** theatre, particularly in continental Europe. The Italian writer/performer Dario ***Fo*** is a modern exponent of a political form of the *Commedia dell'Arte*.	The development of ***Kabuki*** in Japan as a popular form of romance or ***melodrama***. Soon after its introduction women performers were banned. There is much action, costume changing and elaborate scenery. The highly stylised movements of the actors are based on a form of puppet theatre called *Banraku* used by Japanese *shamen* for ritual purposes. *Banraku* also continued to flourish as entertainment.

<table>
<tr><td>1500–1650</td><td>The 'golden age' of Spanish drama with prolific writers such as Lope De Vega and Pedro Calderon de la Barca. Lope De Vega devised a formula for writing hugely popular, action-orientated plays enjoyed by all classes. His masterpiece, Fuenteovejuna foreshadowed the call for greater social justice in the Naturalist plays of T.W. Robertson and George Bernard Shaw in the late nineteenth/early twentieth century.</td><td></td></tr>
<tr><td>1650–1700</td><td>Baroque

French neo-classical theatre dominated European performance. This genre revived the strict observation of the classical rules of tragedy established by Aristotle and Seneca (e.g. the unities of time, place and action). Corneille's Le Cid is a popular example of the genre and later Racine, while observing the classical laws, would begin to allow more flexibility into his play structures (e.g. Phedre). Soon after, the great French playwright Moliere would further flex the classical rules by introducing elements of Commedia dell'Arte into his work as well as new conventions such as indoor settings for his plays. Neo-classicism in Italy led to the development of opera.

The Puritans under Oliver Cromwell had banned theatre of any kind. After Charles II was 'restored' to the throne the brief but important period of Restoration drama flourished. This genre was based on the neo-classical theatre of the French court at Versailles where Charles had spent his exile, but the English version was less lofty and more decadent! Women were allowed on stage for the first time and this often became an excuse for raunchy and titillating dramas based on the manners of the court and featuring licentiousness, adultery and cuckoldry. The dramas were based on the highly developed wit and banter of the aristocratic class. Playwrights of this period included William Wycherley and William Congreve. This short period marked the end of the dominance of the aristocracy both in society and in the theatre. The aristocratic comedies of this period would be challenged and replaced by the sentimental comedies and domestic tragedies which were the staple of the middle-class commercial theatre in the next century.

Aphra Behn, the first English woman playwright, wrote satires, farce operas and spectacles based on the Commedia dell'Arte. Behn had a colourful life; she was born in Surinam, the setting for her play Oroonoko, employed as a spy and imprisoned for debt.</td><td>Kathakali developed as a major Hindu drama form in the early part of this period. Actor training is a long and arduous process which takes as long as ten years to complete. Stress is placed on eye and facial exercises and on memorising 600 different hand movements. Like the other Hindu performance traditions Kathakali is still popular today, and had a major influence on twentieth century practitioners such as Jerzy Grotowski and Eugenio Barba.</td></tr>
<tr><td>1700–1800</td><td>Late baroque/early romanticism

The Golden Age of English acting for both male and female actors such as David Garrick, Sarah Siddons, John Kemble, Edmund Kean and Anne Oldfield. Many of these actors' reputations were based on playing Shakespeare's characters. Garrick inaugurated the glorification of Stratford-upon-Avon as Shakespeare's birthplace in 1769. Theatre was very popular during this period and some theatres in London, such as Drury Lane, had a capacity of 3,000. This period also saw the development of provincial theatres in which touring stock companies would perform from their repertory of plays. From this period the English have laid claim to the art of acting. It was during this period that the social status of actors began to rise – Garrick died a rich man with a state funeral at Westminster Abbey.</td><td></td></tr>
</table>

	European theatre	Non-European theatre
1700–1800	*Ballad-operas* were a popular new genre which had an appeal to all classes. *Ballad-operas* like John ***Gay***'s *The Beggar's Opera* satirised, or parodied, the Italian operas which were popular at the time. They mixed popular songs and melodies together with action-orientated plots, which often poked fun at the government and the establishment. The popularity and satirical nature of this genre led to new censorship laws in 1743 that gave the Lord Chamberlain sweeping powers to approve and ban plays. These laws existed until 1968. The form and popularity of the *Ballad-operas* led to the development of *burlesque* as a popular form of working-class entertainment in America. ***Brecht*** paid tribute to this early genre of a popular theatre, which offered social comment and criticism, in his reworking of *The Beggar's opera* which he retitled *The Threepenny Opera*. Despite the popularity of the *Ballad-operas* and the huge audiences that turned out for the great actors of the period, the theatre became an increasingly middle-class pastime. This audience liked *Sentimental Comedies* like *Sir Richard* ***Steele***'s *The Funeral* and *Richard* ***Sheridan***'s *The School for Scandal*. In these comedies, evil behaviour was seen as the result of bad examples (friends, family, and environment) but righteousness could be achieved through moral instruction and good examples. The rewards of good behaviour were money, titles, property and social status! *Domestic Tragedies* were also popular with the middle class audience, these tragedies also confirmed the middle class view of the world but *George* ***Lillo*** would be the first playwright to base his main characters on non-aristocratic, ordinary people in plays like *The London Merchant*. These two new genres of middle class theatre laid the ground both for ***Realism*** and ***Melodrama***. In the foreword to *She Stoops to Conquer*, the Irish playwright, *Oliver* ***Goldsmith*** attacked the sentimentality of the audience and established through this play what he called *Laughing Comedy* which was a harder edged, less sentimental form of comedy.	The first theatre in America was built in Williamsburg, Virginia, in 1723, despite the vehement opposition of Puritans like William Penn. The first professional company in America was the *London Company of Comedians*, later renamed the American Company, under the leadership of the Englishman Lewis Hallam.
1800–1850	**Late Romanticism** The turn of the century saw the heyday of ***romanticism***, which was an artistic movement based on the philosophical ideas of Kant and Rousseau (and later of Nietzche and Shopenhauer). The romantic artist was judged according to the uniqueness of their personal vision and personality rather than for their technical craft. The flamboyant and colourful *Lord Byron* was a classic example of the romantic artist. He was famously described as 'mad, bad and dangerous to know'!. *Romanticism* in theatre reacted against the constraints of *neo-classicism* and was often based on the representation of the heroic individual's struggle to maintain lofty ideals and virtues in an imperfect and corrupt world. The themes of *romanticism* included nature, the oppression of the poor, liberty and nationalism, the exotic and the heroic rebel. ***Shakespeare*** was the ideal model for the romantic playwright. The plays often dealt with extreme experiences like suicide, infanticide and incest. The most accomplished romantic playwrights were the Germans ***Goethe*** and ***Schiller*** and others in the *Sturm und Drang* (storm and stress) movement. In literature, Coleridge, Shelley, Keats, William Blake and Sir Walter Scott all shared similar ideas and ideals. The romantic movement would have a great influence on the ***post-realist*** theatres of the twentieth century (e.g. ***Brecht***'s *epic theatre*) and is sometimes credited as the birthplace of the modern ***avant-garde*** tradition in theatre.	The *Peking Opera* was established in the early 1800s. The major emphasis was on the performance of the highly trained and athletic actors. Males played all parts. Sets and props were minimal, but the costumes were highly elaborate and stylised. The Peking Opera would have an influence on ***Brecht*** and ***Brook***.

1800–1850	The most commercially successful genre of this period was ***melodrama***. *Melodramas* were a contemporary version of the old *morality plays*, which substituted the morality of the new, powerful and affluent middle classes for religious morality. A melodrama exploits sensational action at the expense of serious thought and character and often ends in a spectacular conflict between 'good' and 'evil' in which 'good' (or at least the middle class's idea of good) always triumphs. *Melodramas* often used spectacular scenery, songs and 'cliff-hanger' curtain scenes in order to heighten the audience's emotional response. In depicting ordinary bourgeois life and settings, the melodramas formed the basis for *Realism* in the next period. Famous examples include: Dion Boucicault's *The Corsican Brothers* and Thomas Holcroft's *A Tale of Mystery*. Later popular melodramas would include *Maria Marten*, or *Murder in the Barn* and *Sweeney Todd*. A more sophisticated form of *melodrama* is to be found in plays that combine elements of both *melodrama* and *realism* like *T.W. Robertson's Caste*. Although his plays would not be performed for another three decades, the German playwright and militant revolutionary Georg ***Buchner*** foreshadowed ***Naturalism*** in a series of plays written in this period including *Danton's Death* and *Woyzeck*. In these plays he expressed his sympathy for the socially downtrodden and explored, as the *Naturalists* would also, the relationship between social class and environment.	William Henry ***Brown*** founded the first African-American theatre in New York in 1821. The theatre and the company were persecuted by the police but managed to stage *The Drama of King Shotaway* in 1832 which dealt with the slaves' revolution in St Vincent and is an early example of *political theatre*.
1850–1910	**Realism and naturalism** Henrik ***Ibsen*** reacted against both ***romanticism*** and ***melodrama*** by writing plays that were concerned with ordinary lives in ordinary settings, and which used everyday speech rather than verse. His plays sought to offer the 'illusion of reality', or ***realism*** on the stage; a 'slice of life' as we would say today. He is often referred to as the 'father of modern drama' because he was the first *realist* playwright of the modern age and his influence still dominates the stage and screen of today. *Ibsen* wrote his plays for a middle-class audience, but he sought to question the constraints and hypocrisy of middle-class morality. Many of his plays were extremely radical and provocative both in terms of their content and structure. *A Doll's House*, for instance, which debated the role of women and women's emancipation was deeply disturbing to audiences of the day. *Ibsen* also wrote romantic plays like *Peer Gynt* and symbolist plays like *When We Dead Awaken*. The new emphasis on realistic settings, characterisation and acting led to major developments in directing, acting and scene design. *The* ***Meiningen*** *Troupe* initiated long rehearsals, actor training and the use of new technologies in stage machinery and lighting. Later ***Antoine*** would develop a new intimate, middle-class theatre based on the presentation of *realist* plays in very lifelike settings at the *Teatre Libre* in Paris. Other 'little theatres' based on *Antoine*'s model would open all over Europe and specialise in offering *realism* to an educated middle-class audience. *Ibsen*'s *realism* was strongly influenced by the behavioural theory of ***naturalism***. This theory, popularised by Emile ***Zola***, suggested that your heredity and environment determined everything in life. In this sense it was a theory of human behaviour based on Darwin's theories of evolution – the survival of the fittest. Your family and the environment in which you lived and were brought up predetermined your life. If you were born into poverty and a poor environment you were bound to end up poor and	

	European theatre	Non-European theatre
1850–1910	probably criminal! *Zola*'s *Terese Raquin* became a model for *naturalism* as a theatrical style. Setting was the key feature of this style – the set was a part of the action, highly detailed and very realistic. The classics of *naturalism* include ***Hauptmann***'s *The Weavers*, ***Gorki***'s *The Lower Depths*, the mine-town plays of D.H. *Lawrence* and the sea plays of Eugene *O'Neill*. Although this period is best remembered for the birth of modern ***realism*** and ***naturalism***, there were other important movements developing too. The French producer *Paul Fort* opened the *Teatre D'Arte* to encourage a non-naturalistic style of theatre. Later *Aurelien* ***Lugne-Poe*** would take over and rename the theatre as *Teatre D'Ouevre* and establish ***symbolism*** in his direction of plays by ***Maeterlinck*** and *Hauptmann*. *Symbolist* plays challenged the claims to truth made by both *realism* and *naturalism*. The *symbolists* believed that truth lay beyond mere appearances, they aimed at producing a new drama that would reflect the mental or spiritual life rather than the crude world of the senses represented in *realism*. The plays were strong on atmosphere and effects, the influence of supernatural powers and the occult and often used non-naturalistic scenery painted by leading painters of the day such as *Bonnard* and *Toulouse-Lautrec*. The most renowned *symbolist* plays of this period were the Dream plays of ***Strindberg***. These early experiments with *symbolism* would have a profound effect on the development of *post-realist* theatres in the twentieth century. Perhaps the biggest shock of this period was the performance of *Alfred* ***Jarry***'s *Ubu Roi*, which was a crude, subversive attack on both *realism* and *symbolism*. Its strong imagery, obscene words and actions and the use of puppet movements and gross make-up would have a profound influence on *Antonin* ***Artaud*** who named his theatre after *Jarry*. In turn both ***Brecht*** and ***Brook*** would also be influenced by this remarkable play. The century closes with the playwrighting of *Anton* ***Chekhov*** and the establishment of the ***Moscow Art Theatre*** (MAT) under the leadership of *Konstantin* ***Stanilavski*** and *Vladimir* ***Nemirovich-Danchenko***. *Chekhov* developed a new form of ***tragi-comedy***, which pictures characters as average and helpless individuals suspended in a web of futile and absurd relationships. He combined the funny with the sad, the absurd and the terrifying, the pathetic and the grotesque. The audience was led to sympathise with the characters' pain whilst laughing at their folly. In order to play *Chekhov*, *Stanislavski* would develop his system of ***psycho-realism*** in acting, although later directors at the MAT such as ***Meyerhold*** and *Andrei* ***Bely*** who directed *Chekhov* in a form of *symbolic-realism* may have got closer to the complexities in *Chekhov*'s work which combines a highly complex use of symbols in realist settings. This was also the 'golden age' of technical theatre. New technological developments in stage machinery and lighting were exploited to both create more realistic illusions on stage and also to create fantastical atmospheric effects in *symbolist* pieces. Amongst the great technical innovators who began their work in this period were the theorist and designer, *Gordon* ***Craig***, the lighting designer *Adolphe Appia* and the director *Max* ***Reinhardt***. The development of cinema in the 1880s would both effect and transform the live theatre of the next century.	

Appendix 3: Webliography

Sites relating to:

Ancient Greek Theatre
didaskalia.berkeley.edu/stagecraft/greek.html
www.perseus.tufts.edu/StartingPoints.html

Artaud, Antonin (1896–1948)
www.hydra.umn.edu/artaud/links.html
www.offroads.com/artaud/home.html

Asian Theatre General
www.usfca.edu/fac-staff/davisr/thtrasia.html

Barba, Eugenio (1936–)
www.odinteatret.dk/background/eugenio.htm

Bread and Puppet Theater (USA)
www.pbpub.com/bread&puppet/bread.htm

Brecht, Bertolt (1898–1956)
www.imagi-nation.com/moonstruck/clsc15.htm
www.kirjasto.sci.fi/brecht.htm
www.optonline.com/comptons/ceo/00675_A.html

Büchner, Georg (1813–1837)
www.imagi-nation.com/moonstruck/clsc29.html

Chekhov, Anton Pavlovich (1860–1904)
eldred.ne.mediaone.net/ac//yr/Anton_Chekhov.html
mockingbird.creighton.edu/NCW/chekwrit.htm

Commedia dell'Arte
www.214b.com/
www.sculpture-ol-brenner.com/lacommd.htm

Design
www.siue.edu/PROJECT2000
uncclc.coast.uncwil.edu/search~b001o001c001i001/d?SEARCH=Theaters--Stage+Setting+and+Scenery

Drama training and careers advice
www.drama.uk
www.metier.org.uk
www.ncdt.co.uk
www.netgain.org.uk

General
www.brookes.ac.uk/theatre/studies.htm
www.brookes.ac.uk/VL/theatre/images.htm
www.imagi-nation.com/moonstruck/index.htm
www.londontheatre.co.uk/
www.optonline.com/comptons/ceo/04746_A.html
sas.auc.eun.eg/actorsbox/main/center.htm
www.uktw.co.uk/main.html
vl-theatre.com/

Ibsen, Henrik (1828–1906)
www.kirjasto.sci.fi/ibsen.htm
www.mnc.net/norway/Henibs.htm

Kabuki
cc.weber.edu/~shopfenbeck/images.htm

Kathakali
members.xoom.com/kathakali/index.htm
www.umich.edu/~hindu/dance/kathakali.htm

Meyerhold, Vsevold Emilievich (1874–1940/3)
www.unet.com.mk/mian/english.htm

Moscow Art Theatre
www.theatre.ru:8080/mhat/eindex.html

Mother Courage
www.bssd.ac.uk/bssd/techreh.htm
www.udel.edu/theatre/pttp/mmineart/mcrev.htm

Noh Theatre
members.tripod.com/tecra34/noh.html
schiller.dartmouth.edu/japanese_studies/amel07/nohdra.html
www.wam.umd.edu/~mgrantha/Noh/

Shakespeare, William (1564–1616)
www.bbc.co.uk/education/archive/lear/index.shtml
daphne.palomar.edu/shakespeare/default.htm
www.shakespeare.uiuc.edu/library/index.cgi

Stanislavski, Konstantin Sergeivich (1863–1938)
www.bemorecreative.com/one/1286.htm
www.optonline.com/comptons/ceo/04529_A.html

Strindberg, August (1849–1912)
www.extrapris.com/astrindberg.html
www.strindbergsmuseet.se/index_eng.html

Wedekind, Frank (1864–1918)
www.imagi-nation.com/moonstruck/clsc16.htm

Index